# Woodrow Wilson
## LIFE AND LETTERS

*Books on Woodrow Wilson
by Ray Stannard Baker*

◇◇◇◇◇◇◇◇◇◇◇◇◇◇◇◇◇◇◇◇◇◇◇◇◇◇

WHAT WILSON DID AT PARIS

WOODROW WILSON AND WORLD SETTLE-
MENT, AN ACCOUNT OF THE PEACE CON-
FERENCE AT PARIS, IN THREE VOLUMES

WOODROW WILSON, LIFE AND LETTERS

THE PUBLIC PAPERS OF WOODROW WILSON,
AUTHORIZED EDITION, SIX VOLUMES,
EDITED WITH WILLIAM E. DODD

WOODROW WILSON
TAKEN ABOUT THE TIME HE BECAME PRESIDENT

# Woodrow Wilson

## LIFE AND LETTERS

*Governor*

## 1910—1913

BY

## RAY STANNARD BAKER

—◆≫✦≪◆—

*Illustrated*

**VOLUME THREE**

*Garden City, New York*
DOUBLEDAY, DORAN & COMPANY, INC.
1931

PRINTED AT THE *Country Life Press*, GARDEN CITY, N. Y., U. S. A.

"*The fundamental faith of democracy is that out of a mass of uncatalogued men you can always count upon genius asserting itself, genius suited to mankind, genius suited to the task. The richness of a democracy is in this—that it never has to predict who is going to save it. It never relies upon those of established influence. The gates of opportunity are wide open and he may enter who is fit.*"

(WOODROW WILSON *at Chicago, February 12, 1912.*)

# PREFACE

This biography is founded upon the private papers of Woodrow Wilson placed without restriction in the author's hands by Mrs. Wilson. A large amount of additional material of the greatest biographical significance, made available by Mr. Wilson's friends, members of his cabinet, and other political associates, and by his relatives, has enriched the original record. This and other generous assistance has been all too poorly acknowledged in footnotes and other references in these volumes.

The author has sought to bring to the service of accuracy the critical advice of many of Mr. Wilson's associates to whom chapters or sections of this narrative have been submitted. While he himself must accept full responsibility for the documents used and the facts set forth, the suggestions of friends having intimate knowledge of the subjects discussed have been of the utmost service.

The author desires to acknowledge especially the assistance in connection with the gubernatorial period of William G. McAdoo, George L. Record, Henry Morgenthau, Frank Parker Stockbridge, McKee Barclay, Robert S. Hudspeth, William O. Inglis, and Charles L. Swem. Parts of the manuscript have been read by Professor William E. Dodd of Chicago University, Norman Hapgood, Bernard M. Baruch, and Vance C. McCormick. Newton D. Baker, Frank R. Kent of the Baltimore *Sun*, and William G. McAdoo have helped check incidents relating to the Baltimore convention.

David F. Houston, Lindley M. Garrison, Albert S. Burleson, Josephus Daniels, Thomas W. Gregory, William C. Redfield, William B. Wilson, together with members of the cabinet already mentioned, have been of much assistance in dealing with situations of which they had special knowledge, or in enabling the author to recapture the atmosphere of the early months of President Wilson's administration. Mrs. William J. Bryan has generously permitted the author to examine her husband's papers.

Senator Carter Glass and Alexander Dana Noyes have made valuable suggestions regarding the chapter on the Federal Reserve Act; Professor Frank W. Taussig has read "The Struggle for Tariff Revision," and Justice Louis D. Brandeis, the section devoted to trust legislation. For suggestions regarding foreign problems the author is indebted to John Bassett Moore, Professor J. Fred Rippy of Duke University, and Denys P. Myers of the World Peace Foundation, and especially to Dr. Joseph V. Fuller, Chief of the Research Section of the Department of State, for painstaking assistance.

Mrs. Woodrow Wilson by her unflagging interest and encouragement has lightened the burden of an often difficult task, and Professor Stockton Axson, in these as in previous volumes, has given unstintingly of his time in reading and commenting upon the manuscript, especially those sections relating to the more intimate family life of Mr. Wilson. Miss Margaret Wilson, Mrs. Francis B. Sayre, and Mrs. William G. McAdoo have made valuable suggestions. Dr. Cary T. Grayson, Mrs. Fred Yates, and Miss Mary Yates of Rydal, England, have given much appreciated information.

In the analysis of the voluminous material placed at his disposal the author wishes particularly to acknowledge the scholarly assistance during several years of Dr. A. Howard Meneely of Dartmouth College. Katharine E. Brand has contributed with discernment and fidelity to the organization of the documents and in the preparation of the copy. Robert A. Cotner and Inez C. Fuller have given faithful secretarial assistance.

The author is much in debt to the Jones Library, of Amherst, and to Charles R. Green, librarian, for facilities so generously placed at his disposal.

Wherever Woodrow Wilson's letters or other papers are used in the text of these volumes, they correspond exactly in capitalization and punctuation with the original documents.

# CONTENTS

# LIST OF ILLUSTRATIONS

# LIST OF TEXT ILLUSTRATIONS

# Woodrow Wilson
## LIFE AND LETTERS

# Woodrow Wilson
## LIFE AND LETTERS

### CHAPTER I

### THE CALL TO LEADERSHIP

The political capacity consists in no small degree in this: in the power and the instinct to generalize the wrongs and the rights of others and translate them into the terms of a Cause, a duty laid upon ourselves, though they now touch our personal interests not at all.

*Notes for an address before the Society of Colonial Wars, Princeton, May 19, 1899.*

It required statesmanship of no mean sort to bring us to our present growth and lusty strength. It will require leadership of a much higher order to teach us the triumphs of coöperation, the self-possession and calm choices of maturity.

*"The Making of the Nation."*

In enumerating the causes why the best men do not enter politics, Mr. Bryce seems to me to omit one of the most important, although he elsewhere repeatedly gives evidence that he is in full view of it, namely, the absence of all great prizes of legislative leadership to be won by sheer strength of persuasive mind and constructive skill.

*Review of James Bryce's The American Commonwealth.*

### I. THE GREAT STAGE

WOODROW WILSON'S emergence upon the great stage of American public affairs came at a moment of extraordinary political unrest. Many observers of the time felt with Wilson himself that, while it was "not a day of revolution," yet it was "a day of change, and of such change as may breed revolution, should we fail to guide and moderate it."

The drama in which Wilson was to play so large a part

had no inconsiderable prologue. The action had begun years before with the rising of the West against the East. It was at first a mere vague thunder of protest and discontent. Vast new forces, dimly perceived, not at all understood, were abroad in the land. Industrialism was rising to power, capital was concentrating, cities full of clotted aliens were expanding at the expense of the country. At the same time free land, free opportunity, those safety valves of unrest, were disappearing. The old pioneer, democratic, town-meeting way of life, faced by the new problems, was proving ineffectual in its mechanism if not in its spirit.

The unrest had begun in the '70's with the Greenbackers: the panic of 1893 was the symbolic explosion. It produced Populists and Socialists; it resulted in vast strikes; it sent out those disconsolate petitions in boots, the Coxey's Armies, marching in drab misery to seek a vain cure at the Capitol.

Bryan was the first great protagonist of the movement. Seizing control of the Democratic party in 1896, he came trumpeting the wrongs of the common man. He was for the farmer against the industrialist, the small dealer against the great merchant, the debtor against the creditor, the West and South against the East. His remedy might be quackery; the problems he heralded were valid. The Spanish War of 1898 momentarily obscured the domestic unrest—and added new difficulties to the old. For it made America, for the first time, a vital factor in international affairs.

War may postpone problems; it rarely solves them. No sooner was it well over than the unrest became more acute than ever. The Muck-rakers and the Reformers appeared upon the stage, the first shouting the ills they saw so clearly, the second eagerly offering remedies. A vast commotion of unrest!

In the midst of this mêlée of a crowded stage appeared a figure on horseback—a figure easily visualized in sombrero and chaps—denouncing the Muck-rakers, and at the same time stealing their thunder; joyously leading all the Reformers, for he could shout louder than any of them. Roosevelt, flourishing his big stick!

Bryan had been beaten with difficulty in 1896 and 1900; Roosevelt was elected in 1904. Both of the old parties were now in the control of bold and hard-fighting reformers. Well might the East tremble for its safety. Corporations, if corporations have even metaphorical sensitiveness, shook in their shoes; money bags, literally enough, shrank in their cool vaults in Wall Street; investigations were afoot, anti-trust laws, anti-railroad laws, anti-tariff laws, were at length a serious possibility.

Such, in general, was the situation in America on that winter evening, February 3, 1906, when Colonel George Harvey, rising in his place at the dinner of the Lotos Club in New York City, proposed Woodrow Wilson, the honoured guest of the occasion, for President of the United States.

## II. THE PLAY BEGINS

The Lotos Club dinner was the first great moment in the drama—as we see it who sit back in the dim orchestra of history. It had all the marks of dramatic surprise. Although the chief actor, now so solemnly introduced, had been preparing for this moment all his life long—preparing as no man in America ever before prepared for the part— he did not know that he was to be presented. "An after-dinner courtesy," he considered it, which, nevertheless, pleased him.

February 3, 1906.

MY DEAR COLONEL HARVEY:

Before I go to bed to-night I must express to you, simply but most warmly, my thanks for the remarks you made at the

Lotos dinner. It was most delightful to have such thoughts uttered about me, whether they were deserved or not, and I thank you with all my heart.

With much regard, sincerely yours,

WOODROW WILSON

The man who presented him was at the moment scarcely more than half in earnest. His address had been the "lightning-rod" of an audacious political prognosticator. He was seeking a safe Eastern leader for the Democratic party with whom to counter the spreading danger of Bryanism. A Parker, perhaps, for 1908.

George Harvey was the quintessential political journalist. He loved events, loved to observe them with an ironic eye, loved to gamble with them. He could support Wilson the Democrat in 1906 and 1910: he could as easily work for Harding the Republican in 1920. Born in Vermont in 1864, he began his career on the Springfield *Republican*, presently going to the *World*, to serve under one of the greatest of journalists, Joseph Pulitzer. He became the representative of the *World* in New Jersey in 1885, where his clever mind and his social gifts won him a gilt-braid appointment as colonel on the staff of Governor Green. It was a little later that another honorary colonel who was to play a large part in Wilson's career was being commissioned in far away Texas—Colonel House. Another colonel who was also to step in—and out—of Wilson's career, Watterson of Kentucky, was already ripe with many honors.

In 1890 Harvey was appointed Insurance Commissioner of New Jersey, and came even more intimately into relationships with the political bosses. Former United States Senator James Smith, Jr., the shrewdest of them all, on whose newspaper Harvey was for a time employed, "Bob" Davis and "Jim" Nugent, his satellites, kept no secrets from Harvey; he knew, to the last trick, the game they played.

Harvey early attracted the attention of several of those familiar and potent figures in American public life—half business men, half politicians—who engineer important enterprises, such as public utilities, which depend more or less upon franchises or may be influenced by political action. They have often been men of striking address and real power—not great, but shrewd, clever—like Harvey himself. One of these was William C. Whitney, a traction magnate who served notably as Secretary of the Navy in Cleveland's cabinet. Another was Thomas F. Ryan of Virginia, who was not only one of the most puissant financiers in Wall Street but also a leader in the Democratic party. Harvey was for a time their associate and pupil in what has been called "franchise politics." He was thus closely in touch with the great moneyed and business interests of the country as well as with the politicians. Presently he became the owner and editor of the *North American Review*, then the foremost conservative journal of America, and later the editor of *Harper's Weekly*, Harper & Brothers being then financed by J. Pierpont Morgan, the Mogul of the financial world. Harvey knew how to organize successful dinners, where he could bring together financiers who desired favours with publicists not averse to supporting them and politicians who might be persuaded to grant what they desired. In short he symbolized that combination of boss politics, big business, and journalism so hateful to the rising West under the titles of "Wall Street government," "The Interests," "Privilege," and the like. It represented everything that Bryan, La Follette, Debs, abominated.

Why did Harvey suggest Woodrow Wilson for President of the United States?

Journalists do not "make" public men: they discover them. Harvey came vividly into contact with Wilson for the first time in 1902 when he attended his inauguration as president of Princeton University. Harper & Brothers, of whom he was the titular head, were Woodrow Wilson's publishers, and about to issue his *History of the American People*. The inauguration was a great event, extraordinarily staged, attended by notabilities of the academic, literary, and business world, including J. Pierpont Morgan himself, who came in a special car and brought his own wine and cigars. Wilson's address upon that occasion, as we have already seen,[1] made a profound impression of power, leadership. Here was a man who could say things that interested the people. He was politically minded: and he was conservative. He was conservative!

Wilson undoubtedly took hold upon Morgan and Harvey upon this occasion—and later—exactly as he had been taking hold upon people all his life. It is of the genius of leadership that it subdues those who come in contact with it. It suggests itself. It stimulates men's imaginations as something to be followed, or to be used. It is in a man or it is not. Even when it repels, even more when it repels, it gives convincing evidence of its force.

"When you come into the presence of a leader of men you know you have come into the presence of fire,—that it is best not incautiously to touch that man,—that there is something that makes it dangerous to cross him, that if you grapple his mind you will find that you have grappled with flame and fire. You do not want sweetness merely and light in men who lead you. . . ."[2]

Sometimes Wilson attracted men who did not even know who he was. Mitchell, of the New York *Sun*, who saw him on a railroad train—he was then president of Princeton—sets down the incident in his *Memoirs:*

---

[1]See *Woodrow Wilson, Life and Letters: Princeton*, p. 141.

[2]Address on Robert E. Lee, delivered at the University of North Carolina, January 19, 1909. *The Public Papers of Woodrow Wilson*, Vol. II, p. 68.

"No face ever interested me more immediately than that of this chance opposite."[1]

"'Watch that man!' was Page's admonition to his friends."[2]

Harvey was by no means the first to suggest Wilson as "a man capable of the greatest national leadership." Long before the Lotos Club dinner he had been many times spoken of as a "possible President." Probably the first of such public suggestions was made on May 5, 1902—just before he became president of Princeton University.

Professor Wilson had visited Indianapolis on April 25th and addressed the Contemporary Club on the subject, "What It Means To Be An American." He was a dinner guest of Booth Tarkington, and was introduced by the president of the club, Mrs. William L. Elder, as a "critical optimist." Afterwards he wrote to Mrs. Elder:

"You said of me just what I should like to believe to be true. I am not so inexperienced or so unkind as to hold introducers responsible for what they say in compliment to a guest, but when exactly the most pleasing thing possible is said, I deem it only decent—as well as a great pleasure—to give my hearty thanks for what is, at least, a most delightful invention."[3]

It was a "lively, amusing and eloquent" speech. On May 5th there appeared an open letter in the Indianapolis *News*, headed "A Suggestion to Democrats: A Man Like Woodrow Wilson Wanted for Leader." The writer, who signed himself "Old-Fashioned Democrat," remarked that "hundreds of thousands of Democrats are longing for a chance to fight a good, old-fashioned Democratic campaign." He then went on to discuss various leaders, Cleveland, Bryan, Hill, Gorman, Olney:

---

[1] Edward P. Mitchell, *Memoirs of An Editor*, p. 384.
[2] *The Life and Letters of Walter H. Page*, Vol. I, p. 104.
[3] April 29, 1902.

"It seems to me that this would be a good time for the Democrats to break entirely away from the older men, and to take one wholly unidentified with past quarrels. . . . The type of man that I have in mind is represented by Prof. Woodrow Wilson, of Princeton University, who lectured in this city a few days ago. . . .

"Of course, I understand that a suggestion like this will be deemed strange and fanciful by many people who have come to take a distressingly practical view of our politics. But if there ever was a time when an infusion of imagination and idealism was needed in our politics it is in these days of railroad mergers, shipping trusts, beef trusts and steel combinations. We need to get back to the old ideals, and in order to get back to them we must enlist under a man before whose eyes they gleam with undimmed brightness."[1]

The suggestion of "Old-Fashioned Democrat" was taken up by other papers in the country. A Californian remarked:

"With Cleveland and Hill clasping hands in New York, Colonel Watterson in Kentucky and Colonel Bryan in Nebraska rearing upon their hind legs and Mr. Gorman in Maryland sawing wood, it is a pleasant diversion of thought, to say the least, to turn towards the man from Princeton."[2]

---

[1] A careful study of the facts has led Stephan C. Noland of the Indianapolis *News*, to whom the author is much indebted, to the conclusion that this letter was written by Louis Howland, now editor of the *News*, with slight additions to the text by Charles R. Williams, then editor, who was a Princeton man. Wilson himself always believed that "Old-Fashioned Democrat" was "absolutely the first Wilson man." He said, in October 1912, just before he was elected President:

"'About that time I was talking to Richard Watson Gilder, who said: "Wilson, I understand you are suggested for the Presidency."

"'"The presidency of what?" I asked.

"'"The presidency of the United States," he replied, "and it was no fool who suggested the idea."

"'Now I told Mr. Gilder,' continued the Governor, 'that the idea was all right, but I did not want it so carefully explained that the man who suggested the idea was not a fool.'"—Indianapolis *News*, October 25, 1912.

[2] Editorial in the Santa Cruz, California, *Surf*, June 27, 1902.

It has been customary to assert that Wilson "knew no one," "had no contacts" in his own state of New Jersey before he became a candidate for governor in 1910. Wilson did not indeed become acquainted with the "rank and file" nor with the political leaders, but he spoke year after year at various points in the state and, for a college man, had an unusually wide acquaintance. In December, 1903, we find him making the principal speech at a dinner given in his honour by the civic committee of the Passaic Board of Trade. Distinguished guests were present, including Senator Kean of New Jersey. Wilson made an address on "Patriotism," urging unselfish devotion to the public life.

"Dr. Wilson began speaking at 9:30 o'clock and did not take his seat until 10:45, but during every moment of his magnificent address he held his audience spellbound. Every sentence was alive with vital force and meaning. There was not a superfluous word. The address was eloquent and scholarly, and had just enough humor in it to make it perfect."[1]

On November 29, 1904—three weeks after the election of Roosevelt—Wilson was the principal speaker at the dinner of the Society of the Virginians at the Waldorf-Astoria in New York. The Governor of Virginia presided. The atmosphere of the time still vibrated with the political excitement of the recent campaign and Wilson used the opportunity to declare his faith. He had been personally stirred by the campaign, personally chagrined that his own Democratic party had behaved with such puerility. His address was what the newspapers referred to as a "clarion call" for the rejuvenation of the Democratic party—which, he declared, was under the domination of unsafe leaders. He meant, of course, Bryan. He would "read them out of the party."

"It is now high time that the South, which has endured

---

[1] Passaic *Daily News*, December 4, 1903.

most by way of humiliation at the hands of this faction, should demand that it be utterly and once for all thrust out of Democratic counsels; that the men of New York, New Jersey, Connecticut, Massachusetts, Indiana, and the prosperous states beyond the Mississippi who wish for reform without loss of stability should join with it to re-assert the principles and return to the practices of the historic party which has always stood for thoughtful moderation in affairs and a careful use of the powers of the federal government in the interest of the whole people. . . ."

Nothing could have been more pleasing to such a New York audience, representing the conservative wing of the Democracy. Bryan was to them anathema; and Roosevelt, to say the least, was suspect. Here was a brilliant leader who could make a fighting speech for conservative national action. Few of those present knew anything at all of Wilson's entire body of opinion; it was enough that he had scored William J. Bryan. The effect of the speech can be best described in the words of the *Sun*, a paper certainly not given to dithyrambs:

"President Wilson's speech was greeted with one of the most remarkable demonstrations of approval that has been manifested at a public dinner in this city for a long time. He was time and again overwhelmed with applause as he was speaking and had to wait until the handclapping ceased long enough to permit his voice to be heard before he could go on. When he closed, in a voice impressive and earnest in its tone, the applause broke loose like a pent-up torrent, and he was called to his feet to bow his acknowl-edgments to the extraordinary ovation tendered him."[1]

During the next year, 1905, although Wilson was absorbed with his university reforms he found time to speak in various parts of the country, as far east as Rhode Island, as far south as Alabama, as far west as Michigan,

[1] November 30, 1904.

and often in New York and New Jersey. Wherever he was, whatever his audience, his message was always the same: the true service of the people. The university must inculcate sound thinking, raise up wise leaders to reinspire the nation with the spirit of its founders.

By the time that Harvey made his "nomination" at the Lotos Club in 1906, Wilson had thus secured a strong hold upon hundreds of thoughtful men throughout the country. He was always his own Warwick. But Harvey's speech, shrewdly staged, spoken at the right moment, precipitated the public interest.

### III. THE CHIEF ACTOR HIMSELF

The public reaction to Harvey's "nomination" astonished Wilson. He could not understand it, nor quite believe it.

"Was Colonel Harvey joking?" asked Mrs. Wilson when he returned to Princeton.

"He didn't seem to be," said Wilson.

He began to receive letters from all parts of the country, some of them enclosing editorials regarding the Lotos Club incident. Harvey published approving comments in his issue of *Harper's Weekly* for March 10th, with a strong reaffirmation of belief in Wilson's availability. He seemed not a little astonished himself! He had evidently played a winning card; and he immediately followed it up. It would be something to be instrumental in choosing a presidential candidate. It would also serve perfectly the interests he had behind him.

Harvey was not the only shrewd editor to awaken to Wilson's possibilities at this time. St. Clair McKelway, of the Brooklyn *Eagle*, a distinguished figure in American journalism, sent a man[1] to Princeton to see Wilson with the

---

[1]George Tirrell, a well-known newspaper man.

possible purpose of giving him his editorial support. Wilson was seriously disturbed. This was going entirely too far! So he wrote McKelway a letter on March 11th which discloses vividly his own reaction to the proposals.

MY DEAR DR. MCKELWAY,

I was very much surprised to learn from Mr. Tirrell, whom you sent last week to see me, that you thought that Colonel Harvey's suggestion that my name be considered in connection with the next Democratic nomination for the presidency might be worth taking up seriously.

It has, of course, been very gratifying to me that Colonel Harvey should have thought of me in that way; and I quite understand that such a man as he would not put forward a suggestion of that kind in the deliberate and formal way in which he has given utterance to it without meaning it in all seriousness. But I have myself interpreted it as meaning, not that he thought that such a suggestion might lead to an actual nomination, but only that he hoped that its consideration might lead to a careful canvass of the possibility of putting in nomination someone who held views and a position like my own: views which would hold liberal and reforming programmes to conservative and strictly constitutional lines of action, to the discrediting of rash and revolutionary proposals; a position disassociated from past contests and suggestive of personal independence, the position of a man whose views had not been formed under the influence of personal ambition. To discuss such a name would be to discuss and perhaps ascertain the possibility of drawing together into common political action the men who wish a change in our present political methods and policies but not in our traditions of statesmanship. Certainly it never occurred to me to attach any other practical significance to the use of my name.

I told Mr. Tirrell that, so far as I was concerned, I should expect that you would take the name up, if you took it up at all, in the same way,—that is, not in the least with the idea that it was desirable to obtain the nomination for me, but only with the purpose of seeing what the country was willing to think of by way of a rehabilitation of some of the older ideals of the Democratic party, or, rather, by way of organizing an

Opposition with which conservative men could without apprehension ally themselves.

And I have feared that if you adopted Col. Harvey's suggestion immediately a misapprehension might arise which would put another colour on the matter. On the sixteenth of April next I am to speak at the annual dinner of the Democratic Club of New York. The club is to celebrate Jefferson's birthday on that date instead of on the thirteenth, this year. I am to respond to the toast "Jefferson"; and it will be necessary for me to speak of Jefferson's opinions as if I were reminding Democrats of the first principles of the party. Such a speech would be flat and pointless were I not to speak also of the proper application of those principles in our own day. I accepted this invitation before Colonel Harvey had made his suggestion; but it occurs to me that if anything more were made of that suggestion before I speak at the dinner of the Democratic Club, my speech would sound like a personal platform and a self-nomination. That would mortify me profoundly.

It would, of course, make me ridiculous. But that is the least of the matter. It would entirely belie my whole character. Nothing could be further from my thoughts than the possibility or the desirability of holding high political office. That is as little in my mind now as it was before Colonel Harvey published his kind editorial characterization of me. I should like to have some part, if only a nominal one, in providing the country with an Opposition which its citizens would some day be glad to put into power, but I should not like to have that part the silly part of seeming seriously to consider myself a presidential possibility.

You know me so well, and I know and trust you so entirely that it is not necessary for me to apologize for writing this letter. You will understand and appreciate it as in all respects meaning what it says and will see how necessary it was for me to write it.

With warmest regard,

Cordially and faithfully Yours,<br>WOODROW WILSON

There is in this letter a shade of meaning not accidental —it appears even more plainly in other letters of the time—that indicates Wilson's fear of being considered a mere conservative, or a reactionary.

He believed reforms to be necessary, had believed it all his life. His first book, *Congressional Government*, was the book of a reformer. He was now trying to reform Princeton University. He wanted, at the very beginning, therefore, to make it clear to McKelway, Harvey, and anyone else who might consider him as a candidate for public office that he stood for the spirit of American institutions, as expressed by Thomas Jefferson. He was for the democratic way of life. But he "would hold liberal and reforming programmes to conservative and strictly constitutional lines of action."

In earlier years, Wilson, though always a Democrat, had leaned toward Hamilton. He had even called himself, when he thought of the dangers of disunion wrought by the Civil War, a "Federalist." But he had never shared Hamilton's economic views, nor his contempt for the people. More and more, as experience and a greater familiarity with the realities of public affairs informed him, he had been "coming around" to Jefferson. To no public address of his life—if the documentary evidence may be trusted—did Wilson give more intensive labour than to this study of Thomas Jefferson.

So important is this address that we should examine what it was, exactly, that he said. He declared first that he did not follow Jefferson "because of his political opinions; for he himself departed from them at will when some favourite object seemed the better served by the departure." He followed Jefferson because of "his objects and his principles." "It is indeed his spirit that rules us from his urn."

He went on to state those principles in the compass of a single sentence:

"His principles were the right of the individual to

opportunity and the right of the people to a development not monopolized by the few."

As to the method of application to the problems of the year 1906, he said:

"If we would act now in the spirit of Jefferson, we must be careful not to depend too much upon the federal government or turn too often from the remedy which is at hand in the power of the states. It is easier to apply morals in limited communities than in vast states, easier for neighbours to understand one another than for fellow citizens of a continent. The best searchings of morals are those which are made at home, about our own doors. We should be careful not to lose our individual sense of responsibility in the aggregate action of the nation. A revitalization of the parts is true Jeffersonian method."

We know that the address made a strong impression upon those who were present—many of them men of influence in the Democratic party. A letter from George B. McClellan, then mayor of New York, expressed warm approval:

"It was the clearest and most forceful and eloquent oration that it has been my good fortune to hear in many a day."[1]

On the following day, St. Clair McKelway answered Wilson's letter of March 11th. While he commended the address, his response was not quite as warm as might have been expected. Was there something disturbing about the seriousness of the man? What, exactly, did he mean by "a development not monopolized by the few"? This was what Bryan was also saying, much more vociferously.

One could make an interesting study of the way in which reputations grow in a democracy; how fitness for political leadership is recognized; how the great leader emerges. Apparently the less attention the man himself pays to

[1]April 18, 1906.

that reputation and the more intently he pursues his own vision, the more certain his advancement. In almost every case in which famous Americans have aimed directly at the presidency they have failed. During the four years that followed Colonel Harvey's "nomination," Wilson paid slight attention to the proposals that were made from time to time regarding his political availability. He even did his best, on several occasions, as will presently be seen, to discourage the use of his name as a candidate for public office. The summer of 1906 saw the breakdown in his health—the rupture of a blood vessel in his eye which was to render him partially blind for the remainder of his life—so that for a time it seemed that his career was ruined; and in the following winter he was to plunge into the struggle for the reorganization of Princeton University which was for nearly three years to absorb his energy. Yet all this time his reputation, the public interest in the man, was steadily and surely growing. "As early as 1906 Joseph Pulitzer, in the course of some general instructions to his editorial writers, suggested that the United States might wisely elect as President a man of the type of Dr. Eliot of Harvard, whom he greatly admired. 'Woodrow Wilson,' he added, 'of course also comes up to the standard, a scholar and a thinker.' The *World* sympathetically watched Mr. Wilson's fight for democracy as a college president in Princeton. . . ."[1]

We find Walter H. Page, a shrewd observer, a progressive thinker, writing in January, 1907:

"A good deal of gossip, certainly not authorized and probably irresponsible, continues to find its way into the newspapers, touching the possible entrance into high politics of President Woodrow Wilson, of Princeton University. . . .

"The suggestion will hardly bear fruit, it is feared;

[1] John L. Heaton, *Cobb of "The World,"* p. 178.

for President Wilson is not a politician, and he is a right-minded man of a safe and conservative political faith. He would not have the government own the railroads; he would not stir up discontent; he has no fortune; he does not speak the language either of Utopia or of riot. But, if the Democratic party should come to its senses again next year and assert its old doctrines and take on its old dignity, and seek real leadership (and pray Heaven, it may!) leaving its Bryans and its Hearsts alone, this suggestion of President Wilson is logical, sound, dignified, and decent. Here is a man of high character, and of the best political ideals, a man who knows our history, our laws, and the genius of our people, American to the core and linked by inheritance and by training to the best traditions of the past, a man who has had such executive experience as a university presidency demands (and that is a good deal), a man of a wide acquaintance, and of a mind of his own. . . . Although his life has been spent in academic pursuits, he is a man of a practical mind and he knows men as well as books. He uses our language with both strength and charm; he has a sense of humour; and he is a Democrat of the best traditions. What if a political miracle should happen and the long-lost old party should find itself by nominating such a man?"[1]

Wilson began to stir two quite different classes of people: the first, thoughtful men, idealists, reformers, who felt his power, accepted his principles, and wished to follow him; the second, the politicians, the practical and selfish men, who likewise felt his power and wished to use him. Walter H. Page was a good example of the first, Harvey and Ryan of the second. All through his political career his support was similarly divided. Wilson himself, as devoted to his principles as John Knox, used both groups for achieving the purposes he had in mind. Some-

[1]*The Life and Letters of Walter H. Page*, Vol. III, pp. 12–13.

times the first discovered that the reforms or the policies
they advocated were not those of Wilson; and the second
were filled with astonished bitterness by awakening to
the fact that instead of using this strange leader with his
mind of "flame and fire" they themselves were being
used.

## IV. THE RELUCTANT LEADER

It would be a mistake, however, to brush aside entirely
the political aspects of Wilson's life from 1906 to 1910.
If the events themselves were unimportant from the public
point of view—they have remained indeed almost wholly
unknown—they proved highly significant in the education
of the man. They gave the political philosopher his first
glimpses into the Cimmerian depths of the practical
politics of that day; they furnish those early clues so
fertile in biographical understanding; they possess many
of the elements of high comedy.

Consider the man: the hard-knit, serious, determined
Scotch-Irish, Presbyterian texture of him—a man to
whom principles, purposes, were everything, his own
ease and comfort, even his friendships, wholly secondary.
He had begun as a boy with high-flown aspirations for
political leadership—aspirations warranted by a sense of
his innate capacities. "Thomas Woodrow Wilson, Senator
from Virginia." Leadership was his deepest and most
powerful impulse; statesmanship his goal.

He had been compelled to renounce these towering
visions of political place and honour before the stern facts
of his birth and environment. He chose deliberately a
"secondary course"—and settled into it with dogged
singleness of purpose. "Profound and public-spirited
statesmanship" was still his objective, but he would make
his influence felt by "literary and non-partisan agencies."

He would become "an outside force in politics." He would train young men for the leadership of American democracy which he himself had renounced.

When his friends began to urge his active participation in politics, it made a tremendous appeal to the deepest instincts and aspirations of his nature. On the other hand, the purpose of his life had become hardened, after nearly a quarter of a century, behind objectives which he now considered more important than anything else. He would not and could not think of anything else until he had won the battle at Princeton.

"I should like to have some part, if only a nominal one," he wrote McKelway, "in providing the country with an Opposition," but "nothing could be further from my thoughts than the possibility or the desirability of holding high political office."

There was thus an inner conflict of spirit as well as overwhelming outer problems which contributed to make the years from 1906 to 1910 among the most difficult of Wilson's entire life. His friends, both those who wished to follow him and those who wished to use him, were earnestly endeavouring to get him into active politics—literally trying to force him into the field of leadership in which his genius truly lay—while he himself was earnestly endeavouring to keep out. It is a comedy without parallel in American annals.

One of the earliest difficulties that beset Wilson's supporters was the fact that he was so densely ignorant of practical politics. He knew none of the lesser leaders: he had never held a public office. How present such a man to the American electorate? How elect him President of the United States? He might have ever so great powers as a leader, ever so great an appeal to the people, still there was a Process and a Method. Wilson himself, confident of the power of his appeal, since he believed he was setting forth eternal principles, was always more or less contemptuous of Process.

The attitude of the bosses toward him—though the expression was of a slightly later time—is summarized in "Jim" Smith's characterization of him as a "Presbyterian priest." "How," asked another shrewd politician, "are you going to elect a monk out of a monastery?" They were practical men and knew what they were talking about. Principles, ideals, service, true patriotism were all right, of course, fine to talk about, but how were you going to carry the downtown wards of Newark, New Jersey?

As a first step, a trial heat, Wilson was appointed in 1906 a member of one of those ornamental commissions with a bright façade of reform, with which practical politicians, busy with their own designs, like to occupy the mind of the people. This was the New Jersey Commission on Uniform State Laws. It was supposed to meet with commissions of other states to promote "uniform legislation among the states on subjects of common interest"—which did not, of course, remotely touch the acute problems of the day. To Wilson it was not in the least interesting.

An appointive office, indeed, was not enough. Wilson must be put forward for some dignified elective office. He must appear to be in the running. Accordingly in the fall of 1906 a movement was started to make him the active candidate for the United States Senate on the Democratic ticket. To this he refused to assent.

"I have so far escaped actual entanglement in politics, though the meshes were spread for me by wireless telegraphy before I landed. An effort more serious than I had anticipated was made to induce me to become a candidate for the Senate; but grace was given me and I declined. I hope that that will quiet other dangers."[1]

[1] Woodrow Wilson to Fred Yates, November 6, 1906.

After the election, in which the Republicans won a majority of the legislature[1] Wilson was again urged to permit his name to be used as the nominee of the party. While he could not, of course, be elected, it would be a distinguished honour and would introduce him to the people of the state and nation. It would also redound to the glory of the local Democratic machine because it would show what kind of man the party in New Jersey favoured—in a year when he could not possibly be elected.

It was a beautiful plan. A group of Wilson's friends, including Harvey, put it up to him. Since he knew little at that time of the ways that were dark in the politics of New Jersey—or anywhere else!—he could see nothing wrong with the proposal. Even though it was wholly honorary, it might broaden his contacts and give him a better platform for presenting his deep-seated political ideals.

While he gave his assent to the plan, he was beginning to be not a little uneasy. How much was there in all this political talk? Exactly what did it mean? Who were really behind him? Did they think of him as a possible candidate for the presidency, or was he being used as a counter in a game that he did not understand?

In December Wilson wrote a letter to George Harvey asking how much fire there really was behind all the smoke. Harvey replied at length on December 17, 1906, naming the various men who had spoken to him regarding Wilson's availability.

"In a word," concluded Harvey, "I have never heard an *unfavourable* comment, the reference almost always being to you as a type rather than as an individual—which also has been the crux of my own expression, even in the little speech at the Lotos Club."

In quite a characteristic way Wilson analyzed Harvey's

[1]United States senators were then elected by the members of the legislature.

letter, writing down in his own hand on the last, blank, page a summary of its findings:

"Interested.                    "Favourable (to type)

"Mr. Laffan                     "August Belmont
"Thos. F. Ryan                  "Henry Watterson
                                "Ochs—Miller
                                "Dumont Clark

"Favourable to Man

"Major Hemphill
"J. H. Eckels
"John G. Carlisle."

Here were the editors of several powerful and conservative journals: Laffan of the *Sun*, Ochs and Miller of the *Times*, Hemphill of the Charleston *News and Courier*, Watterson of the Louisville *Courier-Journal*. Here were also typical representatives of "big business"—Ryan and Belmont. Dumont Clarke and Eckels were bank presidents. There was only one political notability in the group —John G. Carlisle, who had been in Cleveland's cabinet— and he could not certainly be counted as a power in the party as it was then controlled. No one of the group could be suspected of being a "progressive," and several, in the jargon of the day, might be called "reactionary."

It was, in short, support that was strongly conservative: men who feared Bryan, feared labour unions, feared still more the insurgency and "socialism" of the West. This fact, at the time, did not disturb Wilson. He considered himself a conservative, certainly in method, and he was heart and soul opposed to Bryanism. He thought of himself as a "constitutional reformer," as John Fiske called Thomas Jefferson. It was only a little later that he wrote the famous letter to Joline, a prominent New York lawyer, that was to become an issue in the campaign of 1912:

MY DEAR MR. JOLINE:

Thank you very much for sending me your address at Parsons, Kansas, before the Board of Directors, of the Missouri, Kansas and Texas Railroad Company. I have read it with relish, and am in entire agreement. Would that we could do something, at once, dignified and effective, to knock Mr. Bryan, once for all, into a cocked hat.

Cordially and sincerely yours,<br>WOODROW WILSON

Mr. Adrian H. Joline[1]

Wilson was then just beginning the "battle of Princeton," and had not learned the exact nature of the opposition to the reforms he himself believed in. Rich men and conservative men were among his greatest friends, the most generous supporters of Princeton. Wilson was never opposed to great wealth—only to those uses of it which corrupted the state. To the end of his life some of his warmest friends were men of great wealth. He was thus beginning, exactly as Gladstone began, as a conservative, a man naturally of the conservative class, with conservative friends. But like Gladstone, he was also an independent thinker.

The easy—the too easy—offer of the Democratic nomination for the senatorship in New Jersey was to prove an eye-opener. Just before the legislature met in January, 1907, he received a long letter addressed "My dear Tommy," from his old classmate and friend, E. A. Stevens of Hoboken. It developed an astonishing state of affairs.

Colonel Stevens, as nearly one of the old aristocracy as was to be found in America, had been active in the reform movement that was beginning to creep into New Jersey. Both of the old parties had their "insurgents" who were

[1]April 29, 1907.

trying, as yet without avail, to stimulate a revolt from the old absolutism of control. George L. Record and Everett Colby were active in the Republican party and Colonel Stevens and Otto Wittpenn in the Democratic party. The movement had not yet attained great proportions in the state, but the bosses saw the storm sweeping up, a black cloud out of the West. No one could tell how far it might spread and it was well enough to head it off.

As a part of the struggle by the reformers in the Democratic party, Colonel Stevens had taken an active part in the campaign of 1906 with the understanding that if the Democrats won he was to be nominated for United States senator. His consternation and that of the reformers generally may be imagined when it was learned that Woodrow Wilson's name was also to be proposed to the legislature *with the backing of the bosses*. It was the ancient political game of killing off one reformer whom they could not control by putting up another whom they thought they could.

In his letter to "My dear Tommy," on December 29th, Colonel Stevens laid bare the entire scheme, even told Wilson that he, Stevens, had been approached with the intimation that if he "would put up the money necessary" he could receive the support of the Essex County delegation. In short, if he would "play the game" with the bosses, they would drop Wilson and support him. This he had spurned. He said in his letter to Wilson:

"My reasons for troubling you about this are twofold.

"First. I made my run for the avowed purpose of bringing about better party conditions. The very men who opposed me in this, the ones who in the past have controlled the state machine, the ones from whom came the intimation I have mentioned, are the ones who have been and are backing you. It is not because I want the compliment but because I feel that the welfare of the party demands that their methods should not succeed.

"Second. Your name has been mentioned for the Presidency. Your running against me will be taken by my friends under the conditions as an act of bad faith, as a sign of your willingness to allow the use of your name as a club by the very men who every good Democrat feels to have been the bane of the party and whose leadership has made the state hopelessly Republican."

This letter profoundly disturbed Wilson. It laid bare a kind of politics not known to his philosophy. In his reply, "My dear Ned," he spoke of being "an outsider and . . . inexperienced in such matters" and then went on to say:

"When it was a question of actual election to the Senate I felt bound to say that I could not accept the office; but a complimentary vote, tendered by a minority, involves no responsibility on the part of the recipient, and therefore it seems to me that it would be quite gratuitous of me to say that, if it were tendered me, I would not accept it. . . . I have already said with sufficient emphasis that I am not a candidate for anything; and no one, I take it, will venture to doubt my sincerity."[1]

Colonel Stevens replied immediately, however, that Wilson could not thus remain passive. If he did not act he would be forced into the political situation by clever manipulators who were trying to kill the reform movement. Wilson was now thoroughly aroused and alarmed. He felt himself ignorant of the entire situation and responded to a letter from the man who had been designated to nominate him, eagerly seeking information which to any tyro in the politics of New Jersey would have been as simple as his A,B,C's.

"As you know, I have been in no way concerned person-

---

[1]January 2, 1907.

ally in the movements which have led to my name being made prominent in connection with the United States Senatorship. I have thought that I owed it to the University as well as to myself to take no part in politics that would push my own interest. Being a complete outsider, I am necessarily wholly ignorant of the forces at work. I would esteem it a real favour if you would tell me very frankly what lies behind the suggestion of your letter."[1]

He also ran up a flag of distress in a letter to George Harvey:

"MY DEAR COLONEL HARVEY:

"Intimations come to me from so many quarters that were I to consent to receive the complimentary vote of the Democrats of the legislature for the United States Senatorship I would be thought to have acted in bad faith towards Colonel Stevens, to whom I left a free field, and all the work of the campaign, when it was a question of winning an election, that I feel that I must withdraw my name from consideration. I have, as you know, been entirely passive in this matter from the first. I declined to be considered a candidate for the senatorship, and I would have accepted the honour of the complimentary vote only if it could have come to me without casting the least reflection upon my old friend, Colonel Stevens. . . . I can remain passive no longer. I must beg that you will point out to me the most courteous and convenient way in which to convey to the gentlemen who were intending to pay me this honour, my inability to accept their kindness.

"You have played so generous, so thoughtful, so admirable a part in this whole matter that my chief regret is that you will be disappointed. I hope that I may have many opportunities of showing my appreciation and admiration and that you will not think me too exacting

--------
[1]January 6, 1907.

*To Colonel George Harvey*            *Jany 7th, 1907*

Mr. Wilson drafted many of his earlier political letters in short-hand, afterwards transcribing them on his own typewriter.   This is a facsimile of a letter written to Colonel George Harvey, January 7, 1907.   (See transcription on pp. 26, 28.)

a friend in asking you now to show me the way of extrication."[1]

Harvey rose beautifully to the occasion and, on January 10th, drafted a letter which he suggested that Wilson send to "Mr. Black or one of the other gentlemen who waited upon you." Wilson was tremendously relieved; and at once wrote to Charles C. Black, who had been advocating his nomination, using Harvey's suggestions almost literally:

January 11th, 1907.

MY DEAR MR. BLACK:-

It is probable that I shall be leaving for Bermuda at an early date. I think it best, therefore, in view of our recent conversation and in order to avoid the possibility of any misunderstanding, to place in your hands the following statement of my position with regard to a possible nomination by the Democratic members of the legislature, for the United States senatorship.

As you know, I have never been and am not now a candidate for the nomination. I took no part in the campaign, and do not feel that I am in any sense entitled to the honour. I have no information from any Democratic members of the legislature of their intention to vote for me. Consequently, if there be any having such a purpose in mind, I cannot address them directly. But I desire to authorize you to request on my behalf that my name be withheld from consideration in the Democratic caucus.

It is perfectly clear to my mind that the compliment should be paid to someone of those who were active in the canvass whose result so closely approached a complete Democratic victory. If then, as you informed me, some members of the legislature are still disposed to vote for me, I earnestly urge them to reconsider their determination and to give their vote to someone who by his efforts fairly won the tribute of that recognition.

To make certain that no further doubt may exist respecting my attitude and wishes, I think it would be well for you to publish this letter.

With kind regards,

Faithfully yours,
WOODROW WILSON

THE HON. CHARLES C. BLACK
_____
[1] January 7, 1907.

On the same day he wrote gratefully to his old friend Stevens:

MY DEAR NED—

My delay in replying to your last letter has been due to the fact that I have been very busy making such inquiries as would enable me to act upon the fullest possible information in the matter which has disturbed me and you.

I want to thank you for the delightful friendliness and generous spirit of your letter, and to assure you that these puzzles of judgment as to what line I should take, have only bound me closer to you.

I am at last convinced that you are right in saying that to remain passive now is to defeat my own end, which has all along been to maintain a perfect disconnection from the differences which have arisen between Democratic groups in this State. I think that it would be a mistake for me to write to the Speaker of the House, as you suggest, because I have had absolutely no communication with any official spokesman of any of the groups in the legislature. Indeed, so far as I know, I have no acquaintance with any Democratic member of the legislature. I am therefore taking the liberty of writing to Mr. Black, with the suggestion that if he pleases he may print the letter I send him. I know that you will understand my wish to take this action outside politics, so to speak, and I think that you will be convinced that the form of my letter to Mr. Black takes me entirely out of the choice for even a complimentary nomination. I am convinced that I could not accept such a nomination.

Allow me, in closing, to thank you for having done so much and done it so frankly, to set me right in this delicate matter.

Always cordially and faithfully yours,

WOODROW WILSON

COL. E. A. STEVENS.

Wilson had desired that his letter to Mr. Black be published; but it was of course suppressed. The politicians wanted nothing added to Colonel Stevens's support.

It was a narrow escape! It revealed to Wilson his abysmal ignorance of practical politics. It explains, in some degree, his extreme caution three years later when he was again put forward, under even greater pressure, for the governorship.

The rebuff of the politicians, however, in no wise dimmed the interest in Wilson. It even seemed to increase it. Some of the important men behind the scenes in the larger field of New York were beginning to be attracted to him. One of these was William M. Laffan of the *Sun*—a man of powerful, if Machiavellian, intellect, educated as a physician in Dublin, and a lover, like Harvey, of being the "god in the machine." He had addressed to A. B. Parker a searching questionnaire in 1904 as to his political beliefs, and he now wished to "look over" Woodrow Wilson, who seemed a Democratic possibility upon whom conservatives could unite to meet the radical doctrines of Bryan and Roosevelt. The "big interests" cared relatively little which party won the election provided the leadership was "amenable," "conservative."

Accordingly Laffan arranged, through his friend Dr. John A. Wyeth, a celebrated New York physician who was president of the Southern Society, for a little dinner of four, "entirely private," at Delmonico's on March 15, 1907. Laffan brought with him Thomas F. Ryan. Ryan was later anathema to all the "progressives"—regarded as the chief "reactionary" in the Democratic party, the chief representative of the "Wall Street interests."

We may sit down comfortably with this group of extraordinarily able citizens gathered in the most famous American restaurant of that time, with a feeling that we are inside observers of the great game of politics as it is played in this democracy. Notable men, these! Wyeth was what the chemist calls a catalytic agent. He himself knew nothing of the game; he was getting the elements together. Laffan and Ryan were masters of every trick in it, could see the cards with eyes closed, even those they had up their own sleeves. To what extent Wilson was aware of what lay behind this delightful little dinner, it is difficult to say. The letters arranging for the affair give no clue. Wilson loved political discussion, especially with able men who knew what was going on: and he lost no opportunity of meeting rich men like Ryan, who might be interested in the work at Princeton, where he was dreadfully in need of funds to support his preceptorial system. He afterward approached Ryan for a subscription!

During the course of the dinner, Laffan quizzed Wilson sharply, if discreetly; and he set forth his beliefs fully— too fully! Laffan and Ryan came away, as St. Clair McKelway had come away from the Jefferson Day address the preceding spring, not a little doubtful about the man. Was he not too serious? Too independent? He did not satisfy Ryan and Laffan as Parker had done in 1904.[1]

Incidentally, Laffan told of the letter he had written to Parker in 1904, and a few days later a copy of it was sent to Wilson through Dr. Wyeth, who wrote that Laffan was "in great distress over the situation" of the country and wanted "advice and help."[2]

Such an appeal went straight to Wilson's heart. It was exactly the service that he believed the "literary politician," the trained university man, ought to perform; he ought to advise and help the practical man of affairs.

"Let him [the "practical politician"] find a man with an imagination which, though it stands aloof, is yet quick to conceive the very things in the thick of which the poli-

---

[1]Edward P. Mitchell of the *Sun*, in his interesting *Memoirs of an Editor*, gives a hearsay account of this meeting (pp. 387–8) but places it in 1904, when it was really in 1907. He also says that "Elihu Root, from the other camp, dropped in quite casually before the evening was over." This may be so; it would be significant, if it were so, as evidence that similar-minded groups of the two old parties were working in harmony, as we know, of course, that they were; but there are no references in the Wilson documents to indicate that Root did appear.

[2]Dr. John A. Wyeth to Woodrow Wilson, March 24, 1907.

tician struggles. To that man he should resort for instruction."[1]

Wilson was himself as profoundly disturbed by the conditions of the country as Laffan or Ryan at one extreme —or Bryan at the other. He considered that the nation was without leadership. Vast problems of the tariff, the trusts, the railroads, were pressing for solution. Business was in a bad way; the "panic of 1907," which was to break in October, cast its shadow before. He had long been thinking and talking about what to do in such a crisis. It must be his task, as the "outside influence in politics," to apply the spirit of Jefferson's principles—which he considered the essence of democracy—to the problems of the day. What was the use of ideals if they were not made practical?

An invitation to speak at the Jamestown Exposition on July 4th, on the subject, "The Authors and Signers of the Declaration of Independence," afforded him exactly the opportunity he desired. He did not blink the evils so vividly described by the Muck-rakers, by Bryan, by Roosevelt, by Debs. He said:

"The elaborate secret manipulations by means of which some of our so-called 'financiers' get control of a voting majority of the stock of great railroad or manufacturing companies, in order to effect vast combinations of interests or properties, incidentally destroying the value of some stocks and fictitiously increasing the value of others, involve first or last acts which are in effect sheer thefts. . . ."

Sheer thefts! But how would he meet the problem? By applying the principle, set forth by the men of the Declaration, of individual liberty, individual responsibility:

"Every man who signed the Declaration of Independ-

[1]*Mere Literature*, p. 74.

ence believed, as Mr. Jefferson did, that free men had a much more trustworthy capacity in taking care of themselves than any government had ever shown or was ever likely to show in taking care of them; and upon that belief the American government was built."

It was folly to try to regulate or punish corporations for evils committed by individuals:

"When we fine them, we merely take that much money out of their business,—that is, out of the business of the country,—and put it into the public treasury where there is generally already a surplus, and where it is likely to lie idle. When we dissolve them, we check and hamper legitimate undertakings and embarrass the business of the country much more than we should embarrass it were we to arrest locomotives and impound electric cars, the necessary vehicles of our intercourse. And all the while we know perfectly well that the iniquities we levy the fines for were conceived and executed by particular individuals who go unpunished, unchecked even in the enterprises which have led to the action of the courts."

He then went on to say:

"It is the task of finding the individual in the maze of modern social and commercial and industrial conditions; finding him with the probe of morals and with the probe of law. One really responsible man in jail, one real originator of the schemes and transactions which are contrary to public interest legally lodged in the penitentiary, would be worth more than one thousand corporations mulcted in fines, if reform is to be genuine and permanent."

It "is only in this way," he observed, "that we can escape socialism."

Here then was the essence of his doctrine. It was the good solid Democratic dogma of the individual, the "great old tradition." The address found its way into many Southern newspapers. It was republished in full by George Harvey

16181

in the *North American Review* for September, 1907. To
more than one Democrat it was the voice of a prophet.
One old Roman of the party, Burleson of Texas, cut the
article out and carried it in his pocket. It was his first
knowledge of Woodrow Wilson, in whose cabinet he was
afterwards to serve.[1] The conservatives of the North also
regarded it as an eloquent counter-blast to the "socialism,"
the "revolutionary panaceas," of Roosevelt, Bryan, and
others. They were perhaps all the more interested because
they did not at all believe that "personal guilt" could
ever really be established, or "rich malefactors" be put in
jail. It was indeed a traditional rather than a scientific
approach to the new problems: it was dogmatic rather
than creative.

That summer Wilson was in the Adirondacks, engaged
in the beginnings of the quad fight at Princeton,[2] but he
found time to work out a further statement of his beliefs,
not only to clarify his own mind, but to send to Laffan and
others who, as he thought, were really seeking new light
on the problems involved. This exchange of views between
thinking men—after the manner of the founders of the
government, Adams, Jefferson, Madison, Monroe, was
one of his darling projects, often suggested.[3] Men could
come clear on the problems of the country before commit-
ting themselves publicly, and thus meet them with intelligent directness. It might possibly have worked if the frightened Easterners, approaching the panic of 1907, had been
in an objective mood—or if they had really wanted a just
and democratic solution of the problems that everyone
saw.

Wilson called his statement of faith a "credo." He wrote
it out first in shorthand, then on his own typewriter; and

---

[1] A. S. Burleson to the author.
[2] See *Woodrow Wilson, Life and Letters; Princeton*, pp. 254–255.
[3] See *Woodrow Wilson, Life and Letters: Youth*, pp. 280–282.

it was presently sent on to Laffan and his friends. He here came out even more strongly than in his Jamestown Exposition address at Norfolk for freedom of the individual; and expressed vigorously his opposition to the tendency of the times to regulate business by governmental commissions.

It is unfortunate that we have no direct evidence as to how this effort to enlighten Laffan and others was received. It must have seemed highly academic to the "hard-boiled" leaders in New York who were frightened out of their boots by the specter of socialism. Moreover the panic of 1907 broke in October and they were fully occupied with their own distress. Any practical politician of the time could have told Wilson that he was pursuing about the worst method in the world if he wanted to get into politics through the influence of the Eastern leaders. He was asking the people to think! He was demanding that the leaders go back to fundamental principles and preach the essentials of democratic government. What they wanted was to smash Bryan, hamstring Roosevelt, and keep Debs in jail.

Wilson continued, all through 1907 and 1908, to talk upon public affairs wherever opportunity offered—and to discourage any use of his name for public office. His addresses bore such titles as "Ideals of Public Life," "True Patriotism," "The Recent Campaign and the Present State of the Parties." His fight at Princeton was becoming more widely known and understood. Politicians or no politicians, offices or no offices, his hold on thoughtful men throughout the nation was steadily growing.

"If Mr. Bryan is to be eliminated, then the eyes of the Democracy will instinctively turn to Woodrow Wilson, economist, statesman, philosopher, publicist, and advanced student of affairs. . . ."[1]

[1]Editorial in the Wilkes-Barre *News*, April 25, 1907.

In the spring of 1908, there began to be talk of nominating Wilson at the Denver convention of the Democratic party. He was to be used as the conservative upon whom the party might unite to defeat Bryan. Harvey was active in the matter, and proposed to publish a strong article in the *North American Review* urging such action. By this time Wilson had begun to listen with guarded approval to such suggestions—they were naturally pleasing to hear—though without any idea that he could possibly be nominated. He wrote to Henry James Forman, the editor:

April 10th, 1908.

MY DEAR MR. FORMAN:-

I wish very much that you could disobey Colonel Harvey's instructions. I do not feel that it is any longer true that I am being seriously considered as a possible recipient of the nomination at Denver this year, and fear that Colonel Harvey is carrying his generous loyalty to an idea and a high purpose further than the situation makes necessary. I need not say how warmly I appreciate it all or how deeply grateful I am to have been considered worthy of the honour he has done me. I am merely giving expression to my feeling that the suggestion he so generously made is no longer one of the working elements of the political situation.

As for your question whom I would suggest to write an article for the North American Review if not Mr. Cleveland, I am entirely at a loss. I do not know anyone close enough to me to be able to write of me from intimate personal knowledge who would be likely to be an advocate of my candidacy, it happening that most of my closer associates are Republicans and not Democrats. I suppose that it would hardly be within your plan to have the article written by a Republican, though I know one or two Republicans who might *ex thesi* be willing to write it. Perhaps Mr. Laffan of the Sun or Mr. Walter H. Page of the World's Work could suggest someone who would have the requisite political capacity to frame such an article properly.

With much regard,

Sincerely yours,
WOODROW WILSON

Later when it became clear that Bryan would dominate the convention, and probably himself be nominated, it was proposed that Wilson take the vice-presidency on the ticket "Bryan and Wilson." This he spurned with asperity. He felt, and said in public, that Bryan was "foolish and dangerous in his theoretical beliefs."[1] When he departed for Europe in June, 1908, he left positive instructions with his friend, Stockton Axson, to refuse in his name any such proposals. Some of his friends, still thinking there might be a chance for his nomination for the first place on the ticket, urged him not to get too far away from the cables. He complied, not without impatience, remaining in Edinburgh and writing to his wife:

"I shall, as I said, be here till the Democratic convention has adjourned, which will probably be the end of the week, unless Mr. Bryan handles *his* convention more expeditiously than Mr. Roosevelt handled his,—and I do not see how that would be possible. I must admit that I feel a bit silly waiting on the possibility of the impossible happening. . . . There is evidently not a ghost of a chance of defeating Bryan—but since Col. H. *is* there I might as well be here."[2]

Taft was elected in November, 1908, and Wilson became almost wholly absorbed in the fierce struggles at Princeton. His friends bided their time. George Harvey remarked:

"We now expect to see Woodrow Wilson elected governor of the state of New Jersey in 1910 and nominated for President in 1912 upon a platform demanding tariff revision downward."[3]

There is something remarkable, something even great,

---

[1] Interview with Woodrow Wilson, March 10, 1908.

[2] July 6, 1908.

[3] *Harper's Weekly*, May 15, 1909. Harvey's backers, the great bankers of the nation, were not unwilling to see the tariff revised downward.

in the way George Harvey advocated Wilson, in season
and out, during all these years—something that transcends
his evident political and personal interests. The two men
were never on terms of close friendship—Wilson wrote no
such letters to Harvey as he wrote to David B. Jones or
M. W. Jacobus or Robert Bridges—but it was Harvey's
unflagging support that was one of the greatest elements in
getting Wilson finally into public life.

## V. THE OFFICE SEEKS THE MAN

Two powerful influences, quite outside the insistent
urging of his friends, were instrumental in forcing Wilson
into active politics. First, he had certain deep-seated
principles or ideals—a "vision of inner realities"—which
he was endeavouring with all the energy of his intense
nature to bring to realization. He found himself opposed,
and then defeated, in his struggle to make over Princeton
University in the light of those principles. Second, he
discovered that the same forces of money and privilege
which he had been fighting at Princeton were corrupting
the entire fabric of American public life. The "Muck-
rakers" were right in their diagnosis, however wrong the
reformers might be in their remedies. It was the hammering of hard experience, the bitter sense of defeat in a cause
he regarded as immutably right, that produced the change
in the tough fibre of his covenanter spirit.

There was evidence enough in 1909 and 1910 of the
conditions in the nation. Taft's administration, in so far
as it represented any obstacle to "the interests," had
broken down. It had failed to redeem its promise to revise
the tariff. Wilson himself called the new law a "tariff of
abominations." Railroads and trusts challenged the
authority of the government. There had been vast scan-
dals in the control of life insurance companies; the govern-

ment of American cities was a stench in the nostrils of decent men.

A powerful progressive or insurgent movement was indeed growing up in the country: but to Wilson it was a movement that was anti-this and anti-that, vital only in its blind oppositions. It was without leadership.

"We have heat enough; what we want is light. Anybody can stir up emotions, but who is master of men enough to take the saddle and guide those awakened emotions? Anybody can cry a nation awake to the necessities of reform, but who shall frame the reform but a man who is cool? . . ."[1]

More and more Wilson was becoming impatient of what he called the "minor statesmanship" of education.[2] He longed for the greater statesmanship, and yet he was tied close to the struggle at Princeton, committed to faithful friends who had supported him, obligated to win the battle, since it was of his own making. He set forth his situation as it was in 1909 in a letter to a New York lawyer who had urged that it was his duty to enter politics in New Jersey:

"I feel very keenly the necessity for an effective party of opposition and believe with all my heart that the welfare of the country calls for an immediate change in the personnel of those who are conducting its affairs in responsible political positions."

But he goes on to say:

"I am placed, as you will see, in a very embarrassing position, because it is manifestly undesirable that the head of a university should seek a prominent part in party contests. No serious proposal,—I mean emanating from

---

[1]Address on the occasion of the celebration of the hundredth anniversary of the birth of Abraham Lincoln, Chicago, February 12, 1909. *The Public Papers of Woodrow Wilson*, Vol. II, p. 100.

[2]Address at the inauguration of President H. H. Apple at Franklin and Marshall College, January 10. 1910.

authoritative party sources,—has ever come to me that I should allow myself to be a candidate for office, except when the minority in the New Jersey Legislature at one time thought of giving me their complimentary vote for United States Senator. If such an invitation should come, I quite agree with you that it would be my duty to give very careful consideration to the question where I could be of the most service, but I feel that my official connection with Princeton precludes me from active candidacy for any political preferment."[1]

No speeches of Wilson's life had in them more fire than those of the early months of 1910. They bespoke his own internal wrath, the turbulence of balked purpose. He was a man naturally of fierce temper, rigidly controlled. He once said of George Washington, also a man of passionate nature, "He was always well in hand." It was Wilson's own ideal of self-discipline; but in the early months of 1910, he more nearly "let go" than at any other period of his life.

On January 17, 1910, for example, we find him appearing before the veritable kings of the earth—and standing there, like some prophet of his boyhood Bible, to tell them of the handwriting on the wall. This was at a meeting of the bankers of the city of New York at the Waldorf-Astoria. J. Pierpont Morgan was in the place of distinction at the head table. The Secretary of the Treasury, Franklin MacVeagh, was the guest of honour; and scores of men were present whose word was law in the financial world—George F. Baker, A. Barton Hepburn, George M. Reynolds of Chicago, and others. Frank A. Vanderlip was toastmaster. Wilson, in his brief address, told these powerful men exactly what he believed. "He spoke like some old Hebrew prophet."

"Banking is founded on a moral basis and not on a

---

[1]Woodrow Wilson to Adolphus Ragan, July 3, 1909.

financial basis. The trouble to-day is that you bankers are too narrow-minded. You don't know the country or what is going on in it and the country doesn't trust you. You are not interested in the development of the country, but in what has been developed. You take no interest in the small borrower and the small enterprise which affect the future of the country, but you give every attention to the big borrower and the rich enterprise which has already arrived."

He then went on to say:

"There is a higher law than the law of profit. You bankers sitting in this provincial community of New York see nothing beyond your own interests and are content to sit at the receipt of customs and take tolls of all passers-by. You should be broader-minded and see what is the best for the country in the long run."[1]

Morgan, who sat next to Wilson, was deeply offended by the speech. He was seen by a reporter to "look glum and puff his cigar energetically." When Wilson sat down, Morgan let him know that he considered the remarks personal. Wilson responded instantly that he had no idea of making any personal application, he was speaking of principles.

A few days later, on the 21st, Wilson made another great speech at the Hotel Astor, this time to quite a different group—reformers. If he had told the bankers frankly where he thought they were wrong, he now told the reformers with equal assurance where he thought they were right.

It was upon this occasion that the present writer saw and heard Woodrow Wilson for the first time—to him an unforgettable experience. No speaker he had ever heard before made an impression quite so vivid, clear-cut, alluring. It was not so much what the man said—short-ballot

---

[1]From report in the New York *World*.

reform was then in the air, and other men that evening presented its essentials excellently well—but it was the extraordinary sense the orator gave of a fire-like sincerity and conviction. Here was complete understanding; here was the man who in a chaotic world, plagued with evil spirits, knew what to do. Here veritably was the thinking leader the country needed and could trust!

The stormy applause that followed the address gave evidence of the gift Wilson had of convincing men of his powers of leadership. There was after all something, at its best, irresistible in Wilson's oratory. He himself fulfilled in no small degree his own vision of what a political orator should be:

"I wish there were some great orator who could go about and make men drunk with this spirit of self-sacrifice. I wish there were some man whose tongue might every day carry abroad the golden accents of that creative age in which we were born a nation; accents which would ring like tones of reassurance around the whole circle of the globe, so that America might again have the distinction of showing men the way, the certain way, of achievement and of confident hope."[1]

The writer recalls vividly also a discussion that followed the address. Wilson had taken hold upon most of those present much as he had upon him. Two or three remained obstinately critical. He was "too academic." Underneath he was a reactionary. Nevertheless, there was general agreement that Wilson was without doubt the ideal leader for a progressive movement. It is painful to add, in the light of what followed, that there was also general agreement that Wilson was politically impossible! Most of those present believed that La Follette of Wisconsin or Colonel

---

[1]Address delivered on the hundredth anniversary of the birth of Robert E. Lee, at the University of North Carolina, January 19, 1909. *The Public Papers of Woodrow Wilson*, Vol. II, pp. 81–82.

Roosevelt whose "return from Elba" was then imminent,[1] were, practically and logically, the true leaders of the Progressive movement.

One would have thought that after such a bearding of the bankers in their den, such an acceptance by the reformers—to say nothing of the furor just then being raised by Wilson's fight at Princeton—the enthusiasm on the part of Colonel Harvey and his conservative backers would have been smothered. So far at least as the Colonel himself was concerned, it was not. At that very time he was trying harder than ever to get Wilson into the state campaign for governor, with eyes on the nomination for the presidency in 1912. Did Harvey and his backers think that Wilson was insincere in these public addresses? Did they think that they could control him if once they got him elected? Or were they carried off their feet by the power of the man? They clearly saw in him a leader destined, by virtue of his genius, as well as by his strategic position in the party to great place;[2] was the temptation irresistible to gamble upon him?

Possibly all these elements entered into the situation. Suffice it to say that just about the time that Wilson was making these prophetic addresses in New York, Colonel Harvey was inviting the "Big Boss" of New Jersey, former Senator James Smith, Jr., to a luncheon at that political trysting place in New York, Delmonico's. Was it in the very room where three years before Laffan and Ryan had "looked over" Wilson as a possible presidential candidate?

Smith was an extraordinary character. A Chesterfield

---

[1] Roosevelt came out of Africa in April, 1910.

[2] See George Harvey's article, "The Political Predestination of Woodrow Wilson," in the *North American Review*, March, 1911, in which he says: "The finger of Predestination, guided by Logic, Circumstance, Conditions, and History, points unerringly to Woodrow Wilson, Democrat, as the opponent of William H. Taft, Republican, in 1912."

of a man! Six feet tall, immaculately groomed, crowned
with a silk hat, he was the veritable pattern of suave
distinction that befitted a man of power and place. He had
"the face of an innocent child." His rise had been characteristically American. He had begun as a grocer's clerk,
had become the owner of two newspapers, the director of
several manufacturing plants, and finally a bank president.
Though without much formal education himself, having
come from the family of an Irish Catholic immigrant, he
sent three sons to Princeton, and had come on several
occasions under Wilson's spell. He was of the genuine breed
of the city boss—"generous to a fault," dispensing the
money he received from great corporations or from the liquor interests among the little leaders and henchmen upon
whom he depended to carry their precincts for the organization. He was recognized, generally, as political overlord
by Nugent of Newark and Bob Davis of Jersey City,
themselves autocratic local bosses. He was on friendly
terms with the equally influential, though more secretive,
bosses of the Republican party. Both were controlled by,
or worked in harmony with, business leaders, lobbyists,
"Black-Horse Cavalry," who sought privileges and immu-
nities at Trenton. He was as powerful in New Jersey as
Richard Croker of Tammany Hall in New York—more
powerful than elected senators or governors. He was, in
short, besides being a human and likable man, a shining
exemplification of all that was worst, most hopeless, in
American political life.

Smith lived during the summers in the historic cottage at
Elberon where President Garfield had died. Colonel Harvey was not far away at Deal. Harvey had introduced
Smith to William C. Whitney, one of the shrewdest political and business leaders of his time, and when Smith
wanted to go to the United States Senate, Whitney, to
whom the Democratic boss might be useful, employed his

influence with the members of the New Jersey legislature
to see that he was carried in on the Democratic wave that
elected Cleveland in 1892. It was not, however, without
"money as plentiful as ugly rumours."[1] When Smith
reached the Senate he was soon under fire from his own
party leaders, President Cleveland among them, because
of his position on the tariff bill, which the Democrats were
endeavouring to pass. Upon investigation of the scandal of
the so-called "sugar senators," Smith acknowledged that
it was his "impression" that he had "bought a thousand
shares of sugar" while action on the sugar schedule was
pending. But such events as these, even Cleveland's bitter
arraignment, even the attacks of the reformers, had not
broken Smith's domination of the Democratic party
machine in New Jersey.

A powerful and impressive figure indeed it was who
sat down with George Harvey at Delmonico's in January,
1910. Harvey presented all the arguments for choosing
Wilson as candidate for governor on the Democratic
ticket that fall—as a step toward his nomination for the
presidency in 1912. They spent the entire afternoon in
discussing the subject. Smith was skeptical. Wilson was
a planet wholly out of his orbit. How would such a man,
as distant as Jupiter, take with the boys? Yet Harvey's
arguments were persuasive. The Democratic bosses and
the machine in New Jersey were under fierce attack—the
insurgent movement was running wild in the country.
There was a real chance at last for an overturn of the
Republicans in New Jersey. Smith's own personal fortunes
were waning. Political principles were nothing; what was
wanted was a victory. Nevertheless, Smith was doubtful
of this "Presbyterian priest." Wouldn't he break up the
organization?

---

[1] James Kerney, *The Political Education of Woodrow Wilson*. Kerney was editor of
the Trenton *Evening Times* and knew Smith long and intimately.

A week later Harvey exultantly told his friend and assistant, William O. Inglis, that Smith had "come up to the scratch in fine shape."[1]

"He told me," Harvey said, "that he was prepared to go ahead whenever I could assure him that Wilson would accept the nomination. He said, however, that I ought to consider one phase of the situation carefully. That was that if he should force Wilson's nomination there would be, in the first place, a great cry about boss dictation, and a good many people would believe and more would say that he was using Wilson as a stool pigeon in order to secure his own reëlection to the Senate."

Harvey told Smith that this was one of the drawbacks that would have to be met. Smith responded:

"Well, I have thought it all over carefully, and I am ready to go the whole hog. If you think it advisable, I will make definite announcement to-morrow that under no circumstances would I accept reëlection to the Senate."[2]

Having secured Smith's somewhat reluctant assent, the greatest obstacle to Harvey's plan was yet to be met. This was Wilson himself.

Harvey went to Princeton to address a meeting of a women's club in which Mrs. Wilson was interested; he and Mrs. Harvey were guests at Prospect, President Wilson's home. The two men spent the entire evening in Wilson's library discussing the question.

Wilson countered Harvey's suggestion with the arguments so prominent in his letters and speeches of that

---

[1]From an interesting account by W. O. Inglis in *Collier's Weekly*, October, 1916.

[2]Inglis's account, *Collier's Weekly*, October, 1916. As to Smith's senatorial ambitions which were to be so much of an issue after Wilson's election as governor, James Kerney says:

"Not once, but a dozen times, he declared that under no circumstances would he be a candidate for the United States Senate, should the campaign eventuate in a Democratic legislature. His health and the fact that the Washington life bored him were constantly advanced as reasons for his having put all thought of the Senate behind."—*The Political Education of Woodrow Wilson*, p. 26.

time. In the first place he was committed to the struggle at Princeton, then at its very hottest.[1] In the second place he dreaded taking the plunge into active politics— especially such politics as then existed in New Jersey. He felt that a great source of his power, all along, had been his detachment. He could tell the truth remorselessly. He hated to surrender his position as an "outside influence." What he thought the people most needed was a leader "detached from this struggle yet cognizant of it all, sympathetic with it all, saturated with it all," yet one who could withdraw himself, "because only the man who can withdraw himself can see the stage; only the man who can withdraw himself can see affairs as they are."[2]

Compared with the presidency of a great university, where he had both a platform and a fight, how was he to enlarge his influence by becoming the governor of a state? Of course there was the presidency beyond—but it seemed a remote chimera. A chance in a million! Finally he was afraid of having anything to do with the bosses of New Jersey. He had had his lesson in 1907. He felt himself too ignorant of real conditions to cope with them.

Yet he was torn to the depth of his soul. All his old aspirations for active political life were "set throbbing again."

"This is what I was meant for, anyhow, this rough and tumble of the political arena. My instinct all turns that way, and I sometimes feel rather impatiently the restraints of my academic position."[3]

He knew he could lead, he could govern. As governor,

---

[1] The trustees of the university had declined Procter's gift of $500,000 for a graduate college on February 10th.

[2] Address on the occasion of the celebration of the hundredth anniversary of the birth of Abraham Lincoln, Chicago, February 12, 1909. *The Public Papers of Woodrow Wilson*, Vol. II, pp. 99–100.

[3] Woodrow Wilson to Mary A. Hulbert, September 5, 1909.

far more as President, he could perhaps realize some of the principles he held most dear.

Harvey himself relates exactly what he finally said to Wilson:

"'It all resolves to this: If I can handle the matter so that the nomination for governor shall be tendered to you on a silver platter, without you turning a hand to obtain it, and without any requirement or suggestion of any pledge whatsoever, what do you think would be your attitude? That is all that is necessary for me to know. I do not ask you to commit yourself even confidentially.'"

Mr. Wilson, according to Colonel Harvey, walked up and down the floor for some minutes in deep thought, apparently weighing all considerations and possibilities with the utmost care. Finally he said slowly:

"'If the nomination for governor should come to me in that way, I should regard it as my duty to give the matter very serious consideration.'"[1]

It was an assent as shadowy, as evasive, as any man ever gave, but Harvey—and Smith, whom he straightway informed—had to accept it or nothing.

Wilson gave the matter no further consideration, but the office was now seeking him in dead earnest. Although Harvey had gone off to Europe, the pressure upon Wilson for public addresses and for political leadership continued to grow. Enthusiasts at Elizabeth, New Jersey, organized a Democratic dollar dinner for March 29th and persuaded Wilson to address them. One of the leaders went to Washington and, after talking with a number of senators and representatives, induced Senator Gore to come to Elizabeth for the purpose, as he wrote Wilson, of "launching you as a candidate for Governor."

". . . they believe you should make the sacrifice and accept the nomination for Governor of New Jersey, feeling

---

[1] Inglis's account, *Collier's Weekly*, October 7, 1916.

assured you could easily be elected; and as such Governor you would stand a full even chance for the nomination of President in 1912. . . ."[1]

To this proposal to "launch" him, Wilson responded with an emphatic refusal. But he could not prevent the audience, when he arose to speak, from shouting, "Our next Governor!" His address, "The Living Principles of Democracy," made a deep impression upon those present, and was published in *Harper's Weekly*[2] and elsewhere. It was a ringing appeal to the Democratic party to reassert its leadership, reaffirm its great principles:

"These signs of changing public opinion should not make us eager for office, but eager for an opportunity to see the principles we believe in realized in action. . . .

"We must supply efficient leaders and eschew all the lower personal objects of politics. . . . If the Democratic party sees this opportunity and takes advantage of it without selfishness, with patriotic enthusiasm, with an ardor for the things a new age is to bring forth, it will win not mere party success, but a glory which it will itself be glad to see merged and identified with the glory of the nation itself."

One of those present at the dinner was the "Big Boss" himself. He was "carried away by the speech." After it was over he told a friend that Wilson was a great man— "but what can be done with him in politics?"[3]

In April the Princeton fight was again turning against Wilson. On the 7th came his address to the New York alumni who were "fighting mad." They were almost solidly opposed to his reforms; and they "held the money strings." They were of the same class, some even of the same group, that he had met at the bankers' dinner in

---

[1]L. T. Russell to Woodrow Wilson, March 23, 1910.

[2]April 9, 1910.

[3]Judge Robert S. Hudspeth to the author.

January. They "sided with dollars rather than with ideas." "A university does not consist of money," he told them, demanding that the real purpose of the university, the education of leaders for the democracy, be restored.[1]

Ten days later he was in Pittsburgh, even more hotly in revolt. "There are certain principles which I feel I cannot yield." He had been defeated again in the meeting of the Princeton board of trustees on the 14th. He felt that he was at the end of his rope; and in his wrath he let go all the reins as in no other speech in his life.

"The people are tired of pretense, and I ask you as Princeton men to heed what is going on."

A Pittsburgh paper thus reported the address:

"It is probably putting the matter mildly to say that it was such a speech as they had not expected to hear. A more unsparing denunciation of the churches of the country could scarcely have come from the lips of the most radical Socialist leader. He was equally severe with the privately maintained colleges, of which Princeton is one, while with fiery breath he literally wiped the political parties and their leaders out of existence. When he ended by predicting revolution, either peaceable or bloody, for the country, his audience seemed to sit as though stupefied with surprise."[2]

The address was seized upon by the newspapers and its sensational statements set forth in flaring headlines.

### DISASTER FORECAST BY WILSON

#### PRINCETON PRESIDENT'S FIERY SPEECH RECEIVED IN SILENCE BY LOCAL ALUMNI.

### DENOUNCES CHURCHES[3]

---

[1] See *Woodrow Wilson, Life and Letters: Princeton*, pp. 336-338.
[2] Pittsburgh *Dispatch*, April 17, 1910.
[3] *Ibid.*

Wilson's Princeton enemies republished extracts from the address in a pamphlet headed, "That Pittsburgh Speech," and circulated it among the students and alumni of Princeton.

Wilson was afterwards deeply chagrined at having let himself go. ". . . in my deep excitement, I did not think of how it would sound in the newspapers."[1] But if the expression was intemperate, he nevertheless believed that what he said was true, and would offer no excuse for it.

Years later, Lawrence C. Woods wrote to Mr. Wilson:

"Do you recall how, after 'That Pittsburgh Speech' April 17th 1910, motoring down the next morning (Sunday) to our home, you were so disheartened that you said that you felt your life had been a *failure?* And only two years later I heard Judge Wescott at Baltimore close his great speech, nominating you, by quoting from that same 'Pittsburgh Speech' which you had made in the depths of despair."[2]

The Pittsburgh meeting was the turning point. He knew now where he stood; what the fight really was. He did not, indeed, propose to give over the struggle at Princeton; but if he were defeated there, he could carry the fight into the larger field.

## VI. THE RECEPTIVE CANDIDATE

A peculiar power and fire marked Wilson's addresses during the spring of 1910. While he dealt almost wholly with problems of education—he was then at the climax of his struggle at Princeton[3]—or with the larger principles and issues of public life, he was irresistibly drawing men to him—strong men, thoughtful men, who were as anxious as he to find a new leadership for the nation.

[1]Woodrow Wilson to I. H. Lionberger, April 28, 1910.

[2]December 22, 1921.

[3]The Wyman bequest which sealed his defeat came on May 22nd.

On May 12th he spoke before the Princeton Club of Chicago:

"When . . . will leaders arise? When will men stop their questionings and recognize a leader when he rises? When will they gather to his standard and say, 'We no longer question; we believe you; lead on, for we are behind you'?

"America needs men of that sort. Will you encourage them? Will you make your universities such places as can produce them? Will you inject into everything you are connected with, so far as Princeton is concerned, the utter seriousness which is indispensable in such circumstances? . . . You are your own saviors, and when you have come to the determination to save yourselves you will know your leader the moment you meet him, for you will find if he is of your sort and of your purpose."

It was the kind of flaming eloquence that not only set men to thinking, but roused them to action. One of those present was John Maynard Harlan, a man of power and influence in Chicago, once a candidate for mayor. Although himself a Republican he "felt like saying to Wilson after the great applause had subsided, 'Lead on, for we are behind you.'"

He acted, indeed, at once. He sought out his friend Edward N. Hurley, an independent Democrat and an influential business man, and brought him and Wilson together. Hurley was as powerfully attracted as Harlan had been,[1] and went at once to see Roger C. Sullivan, the Democratic boss of Illinois. Sullivan had heard of Wilson but was skeptical. Hurley's enthusiasm was contagious and finally a luncheon with Smith of New Jersey, Sullivan's old friend, was arranged. When Hurley began to talk of Wilson, Smith remarked:

---

[1]Hurley became Wilson's devoted friend and afterwards played an important part in the war-time administration of Woodrow Wilson, as chairman of the United States Shipping Board.

"I think very well of him. While he has had no practical experience in politics, he is a wonderfully able man, and under certain conditions I would be glad to see him nominated for the governorship of New Jersey."[1]

He expressed his fear, however, that Wilson might be antagonistic to the Democratic organization in New Jersey:

"I'll see if Harlan cannot get a definite statement from Wilson on that subject," said Hurley.

Harlan was not only willing but eager to help. He wrote to Wilson on June 11th:

"Mr. Hurley said very positively that Mr. Smith had not the slightest desire that you commit yourself in any way as to principles, measures or men, but that he would wish only to be satisfied that you, if you were elected Governor, would not set about fighting and breaking down the existing Democratic organization and replacing it with one of your own."

Wilson replied on June 23rd:

MY DEAR MR. HARLAN:

I owe you an apology for not having replied sooner to your letter of June 11th. The Commencement season began, as you know, on June 10th, and ever since it began I have been in the throes of the busiest part of the season.

I need not say that I read your letter with the greatest interest. I would be perfectly willing to assure Mr. Smith that I would not, if elected Governor, set about "fighting and breaking down the existing Democratic organization and replacing it with one of my own." The last thing I should think of would be building up a machine of my own. So long as the existing Democratic organization was willing to work with thorough heartiness for such policies as would re-establish the reputation of the State and the credit of the Democratic Party in serving the State, I should deem myself inexcusable for antagonizing it, so long as I was left absolutely free in the matter of measures and men.

---

[1]Edward N. Hurley, *The Bridge to France*, pp. 3-4.

I have been so extremely busy and business has brought me so near the eve of my vacation, that I do not see how it would be quite possible for me to arrange to lunch with Mr. Hurley and Mr. Smith in New York, but I should be very pleased to do so if it should turn out to be possible. My address will be care of Miss Florence Griswold, Lyme, Conn.

I deeply appreciate your kindness in keeping these political matters in mind. You are certainly most generous and I appreciate your interest and friendship very warmly indeed. It seems to me as if the developments in Princeton make it pretty certain that my duty lies here in the immediate future and not in the political field, but I am as eager as ever to do anything that is possible, consistent with my other obligations, to help forward the rehabilitation of the great party in which I have always believed.

With warm regard,

Cordially and faithfully yours,
WOODROW WILSON

MR. JOHN M. HARLAN,
Chicago, Illinois.

Upon the receipt of this letter, Hurley, to whom Harlan gave it, went at once to New York and showed it to Smith, who said that "it was entirely satisfactory."

Wilson, however, was loath to take the final plunge. By the last of June, Smith and the other political leaders in New Jersey were on tenterhooks. The convention was to take place in the middle of September and their would-be candidate seemed not to care whether he was being considered or not. Smith, at his wits' end, was about to choose another candidate—Judge Hudspeth of Jersey City—when Colonel Harvey returned from Europe. Smith sought him out immediately and told him that he couldn't hold his people a moment longer. He must know positively whether Wilson would accept.

Wilson was called on the telephone and asked if he could come to Deal for a conference with Smith on Sunday, June 26th. Colonel Watterson of Kentucky, whom Harvey regarded as one of the shrewdest political judges and prophets in the country, was to be there. Harvey wanted him to meet Wilson and to help persuade him to be a candidate.

Everything being thus in readiness, Harvey was dismayed on Saturday to receive this telegram:

Lyme, Conn., June 25, 1910.
Colonel George Harvey, Deal, New Jersey.
Sorry to find there is no train from here to-morrow. Deeply regret I shall not be able to attend dinner.
WOODROW WILSON

Wilson apparently did not want the governorship, even on a silver platter.

What was to be done? Inglis suggested that he might go over to Connecticut and bring Wilson down. It was already Saturday evening, but there was still a chance.

"If you don't fetch him," Harvey called to Inglis at parting, "don't come back. Go and commit hara-kiri!"

Inglis arrived at New London in the middle of the night, and made a dash for Lyme in the only motor cab in town on Sunday morning. He knew that he had to get back to New London with Wilson—if he would come!—for the 12:25 train.

When he arrived at the Griswold home in the sleepy old town of Lyme, where the Wilson family were spending the summer, Wilson himself opened the door. He and his family were just starting for church.

"Colonel Harvey has asked me to drop in and bring you down to dinner this evening."

Wilson seemed in no way surprised. Inglis had considered an eloquent and persuasive speech urging Wilson to come to Deal and be governor and President. He was given no opportunity to deliver it, for Wilson responded immediately:

"I'll have to put some things in a bag."

They caught the fast train at New London by a margin of ten minutes, and arrived at Deal just in time for dinner. Colonel Watterson and Senator Smith were already there. It was a delightful dinner, with Wilson at his best. Colonel Watterson was fascinated; and though he had come to Deal favouring Harmon of Ohio for the Democratic nomination for the presidency in 1912, he left committed to Wilson.

The conference that followed the dinner lasted until midnight. Wilson agreed finally to take up the matter of the governorship with his loyal friends of Princeton University. They had been faithful in their support and he felt that he could not withdraw from the fight, especially now that the tide was against him, without their approval.

Cleveland H. Dodge, when Wilson discussed the situation with him, was without qualification for his acceptance of the nomination. More than that, he offered to help him in every way he could.[1] Wilson wrote to David B. Jones of Chicago, who was one of his closest friends, a trustee of Princeton University, and a supporter of unwavering loyalty.

> 27 June, 1910.
> Lyme, Connecticut
> Care Miss Florence Griswold

MY DEAR MR. JONES,

I find that the political question I put to you in my brief note the other day has become acute; and I think that I ought to make a full statement of it to you.

It is immediately, as you know, the question of my nomination for the governorship of New Jersey; but that is the mere preliminary of a plan to nominate me in 1912 for the presidency.

---

[1] No one ever redeemed a promise more effectively. Dodge did yeoman service for Wilson, with both money and brains, throughout his political career, and would never accept any office or other favour at Wilson's hand.

It is necessary, if I would be fair to all parties, that I should decide this week whether I can accept the nomination for the governorship. There are some half dozen other men who desire it, but they have all told the State Committee that they are willing to withdraw and allow me to have it by acclamation if I will accept it. If I will not, they wish at once to rally their forces, and it is only fair to give them the chance. The convention meets in September.

What appear to be the facts (reinforced by additional evidence since I saw you and talked it over in Chicago) are, that the representative politicians of Indiana, Illinois, Ohio, Minnesota, and Iowa prefer me as a presidential candidate to Harmon and have urged the party men in New Jersey to nominate me for the governorship, in order to elect me by a substantial majority and so make it necessary to consider me; that the New Jersey men are confident that I can be elected by a majority so large as to be very impressive and convincing and are willing to give me the nomination unanimously, without the raising of a finger on my part; and that my chances for the presidential nomination would in such circumstances be better than those of any other man.

Last evening I dined with Colonel Watterson, of the Louisville Courier Journal, Colonel Harvey, of Harper's Weekly, and James Smith, the reputed Democratic boss of New Jersey. Whatever one may think of Colonel Watterson, there can be no doubt of his immense political influence in his section of the country, and indeed throughout the whole South. He came on to make my acquaintance, and before the evening was over said that, if New Jersey would make me Governor, he would agree to take off his coat and work for my nomination in 1912. The opportunity really seems most unusual.

I have promised nothing. In order to go into this thing, I feel that I must get the free consent of yourself, your brother, McCormick, Dodge, Sheldon, and the other men who have been such splendid friends of Princeton and of mine, who have guaranteed money to the University, and who ought not now to be embarrassed by any action of mine. It will be necessary, too, if I am to withdraw from the presidency of the University (now, of course, without the least intimation that I am withdrawing with any criticism of the University itself) that we agree upon concerted action in the matter of a successor to the presidency of the University, in order that no reactionary be chosen and our present advantage lost; but that can be done later, when my own choice is decided. Nothing of this need be known until the autumn.

Will you do me the very great favour, therefore, of laying this whole matter before your brother, Mr. McCormick, and Mr. McIlvaine and asking them to give me their absolutely frank opinion and wish in the premises, in view of the whole circumstances in their entirety, indicating, as they seem to do, as definite a prospect of the Democratic nomination in 1912 as it is possible to have in the nature of the case and the conditions of the time? If it is necessary, and you will telegraph me that I may find you and the other gentlemen I have mentioned in Chicago, I will come on at once for a conference, since I really feel bound to give my answer, if possible, by the end of the present week.

I cannot throw off the feeling, perhaps I should say the fear, that I am in some way imposing upon your kindness and that of the other men by even suggesting that I take the liberty at this juncture of withdrawing from Princeton. Perhaps it is the fear that this will look to you like a mere case of personal ambition. To my mind it is a question of which is the larger duty and opportunity. At any rate, I am sure that you will all judge leniently and will understand.

With warmest regard,

Faithfully Yours,
WOODROW WILSON

The next day he went down to New York to see his old friend and classmate, Edward W. Sheldon, also a trustee of Princeton, whom he regarded as one of the wisest men he knew, and sought his advice. He found Jones's telegram in reply to his letter on his return to Lyme: and expressed his joy and relief in a letter to Cleveland Dodge:

"Last evening I got the following telegram from David Jones, after a conference he had held with Cyrus, Tom. Jones, and McIlvaine.[1] Can you imagine anything finer?

---

[1] Cyrus H. McCormick, Thomas D. Jones, and William B. McIlvaine, all trustees of Princeton.

'Chicago, 30 June, 1910.

'All four concur unreservedly in the opinion that no obligation whatever exists on your part, either to any individual supporter or to the University as a whole, which should deter you from following your own inclination. Question what you had better do is largely personal to yourself. We do not feel sufficiently clear on the subject to advise. We appreciate your perplexity and our sympathies are and will continue to be with you. Whatever your conclusion may be, you can rely on our hearty support in any field of service you may enter upon. 'D. B. JONES'.

I feel a richer man for having had this experience in dealing with noble, public spirited men. Whatever I may decide, I shall have steadier hopes and confidences."[1]

He also wrote to David B. Jones:

Lyme, Connecticut,
1 July, 1910.

MY DEAR MR. JONES,

Your two telegrams reached me yesterday. How can I sufficiently thank you for them or adequately express my admiration of the generous group of friends for whom you sent the second telegram? Dodge and Sheldon of course acted in the same way. I am specially privileged in having earned the friendship and confidence of such men, and I want to express my deep and lasting gratitude. The question is, if anything, all the harder to decide; but, whichever way I decide it now, my heart will be stronger for the work to come.

Your letter and your brother's letter have been of real service to my thought. They are wise and full of the real gist of the matter. They add to my obligation and to my admiration.

I will, of course, write the moment I come to a conclusion. This is only to tell you how I feel.

With affectionate regard,

Gratefully and faithfully Yours,
WOODROW WILSON

---

[1]For full text of this letter, see *Woodrow Wilson, Life and Letters: Princeton*, p. 353.

In the meantime one other staunch friend, upon whose judgment Wilson always counted, remained to be consulted. This was Dr. M. W. Jacobus of Hartford Theological Seminary, likewise a trustee of Princeton. Wilson asked him to come down to Lyme and the two men talked over the entire situation at great length. He told Dr. Jacobus that he "had always held before his classes in Jurisprudence the imperative obligation which rested upon a man when there came to him the call of the State to its service, so that he could not face his classes again if he rejected this summons."[1]

From this time onward events moved swiftly enough.

Whatever doubts Senator Smith had entertained regarding Wilson were dissipated at the dinner at Deal. He was even so anxious to get Wilson committed that he wrote to his friend Hurley, in Chicago:

June 28th, 1910.

MY DEAR FRIEND:-

I understand our mutual friend is going to see Messrs. Cyrus H. McCormick, Thomas D. Jones and William B. McIlvaine of your City, as to the advisability of his candidacy. Wouldn't it be well to have Mr. Harlan see them before our friend meets them?

With kind personal regards, believe me

Sincerely yours,
JAMES SMITH, JR.[2]

Upon Hurley's suggestion, Harlan went to New York and had a long talk with Wilson, urging him strongly to enter the fight, and telling him of the support he would certainly receive in Illinois.

Wilson was still hesitant. He tramped the country roads around Lyme, he played golf on the sheep-pasture links of the Vreeland farm, and in the evening, sitting on the

---

[1] Dr. M. W. Jacobus to the author.
[2] Edward N. Hurley, *The Bridge to France*, p. 10.

wide porch, read aloud Browning's "Saul," or he and his daughter Nell matched each other in repeating the "Bab Ballads."

He was extremely fond of the freedom and beauty of Lyme—"a jolly, irresponsible lot of artists"—a "haven of rest"—to which he loved to retire.

There had already been widespread speculation in the newspapers as to what was really going on; and confident reports, extraordinarily near the truth, that there had been conferences between the most powerful bosses of the Democratic party outside of New York—Sullivan, Smith, and Taggart were mentioned—the purpose of which was to make plans for electing Wilson governor as a "springboard" for the presidency in 1912. It was extremely disturbing to Wilson to find Hearst's New York papers spreading abroad such news as this:

## WALL ST. TO PUT

## UP W. WILSON

## FOR PRESIDENT[1]

He could not indeed help asking himself why these bosses were supporting him. What did they want? What lay back of it all?

"I was asked to allow myself to be nominated, and for a long time it was impossible for me to understand why I had been asked. The gentlemen who wanted to nominate me were going outside the ranks of recognized politicians and picking out a man who they knew would be regarded as an absolutely independent person and who I thought they knew was an absolutely independent person. I tried to form a working theory as to why they should do it. I asked very direct and impertinent questions of some of

[1]New York *Journal*, July 8, 1910.

the gentlemen as to why they wanted me to make the run. They didn't give me any very satisfactory explanation, so I had to work one out for myself. I concluded on the whole that these gentlemen had been driven to recognize that a new day had come in American politics, and that they would have to conduct themselves henceforth after a new fashion. Moreover, there were certain obvious practical advantages to be gained by the old-time managers. Whether they could control the governor or not, a Democratic victory would restore their local prestige. . . ."[1]

There was another highly important consideration that affected the situation. Wilson was a poor man. He had practically no means beyond his Princeton salary. He had been educating his three daughters and assisting in the education and support of numerous young relatives. There had been more or less ill health and expensive vacations in Europe and elsewhere. Even with his added earnings from his literary work, it had sometimes been difficult for him to balance his budget at the end of the year. Wilson quoted humorously Mr. Dooley's advice:

"If anny Dimmicrat has a stiddy job he'd better shtick to it!"[2]

The pressure, however, continued, and on Tuesday, July 12th, came the decisive conference in New York. They had to "beg him to attend." Harvey and Smith called the group together for luncheon in a private room at the Lawyers' Club at 115 Broadway. Smith sent his friend Judge Robert S. Hudspeth, whom he hoped to run for governor if Wilson refused. Hudspeth occupied the important position of national Democratic committeeman from New Jersey. He knew well upon what points Smith was most anxious for assurance. First, what would be

---

[1] William Bayard Hale, *Woodrow Wilson; the Story of His Life*, pp. 166–167. Wilson made the same explanation to several friends.

[2] Dr. Edward M. Chapman of Lyme, Connecticut, to the author.

Wilson's attitude toward the organization in New Jersey. Second, what were his views on the liquor question. Smith told Hudspeth:

"Unless we can get the liquor interests behind the Doctor, we can't elect him."[1]

Smith also sent over his chief lieutenant and kinsman, James R. Nugent, boss of Newark, who was state chairman of the party, Eugene F. Kinkead, Congressman, and Richard V. Lindabury, the foremost lawyer of the state, associated with the bosses at one extreme and with the great financial leaders of New York at the other. He was of the counsel for the United States Steel Corporation and J. P. Morgan. Others who were there were Milan Ross, a lesser political leader, and of course George Harvey. Every man in the group except Wilson was a practical politician.

Every man present was also keenly on his guard—all more or less suspicious of this extraordinary, brilliant, persuasive outsider, this scholar and author, this "Presbyterian priest"—but they were not more suspicious of him than he was of them.

"I will not accept this nomination unless it comes unanimously. I am not seeking this office," said Wilson.[2]

Judge Hudspeth then raised the important liquor question and Wilson responded instantly:

"I am not a prohibitionist. I believe that the question is outside of politics. I believe in home rule, and that the issue should be settled by local option in each community."

"You know, Dr. Wilson, that the Democratic party in New Jersey has been fighting local option for years. It is our *bête noire*."

Hudspeth then explained Smith's position and his very strong feeling on the subject.

---

[1] Judge Robert S. Hudspeth to the author.
[2] Judge Robert S. Hudspeth to the author.

"Well," said Wilson, "that is my attitude and my conviction. I cannot change it."[1]

When Hudspeth later reported this conversation to Smith, the "boss" shook his head dubiously, but did not withdraw his support. He thought he could "smoke out" Wilson later in the campaign—with results, as will be seen, that astonished him.

As to the other point, Wilson's attitude toward the organization, we have the positive evidence not only of Wilson, but that of Judge Lindabury in a letter to James Kerney in which he said that he did not "recollect that Mr. Wilson promised in any way to accept organization recommendations or that anyone asked him to do so."[2]

Wilson on his part wrote to his friend David B. Jones:

Lyme, Connecticut,
14 July, 1910

MY DEAR MR. JONES,

After much doubt and perplexity, I have told the New Jersey men that, if the nomination for governor comes to me without any effort on my part, unanimously, and with no requirement that I pledge myself to anybody about anything, I will accept it. I did not see, in the circumstances, how I could say anything else, particularly in view of my life-long teaching, in my college classes, that it was the duty of educated men to accept just such opportunities of political service as this.

The decision cost me a deep pang; and the heart of the hurt is that I am about to lose the close association I have had with the splendid friends who have honoured me with their confidence and affection during my life and work at Princeton. Surely no man ever had finer or nobler friends. It makes me very proud and very deeply grateful to think of them. I do not know what ability I shall show in the new work, if it is put upon me, but I shall strive with all my heart to disappoint none of you in respect of my character and principles.

---

[1]Judge Robert S. Hudspeth to the author.
[2]July 21, 1924. See James Kerney, *The Political Education of Woodrow Wilson*, p. 46.

Will you not be kind enough to give my warm regards to your brother and to beg him to regard this letter as also written to him.

Faithfully and gratefully Yours,
WOODROW WILSON

He was now under greater pressure than ever for some public statement. His friend, H. E. Alexander of the Trenton *True American*, who had been for some time an enthusiastic supporter, argued that such a statement would appeal to the people of the state, and he could soon determine whether or not there was a real and popular call for him. Accordingly on the 15th, he took the plunge and sent the following statement to the *True American* and the *Newark News:*

There has recently been so much talk of the possibility of my being nominated by the Democrats of New Jersey for the Governorship of the State, and I have been asked by so many persons, whom I respect, what my attitude would be towards such a nomination, that it would be an affectation and discourtesy on my part to ignore the matter any longer. I need not say that I am in no sense a candidate for the nomination, and that I would not, in any circumstances, do anything to obtain it.

My present duty and responsibilities are such as should satisfy any man desirous of rendering public service. They certainly satisfy me, and I do not wish to be drawn away from them, but my wish does not constitute my duty, and if it should turn out to be true, as so many well-informed persons have assured me they believe it will, that it is the wish and hope of a decided majority of the thoughtful Democrats of the State that I should consent to accept the party's nomination for the great office of Governor, I should deem it my duty, as well as an honour and a privilege, to do so. I cannot venture to assume that this is the case. It remains to be seen whether it is or not. I should not feel personally disappointed if it should turn out otherwise.

But it is clearly due to the many public men and the many representatives of the public press who have urged me to say how I feel about this very important matter that I should make this statement rather than seem to avoid their legitimate inquiries.

WOODROW WILSON

Even after this he was doubtful. His old friend Walter H. Page went up to Lyme to see him a few days later.

"His visit was a plea that Mr. Wilson should accept his proffered fate; the governorship of New Jersey, then the presidency, and the opportunity to promote the causes in which both men believed.

"'But do you think I can do it, Page?' asked the hesitating Wilson.

"'I am sure you can': and then Page again, with his customary gusto, launched into his persuasive argument. His host at one moment would assent; at another present the difficulties; it was apparent that he was having trouble in reaching a decision."[1]

On July 20th Wilson wrote to his friend McAlpin, secretary of Princeton University:

"I hope you have not been grieved by what I have felt obliged to do about the governorship. It cost me many an anxious hour before I could see what appeared to be my duty; and I may have mistaken it. What made me most loath was the thought of the men, like yourself, whom I *might* be losing my close associations with."

The reaction to Wilson's announcement was most illuminating; in one way reassuring, in another alarming. One thing was certain: the country was intensely interested; and interest is the breath of life to the political leader. Here was an entirely new type of leader stepping out upon the stage of public life—the scholar, the thinker. People had lost faith in politics and politicians; here was the prospect of a new and hopeful statesmanship.

---

[1] *The Life and Letters of Walter H. Page*, Vol. I, p. 106.

"Whatever the event, there can be no question that leadership of the Woodrow Wilson type is the one thing that would rehabilitate the Democratic party and place the coming campaign upon a dignified level."[1]

"Woodrow Wilson's announcement that he would accept the Democratic gubernatorial nomination if sufficient popular demand for his candidacy developed, is one of the biggest political surprises of the year.

"To be governor would confer no honour upon a man whose fame as an educator and historian and authority on government is international. It would mean much that is disagreeable for him. His attitude, it is recognized, is that he is prepared as a patriotic duty to make the sacrifice, if necessary, in order to end the frightful present conditions resulting from misrule."[2]

"It is prophetic of the day when statesmen will displace the puny politicians who make the administration of affairs at Trenton sometimes disgusting and sometimes alarming."[3]

The interest in papers outside of New Jersey was quite as cordial:

"Whether or not Woodrow Wilson is the next Democratic candidate for governor of New Jersey, whether or not, that is, the nomination goes to him on his own terms as representing 'the wish and hope of a decided majority of the thoughtful Democrats' of his state, the fact that he is willing to take it, so offered, and would regard it as 'an honour and a privilege' as well as a duty, is one of not a few happy omens for the national Democracy.

"Too long that party has been the object, and the just object, of general contempt, of its own contempt. Futile,

[1] Newark *Evening News.*
[2] Long Branch *Record.*
[3] New Brunswick *Times.*

impotent, Bryanized, bedlamized, it has held out nothing to honourable ambition."[1]

All this comment, reënforced by an avalanche of letters, convinced Wilson for the first time that there was a genuine and popular demand for him. He had hesitated long, fearing that he was being used by the bosses: he hesitated and doubted no longer.

He was not unprepared for the doubt—even dismay—expressed by certain newspapers in New Jersey and elsewhere, which charged him with being the tool of the bosses. He was mere "window-dressing" for the discredited machine. The *Observer* of Hoboken remarked that he was "afloat on a bad hull":

"There is no denial of the fact that Dr. Wilson was induced to enter the race by a combination of the very elements which the Progressives are fighting, and that these elements have assumed charge of his candidacy. . . .

"When it is remembered that the leading corporation lawyer in the state, Richard V. Lindabury, who has taken no interest in Democratic politics for fifteen years, and George B. M. Harvey, who is closely affiliated with the Morgan railroad interests, were active with the bosses in the exclusive conference at which Mr. Wilson's candidacy was decided upon: that the Professor has himself alienated all of the union labour men of the state, of which the party is largely composed, by his recent address at Princeton University, and that his position on every other local question is at the time unknown, he will understand the great wave of doubt and opposition which is sweeping through the state."[2]

It was with this extraordinary interest, these strong cross-currents of opinion, that the campaign for the nomination went forward.

---

[1] New York *Sun*.
[2] July 18, 1910.

# CHAPTER II

# CANDIDATE FOR GOVERNOR

You must take your leaders in every time of difficulty from among absolutely free men who are not standardized and conventionalized, who are at liberty to do what they think right and what they think true; that is the only kind of leadership you can afford to have.

*Address on Abraham Lincoln, February 12, 1909.*

We need good leaders more than an excellent mechanism of action in charters and constitutions. We need men of devotion as much as we need good laws. The two cannot be divorced and self-government survive.

. . . the excellence of a polity might be judged by the success with which it calls the leading characters of a nation forth to its posts of command.

*Address at Trenton, December 26, 1901.*

Neither men nor society can be saved by opinions; nothing has power to prevail but the conviction which commands, not the mind merely but the will and the whole spirit as well. It is this and this only that makes one spirit the master of others and no man need fear to use his conviction in any age."

*Address at Middletown, Connecticut, June 30, 1903.*

## I. THE TRENTON CONVENTION

THE Democratic state convention was set for September 15th at Trenton. Although Wilson, in his cool retreat among the elms of Old Lyme, was unaware of it, the political pot in New Jersey had never bubbled more furiously than it did that summer. Powerful as the bosses were it soon became apparent that they would need to strain their machine to the uttermost to nominate their chosen candidate. Wilson was unknown to the "rank and file" of the battle-scarred Democrats of the New Jersey cities, who must be depended upon to support him. The tribal law of the machine is personal allegiance. Reward those who have faithfully served the organization; help those who will help you. Here was a man who had never had anything whatever to do with "the boys." He had no political support even in his own town. When the Democratic committee of Wilson's county of Mercer met in August, they passed a resolution declaring it "the practically unanimous sentiment of the voters of the county" that Frank S. Katzenbach, Jr.—Wilson's chief rival—be the Democratic gubernatorial candidate. Katzenbach had served long and faithfully in the party ranks, he had spent his time and money, he was the "logical candidate."

Moreover Wilson had offended the well-organized battalions of labour which marched ordinarily in the ranks of the Democracy. They were attacking him hotly. Extracts from his baccalaureate address of the previous year were being anonymously circulated. On August 16th the New Jersey Federation of Labor, at its Newark meeting, passed a resolution denouncing Wilson as a foe of labour. This was most disturbing. Wilson felt that his views were being grossly misrepresented. The subject of his address had been "Unprofitable Servants" and the paragraphs regarding trade unionism, lifted out of their context, were indeed easy ammunition for the enemy. He had said:

"You know what the usual standard of the employee is in our day. It is to give as little as he may for his wages. Labour is standardized by the trades unions, and this is the standard to which it is made to conform. No one is suffered to do more than the average workman can do: in some trades and handicrafts no one is suffered to do more than the least skillful of his fellows can do within the hours allotted to a day's labour, and no one may work out of hours at all or volunteer anything beyond the minimum."

But Wilson had treated the "unprofitable servant" as a broad human problem. It was the failing on the part of

*Photo. by Underwood & Underwood*

WOODROW WILSON, CANDIDATE FOR GOVERNOR,
AT PRINCETON.

men in every walk of life, business men, college men, students, that they did merely what they were expected to do, and nothing more.

"But we do not need to turn to the trades unions to illustrate our disregard for the true meaning of duty. You know how some men cheapen their college diplomas by getting them for as little work as possible. . . . They cheat nobody but themselves."

While Wilson's determined policy was one of silence—not to "lift a finger to get the nomination"—these charges were too much, and his only public utterance before the convention dealt with these "willful and deliberate misrepresentations."

"I have always been the warm friend of organized labour. It is, in my opinion, not only perfectly legitimate, but absolutely necessary that Labour should organize if it is to secure justice from organized Capital; and everything that it does to improve the condition of workingmen, to obtain legislation that will impose full legal responsibility upon the employer for his treatment of his employees and for their protection against accident, to secure just and adequate wages, and to put reasonable limits upon the working day and upon all the exactions of those who employ labour, ought to have the hearty support of all fair-minded and public-spirited men."[1]

He had criticized some of the things trades unions had done:

". . . but I have criticised them as a friend and because I thought them harmful to the labourers themselves and harmful to the country. I know of no other standard by which to judge these things than the interest of the whole community. The labouring man cannot benefit himself by injuring the industries of the country."

He made another point quite clear:

---

[1]Letter to Edgar Williamson of Orange, New Jersey, August 23, 1910.

"I am much more afraid that the great corporations, combinations, and trusts will do the country deep harm than I am that the labour organizations will harm it; and yet I believe the corporations to be necessary instruments of modern business. They are good things so long as they act in the common interests, and very bad things when they do not."

He concluded with an appeal for "criticism which is not intended to damage but to create a better understanding all around."

This letter did not, of course, reach the mass of the workers, did not certainly change their views or bring them at that time to Wilson's support.

Not only were the "rank and file" suspicious of Wilson as a candidate—this "professor," this "Presbyterian priest"—but many of the respectables of New Jersey, men who would naturally have been his supporters, but who were in revolt against the bosses, were opposed to him. Some of them were for Katzenbach, some for Otto Wittpenn, an out-and-out reformer, then mayor of Jersey City, and some for Judge Silzer. A cartoon published in the Newark *Evening News*, expressing the views of some of these reformers, irritated Wilson extremely. It represented him as a weary cart horse, "candidate for governor," dragging a cart into which a diminutive Colonel Harvey was helping a huge Boss Smith on his way to the United States senatorship.

Wilson clearly understood, of course, that Smith had agreed not to run again for the senatorship. Meeting Colonel Harvey in Boston, Wilson showed his irritation.

"You must make up your mind for more of that," responded Harvey, "for it cannot be avoided. I have the Senator's authority to withdraw him absolutely whenever, if at all, I should consider it necessary, but I don't dare to do it before the convention. . . . There is nothing to do but grin and bear it."[1]

Wilson did "grin and bear it"; but the inactive part he was forced to play irked him extremely. He longed to get into the fight himself.

"The task you have in hand in Bergen appeals to me most strongly, to the fighting instinct that is in me and which makes the uphill business the really interesting one. But it is my very clear judgment that the best impression on the voters of Bergen, as of all other parts of the State, so far as I am concerned, would be made by my keeping off the stump until the convention has met,—by my keeping consistently in the background."[2]

If the opposition to Wilson in the convention promised to be strong, it was divided. The bosses had the regular army. On the morning of September 15th, they marched down upon Trenton with bands playing and banners flying. The Big Fellow was there in his silk hat; on either hand his lieutenants, Nugent of Newark, "Little Bob" Davis of Jersey City, and "Plank-Shad" Thompson of Gloucester. Little Bob had for a time been somewhat hard to discipline.

"Who the hell is this Wilson?" he had inquired.

When someone asked him later whether he thought Wilson would make a good governor, he replied:

"How the hell do I know whether he'll make a good governor? He'll make a good candidate, and that's the only thing that interests me."

But the orders had gone forth that Wilson was the candidate of the machine; and the word of the boss was the word of God.

The Opera House was packed to the roof. Wilson was not there, of course; but he had come down from Lyme

---

[1] Inglis's account, *Collier's Weekly*, October 14, 1916.
[2] Woodrow Wilson to Dan Fellows Platt, July 23, 1910.

and was twelve miles away, quietly playing golf on the links at Princeton. He was so confident of being nominated that he had already written out his speech of acceptance. But Colonel Harvey was there; he had taken a room at the Trenton House, not distant from that of the Big Boss, and he was now occupying a box at the Opera House, where he could easily step behind the scenes. While the bosses had made confident predictions as to the result of the convention—"It will be Wilson on the first ballot"—they were secretly worried. There were revolts in several of the delegations; and hot resentment because certain delegates opposed to Wilson were not seated. Among those present was an ardent young Irish lawyer from Jersey City, the leader of a group of Democrats who were fighting the "old gang." He had been a member of the legislature, but was so hostile to the candidacy of Woodrow Wilson that he had not been chosen as a delegate to the convention. He was supporting Judge Silzer. His name was Joseph P. Tumulty.

When the perspiring and restless delegates gathered for the afternoon session, many shrewd observers believed that Wilson was defeated. But the Big Boss, "handsome, cool, dignified," rising from his place on the floor, had the convention well in hand. He knew exactly what to do; he was prepared to force Wilson's nomination over any opposition. The delegates from Wilson's own county being opposed to him, Smith had chosen a man to nominate him from the delegation that would, according to alphabetical order, first be called upon. This was Clarence L. Cole of Atlantic, who had never even seen Wilson, and who was so long working up to his climax that the convention began to jeer and shout, "Who's your man?" "Name him: name him!" When he mentioned Woodrow Wilson, the cheering, well staged in advance, swept the hall. A group of Princeton college students, strategically placed on the stage, began to siz-boom for Wilson—with entire sincerity. In the midst of the applause, however, one of the other delegates from Atlantic, a giant of an old man—Judge Crandall—struggled to his feet and asserted vociferously that not all Atlantic County was for Wilson; that he was for Katzenbach. It was the signal for a joyous row. Other delegates tried to pull Crandall down; but he laid about him with his cane, hitting a fellow patriot so hard on his bald head that his cane broke in two. No one can tell what might have happened next if the Big Fellow himself had not stilled the stormy waters, and in his rich low tones seconded Wilson's nomination. He remarked that he and Mr. Wilson did not move in the same world, he did not presume to claim intimate acquaintance with him. He would have preferred a candidate more closely identified with the Organization; but it was necessary to find a man who would appeal to all the voters of the state and who could be elected. Wilson was that man. He was a good Democrat. He was a great man.

More cheering, led by all the little leaders from Essex and Hudson, who were faithfully following instructions. The other men nominated were Katzenbach, Silzer, and Wittpenn. One of the nominators of Katzenbach was Judge John W. Wescott, who made a virulent attack on Wilson and the tyrannical procedure of the bosses in forcing him upon the convention. Wescott so exposed the "immorality" of the situation "as to throw the convention into a state of almost uncontrollable frenzy."[1]

"The supporters of Woodrow Wilson were in a state of panic. Men were on their feet shaking their fists and howling like mad. The storm of protest threatened to carry everything before it. The insurgents were jubilant and

[1] John W. Wescott, *Woodrow Wilson's Eloquence*, p. 22.

confident of victory. It was the happiest day of my life because it seemed certain that the good influences of the State were to come into control of its affairs."[1]

But the machine had weathered many another storm, and the well-disciplined men of Essex and Hudson and Gloucester sat firm and kept their eyes on their leaders. When the vote was called for, after the hammered admonitions of the chairman, Judge Hardin, the well-oiled mechanism of the organization began really to work. Wilson had the votes!

| | |
|---|---|
| Wilson | $749\frac{1}{2}$ |
| Katzenbach | 372 |
| Silzer | 210 |
| Wittpenn | $76\frac{1}{2}$ |

Upon a motion by one of the men of Mercer, the nomination was made unanimous. The members of the convention, a large proportion of whom were thoroughly bitter and resentful, were on the point of bolting from the hall, when they were called to order by Judge Hardin who announced in a stentorian voice:

"We have just received word that Mr. Wilson, the candidate for the governorship, *and the next President of the United States*, has received word of his nomination; has left Princeton, and is now on his way to the Convention."

Everything had been perfectly arranged. It would never have done to let the delegates get away disgruntled, without ever having seen their candidate. Colonel Harvey had made all the plans to produce Wilson at the dramatic moment. He had told his friend and assistant, Inglis:

"For God's sake don't let a whisper get out about Wilson being at Princeton. Think what it would mean if, after all, he is not nominated. He has relied absolutely on our

[1]John W. Wescott, *Woodrow Wilson's Eloquence*, p. 22.

assurances. Think what a personal tragedy, if we failed."[1]

But Wilson must nevertheless be near at hand so that he could be brought to the stage at the right moment—if nominated! At Harvey's direction, Inglis drove to Princeton[2] early in the afternoon. Wilson appeared immediately at the door of Prospect:

"Gentlemen, I am ready."

He was in the pink of condition. He had been resting during the summer; and that morning he had been playing golf. He was still wearing a knitted golf jacket under his coat; and a soft hat with a narrow brim. Good democratic costume!

They drove swiftly to Trenton and to avoid observation Wilson entered the hotel by a side door and went to Colonel Harvey's room.

Wilson knew nothing at that time of the difficulties the bosses had met in the convention, or of the "steam-roller" methods they had used in forcing his nomination. The toil that George Harvey had given to the enterprise! The determined purpose of the Big Boss! Surely nothing could have been more extraordinary than the way in which Wilson was pushed—forced!—into public life. The conflict up to this time, so far as it had affected him, had been in his own soul.

From this moment onward, however, everything was to change. He was now to appear as an active politician: and he was well enough aware of the test he was facing. Everything depended upon the initial impression he made upon men of a type wholly unfamiliar to him.

"Yet there he sat at ease and chatted on indifferent topics as casually as if he were making an ordinary afternoon call."[3]

[1]William O. Inglis to the author.

[2]Edward W. Kemble, the cartoonist who had come to make drawings for *Harper's Weekly*, went with him.

[3]Inglis's account, *Collier's Weekly*, October 14, 1916.

There was in Wilson a curious strain of fatalism, or faith, or courage, or self-discipline—call it what you will—often marked in crises of his career. In great emergencies, where his own fortunes seemed trembling in the balance, he was invariably the least concerned of men.

Wilson's companion, overwrought with anxiety by the slow progress of the convention, suggested a cup of tea, or Scotch, or rye, or a glass of water.

"No, thank you, better without it."

At length, after long waiting, there came a nervous rapping at the door. It was Cole of Atlantic.

"'Dr. Wilson,' said Mr. Cole, 'I have the pleasant duty to inform you that you have been nominated for governor of New Jersey on the first ballot and it has been made unanimous.'

"'Thanks,' answered Wilson. 'I am ready.'"[1]

Five minutes later, Wilson appeared upon the stage of the crowded Opera House—a slim, well-knit figure still wearing his golf jacket. It may be imagined with what curious eyes, resentful, suspicious, hostile, questioning eyes, the assembled delegates, so recently dragooned into making him their candidate for governor, now looked upon him. The burst of applause died down into an intense silence.

Wilson began quite simply, in a voice that carried, without exertion, to the uttermost limits of the great auditorium:

"You have conferred upon me a very great honour. I accept the nomination you have tendered me with the deepest gratification that you should have thought me worthy to lead the Democrats of New Jersey in this stirring time of opportunity."

---

[1] Inglis's account, *Collier's Weekly*, October 14, 1916. The author is also indebted to several other New Jersey leaders who were present at the convention for the facts here given.

It was a speech wholly without the familiar oratorical clap-trap, but delivered with that peculiar sense of direct contact with his hearers which was of the essence of Wilson's genius.

"As you know, I did not seek this nomination. It has come to me absolutely unsolicited, with the consequence that I shall enter upon the duties of the office of Governor, if elected, with absolutely no pledges of any kind to prevent me from serving the people of the State with singleness of purpose. Not only have no pledges of any kind been given, but none have been proposed or desired."

To many of those present, the little ward heelers, the "boys out for the jobs," some of the things that Wilson said must have seemed strange doctrine indeed—and yet, as his speech progressed, the applause became louder and louder.

"The future is not for parties 'playing politics,' but for measures conceived in the largest spirit, pushed by parties whose leaders are statesmen not demagogues, who love, not their offices but their duty and their opportunity for service. We are witnessing a renaissance of public spirit, a reawakening of sober public opinion, a revival of the power of the people, the beginning of an age of thoughtful reconstruction that makes our thought hark back to the great age in which democracy was set up in America. With the new age we shall show a new spirit. We shall serve justice and candour and all things that make for right. Is not our own ancient party the party disciplined and made ready for this great task? Shall we not forget ourselves in making it the instrument of righteousness for the State and for the Nation?"[1]

It is the universal testimony of those who were present that the speech, brief and simple as it was, produced an extraordinary effect. It was not so much what the man

[1]From original document, written by Mr. Wilson.

said, as it was the sense of power and of sincerity that he gave. "Go on," shouted the crowd when he had finished. "Go on, go on!" He literally brought around his bitterest opponents. Young Tumulty and his friends were converted on the spot. "Thank God at last a leader has come." Tumulty himself tells of the effect upon sturdy old Judge Crandall of Atlantic who had so recently endeavoured to prevent Wilson's nomination:

"As I turned to leave the convention hall there stood at my side old John Crandall, of Atlantic City, like myself a bitter, implacable foe of Woodrow Wilson. . . . [He was] waving his hat and cane in the air, and yelling at the top of his voice, 'I am sixty-five years old, and still a damn fool!'"[1]

Wilson seems to have won even the typical roughnecks of the cities. There was a kind of audacity about the man, the mark of the fighter who loves the fight, that they recognized instinctively.

"God, look at the man's jaw!"[2]

Judge Wescott, who had so bitterly attacked Wilson on the floor, had left the convention in disgust. His brother, also a delegate, had remained to hear Wilson speak, and was won over.

"John, we may be wrong about that man. He made a great speech. It was amazingly candid and forceful, exactly in line with your views and those of every real reformer in the state."[3]

Wescott began at once to study Wilson's address, went to see him at Princeton, and became his devoted friend and supporter. It was he who nominated Wilson for the presidency at the Democratic convention in 1912, and again in 1916.

---

[1] Joseph P. Tumulty, *Woodrow Wilson as I Know Him*, p. 22.

[2] Remark overheard by Professor Stockton Axson, who was standing in the stage wings.

[3] John W. Wescott, *Woodrow Wilson's Eloquence*, p. 23.

When Wilson left the stage, "almost mobbed by the excited Democrats," he had stepped into a wholly new world. It was the world to which he was destined by his genius; it was the world which he knew instinctively how to command. All the inhibitions of earlier years, the dogged loyalty to secondary courses, were flung to the winds. Here he was in his element. He was master. And he knew at length that high, stern happiness which comes to the man who has cast doubt behind him, has come to the full realization of his powers.

## II. THE CAMPAIGN BEGINS

Wilson awakened on the morning of September 16th a political celebrity. No state convention in the history of the country, perhaps, was ever so emblazoned in headlines or acclaimed in editorials. It was everywhere assumed that in choosing a Democratic nominee for governor the party was developing a leader for the presidential campaign of 1912. The man himself as a figure unique in American political life—the scholar, the philosopher—awakened the widest curiosity and interest.

"It is a great day for New Jersey and a great day for the nation when a man like Woodrow Wilson comes forward to help reclaim and vivify our political life."[1]

An avalanche of congratulatory letters and telegrams descended upon the astonished nominee.

"Louisville, Kentucky, September 16.
"Hurrah for Wilson. Am going to do my best.
"HENRY WATTERSON"

He was soon to hear the tramping feet of reporters on the broad stairways of the dignified old home of the presidents of Princeton.

[1] New York *Evening Post*, September 16, 1910.

He dreaded reporters—then and always—though there were reporters whom he later came to know and to trust absolutely. So many of them did not "deliver what they received." They were not "accurate-minded." He had decided in his innocence not to talk for publication at all. He would write out what he wished to say and would thus be assured of accuracy. He worked out in shorthand a "Mem. for Interview"—and this was the first sentence of it:

"When asked if he thought the widespread corruption now being exposed was proof of hopeless demoralization in our politics . . . he said:

"'The revelations being made on every hand, by inquiry after inquiry, of the maintenance of business by corruption should fill the whole nation with sorry shame; but they afford no ground for despair.'"

It may be imagined how long his defenses held. A jaunty reporter for the Hearst newspapers asked him baldly why he had permitted himself to be nominated by the "interests." He responded without premeditation, instantly, hotly:

"It is a humiliating and absurd thing to say that I am the Wall Street candidate for governor of New Jersey."[1]

Other correspondents sought interviews, photographs of the candidate, his home, his garden, his family.[2]

"I can see," said Mrs. Wilson ruefully, "that our beautiful private life is gone."

On the 19th the politicians descended upon him. Smith and Nugent, the generals of his campaign, came first to prepare the way for the resentful leaders of Wilson's home county who had opposed him in the convention. It would

---

[1] Hearst's New York *American*, September 16, 1910.

[2] See article in the York New *Times*, September 25, 1910, "Wilson—A Tilden, But a Tilden Up To Date."

never do to go into the battle with his neighbours sniping at him. They were ushered into the fine old library that was Wilson's study. It was lined to the ceiling with books —it had the very atmosphere of books that Wilson and his father and grandfather before him had loved. It was the peaceful stronghold of the scholar. All this, and the quiet and beauty of the trees that sheltered the old house and the terraced garden below it—the garden that Mrs. Wilson had herself planned and kept—made a powerful impression upon these leaders of the hurly-burly world.

"Can you imagine anyone," remarked the Big Fellow, "being damn fool enough to give this up for the heartaches of politics?"[1]

Smith and Nugent—with James Kerney, who had accompanied them—went over the plans of the campaign with Wilson. They found him an eager questioner. He wanted to know all about the local leaders who were coming in a little later:

"The manner in which he grasped every suggestion was a revelation. When the Mercer leaders had in turn been formally presented by Nugent and had taken seats in the library, Wilson proceeded to discuss local political affairs as if they were the one thing in all the world in which he had been taking an interest. He called the various leaders by name and displayed an apparent familiarity that made them feel very much at home. We spent altogether about three hours outlining the campaign. We were charmed by the reception he had given us."[2]

Wilson found it necessary, also, in these first days, to consider another and more intimate problem—that of money. Even a man devoted to the highest service, doing his duty as he saw it, must live—and his family must live.

---

[1] James Kerney, *The Political Education of Woodrow Wilson*, p. 62.
[2] Ibid., p. 64.

He had been able to put aside during his service at Princeton almost no money. In November, 1908, he had written to a friend: "Two years from now I can retire on a Carnegie pension of $4,000. I have $2,000 of my own." He was soon to resign from Princeton University. What was he to do? One of his devoted friends sensed the difficulty at once and sought to remedy it. Wilson replied:

MY DEAR FRIEND,

I have been overwhelmed with letters that were very encouraging to receive but that did not matter. Yours does matter, and I have had to wait till Sunday to get the leisure of heart and mind to reply to it as I wished,—in a letter written by myself, with this mechanical pen of mine.

I know that you will forgive me for returning the cheque, because I know the spirit in which it was sent, and hope that I know the trust and affection it stands for. I do not remember anything that ever touched me more or made me happier. You have treated me as you would have treated your own brother. I feel as I never did before the value and the beauty of the friendship you have honoured me with.

But I want to say, if possible, that I paid every cent of my own personal expenses in this campaign out of my own pocket. I do not think that they will run above a few hundred dollars; and I have arranged to deliver three addresses after the election which will net me five hundred dollars in fees. I made the engagements with the express purpose of earning the money for that object. Friends at every turn are putting their automobiles at my service; I shall have only hotel bills, the fares for short railway journeys, and the fees for extra stenographic services to pay. It will not come to much, all put together. If I get stuck, I will not hesitate to call on you for what I cannot do. You have made that possible by the way you have done this and by what I see between the lines of your generous letters.

I only hope that I shall prove worthy of such trust and friendship. It warms my heart securely against the chills and discouragements that are sure to come in this distracted field of politics. I am grateful with a deep gratitude that I hope will make me a better man.

I am booked for twenty-seven speeches in the next four and a half weeks; but if you are to be East I simply must have a talk with you about what is to be done here.

Please give my warmest regards to your brother.

Gratefully and affectionately Yours,

WOODROW WILSON[1]

A little later, however, when he began to understand the difficulties—the expense!—of campaigning that fell upon his managers, he welcomed contributions made to the organization by old friends like Cleveland H. Dodge and he was delighted when Judge Wescott told him of several small sums of money sent in by unknown supporters and admirers. But he took none of it for his own expenses.

Crowded days, they were, indeed. He opened the fall term of the university on the 22nd with a reading of the First Psalm and spoke of the relationships of "true religion and sound learning."

A few days later he made his last address before the student Christian association, an audience of undergraduates that crowded Murray Hall to its capacity. It was marked by deep feeling. ". . . therefore endure hardness as a good soldier. . . ."

"Don't go about seeking to associate only with good people. Endure hardness. . . . The man who is worthy is the man who goes out and joins battle. He doesn't allow himself to be turned aside by immaterial things, but keeps his eye on the main point that he seeks to gain, and cuts his way to that."

Up to the time his campaign actually began—when he surrendered himself wholly to the new cause—he had moments of profound doubt. He loved the university, he felt himself committed to the struggle there and the new

_____
[1]Woodrow Wilson to David B. Jones, September 25, 1910.

venture was full of uncertainty. He wrote his friend, President Lowell of Harvard University, on September 20th:

"MY DEAR LOWELL:

"Yes, I have gone and done it and am already experiencing many pangs of doubt as to whether I have done the right thing or not but apparently there was nothing else for it in the circumstances and I shall start out upon the new career as bravely as possible.

"I shall see less of you and feel less close to you in the work of each day but I shall hope to have many opportunities to strengthen myself by consulting with you on public affairs and I shall not lose my grip on university affairs, if I can help it."

About this time he found for his comfort in a current magazine[1] the latest poem by Kipling. It was entitled "If——." He read it aloud and carried it for months in his pocket:[2]

If you can dream—and not make dreams your master;
   If you can think—and not make thoughts your aim,
If you can meet with Triumph and Disaster
   And treat those two impostors just the same;
If you can bear to hear the truth you've spoken
   Twisted by knaves to make a trap for fools,
Or watch the things you gave your life to, broken,
   And stoop and build 'em up with worn-out tools: . . .

If you can talk with crowds and keep your virtue,
   Or walk with Kings—nor lose the common touch,
If neither foes nor loving friends can hurt you,
   If all men count with you, but none too much;
If you can fill the unforgiving minute
   With sixty seconds' worth of distance run,
Yours is the Earth and everything that's in it,
   And—which is more—you'll be a Man, my son!

---

[1] *American Magazine*, October, 1910.

[2] Later he had a copy framed and kept it in his study at the White House. It was in his room the day he died.

### III. THE PROFESSOR IN POLITICS

Wilson was scheduled for the "opening gun" of the campaign for September 28th at Jersey City. He dreaded it acutely.

"I have been asking audiences all my life to accept certain ideas and principles, and I have a curious hesitation about asking anyone to vote for me. It smacks of a personal appeal when I want to bring about a change of view."[1]

When he stepped out before the cheering audience in St. Peter's Hall, he was plainly embarrassed. A friend who heard him says he was nearer failure as an orator than on any other occasion, except one, in his life.

"He fumbled, hesitated, dragged in a story that had no connection with what he was saying."[2]

He soon recovered himself and, before he had finished, had captivated his audience. "It was something new in stump speeches."[3] It was naïve in its directness and sincerity.

"I never before appeared before an audience and asked for anything, and now I find myself in the novel position of asking you to vote for me for governor of New Jersey."

And at the end he took the audience completely into his confidence:

"And so, gentlemen, I have made my first political plea. I feel that I am before a great jury. I don't want the judge to butt in. I am content to leave the decision in your hands."

"He was permitted to go no further. From every quarter of the hall there sprang applause that came straight from the hearts of the people. It was an unasked-for expression

---

[1]Professor Stockton Axson to the author.
[2]*Ibid.*
[3]Trenton *True American*, September 29, 1910.

of the people's approval of Wilson's 'first political plea,'
and it lasted many minutes and grew in volume. . . ."[1]

He never faltered again throughout the campaign. His
speeches were without precedent in New Jersey politics.

"There was not a word . . . about 'sweeping the state';
not a syllable about 'driving the Republican hosts into the
sea.' . . . There was not a mention of 'the enemy.'"[2]

His words regarding the Republican party indeed occa-
sioned "a gasp of surprise . . . from the old war horses"[3]
of Democracy:

"I hope sincerely that you will never hear me, in the
course of this campaign, say anything against that great
body of our fellow citizens who have believed in the principles of the Republican party. What I want you to understand me as doing is this: I believe that that great body of
citizens is now led by persons who are not capable of
realizing in a proper spirit the great principles of the
Republican party any more than they can win the acquiescence of those persons who believe in the great principles
of the Democratic party."

In some respects this first New Jersey campaign was his
greatest. Suddenly released from the cramping atmosphere
of the college, his powers expanding in the field for which
his genius and his preparation best fitted him, he adapted
himself with astonishing facility to popular oratory, trans-
lating into the language of the people the teachings of a
quarter of a century. In the beginning his speeches undoubtedly smacked of the academic: he had been too long
a lecturer to students. One who reads the early addresses
one after another finds them curiously connected—like a
course of lectures in college—the whole being an exposition

[1]Trenton *True American*, September 29, 1910.
[2]*Ibid.*
[3]New York *Sun*, September 29, 1910.

of the basic principles of American government. Occasionally he introduced a rhetorical passage, like the glorification of the flag in his acceptance speech. His young followers glowed over such "perorations": but few of his actual campaign speeches contained such predevised flights. "Yes, I know, those boys are strong for perorations." But he himself was more concerned with lucid expression than with perorations.

While Wilson's audiences found something unique, alluring, in this unfamiliar political oratory, his method soon began to irritate the reformers. "Academic lectures on government!" Men like George L. Record who had been working, agitating, organizing, against the evils of the body politic, who knew specific conditions as Wilson did not, and who had certain clearly defined legislative objectives, considered that Wilson's speeches were "glittering generalities, beautifully phrased, but having nothing to do with the political campaign in New Jersey." They wanted him to "come out" for direct primaries, a corrupt practices act, employers' liability, and other advanced measures. These remedies struck at the roots of boss government and privilege in New Jersey. The reformers had been advocating them for years and Wilson, though one of the leading residents of the state, had never helped them, never even shown any interest in their activities. He was now appealing to the progressive spirit which they had been so active in arousing and yet refusing to declare himself on their specific measures.

The reformer has always been a severe critic of the political leader. Lincoln irritated the abolitionists. He hesitated, sought conciliation, talked general principles. Garrison was an uncompromising critic.

"For every blow that Abraham Lincoln ever struck against the system of slavery," said Wendell Phillips, "the martyr of Marshfield may claim that he struck a hundred."[1] Lincoln was even called the "slave-hound of Illinois."[2]

But he finally wrote the Emancipation Proclamation.

The reformer is a pioneer, he knows facts and conditions, he feels deeply, he believes strongly; he has devised remedies of which he is absolutely sure. The political leader, with a genius for uniting men behind a cause, for getting action, seizes upon his precious reforms as mere items of a programme. To the reformer, he appears careless of details, he compromises, he will accept a part of the perfect plan when he cannot get the whole of it. And he takes what he will without giving credit!

As a matter of fact, reformers and political leaders are both indispensable. Their work is not antagonistic; it is supplementary. It is often through the unrelenting criticism of the reformer that the statesman emerges into power, the demagogue withers.

Whether Wilson satisfied the reformers or not, he was proceeding according to the pattern of his own mind. He was interested in general principles rather than in specific measures. He disliked what has been called "statistical reasoning" upon specific subjects; he did not do it well. It had been so throughout his life. He excelled in the exposition of fundamentals, where LaFollette, for example, could hold an audience spellbound for hours with the recital of complicated facts and statistics.

While Wilson's sympathies were all on the side of the people, his political method then and always afterward was to base his appeal upon broad and simple principles that could be easily grasped, avoiding commitment upon specific measures, the details of action, until he was absolutely sure of his ground. It is a method that has im-

[1] *The Liberator*, June 8, 1860.
[2] *Ibid*. June 22, 1860.

mense advantages—and disadvantages—as Wilson himself learned. It is not so difficult to carry your following with you, for example, on the broad principle of democracy in education, ill enough when it becomes necessary to advocate the abolition of an established club system, the breakdown of social privilege, in order to realize the ideal; it is not difficult to demand the reformation of a currency system, bitter indeed to strike at private control of credit; it is not so difficult to carry a nation on the issue of peace, almost impossible to exact the immediate sacrifice of selfish interest involved in joining a world coöperative movement.

There were other reasons why Wilson did not "come out" earlier. He had entered the campaign ignorant of local conditions, unfamiliar with state leadership, above all uncertain regarding the specific measures proposed for meeting the evident evils the Progressives perceived so clearly.

But Wilson was a swift learner. He soon saw that he must make his position both clear and specific upon the two burning issues of the campaign: first his attitude toward the bosses, second, his approval or disapproval of the programme of the progressives. He had from the first been telling the people that his only purpose was to serve their interests; that he had made no pledges, and was under no obligations. But these assertions, as the bosses well knew, were the common coin of campaign oratory. They listened with their tongues in their cheeks. On the other hand, the progressives, especially the Republican progressives, were attacking him hotly not only for his support by the bosses—he was a "decoy-duck" for Smith —but they wanted to know where he stood upon the measures they were advocating.

Wilson chose his time: and acted with devastating vigour.

### IV. WILSON DECLARES WAR ON THE BOSSES

Within two days after Wilson's first speech, when it was plain that he was going to be unexpectedly successful as a campaigner, the Big Boss began to bring pressure upon him. Smith was worried about the liquor question—as were the brewers and saloon-keepers behind him. Wilson was to speak at the Krueger Auditorium at Newark on September 30th. Smith sent for Hudspeth and said:

"The Newark meeting is going to be packed with people who are interested in the liquor question. They are against local option. They are not going to be satisfied unless Wilson changes his views. If he is elected he has got to stand with the party on this subject. Do you think you can get him to come out on the right side?"

"No," answered Hudspeth, "I don't think he is that kind of man."

Smith, however, was insistent. He said he feared the crowd at Newark would break loose and heckle Wilson. He asked Hudspeth and Nugent to explain to Wilson that his attitude on the liquor question was beginning to be used against him among the very people whose support he must have. Wilson listened patiently and responded:

"You know exactly where I stand. I told you in New York."

He then argued that the liquor question was not the real issue in the campaign; that the people were stirred by far more important problems, and that it was good politics and good sense to keep hammering at the main issues. He also elaborated patiently the reasons for his uncompromising position in favour of local option. When he had finished Nugent said:

"It is a nice idealistic position, but we must face the hard facts. Nine tenths of the people who are going to be at that meeting are opposed to it, to say nothing of nine tenths of the Democrats of the state. And they are going to inquire."

Wilson responded instantly:

"I cannot change my position. It is a conviction with me and I must stand upon it."[1]

On the evening of September 30th, the auditorium was packed with a typical lower-ward audience. But there were no "inquiries" regarding the liquor question! Wilson gave them no time. He launched at once into his address. It was one of the great meetings of the campaign. Wilson "held the audience breathless." The newspaper reports, read years afterwards, seem exaggerated, and yet they were written by men on the spot:

"'Ye gods, but that was a great speech,' gasped Judge Simon Hahn, former assemblyman from Essex, who occupied one of the boxes. 'It held me gripped as though I was fascinated and I could hardly move. I didn't expect it, and I enjoyed it all the more.'"[2]

After it was over Smith waited for Wilson, shook hands with him, and remarked, "That was a magnificent speech. You certainly got the crowd." But a moment later he remarked to Hudspeth, "He'll have to stand the consequences of not coming out on local option."[3]

This effort of the bosses to influence his course evidently opened Wilson's eyes. After the meeting, Hudspeth was to take Wilson home. When they got into the automobile, he remembers that Wilson, being overheated, wrapped himself in a plaid rug. Having settled down in the car, Wilson said:

"I want you to tell me more about Smith, Davis, and Nugent, and what they are up to."

[1] Judge Robert S. Hudspeth to the author.
[2] Charles Reade Bacon in the Philadelphia *Record*. See *A People Awakened*, pp. 36–37.
[3] Judge R. S. Hudspeth to the author.

Hudspeth told him what he could, Wilson asking eager questions. Finally Hudspeth remarked:

"You owe your nomination to these men, and they can elect you or defeat you."

To this Wilson responded doggedly:

"I went in without pledges, asked or given, and it is the people, not the bosses, who will elect me if I am elected, and to whom I shall be responsible."

"If you are elected," responded Hudspeth dryly, "you are going to hear a lot from Jim Smith."[1]

If the bosses were alarmed at Wilson's independence, yet they gloated over the prospect of a coming victory. The Democratic party in New Jersey had been wandering in the wilderness for years—and here was the Moses who was leading them out. But, as Nugent remarked, he was "a terrible man to manage." He insisted on going his own way, and paying little or no attention to the solemn business of the organization. The bosses went through all the usual little processes of "getting the organization in line," "rounding up the boys," but no one paid much attention to them. Wilson, as one commentator expressed it, was the "whole show." The vigorous younger men of the party who were opposed to the bosses, Joseph P. Tumulty among them, were Wilson's leading campaigners. Even the campaign funds came largely from Wilson's friends and from people in no way connected with politics who drew a long breath of relief that an able and decent leader had at last appeared in a state campaign.

But the old bosses had learned nothing. When it began to look as though Wilson might not only be elected governor, but might carry into office a wholly unexpected Democratic majority in the legislature, there began to be intimations that Smith would after all claim election to the United States Senate, in spite of his earlier renuncia-

[1]Judge R. S. Hudspeth to the author.

tion of that ambition, in spite of his own palpable unfitness for the place, in spite of the fact that another Democrat—Martine—had received an overwhelming majority of the Democratic votes cast in the September primaries.

At first Wilson gave no credence to the rumour, but if it was true, it was another confirmation of the intention of the bosses, in case of his election, to do what they pleased with the party and with the state government. He could see his administration wrecked on the very issue that was convulsing the nation. He wanted no quarrel with the bosses; but domination by them would be fatal to everything he was, and stood for; he could see that he must make the issue, and his position, absolutely clear.

Machine politics is founded upon organization, and organization upon interest. The end sought is immediate advantage. "You help me and I will help you." Wilson's concern was with principles: he cared little for organization, and the whole business of political reward for service done to the organization was repugnant to him.

The two codes are not only different, but antagonistic. It is easy to see the point of view of the clan-loyal bosses. They had nominated Wilson, they were helping to conduct his campaign, they were contributing some of their own money, and relying on their friends the brewers and the corporations for still more, to elect him. According to their code he must repay them, not only with favours but with submission. The dean of all the bosses, Richard Croker of Tammany Hall, succinctly expressed the code when he remarked a little later, referring to Wilson:

"An ingrate in politics is no good."

According to Wilson's code, on the other hand, politics was intensely impersonal. The idea, the principle, the service of the people generally, was what counted. The individual and his interests mattered little. He hated personal issues always. All a man had to do was to be right and his cause would prevail. As he said in one of his great addresses of a later period:

"The way to success in this great country, with its fair judgments, is to show that you are not afraid of anybody except God and His final verdict. If I did not believe that, I would not believe in democracy."[1]

It was not until the campaign had been under way for six weeks—two weeks indeed before the election—that Wilson publicly met the issue. The attacks of the opposition by this time were finding the politically vulnerable points in his armour. Former Governor Griggs[2] was asserting with more and more vehemence that Wilson was a man without any experience in public affairs, a "man of the library" unacquainted with practical politics or the business of the state. These statements, being uncomfortably near the truth, stung Wilson to the quick, and the next night he challenged any politician in the state to debate any public question with him. The response came from a somewhat unexpected quarter—in a letter from George L. Record:

"The newspapers announce that you have publicly challenged any politician in New Jersey to debate with you upon the public platform any question of public interest.

"I am keenly interested in public questions, and I hope I am enough of a politician to qualify under your challenge.

"At all events, I accept your challenge, and am willing to meet you in public discussion at any of your meetings, or at such other time and place as you may suggest."[3]

Record was the stormy petrel of New Jersey politics.

---

[1] Address at Philadelphia, July 4, 1914. *The Public Papers of Woodrow Wilson*, Vol. III, p. 146.

[2] John W. Griggs.

[3] October 5, 1910.

A tough-minded State of Maine man, an able lawyer, he had been an outstanding reformer, a leader of the "New Idea" movement. He was then running for Congress as a Progressive Republican.

Wilson replied shrewdly enough that if the Republican party would accept Record as its representative, he would gladly meet him. This the Republican bosses were entirely unwilling to do. They liked Record quite as little as they liked Wilson. On October 11th, Wilson wrote to Record:

"Senator Briggs'[1] reply to my letter . . . is so evasive and inconclusive that it confirms me in the impression that we shall have to deal with one another as individuals and not as representatives of any organizations of any kind."

Wilson therefore proposed to Record that he set forth a series of questions to which "I would take pleasure in replying, in a letter which you would be at full liberty to publish." He then went on to say:

"From what I know of your views upon public questions, I think it very likely that we are essentially at one in regard to the substance of our views, and probably differ only in practical detail. Debate, therefore, would seem to be less suitable then a frank interchange of views in a form that can be very simply handled."

Record jumped at the chance and on October 17th sent Wilson a series of nineteen questions calculated to bring out his views on the most delicate and important questions of the campaign—his relationships to the Democratic bosses, his attitude toward the money interests.

Some of Wilson's supporters took alarm and begged him not to reply. They regarded Record's questions as a trap which might easily catch an inexperienced politican. He would injure the cause, he would alienate large elements of the party, he would antagonize the leading men in the organization.

---

[1] Frank O. Briggs, chairman of the Republican State Committee.

Wilson refused to listen to them. He wrote out his answers in shorthand on Record's letter, and on October 24th they were given to the public. He not only answered every question in full, and with absolute candour, but responded to questions that Record had not asked. While he told a friend that it was "only being honest with the people," it was an astounding example of political audacity and sagacity. It was the kind of thing that went all over the country and set people to laughing, to arguing, to praising, to criticizing. It took the wind out of the sails of the Progressives: it brought over the doubtful Republicans: it turned the tide irresistibly in Wilson's favour.

Wilson's position regarding boss control was unequivocal:

Record's question, 14:

"Do you admit that the boss system exists as I have described it? If so how do you propose to abolish it?"

Wilson's answer:

"Of course, I admit it. Its existence is notorious. I have made it my business for many years to observe and understand that system, and I hate it as thoroughly as I understand it. You are quite right in saying that the system is bi-partisan; that it constitutes 'the most dangerous condition in the public life of our state and nation to-day;' and that it has virtually, for the time being, 'destroyed representative government and in its place set up a government of privilege.' I would propose to abolish it by the above reforms, by the election to office of men who will refuse to submit to it and bend all their energies to break it up, and by pitiless publicity."

Record's question, 15:

"In referring to the Board of Guardians, do you mean such Republican leaders as Baird, Murphy, Kean, and

Stokes? Wherein do the relations to the special interests of such leaders differ from the relations to the same interests of such Democratic leaders as Smith, Nugent and Davis?"

Wilson's answer:

"I refer to the men you name. They differ from the others in this, that they are in control of the government of the state, while the others are not and cannot be if the present Democratic ticket is elected."

Record's question, 16:

"I join you in condemning the Republican Board of Guardians. I have been fighting them for years and shall continue to fight them. Will you join me in denouncing the Democratic Overlords, as parties to the same political system? If not, why not?"

Wilson's answer:

"Certainly; I will join you or anyone else in denouncing and fighting any and every one, of either party, who attempts such outrages against the government and public morality."

Record's question, 17:

"You say the Democratic party has been reorganized, and the Republican party has not. Can a political party be reorganized without changing either its leaders, or its old leaders changing their point of view and their political character? Will you claim that either of these events has taken place in the Democratic party? If yes, upon what do you base that conclusion?"

Wilson's answer:

"I do remember saying that it was seeking reorganization, and was therefore at the threshold of a new era. I said this because it is seeking to change its leaders, and will obviously change them if successful in this

election. If I am elected I shall understand that I am
chosen leader of my party and the direct representative
of the whole people in the conduct of the government.
All of this was distinctly understood at the very outset,
when my nomination was first proposed, and there has
never been the slightest intimation from any quarter to
the contrary since. The Republican party is not seeking
to change its leaders, and, therefore, is not even seeking
reorganization."

Record's question, 18:
"Is there any organized movement in the Democratic
party in this state which corresponds to the progressive
Republican movement of which you have favourably
spoken?"

Wilson's answer:
"I understand the present platform and the present
principal nominations of the Democratic party in this
state to be such an organized movement. It will be more
fully organized if those nominees are elected. This is, as
I interpret it, the spirit of the whole remarkable Revival
which we are witnessing, not only in New Jersey, but in
many other states.

"Before I pass to my next question, will you not permit me to frame one which you have not asked, but
which I am sure lies implied in those I have just answered? You wish to know what my relations would be
with the Democrats whose power and influence you fear,
should I be elected governor, particularly in such important matters as appointments and the signing of
bills, and I am very glad to tell you. If elected I shall
not, either in the matter of appointments to office or
assent to legislation, or in shaping any part of the policy
of my administration, submit to the dictation of any
person or persons, special interest or organization. I

will always welcome advice and suggestions from any citizen, whether boss, leader, organization man, or plain citizen, and I shall constantly seek the advice of influential and disinterested men, representative of their communities and disconnected from political 'organizations' entirely; but all suggestions and all advice will be considered on their merits, and no additional weight will be given to any man's advice or suggestion because of his exercising, or supposing that he exercises, some sort of political influence or control. I should deem myself forever disgraced should I in even the slightest degree coöperate in any such system or any such transactions as you describe in your characterization of the 'boss' system. I regard myself as pledged to the regeneration of the Democratic party which I have forecast above.''

Record's question, 19:
"Will you agree to publicly call upon the Republican and Democratic candidates for the legislature to pledge themselves in writing prior to election in favour of such of the foregoing reforms as you personally favour? If not, why not?''
Wilson's answer:
"I will not. Because I think it would be most unbecoming in me to do so. That is the function of the voters in the several counties. Let them test and judge the men, and choose those who are sincere.''

Wilson was equally outright regarding the problems, then red-hot, of public utilities, corporations, trusts. He took the progressive position regarding state control of utilities, workmen's compensation, the direct election of United States senators, and in favour of a corrupt practices act.

It might have been expected that such an indictment of

the bosses would have alienated Smith, Nugent, Davis, and the others. It did not! They plainly did not believe that Wilson meant what he said. They regarded it as "wonderful campaign stuff"; it would "put him over." On one occasion Smith sat with Harvey in a box at one of Wilson's meetings and smiled broadly and benevolently while Wilson was reasserting his views on boss control of politics. To the end of the campaign Wilson literally fascinated Smith by his powers as an orator and campaigner. The veteran politician had never seen anything like it.

### V. WILSON SWEEPS THE STATE

The New Jersey campaign was the making of Wilson politically. His power with his audiences from the beginning was consummate. This is a fact upon which every commentator of the time, enemy or friend, agrees. "He was the only orator I ever heard who could be confidential with a crowd." From the very beginning he made the campaign so interesting, so amusing, so stirring, that he focussed the attention of the entire country to a degree unprecedented in a state election.

"A perfectly frank candidate for office is a rarity, so rare that very few persons can recollect ever listening to one. Dr. Wilson is one. . . . What he really does is to stand up before his audience and think out loud. . . .

"There is a genuine ring to every word he utters. The hallmark of sincerity is stamped on his face and he makes you feel his force and earnestness."[1]

The metropolitan newspapers of New York, Philadelphia, and Baltimore sent men into the field to report his meetings. Extracts from his addresses were published in papers all over America. In far away Texas, the Waco

[1]Frank R. Kent, in the Baltimore *Sun*, November 4, 1910.

*Times-Herald*, after publishing a three-column editorial on the campaign, remarked:

"In Woodrow Wilson we have the clear thinker, the true patriot, and the right sort of a Democrat, and we are hoping for his election as governor of New Jersey, having in mind the possibility of his going to live in the White House at Washington."[1]

He began to strike off the kind of phrases that stick and cling in the popular mind. On September 20th he referred to the trust problem as "corporation joy-riding": on October 10th he first used the expression "pitiless publicity" as a cure for the evils of big business.

One element of Wilson's power on the platform was a gift of mimicry; he could tell a Negro or Scotch story to perfection. When he wanted to illustrate the lack of purpose or leadership in the Republican party he told the story of the mule on a Mississippi River steamboat that ate the destination tag attached to its collar.

"Cap'n," cried out the Negro deckhand in great excitement, "dat mule done ate up whar he gwine to!"

He had an extraordinary aptness in swift repartee. Speaking of "political optimists," someone in the audience called out, "What is an optimist?"

"An optimist," he responded instantly, "is a man who is able to make pink lemonade out of the lemons handed him by his enemies in politics."

He had apt illustrations for the policies he was advocating —like that of "personal guilt," as applied to the problem of the trusts:

"If an automobile breaks the speed limit it surely would not be logical to lock up the automobile. Automobiles are useful, but sometimes the men who run them make them harmful. . . . every time that a corporation violates the law

[1] October 7, 1910.

you may be pretty sure that it is a single person's mind which prompted that violation."[1]

The last and greatest speech of the campaign was at Newark, on November 5th, three days before the election. The audience was immense, a gathering "totally unmatched . . . [in] New Jersey history."[2]

". . . Mr. Wilson stepped out into the glare of electric light, the immense audience 'cut loose for fair,' as one on the stage expressed it. They shouted and cheered and threw their hats in the air, stood on chairs, and kept cheering and calling his name till it seemed the candidate must be embarrassed. Then he started it going all over again when he said:

"'It sounds like the cheering on the homestretch.'

"'And Wilson wins!' cried an enthusiast, as the thousands of throats broke into another roar."[3]

He was at once on intimate terms with his hearers:

"I want to speak very plainly to this audience to-night. I have now been into every county of the state, and I have seen audiences that would move the heart of any man, thronging in numbers and rallying around, not a party, not a person, not to accomplish some selfish purpose of interest, but to enjoy the experience of hearing the genuine interest of the entire commonwealth candidly discussed. I have tried throughout this campaign to be as candid and as fair as I knew how to be; I have tried always to dwell upon the merits of every question. . . ."

He went on to put his idea of party leadership straight to the voters—a party leadership plainly designed to shelve the bosses:

---

[1] This illustration, first used at a Princeton alumni luncheon by Dr. Samuel M. Crothers of Boston, delighted Wilson. After the "joy-riding" simile became completely identified with his name he remarked ruefully to his friend Axson, "I am afraid it is often like this: a good thing belongs not to the inventor but to the person most conspicuous in the public eye who uses it."

[2] Charles Reade Bacon in the Philadelphia *Record*. See *A People Awakened*, p. 220.

[3] *Ibid*.

"I want to say, therefore, that I understand the present campaign to mean this—that if I am elected governor I shall have been elected leader of my party and shall have been elected governor of all the people of New Jersey, to conduct the government in their interest and in their interest only, using party and party coherents for that service. If the Democratic party does not understand it in that way, then I want to say to you very frankly that the Democratic party ought not to elect me governor. . . ."

Those who heard this last address have never forgotten the strange lift, the aspiration, the fire of enthusiasm Wilson communicated to his hearers:

"We have begun a fight that, it may be, will take many a generation to complete, the fight against special privilege, but you know that men are not put into this world to go the path of ease; they are put into this world to go the path of pain and struggle. No man would wish to sit idly by and lose the opportunity to take part in such a struggle. All through the centuries there has been this slow, painful struggle forward, forward, up, up, a little at a time, along the entire incline, the interminable way. . . .

"What difference does it make if we ourselves do not reach the uplands? We have given our lives to the enterprise, and that is richer and the moral is greater."

"At the end of this memorable and touching speech old Senator James Smith, seated alongside of me, pulled me by the coat and, in a voice just above a whisper and with tears in his eyes, said: 'That is a great man, Mr. Tumulty. He is destined for great things.'"[1]

When Wilson returned to Princeton on that Saturday night following the Newark speech, no one doubted that he would be elected: but no one dreamed that the victory would be so stupendous. His majority at the election was

[1] Joseph P. Tumulty, *Woodrow Wilson As I Know Him*, p. 45.

49,056—the largest ever given a candidate for governor, with a single exception. He carried 15 of the 21 counties, some of which had never before given a Democratic majority. The legislature in which there had been a Republican majority of 31 in joint ballot in a total of 81, now had a Democratic majority of 21. It was the more remarkable in that the state had been for seventeen years steadily Republican, Taft's plurality two years before having been 82,776. While there had been a Democratic landslide in other states, Wilson's campaign and his victory were the outstanding political events of the year.

To Wilson himself the most affecting incident of the election was the enthusiasm of the students of Princeton. When the result was assured, they formed a parade, "the largest ever seen in Princeton," because it included the townsfolk, and marched with torches and banners, headed by the band, to the new Governor's home. Here they gave the college cheer and Wilson, appearing in the window, spoke with deep feeling to the men of the university.

"It is my ambition to be the governor of all the people of the state, and render to them the best services I am capable of rendering."

### VI. THE BIG BOSS SEEKS CONTROL

While Wilson's victory at the polls had been decisive, he discovered immediately that the real fight had only begun. The campaign had drawn heavily upon his physical resources, and he was now inundated with congratulatory letters and telegrams from every part of the country. No one of them pleased him more than the message, received before the election, from his father's old Negro servant in North Carolina:

"I am praying for your election as governor of New Jersey. David Bryant, your father's old servant."

Another was from the Governor of Indiana:

"I welcome you into the Company of Governors who think that principles are worth maintaining. Congratulations.

"THOMAS R. MARSHALL".

He was to learn for the first time what it meant to be elected to office in America—the supporters who came to tell him whom he must appoint, the friends eager with warnings, the former opponents darkening his doorway with hat in hand to prove that they were now his devoted friends. Mrs. Wilson, fearing for his health, demanded that he escape for a fortnight's rest.

"You've been elected; why shouldn't you take a vacation?".

Wilson was preparing to leave Princeton, when he received an altogether astonishing visit from the Big Boss himself. In spite of Wilson's attacks on the boss system during the campaign, Smith had rejoiced in the swelling success of the campaign and on the day after the election had sent the new Governor the following telegram:

"The result of the election affords convincing proof of your ability to lead. Your campaign has been without precedent. . . . Every well wisher of good government will hail the result as a personal gain. You have now earned a rest which I hope you will permit yourself to take before assuming duties that are to bring you further honour."

A day or so later, the Big Boss arrived in Princeton, suave, immaculate, to offer his felicitations in person; and also, as if by chance, to remark that his friends were now urging him strongly to become a candidate for United States senator, that his health was much improved, and that he "hoped the legislature would offer him the seat."

While Wilson had had intimations of Smith's intention during the campaign, the bland assurance of his course was astounding—the more so when he discovered that Smith and Nugent, losing no time upon vacations such as Smith was recommending for him, were already bringing pressure to bear upon the newly elected legislators. We have Wilson's own account of this meeting:

"I pointed out to him that this action on his part would confirm all the ugliest suspicions of the campaign concerning him, and urged him very strongly not to allow his name to be used at all: but my arguments had no effect upon him."[1]

Wilson had taken no public position on the question of the senatorship—it had not arisen in the campaign. He had rested upon Smith's positive declaration made before the convention in September that he would not be a candidate. The Democratic party at the preferential primary in September had given James E. Martine an overwhelming majority of the votes cast for United States senator and Smith had not even offered his name as a candidate. While the preferential vote was advisory and not legally binding upon the legislature, the method had had the approval of the Democratic platform and it represented the only available expression of the wishes of the people.

During his conversation with Wilson, Smith had argued that the primary was a joke.

"It was very far from a joke," rejoined the Governor-elect. "But assume that it was. Then the way to save it from being a joke hereafter is to take it seriously now. . . . The question who is to enjoy one term in the Senate is of small consequence compared with the question whether the people of New Jersey are to gain the right to choose their own senators forever."

Smith had plenty of courage: he knew well enough that he must assert his power or lose it. The contest had to be.

---

[1] Trenton *True American*, December 24, 1910. Statement given out by Governor-elect Wilson, dated December 23, 1910

He had no moral power, no claim upon the faith of the people; his strength rested upon personal favours given and received. He knew that his following would desert him —as indeed it did—when he could no longer "deliver the goods."

Wilson was also aware that the contest was inevitable. It was not enough to declare his opposition to the bosses; it was not enough to be elected on that declaration; he had now to act. His cherished plans for a vacation ended on the spot; he made up his mind to remain at Princeton and see the fight through.

He could, it is quite true, have avoided the issue. He could have argued that it was for the legislature to decide; that he had no constitutional or legal right to interfere. It would have been easy for him as a politician to slip away among the mazes of the American system of divided powers, "checks and balances," from that "responsible leadership" of which he had been talking and writing all his life. He argued out the situation, presenting all sides of the case, "thinking aloud," with several visitors who came to see him during the week after election.[1]

Dix of New York, who had been swept into the governorship on the same Democratic landslide, pursued exactly that policy, kept his hands off the senatorial contest—and was never heard of again! Dix said in an interview at that time:

"I do not agree with Governor-elect Woodrow Wilson, of New Jersey. I think the legislature is amply able to take care of itself in the selection of a United States senator and I see no reason why I should interfere."

It was a difficult position indeed for an amateur in politics. Wilson had no organization behind him, no money, only slight acquaintance with the leaders, few supporters he could be sure of; he had been less than two months in

[1] Dan Fellows Platt, on November 12, 1910, among them.

active politics. And he was pitted against one of the most astute, experienced, and powerful political bosses in the country. Some of his friends argued strongly against an "irretrievable break." He might indeed beat Smith for the Senate, but could he go on and get the reforms he sought from a restive legislature? Above all, what hope would there be in a coming national campaign if his own state organization was fighting him? Several of the "wise writers" for the New York newspapers were already, and quite cynically, prophesying Smith's election to the Senate. It was with a distinct sense of renunciation that Wilson went into the fight.

The senatorial situation was further complicated by the fact that the candidate whom he must support in opposition to Smith was ill-fitted for the high office of United States senator. Many citizens of New Jersey who were opposed to Smith could not stomach Martine. A man of independent means, Martine lived in a fine country place and had upheld for years the banner of the Democracy in a district overwhelmingly Republican. He had been a candidate for every office from sheriff up and had never been elected to anything. He was known throughout the state as "Farmer Jim." An honest, noisy, whole-hearted and not unlovable man, a vociferous follower of Bryan, it was his tragedy that no one took him seriously. As a talker he was utterly incontinent. Wilson said of him ruefully after an interview:

"The trouble with Martine as a talker is that he has no terminal facilities."

Finally, Wilson hated personal controversy. Personal controversy obscured principles and measures; and he had nothing personal against Smith; it was the boss system and boss control that he was fighting.

In spite of all these difficulties and dangers, it is clear, from the very first, that Wilson was unalterably determined to assert his leadership—boss or no boss. If he could secure it by reason, by argument, by persuasion, well and good; if not, he was prepared for the rough-and-tumble of what must be a fight without gloves.

## VII. WILSON TRIES PERSUASION

On November 14th, Wilson acted. He wrote an appreciative letter to Martine which he knew would be published immediately. While he did not mention the senatorship, the warmth of the letter was unmistakable:

MY DEAR MR. MARTINE:

It was a very great victory, and you were one of the most valiant fighters in it. Words of appreciation do not pay the debt; but it is delightful to speak them where they are so well appreciated and deserved. We shall now lift the old party to new success.

With warmest regards and appreciation,

Faithfully yours,
WOODROW WILSON

His next step was to bring friendly pressure to bear upon Smith to get him to withdraw as a candidate for senator. He appealed to several of his trusted friends, among others Cleveland H. Dodge, who, though no politician, knew men in New York who could bring powerful influence to bear on Smith; and he corresponded with Henry Watterson and George Harvey. His letter to Harvey of November 15th— a letter almost certain to reach Smith's eyes—while it referred to the Boss in courteous, even complimentary, terms, left no doubt as to Wilson's determination:

"I am very anxious about the question of the senatorship. If not handled right it will destroy every favourable impression of the campaign and open my administration with a split party. I have learned to have a very high opinion of Senator Smith. I have very little doubt that if he were sent to the Senate he would acquit himself with honour and do a great deal to correct the impressions of his former term. But his election would be distasteful to the very people who elected me and gave us a majority in the legislature. . . . They count upon me to prevent it. I shall forfeit their confidence if I do not. All their ugliest suspicions, dispelled by my campaign assurances, will be confirmed.

"It was no Democratic victory. It was a victory of the 'progressives' of both parties, who are determined to leave no one under either of the political organizations that have controlled the two parties of the state. . . . It is grossly unjust that they should regard Senator Smith as the impersonation of all that they hate and fear; but they do, and there is an end to the matter. If he should become a candidate, I would have to fight him; and there is nothing I would more sincerely deplore. It would offend every instinct in me, except the instinct as to what was right and honest from the point of view of public service. I have had to do similar things in the University.

"By the same token, ridiculous though it undoubtedly is, I think we shall have to stand by Mr. Martine. . . .

"I have stripped my whole thought and my whole resolution naked for you to see just as it is. Senator Smith can minimize the biggest man in the state by a dignified refusal to let his name be considered. I hope, as I hope for the rejuvenation of our party, that he may see it and may proceed to do so.

"It is a national as well as a state question. If the independent Republicans who in this state voted for me are not to be attracted to us they will surely turn again in desperation to Mr. Roosevelt. . . ."[1]

Wilson secured no help from Harvey. Harvey was a friend of Smith's; he refused to take sides in the senatorial

---

[1] Transcribed from Mr. Wilson's original stenographic copy.

struggle, and from this time onward the relationships between the two men began to change.

Meanwhile, Cleveland H. Dodge had indirectly brought pressure to bear on Smith "without any satisfactory result, and it is evident that Smith proposes to go to the Senate. I hear from a reliable source that all the Democratic Assemblymen, but six, are under such financial obligations to him that he owns them absolutely."[1]

Henry Watterson went personally to see Smith to "impress the wisdom of accepting the inevitable with good grace." Smith did not budge.

In the meantime, Wilson was receiving letters from all parts of the state protesting against Smith's candidacy; the progressive newspapers were urgent.

"For at least thirty years New Jersey has not been represented at Washington by a single man who had the common good at heart. Every one of them was selected, not by men, but by money; not to look after the common good, but property."[2]

Some of the progressives, and even more, the radicals, were beginning to attack Wilson hotly for "playing fast and loose," for not "coming out." But as on so many other occasions in his political career, he held back, trying his best to prevent an open break, seeking "accommodation," trying to persuade Smith to withdraw. He was losing no time in widening his acquaintance among the public men, especially the editors, of the state. He began inviting them by twos or threes to visit him at Princeton to talk over the senatorial situation. He had already secured an astonishing grasp of the "lay of the land" in New Jersey. Although he himself had always been an extremely sparing reader of newspapers, confining himself at that time almost

---

[1] Cleveland H. Dodge to Woodrow Wilson, November 18, 1910.

[2] The *Observer* of Hoboken, November 17, 1910. The *Observer* was edited by Matthias C. Ely, one of the able Democrats of the state, at first a critic of Wilson, afterwards his supporter.

exclusively to the New York *Evening Post*,[1] Mrs. Wilson followed indefatigably, as she had been doing for years, everything in the press that she thought would interest or assist her husband. She saw practically all the important papers of the state, to say nothing of the New York newspapers, and clipped out everything relating to the campaign. She would go over the assortment with Mr. Wilson every day, often giving him suggestions as to people to see, Mr. Wilson making memoranda in the little book he carried always in his vest pocket. The clippings she made during these weeks, to the number of many hundreds, are to be found to-day in Wilson's files.

At this time Wilson was still living at Prospect, the residence of the presidents of Princeton, but he must now give over his educational work. It proved a "sad business"; but on October 20th he had formally presented his resignation from the presidency of the university "I have so long loved and sought to serve."

"In view of Princeton's immemorial observance of the obligation of public service, I could not have done otherwise."

He asked that the board "act upon the resignation at once."

"It is my earnest prayer that the University may go forward without halt or hindrance in the path of true scholarship and thoughtful service of the nation."[2]

The board of trustees met on November 3rd and, after accepting the resignation, placed on record "its high appreciation of the great service which he has rendered to the educational life of the University and the higher education of the country at large during these eight years of his administration." In view of the absurd stories later circulated by Wilson's enemies to the effect that his res-

---

[1] At other times he depended on the Springfield *Republican* or the Baltimore *Sun*.
[2] *The Public Papers of Woodrow Wilson*, Vol. II, p. 269.

ignation was "forced,"[1] the resolution of the board is here presented:

"Resolved, That the salary of Woodrow Wilson, as President of the University, be continued until the end of the first term of the present academic year, that he be invited to continue to occupy the premises at Prospect, and that he be requested, in so far as he may find it possible in such duties as may devolve upon it, to continue his present professorship of Jurisprudence and Politics, which he has made of such service to the student body."

At the same meeting the board further honoured him by conferring upon him the degree of Doctor of Laws.

Wilson refused, however, to accept any salary, either as president or as professor, after the date of his resignation on October 20th, "in view of the financial needs of the university," and he was soon to move into Princeton Inn, where he was to make his home for many months. His entrance into politics represented a real financial sacrifice.

## VIII. THE BATTLE BEGINS: WILSON'S ULTIMATUM

Wilson soon saw that he could not rely merely upon "public pressure" in his campaign to prevent Smith's nomination, for the Boss was busily engaged in tying up the members of the legislature.

"Ever since the election he has been using every means at his disposal to obtain the pledges of Democratic members of the legislature to vote for him as senator. He has assumed, in dealing with them, that the state organization

---

[1] Senator Henry Cabot Lodge was instrumental in spreading abroad this small beer of misrepresentation. See *The Senate and the League of Nations*, by Henry Cabot Lodge, p. 219. President John Grier Hibben of Princeton University had finally to meet the lie with the public statement:

"I shall be very glad to answer that the resignation of President Wilson as president of Princeton University was handed to the board of trustees in October, 1910, when he made the race for governor of New Jersey. He resigned for that purpose and his resignation was not 'forced.' It was voluntary."

would be in control of the legislature; that its offices would be distributed as he should suggest; that members would be assigned to committees and the committees made up as he wished them to be. He has offered to assist members in obtaining membership on such committees as they might prefer. In brief, he has assumed that he and other gentlemen not elected to the legislature by the people would have the same control over the action of the houses that is understood to have been exercised by the so-called Board of Guardians of the Republican party in recent years."[1]

Wilson saw that he must get down into the sweat and dust of direct political combat. On November 25th he appeared in the office of Joseph P. Tumulty in Jersey City —to that ardent young man's astonishment. He wanted to see "Little Bob" Davis, who was sometimes in revolt against the Big Boss. Possibly Davis could be won away. Tumulty went with him to the little red-brick house among the plain people from which for years "Little Bob" had ruled the political destinies of Hudson County. Davis was dying of cancer; his face was pinched and white; but his political militancy was undimmed. He suggested that Wilson keep his hands off the senatorial situation.

"If you do, we'll support your whole legislative programme."

"How do I know you will?" responded Wilson. "If you beat me in this first fight, you will be able to beat me in everything."

Davis laid his hand almost affectionately on Wilson's arm, and expressed the only code he knew—that of clan loyalty:

"I've given my word to Smith; I can't go back on him."

---

[1]Trenton *True American*, December 24, 1910. Statement given out by Governor-elect Wilson, dated December 23, 1910.

Wilson's method of dealing with the legislators was as far removed as possible from that of the bosses. He invited them in small groups to meet him at Princeton or at the Collingwood Hotel in New York. He did not threaten, he offered no rewards; what he did was to reason with them, impress upon them their duty to serve the people who elected them.

"That your visit to Jersey City has helped the cause, no one can doubt, for even the closest friends and advisers of Mr. Davis have counselled him to go slowly and to repudiate Senator Smith. The sentiment in our county is daily growing and the people await your announcement with patience and great expectation, and evidence their willingness to follow 'the true and courageous.'"[1]

Progressives outside the state were watching Wilson's course with anxious eyes. Would he prove big enough, strong enough, to meet the situation? Or would he be downed by the bosses? "The First Test of Woodrow Wilson" was a heading in the Philadelphia *North American*.[2]

On December 5th, Wilson had made such progress with the fight that he could write in no uncertain words to the editor of the New York *Evening Post:*

"It looks as if we had Smith safely beaten for the Senatorship. It is equally clear that we have sufficient majority to elect Mr. Martine. . . .

"I hope tomorrow to see Senator Smith, and tell him very plainly what my position is in order to induce him, if possible, to decline the candidacy. If he will not do that I will come out openly against him."[3]

He was now ready to beard the lion in his den. He went to Newark on December 6th and called on Smith. It must

---

[1]Joseph P. Tumulty to Woodrow Wilson, November 30, 1910.
[2]December 5, 1910.
[3]Woodrow Wilson to Oswald Garrison Villard, December 5, 1910.

have been a beautiful meeting! Wilson, thin, lithe, scholarly
in appearance, with a gaunt, ascetic, sharply cut Scotch
face; Smith, huge, sleek, rich, well-fed, cherubic-faced,
suave in manner—two more courteous gentlemen were
not to be found in New Jersey: nor two more determined.
Both of them were fighting for their lives; and yet neither
raised his voice. Wilson began by saying that although
he had as yet taken no public stand, it was his intention,
unless Smith withdrew, to announce his open opposition.

"Will you be content in having thus publicly announced
your opposition?" asked the aspirant.

"No. I shall actively oppose you with every honourable
means in my power," replied the Governor-elect.

"Does that mean that you will employ the state patronage against me?" inquired Mr. Smith.

"No," answered Wilson. "I should not regard that as an
honourable means. Besides, that will not be necessary."

The Governor-elect then laid down this ultimatum:

"Unless I hear from you, by or before the last mail delivery on Thursday night... I shall announce my opposition to you on Friday morning."[1]


## IX. OPEN WAR

Wilson waited his two days—busily! He kept on seeing
legislators, he attended an affecting ceremony at Princeton
at which the senior class presented him with a loving cup,
and he made ready for his announcement in case he did
not hear from Smith. "... Smith proves to be the tough
customer he is reputed to be," he wrote to his friend
Thomas D. Jones.[2]

When the last mail on Thursday night brought no
message from Smith, Wilson released his statement:

[1]From the account given by William Bayard Hale, and from interviews with New
Jersey leaders.

[2]December 8, 1910.

"The question, Who should be chosen by the incoming legislature of the state to occupy the seat in the Senate of the United States, which will presently be made vacant by the expiration of the term of Mr. Kean, is of such vital importance to the people of the state, both as a question of political good faith and as a question of genuine representation in the Senate, that I feel constrained to express my own opinion with regard to it in terms which cannot be misunderstood. I had hoped that it would not be necessary for me to speak, but it is.

"I realize the delicacy of taking any part in the discussion of the matter. As governor of New Jersey I shall have no part in the choice of a senator. Legally speaking, it is not my duty even to give advice with regard to the choice. But there are other duties besides legal duties. The recent campaign has put me in an unusual position. I offered, if elected, to be the political spokesman and adviser of the people. I even asked those who did not care to make their choice of governor upon that understanding not to vote for me. I believe that the choice was made upon that understanding; and I cannot escape the responsibility involved. I have no desire to escape it. It is my duty to say, with a full sense of the peculiar responsibility of my position, what I deem it to be the obligation of the legislature to do in this gravely important matter.

"I know that the people of New Jersey do not desire Mr. James Smith, Jr., to be sent again to the Senate. If he should be, he will not go as their representative. The only means I have of knowing whom they do desire to represent them is the vote at the recent primaries, where 48,000 Democratic voters, a majority of the whole number who voted at the primaries, declared their preference for Mr. Martine of Union County. For me that vote is conclusive. I think it should be for every member of the legislature.

"Absolute good faith in dealing with the people, an

unhesitating fidelity to every principle avowed, is the highest law of political morality under a constitutional government. The Democratic party has been given a majority in the legislature; the Democratic voters of the state have expressed their preference under a law advocated and supported by the opinion of their party, declared alike in platforms and in enacted law. It is clearly the duty of every Democratic legislator who would keep faith with the law of the state, and with the avowed principles of his party, to vote for Mr. Martine. It is my duty to advocate his election—to urge it by every honourable means at my command."

Smith was apparently dumbfounded. So sure was he of his power that he seemed not to have believed up to that time that Wilson was in earnest. He came back hotly:

"I have read Governor-elect Wilson's statement on the United States senatorial situation. . . . It is a gratuitous attack upon one who has befriended him, but whose candidacy has not been announced. And it is an unwarranted attempt to coerce the legislature. . . .

"The Governor-elect has given striking evidence of his aptitude in the art of foul play. Gratitude was not expected of him, but fairness was, and his act denies it. . . .

"His reasons, when analyzed, cease to be reasons. They are merely excuses for an act which marks his initial step as governor-elect with worse than a blunder—with an assault that is neither fair nor honourable."

Wilson went into the fight with regret but with determination:

"Smith has at last come openly out and defied me to defeat him: and defeated he must be if it takes every ounce of strength out of me. I feel pretty confident it can be done; but a nasty enough fight is ahead, and I shall have to do some rather heartless things which I had hoped might be avoided. They are against all the instincts of kindliness in me. But you cannot fight the unscrupulous without using very brutal weapons. I only hope I shall use them like a gentleman and a man of honour. Probably I shall have to go out on the stump again and conduct something like a systematic campaign against the whole gang: for Smith is only one of a gang that has had its grip upon the throat of the State for a generation. He is no Democrat. He has been in close alliance with men calling themselves Republicans and their purposes have been wholly non-partisan, as non-partisan as those of the plain (and much more picturesque) highwayman.

"I cannot say whether I relish the new job or not. It is grim and forbidding in many ways, and there is a certain indomitable something in me that gets satisfaction out of it all; and, for the rest, I have not time to think whether I like it or not. It does not matter. It has to be faced and carried through."[1]

The battle was now on—and there were no tips on the foils. The public loves a fight; and the attention of the entire country was more than ever attracted by the contest. The "wise writers," knowing the power of the boss system, still predicted Smith; but a shout of joy went up from the progressives:

"It is going to be a splendid fight. Those who thought that it could be averted or compromised did not know how thoroughly the people are aroused or how alarmed are the bosses and the interests which they represent. . . ."[2]

Wilson's friend John Sharp Williams[3] wrote:

"I see Smith thinks you are not 'polite.' Polite! Heavens! When the question is about balking the publicly expressed will of a Party & furthermore of preventing the return to the Senate of one of the four men who in '93

---

[1]Woodrow Wilson to Mary A. Hulbert, December 16, 1910.

[2]The *Observer* of Hoboken, December 10, 1910.

[3]Congressman, afterwards senator from Mississippi and a loyal friend and supporter.

& '94 as members of that august body converted tariff revision & reformation into a *fiasco* that made the very gods on Olympus hold their sides with piteous laughter— so piteous that in the end it became strangely like tears. You did exactly right."[1]

There were hot exchanges between Smith and Wilson; and even an attempt by Wilson's enemies to raise the religious issue, Smith being a Roman Catholic with a strong Roman Catholic following, and Wilson a Scotch Presbyterian—types as antagonistic as any could well be. Wilson met the issue with political wariness. He welcomed the support of progressive Catholics like Mark A. Sullivan, John J. Treacy, Martin Devlin, and James Kerney; and he chose Joseph P. Tumulty as his private secretary:

". . . the plot thickens about me here; the Smith forces are trying to coil me about with plans of their own which it will take more knowledge of past transactions here than I now have to checkmate and defeat. I am therefore going to ask one of the ablest of the young Democratic politicians of the State if he will not act as my secretary in order that I may have a guide at my elbow in matters of which I know almost nothing."[2]

The attack that proved most devastating of all to the Smith forces was the public mass meeting held on January 5th in the heart of the enemy country, at St. Patrick's Hall, Jersey City. It was bitterly resented by the bosses, but the people were there in force. The "ordinary man" understood the issue exactly:

"If Senator Smith, and those interested in his personal fortunes, reduce politics to the principle of gratitude, and quid pro quo, I would like to know how the disinterested and noble services of ordinary men are to be rewarded?"[3]

---

[1] December 14, 1910.

[2] Woodrow Wilson to Oswald Garrison Villard, January 2, 1911.

[3] Judge John W. Wescott to Woodrow Wilson, December 10, 1910.

One of the many cartoons of Woodrow Wilson published at the
beginning of his political career.    This is from the St. Louis *Post-
Dispatch*, December 29, 1910.

The meeting had been so widely heralded that prominent people came from New York and Connecticut. Mrs.
Wilson, who knew how nervous her husband sometimes
became when any member of his family was present, was
a concealed spectator. Most of the progressive leaders of
the state, Republican as well as Democratic, were there.
Some of Wilson's staid university friends were amazed
by the rough-and-tumble political skill he had acquired as
a speaker since he began his campaign.

"At every reiteration of his determination to fight to
the last for the election of James Martine to the United
States Senate he was cheered to the echo. Turning to Mr.
Martine, who sat on the platform, he said:

"'I appeal to Mr. Martine never under any circumstances to withdraw.' The audience went wild in applause."

Wilson made it clear that he was animated by no personal feeling toward Smith:

"If I understand my own heart, ladies and gentlemen,
I do not entertain personal animosities in this matter. It
is not a question of persons and their faults. . . ."[1]

What he was against was the system of control by selfish
interests:

". . . I want to point out to you that Mr. James Smith,
Jr., represents not a party but a system—a system of
political control which does not belong to either party . . .
it is the system that we are fighting, and not the representatives."[2]

The reaction of Wilson's address in the state was impressive:

"No such assemblage was ever before held in this
county. It exceeded in size any ever held in a single hall,
and enough people were turned away by the police to fill
the auditorium a second time. . . .

[1]Baltimore *Sun*, January 6, 1911.
[2]*Ibid.*

"For once the people of New Jersey are awake under a fearless leader; they do not intend to be dictated to by corrupt bosses or to send an agent of the Sugar Trust to Washington, and they mean, as Dr. Wilson pointed out, to pillory every coward and label and brand every traitor who misrepresents them at Trenton."[1]

Smith replied hotly to Wilson, charging him "with resorting to the trick of attempting to deceive the people that he might strike down one who had befriended him and up-build an ambition that has mastered him." The legislators pledged to the Boss were now showing unmistakable signs of breaking away from his control. Wilson pursued his advantage and on the 14th carried the battle into Smith's own city of Newark. In spite of predictions of disturbance by Smith's partisans, the mass meeting was scarcely less successful than the Jersey City demonstration. Wilson's responses to Smith's attacks were marked by good-humoured resourcefulness and no little wit.

"I am told by the press that I have been called a liar. The only one disturbed by being called a liar is the liar himself. I beg you will observe the equanimity of my disposition!"[2]

### X. VICTORY

Wilson proved relentless as a fighter. To most of the legislators who had grown up under the old system of political control, it was an experience without precedent. They could not understand the smiling defiance, the audacity, of this novice, this college professor, who was fighting the Big Boss—and yet they could not resist him.

"Do not allow yourselves to be dismayed. You see where the machine is entrenched, and it looks like a real fortress. It looks as if real men were inside, as if they had real guns. Go and touch it. It is a house of cards. Those are

[1]The *Observer* of Hoboken, January 6, 1911.

imitation generals. Those are playthings that look like guns. Go and put your shoulder against the thing and it collapses."

On the day before the legislative election, the Big Boss, still convinced that he could win, marched into Trenton with an army of his supporters, headed by a brass band, the parade passing in review before their majestic leader who stood upon the steps of his hotel. It was the ancient and accepted method, that had rarely, in the past, failed to work. Smith began sending for members of the legislature and he and his helpers made them feel the power of the organization.

Wilson, who had been inaugurated as governor the week before, was at his office in the State House. He, too, was closely in touch with the men in the legislature on whom he knew he could depend. Neither side was absolutely sure of a majority. Wilson could not be certain that the Boss had not obtained a hold on enough members to defeat Martine, if not to elect himself.

On the following morning Smith made a triumphant speech to the Essex County delegation, on its way to the capitol. The Houses met separately, with the galleries thronged. They began to ballot at noon. Martine received 40 votes in all—31 in the House, 9 in the Senate—against 10 for Smith, all in the House. Martine was short only one vote of the majority of 81 members. It was plain enough that Martine would win, and that afternoon Smith slipped away quietly for his home in Newark. The next day, at the joint session of the legislature, Martine was elected. He had 47 votes, 6 more than necessary, against 3 for Smith, 21 for Stokes, the Republican nominee, and several scattering.

"I pitied Smith at the last. It was so plain that he had few real friends,—that he held men by fear and power and the benefits he could bestow, not by love or loyalty or any genuine devotion. The minute it was seen that he was defeated his adherents began to desert him like rats leaving a sinking ship. He left Trenton (where his headquarters had at first been crowded) attended, I am told, only by his sons, and looking old and broken. He wept, they say, as he admitted himself utterly beaten. Such is the end of political power—particularly when selfishly obtained and heartlessly used. It is a pitiless game, in which, it would seem, one takes one's life in one's hands,—and for me it has only begun!"[1]

It was a spectacular victory; the sort that demands enlargement in the press. The "Cloistered Professor Vanquishes the Big Boss!" One exuberant writer related how this scholar, "his garments odorous with the vapours of Parnassus, his lips wet with the waters of Helicon—this long-haired bookworm of a professor who had just laid his spectacles on his dictionary, came down to the Trenton State House and 'licked the gang to a frazzle.'"

As for Smith, the Big Boss never seems to have understood what happened. His dependable world, his entire scheme of things, crumbled to earth. He never recovered from the blow. In after years, when Wilson was discussed, he had not a word of bitterness. He would observe: "Wonderful man, wonderful mind, wonderful fighter—but . . ."

And what a shout of joy went up from Wilson's old and devoted friends:

Jan 26th 1911

DEAR WOODROW

You poor dear scholar and amateur in politics! I feel so sorry for you. Why don't you get an expert like Smith to advise you? You are getting to be rather tiresome as one spends too much time congratulating you. If you keep on doing such impossible

---

[1] Woodrow Wilson to Mary A. Hulbert, January 29, 1911.

stunts I think I will hereafter write you an omnibus letter once every six months or else get a stereotyped form.

Anyhow your latest is perfectly glorious and I rejoice with you.

God bless you

Yrs affly

C. H. DODGE

It is not too much to say that it was Wilson's victory over the bosses, by which he became one of the outstanding leaders of the progressive movement of the nation, that made him President of the United States. If he had failed in the struggle with Smith, he could not have secured from a reluctant legislature the reform measures he desired, he could not have challenged in the national field Roosevelt's or La Follette's or Bryan's power as the spokesman for liberalism.

# CHAPTER III

## GOVERNOR OF NEW JERSEY

Absolute good faith in dealing with the people, an unhesitating fidelity to every principle avowed, is the highest law of political morality under a constitutional government.

*Statement given to the press on December 8, 1910.*

I shall, of course, put every power I possess into the service of the people as governor of the state. It will be my pleasure and privilege to serve them, not as the head of a party but as the servant of all classes and of all interests, in an effort to promote the common welfare.

*Statement at the time of his election as governor, November 8, 1910.*

The only ideal politics, to my mind, is that which is real,—which takes men as it finds them, and finds them spirit as well as matter, and so discovers the best men both to themselves and to the world.

*Woodrow Wilson to H. A. Garfield, September 1, 1903.*

Even a reformer need not be a fool.

*Quoted in World's Work, May, 1911.*

### I. THE CRUSADING REFORMER

WILSON began his fight for reform legislation before he was assured of victory in his struggle with Boss Smith.

Some of his alarmed supporters advised caution. One thing at a time. Beat Smith for senator first of all. They were concerned lest his inexperience lead him into irretrievable errors. There was, after all, a political method; it would not do to crowd human nature too hard.

Wilson's response was to force the fighting. On the day before his inauguration—a week before his victory over

Smith—he called a "little conference of a few gentlemen particularly interested in formulating bills for consideration of the legislature before my actual entrance upon my office as governor."[1]

As it was easier for many Jerseymen to reach New York City than Princeton, he appointed the Martinique Hotel on Broadway as the place of meeting, and invited several of the strongest members of the legislature and a number of editors who had helped him. He included in the list George L. Record, rampant Republican progressive.

It was a stirring meeting. Wilson was so intent upon the discussion that he never thought about luncheon—which was quietly ordered and paid for by one of those present. The talking was done mostly by Wilson and Record. Wilson made it plain that he wanted to carry out absolutely, item by item, the reforms pledged in the platform on which he had been elected; direct primaries, a corrupt practices act, laws regulating public utilities, and an employers' liability act. It was an outright progressive, even radical, programme.

Wilson spoke of his recent meeting with William S. U'Ren of Oregon, who had been a leader in his own state in the introduction of the "new tools of democracy"— the initiative and referendum, the recall, and direct primaries. U'Ren, a Westerner of Westerners, born in Wisconsin, a blacksmith turned lawyer, represented the "revolt of the unprivileged." He was a devoted follower of Henry George, with a genius for organization and persuasion. U'Ren had found Wilson an eager listener; it was unnecessary to go into the theory or the history of the initiative and referendum, for Wilson had given these devices painstaking study many years before, setting down the experience of Switzerland and even recalling ancient Greek experiments, in his book, *The State*, first published

---

[1] The meeting was held on January 16, 1911.

in 1889.[1] He had told U'Ren quite frankly, as he now told the politicians gathered at the Martinique, that he had severely criticized the initiative and referendum in his lectures to students, but that the experience in Oregon showed that, in practice, they had worked. They were not to be considered a cure-all, nor yet a substitute for representative government, but they were "useful tools for an emergency."

Few of those present except Record had any interest in these new devices or, indeed, in the reforms proposed. Several were practical politicians, trained in the old school, who were bending to the new wind of progressivism not because of conviction, but because it was at the moment good politics. However, they all agreed to the four or five specific items of the programme, and Record was asked to prepare the necessary bills for presentation to the legislature.

It may be imagined what an uproar the reports of the meeting caused among Wilson's enemies in New Jersey. Here was the new Democratic Governor-elect determining, by "secret conference" with a group of insurgent Democrats and a Republican radical, what was to be "put over" on the legislature. He had entirely disregarded the organization. And he had held the meeting outside of the state! Smith's newspaper, the *Star*, of Newark, began a whirlwind attack. It was nothing to the point, of course, that the bosses had for years been determining by secret conferences, often outside the state, and often with representatives of the Republican machine, what was to be done by the legislature—but when Wilson sought a conference of liberals to discuss proposed legislation in behalf of the people, it was quite a different matter. The *Star* published cartoons showing Wilson, the sharp-nosed pedagogue, instructing his "editorial chorus."

Wilson countered with a public statement:

[1] See *The State*, first edition, p. 310 et seq.

"There was absolutely nothing secret about the conference held in the Hotel Martinique, New York. It was simply a continuation of the policy I have followed ever since my election of consulting everyone who was interested in the reforms which concern the whole state."

He also defended Record:

"Mr. Record is well known to be one of the best-informed men in this state with regard to the details involved in most of the reforms proposed. He is particularly versed in legislation elsewhere, as well as in New Jersey, with regard to ballot reform and corrupt practices, as well as with regard to the regulation of primaries. He generously consented to put his unusual store of information at the service of the conference, which was non-partisan in its purpose and meant in the public interest."

In calling this meeting, Wilson might indeed have been the "blatant amateur," the "political innocent," he was charged with being, but if he had tried with all the cunning of long training he could have devised nothing that would have given wider publicity to his purposes, or more firmly convinced the people of the state that he was working for their interests. People love a fighter; and this fight was being dramatized in a way that was different, interesting, exciting. Afterwards, when Wilson had succeeded in his objectives, he was charged with "playing politics." As a matter of fact, he won because he did not try to play politics at all, but went after what he wanted in the most direct way he could conceive. As it happens in the arts other than politics, the amateur, if he has genius, knows best what to do.

## II. INAUGURATION AS GOVERNOR OF NEW JERSEY

On the day following the Martinique conference,[1] Wilson was inaugurated as forty-third governor of New

[1] January 17, 1911.

Jersey. It was the customary grandiose ceremony with huge crowds brought into Trenton by special trains, the Governor-elect riding with the retiring Governor[1] in an open landau drawn by four prancing horses.

A brass band of tremendous proportions—"three bass drums"—led a highly decorative escort of state troops. The "conquering hero" was given a "salute of seventeen guns"! We have glimpses of a dreadfully solemn state dinner and a "levee" held by Mrs. Wilson and her daughters.

The Opera House was decorated as usual with "flags and evergreens and Southern smilax," and all the dignitaries of the state were there, sitting magnificently in the boxes—all except one. The Big Boss was absent.

Wilson read his inaugural address. It was difficult for him to prepare a speech in advance; he spoke most naturally from notes which he never looked at. He liked to "feel his audience"; he knew how much an audience often contributes to the power of the most accomplished orator. But he began in New Jersey a practice which continued throughout his service at Washington, of preparing in advance his formal legislative addresses.

In substance, the inaugural was an earnest reaffirmation of his determination to carry out the promises of the Democratic platform. He referred with approval to the Oregon laws "whose effect has been to bring government back to the people and to protect it from the control of the representatives of selfish and special interests."

But the core of the address, as it was the vital spark of Wilson's entire policy as governor, was concentrated in a single sentence added in lead pencil to his speaking copy:

"I shall take the liberty from time to time to make detailed recommendations to you on the matters I have

---

[1] J. Franklin Fort.

dwelt upon, and on others, sometimes in the form of bills if necessary."

In this apparently mild statement of his purpose Wilson set forth his determination to lead his party in its legislative programme. In his view, the function of a governor or President should not be merely advisory, with a negative power of veto. He should be a kind of prime minister.

But the constitution of New Jersey was one of the most antiquated in the Union, following the French revolutionary model, with its emphasis upon the separation of governmental powers—a method long extinct in Europe. As Wilson had often pointed out in his writings, this system made for inefficiency; it also furnished an opening, since real leadership must exist somewhere, for the development of an extra-constitutional system of practical control or guidance—to wit, the political machine and the Boss.

During the campaign, Wilson's opponent, the Republican candidate, Lewis, shrewdly counting upon American worshipfulness of the letter of the constitution, had announced that he would be a "constitutional governor." He would live up to the literary theory of the separation of powers—that is, he would keep to his executive chamber and use no influence on the legislature. Wilson responded that if that was what was meant by being a constitutional governor, then he intended to be an "unconstitutional governor." It was the only way, as he saw it, to overturn the old and evil rule of the machine.

He himself set forth his reactions to the new task in a letter written on January 22nd:

"I got into harness last Tuesday. The ceremony was simple enough: the exercises of the inauguration were over in an hour. Only the all-afternoon and all-evening receptions were fatiguing; and even in them there was variety enough to take at least monotony away and afford constant amusement, and, better than amusement, constant human interest. All sorts and conditions of people came, men, women, and children, and I felt very close to all of them, and very much touched by the thought that I was their representative and spokesman, and in a very real sense their help and hope, after year upon year of selfish machine domination when nothing at all had been done for them that could possibly be withheld! Since Tuesday I have been in Trenton every day, except yesterday, getting into harness and learning the daily routine of the office; and all the while deeply moved by the thought of my new responsibilities as the representative and champion of the common people against those who have been preying upon them. I have felt a sort of solemnity in it all that I feel sure will not wear off. I do not see how a man in such a position could possibly be afraid of anything except failing to do his honourable duty and set all temptations (if they were disguised enough to be temptations) contemptuously on one side. I shall make mistakes, but I do not think I shall sin against my knowledge of duty. May I not say that to you, who will know that I am not speaking with the least touch of pride or of self-confidence, but only as one who is obliged to see and know his duty by mere plainness of circumstance and force of education?"[1]

### III. THE LEGISLATIVE BATTLEGROUND

Record promptly prepared bills for the new legislation. Some of the Governor's political advisers, taking alarm at the attacks upon him for his relationships with a "Republican and radical," urged him to "soft-pedal Record." Record himself wrote to Wilson saying that if his assistance should prove embarrassing, he would not press it,

[1]Woodrow Wilson to Mary A. Hulbert, January 22, 1911.

since it was the cause which was to be considered first of all. Wilson responded, on January 27th:

MY DEAR MR. RECORD:-

Thank you sincerely for your letter of yesterday. It does you honour. I am sure that I understand your position thoroughly and I have been very grateful to you for exercising the good taste you have exercised, in view of the unreasonable, but nevertheless, very mischievous representations recently made by the Star.

I have been handed copies of the bills you drew up and shall read them with greatest attention. My hope will be to get them introduced and to get them out as Committee reports, if that is possible. We are working for the same end, although along somewhat different lines which policy dictates and principle does not condemn.

In haste,

Cordially and sincerely yours,
WOODROW WILSON

He was as good as his word; and the bills were promptly introduced—the election bill by E. H. Geran.

It became apparent immediately that Wilson must meet the powerful opposition of the bosses and the machine. Not only did they oppose the legislation itself—for the new election and corrupt practices acts were aimed to destroy the system upon which they thrived—but they must continue to control the legislature or abdicate. It was nothing to them that the platform of their party had promised the passage of such legislation, or that Wilson had pledged his good faith in the campaign to its enactment; platforms were only pious sops thrown to the people for election purposes.

Boss control of the legislature by one party or the other, mostly Republican, had been for years the accepted method. It worked easily and profitably with a minimum of responsibility or labour upon the part of the individual legislator. The Big Boss and his satellites haunted the capitol, often sitting in the lobbies or on the floors of the houses, sometimes actually directing legislation at the elbow of the speaker. The really important bills originated in the offices of corporation lawyers, and the Big Boss of one party or the other had them introduced by certain dependable members. Debate was usually farcical and when the moment for voting came the Boss and his lieutenants would assume command.

"Number 20 is up at ten o'clock. Get in line. Go in and vote."

There were plenty of ways of silencing objectors, even without the crude use of money. Legislators could be threatened with the powerful opposition of the machine in their own districts; and there were offices and patronage as rewards for faithful service. The bosses had acquired great experience and adroitness in the secret achievement of their purposes so as not unduly to arouse the sluggish electorate. As for the press, some of the papers, like the *Star* of Newark, were directly owned by the Boss or his friends; others were influenced in the hundred and one ways by which money interests obtain what they desire.

While the state was now wide awake, and in full revolt, the old leaders, confident of their long-practiced technique, appeared as usual at Trenton. They could scarcely be blamed; it was the custom. When the party won the election, the Boss assumed of course that he was to take command.

Wilson had against him not only this well-settled procedure, but there were other serious obstacles. While the House had a strong Democratic majority, the Senate was still Republican—and the Republican bosses could be depended upon to help the Democratic bosses. Many of the legislators had long been cogs in the old machines; if they did not actually oppose the new legislation, they were

timid and fearful. Would it pay in the long run to support
a governor who had ridden in on a wave of popular feeling
and whose career might cease with the end of his term?
Or would it be better to stand by the old and well-
established Democratic machine, which would continue
to exist and function long after a meteoric governor had
gleamed in the heavens and disappeared in darkness?

Wilson described the battle in a letter on March 5th:

"Things are getting intense and interesting again. The
bills for which we are pledged and on whose passage the
success and prestige of my administration as governor
largely depend are ready for report to the legislature, and
the question is, Can we pass them? I think we can, and
my spirits rise as the crisis approaches: it is like the senatorial contest all over again,—the same forces arrayed
against me; and no doubt the same sort of fight will enable me to win. I have begun my speech-making (this time
at various dinners of boards of trade, which afford me a
convenient platform) and am pouring shot into the enemy
in a way which I hope reaches the heart of his defenses.
To-morrow I meet all the Democratic members of the
Assembly in conference and shall have my first shot at
them direct. Besides that, I shall draw various individuals
into my office and have talks with them. After the difficulties of the House are overcome, there is the Senate to deal
with, which is Republican, by a majority of three. I do
not know just how they will act. The senators gave me a
dinner on Friday night (the customary thing, it seems) at
the new Ritz-Carlton hotel, 46th. St. and Madison Avenue,
and in the little speech I made them I established as
natural and cordial relations as I knew how to suggest.
They are good and honest men, for the most part, and I
could warmly feel all the things I said. I am hoping for the
best even with them,—though from just which of them
I am to get the necessary votes I do not yet know. There

are so many 'personal equations' to bring into these
puzzling calculations that I do not know till the last moment how the 'sum' is going to work out. It's a fascinating,
as well as nerve-racking, business. . . . And somehow,
through all of it, I keep my stubborn optimism. I cannot
manage to think ill of my fellow men as a whole, though
some of them are extraordinary scoundrels. Fortunately in
this strange game most of the scoundrels are cowards also.
The right, boldly done, intimidates them. Above all, they
shrink away from the light. I spoke at three dinners last
week: on Tuesday night before the West Hudson Board of
Trade; on Thursday night before the Hoboken Board of
Trade; on Friday night to the senators."[1]

### IV. THE STRUGGLE WITH BOSS NUGENT

The Big Boss himself did not appear at Trenton after
his defeat for the Senate on January 25th; but he sent his
first lieutenant, Nugent, who was an even cleverer manip-
ulator of the legislature.

"When the Democrats were in control of the Assembly
in 1907 he perched upon the floor of the House and remained there through the entire session. He was in command. The Essex delegation would do as he said. No bill
could pass without his consent, and any bill he opposed
was pretty sure to be beaten."[2]

Nugent began at once to "line up the boys" against
Wilson's "crazy laws." A reckoning between the new
leadership and the old was inevitable. On the very day of
the introduction of the election law[3] Wilson and Nugent
met in Wilson's office. Nugent was a large man, a virile and
dictatorial leader. A nephew of James Smith, he was far
better educated than most of the machine leaders of the

[1]Woodrow Wilson to Mary A. Hulbert.
[2]*Jersey Journal*, February 8, 1911.
[3]February 6, 1911.

state. During the campaign Wilson—and Mrs. Wilson—
had come to have a personal liking for the man, and hoped
now to be able to reason with him. Why should there be a
conflict between them? The election law had been solemnly promised to the people, agreed to in the platform.
He, the Governor, had been elected on that promise. He
had also been chosen by the people as their leader. Why
should Nugent, who was not a member of the legislature,
have access to the floor of the Houses—denied to the
governor—and use that privilege to work against the laws
to which both were pledged? But Wilson's reasoning was
all in vain. Nugent cared only for the maintenance of the
power of the organization. He left Wilson angrily, declaring open war. A sensational report appeared in a newspaper
that Wilson had "threatened to use fisticuffs," for which
Wilson called the writer sharply to account—"the worst
ten minutes a reporter ever had"—causing his withdrawal
from New Jersey and an apology by his newspaper.

If it was war to the knife, Wilson was prepared for it.
Both sides began a vigorous campaign to convince the
legislators. On March 6th, a caucus of Democratic members of the Assembly was called to discuss the new election
law—which many of them, even some who favoured the
general purpose of it, considered too radical. If it could not
be entirely headed off, the opposing leaders might induce
the caucus to agree on amendments that would draw its
teeth.

"All right," said Wilson when he heard of the meeting.
"It's a good idea. Why not invite me?"

Such a joint conference of the executive and legislative
departments was exactly in line with his long-held belief.
He had already been conferring informally with members
of the legislature; why not a formal conference? But to
them it was unprecedented, if not actually unconstitutional. A governor at a legislative caucus! What had be-

come of the old idea of the "separation of the powers"? But if Wilson was party leader why should he not attend a party caucus?

When the caucus met the opposition left no doubt as to where it stood.

"What constitutional right has the Governor to interfere in legislation?" demanded one of the legislators bluntly.

"Since you appeal to the constitution," responded Wilson, "I can satisfy you."

He drew from his pocket a copy of the constitution and read the following clause:

"The governor shall communicate by message to the legislature at the opening of each session, and at such other times as he may deem necessary, the condition of the state, and recommend such measures as he may deem expedient."

Another of Wilson's bitterest opponents remarked cynically:

"The sponsor for this bill would wreck the organization that nominated him."

Wilson countered instantly:

"It is true that the organization nominated me, but fortunately it was the people who elected me. Does the gentleman charge that this bill attacks the interests of the people?"

The Governor's exposition of the election bill lasted for nearly three hours. He had made a minute study of the whole subject, the experience of other states and of foreign countries, and he countered every objection and inquiry frankly and readily.

It was not only his reasoning that gave him power, but his fiery determination to carry on the fight no matter what happened, taking it if necessary to the people of the state, that set his politically minded listeners to thinking hard:

"You can turn aside from the measure if you choose; you can decline to follow me; you can deprive me of office and turn away from me, but you cannot deprive me of power so long as I steadfastly stand for what I believe to be the interests and legitimate demands of the people themselves. I beg you to remember, in this which promises to be an historic conference, you are settling the question of the power or impotence, the distinction or the ignominy, of the party to which the people with singular generosity have offered the conduct of their affairs."

The caucus made a never-to-be-forgotten impression upon those who were present. One of them remarked:

"We all came out of that room with one conviction; that we had heard the most wonderful speech of our lives. . . . Even the most hardened of the old-time legislative hacks said that. It has been said that debate no longer accomplishes anything in American legislation, that nobody is now persuaded by talk. Here was a case, however, which refutes this idea. When we went into that caucus we had no assurance as to what the result would be. But opposition melted away under the Governor's influence. That caucus settled the fate of the Geran bill, as well as the whole Democratic programme."[1]

When the vote was taken, there was a majority of 27 to 11 in favour of supporting the Geran bill as a party measure.

While it was a victory that astonished everyone, the struggle was by no means over. Nugent had a block of about a dozen votes he could absolutely control, and he now began to dicker with the Republican machine. If the Republican organization could keep every member of the Senate in line—hold them against Wilson's persuasiveness—he could still win. For a few days the Wilson forces were badly worried; and on March 20th the Governor again sent for the boss. He came sullenly.

[1]See Burton Hendrick in *McClure's Magazine*, December, 1911.

Photo. by Brown Brothers

WOODROW WILSON IN HIS OFFICE IN THE STATE HOUSE
AT TRENTON, WITH HIS SECRETARY, JOSEPH P. TUMULTY.
WILLIAM BAYARD HALE, SITTING.

"Don't you think, Mr. Nugent," said the Governor, "that you are making a grave mistake in opposing the election bill?"

"No," said Nugent, "and you can't pass it without using the state patronage."

Nugent could have said nothing that would have cut deeper. He was accusing the Governor of bribing the legislators with promises of offices. Wilson met the charge in white heat. He rose from his chair and pointed his hand at the door.

"Good-afternoon, Mr. Nugent."

The boss hesitated, trembling with passion.

"You're no gentleman!" he shouted.

"You're no judge!" responded the Governor.[1]

The report of the meeting spread like wildfire. The boss was seen "tearing down the corridor, apoplectic with rage." The Governor had "fired out of his office" the chairman of the Democratic State Committee! If he had any presidential aspirations, how was he to secure the support of the New Jersey delegation after such a break?

"It was a most unpleasant incident, which I did not at all enjoy; but apparently it did a lot of good. It has been spoken of with glee all over the country, and editorials written about it, of which the enclosed is a specimen. One paper had a cartoon entitled 'Good afternoon,' in wh. Nugent was to be seen flying head foremost from a door out of which protruded a foot marked 'Wilson.' In the distance, nursing his bruises, sat Smith. It is all very well to get applause and credit for such things, but I need not tell you that they are not at all to my taste. I cannot help feeling a bit vulgar after them. They commend me to the rank and file, and particularly to the politicians themselves, I believe, but they do not leave me pleased with

---

[1] In statements of what happened, made by both men after the event, this last heated exchange was not set down, but there is little doubt as to what was actually said.

myself. I feel debased to the level of the men whom I feel obliged to snub. But it all comes in the day's work."[1]

## V. WINNING THE LEGISLATURE

Wilson's open break with Nugent served again to clarify the struggle, and there was a chorus of approval in the press of the state. It put backbone into every member of the legislature who wished but feared to follow the new leader. One member of the Assembly, an eighteen-dollar-a-week workman in a factory, had been asked by his employers, during the senatorial contest, to vote for Smith. He knew well enough that the request involved the bread and butter of his wife and children. He came to Wilson and told him what the situation was.

"I can't advise you," said the Governor. "I have no right to ask you to sacrifice your family. If you vote for Mr. Smith I shall not hold it against you."

When the test came, the workman defied his employer and voted against Smith. His pay was immediately reduced. A few weeks later, when Wilson's election bill came up for vote, his employers advised him to oppose it. Again he appealed to Wilson, saying that he wanted to do what was right. Wilson answered him exactly as he had before. It was a hard problem for a poor man, a legislator who never before had shown any independence; but he again defied his employer, and was promptly discharged. Those who brought the news to Wilson "heard language flow in a vigour drawn from resources not commonly tapped by Presbyterian elders."[2]

Wilson's final victory was uncomfortably close to defeat. Ten Democrats in the Assembly fought him to the bitter end, following Nugent. Everything depended upon what the Republican Senate would do.

[1] Woodrow Wilson to Mary A. Hulbert, March 26, 1911.
[2] William Bayard Hale, *Woodrow Wilson*, p. 209.

Wilson gives a vivid account of his effort to win the Republican senators:

"The Senate of the State has, you must know, a Republican majority of two: I must obtain at least two votes to get my bills through. The senator from ——— is one ———, a sly old fraud who likes to increase his consequence by posing as something of an independent. At an early stage of the game he came to me and intimated that he was going to stand by me and vote for the administration measures. He dropped into my office frequently, and I began to realize that something was in the wind. As if to assist my diagnosis, the sheriff of ——— up and died. The senator promptly showed his hand. He came to me and said very plainly that, since he was going to vote for my bills, he expected to be allowed to say what the appointments in his county should be. Needless to say, I did not indulge him. I appointed the man who seemed to be most acceptable to the Democrats of good standing in the county. He thereupon renounced me. I was not the broad man he had taken me to be, he said. He was loud and not at all parliamentary in speaking of the breach. He certainly would not vote for the bills. A day or two after his disappointment, I was invited, by the Adjutant General, Sadler, to go out with the senators to the country club and eat a fried chicken and waffle supper (which was delicious, by the way), and at the supper things happened! The senators are as jolly as boys when they let themselves 'go' on such an occasion, and that night they were in fine fettle. In the middle of the meal Frelinghuysen, of Somerset, got up and said, 'By special request, Senator ——— has consented to sing 'I Love Him No More.'' Then the fun began! ——— got up to speak, but for almost five minutes they would not let him, throwing all sorts of jibes at him, very good natured and very witty, but very teasing. When they let him, he said that the trouble was, not that he did not love me more, but that I loved him less. I reminded him that I had high example, for 'Whom the Lord loveth he chasteneth,'—and then we were off! The rest of the evening was one unbroken romp. After we got up from the table we danced in every comical combination anyone could think of, and I led Senator —— several times around the big dining room in a cakewalk, in which we pranced together to the perfect content of the whole company. He seemed quite mollified before we got through with him. Such are the processes of high politics! This is what it costs to be a leader! But it remains to be seen whether the sly old fox votes for the bills or not. I would not trust him out of my sight. But this at least seems gained: I am on easy and delightful terms with all the senators. They know me for something else than 'an ambitious dictator.'"[1]

When the final vote came in the Senate—to the astonishment of everyone—it was unanimous in favour of the bill, the Republicans voting to a man with the Democrats.

The news of the passage of the bill by the Senate reached Wilson at Indianapolis where, as a guest of Governor Marshall, he was about to begin speaking to a large audience. The toastmaster "read the telegram aloud and the crowd stood up and shouted for Wilson." It is a singular thing how many events of those early years were dramatized to Wilson's advantage without a turn of the hand upon his part. His New Jersey successes indeed played an immense part, as will be shown later, in adding to his growing prestige as a national leader.

"The 'scholar in politics' in New Jersey is demonstrating that he is made of sterner stuff than either his friends or his enemies expected. He is meeting the bosses at every

---

[1]Woodrow Wilson to Mary A. Hulbert, April 2, 1911.

salient point with the bristling guns of argument and with a serenity of courage and confidence that appalls them. There is no doubt of the result in Jersey. The old regime of corruption and trickery has had its day."[1]

Part of Wilson's success, as he himself said, was due to an electorate aroused by years of agitation by the Muckrakers, by Roosevelt's stirring appeals, by La Follette's spectacular struggles in Wisconsin, by the unremitting campaigns of William J. Bryan. People were in revolt and wanted reform. "Programmes are taking the place of philippics." But without Wilson's leadership New Jersey could never have been placed, in one session of the legislature, at the forefront of progressive states. Other governors came in at the same time, on the same wave of revolt, only to surrender, as Governor Dix of New York had done, to the bosses. Wilson's success was all the more astonishing because he used none of the old political devices; he made no threats, he promised no rewards, he had no secret understandings. What he did was to make his proposals so clear and reasonable that no one could misunderstand them, no one could doubt that they made for a broader, more honest control of affairs in the interest of the people of the state.

"The main object of what we are attempting . . . is to establish a close connection, a very sensitive connection, between the people and their governments, both in the states and in the nation, in order that we may restore . . . liberty and . . . opportunity. . . ."

He was able to give the impression of being a strong progressive, without frightening his more conservative following with extreme or revolutionary proposals. He kept the confidence of both groups: he gave them a sense of being a leader who knew not only exactly where he was

[1]New York *American*, March 18, 1911.

going and why, but how he was going. He clearly placed himself:

"RADICAL—one who goes too far.

"CONSERVATIVE—one who does not go far enough.

"REACTIONARY—one who does not go at all.

"Hence we have invented the term, label,

"PROGRESSIVE, to mean one who (a) recognizes new facts and adjusts law to them, and who (b) attempts to think ahead, constructively. Progress must build, build tissue, must be cohesive, must have a plan at its heart."[1]

More potent than almost anything else was Wilson's absolute faith in his own objectives, as well as in himself. It was part and parcel of the tough-fibred Scotch religious conviction in which he had been nurtured. What was right was right and must prevail. Men who, like Savonarola, or Calvin, or Cromwell, feel that God Almighty is behind them and with them, are hard customers to deal with.

"I have heard it said that it required courage to stand fast for the right. As I conceive it, it would require courage to do anything else. It would require courage to turn away from the shining path and plunge again into the darkness. Do you suppose that it requires courage when you have once seen the light to follow it?"

Out of such a belief, held with all the power of a determined nature, arises the conviction that everyone on the side of the people, his side, was right; everyone on the other side was wrong. There was no room for doubt. He could say of the opposition to the Geran bill:

"It will come from outside the legislature, and will admirably serve to distinguish the friends of the people from the friends of private management. It will be thoroughly worth while to observe the persons who interest themselves to oppose it. Their names will make an excellent list, easily

---

[1]Notes for an address before the Kansas Society, New York City, January 28, 1911.

Kansas Society, New York City, 28 January, 1911.
-----------------------

Why come away from Kansas?  You look fit to stay!
    Have you ceased being Kansans?  A qn. of spirit
        not of mere physical or business or blood
        or sentimental connections.

An age of movement and readjustment, in wh. we are
    apt to quarrel in labels.  We call names; but
    that is not thinking.
    RADICAL = one who goes too far.
    CONSERVATIVE = one who does not go far enough
    REACTIONARY = one who does not go at all.
        Hence we have invented the term, label,
    PROGRESSIVE, to mean one who (a) recognizes new
        facts and adjusts law to them, and who
        (b) attempts to think ahead, constructive-
        ly.  Progress must build, build tissue,
        must be cohesive, must have a plan at its
        heart..

The right attitude, not hostility, not contest, not
    concession, but frankness, publicity (= dis-
    cussing everything as part of the public bus-
    ness, the public welfare), and voluntary ad-
    justment all along the line.  Who sulks and
    stays out of the game must take the consequen-
    ces, — will not be considered.

What breath of new spirit does Kansas-in-New-York
    lend to the new processes?

                                        1/28/'11

Facsimile of Mr. Wilson's notes for an address to the Kansas
Society, January 28, 1911, written on his own typewriter.  Such
notes were made for nearly all of his public addresses.

accessible, of those who either fear to establish the direct rule of the people or who have some private and selfish purpose to serve in seeing that the more concealed and secret methods of politics are not taken away from them and made impossible."[1]

Such a position might infuriate his enemies; might alienate some of those who doubted honestly whether every provision in the new legislation was wisely considered, whether progress toward direct control by the people might not be too swift, might not even tend to destroy representative government; but it was nevertheless an impregnable position for a leader to take. To be sure in a doubtful world!

Another element in his success was the refreshing sense he gave of letting in the air upon old and stale processes of political manipulation. The door of the Governor's office at Trenton literally stood open. Wilson seemed eager to consult any citizen who might care to see him. He was later to discover the difficulties in practice of being accessible to anybody—any man with an axe to grind, any crank with a panacea, any little politician begging a favour— but in these great early days no governor's office in America was freer than Wilson's. He took the people fully into his confidence. He had the gift of turning opposition, often at a single conference, into almost fanatical support. Certain labour leaders were opposed to his employers' liability bill. One of them attacked Wilson hotly—accused him of playing into the hands of the "interests"—until someone suggested that he call on the Governor. He walked into Wilson's office and spent an hour, coming out with the assertion:

"That's the greatest man in America. He's dead right about his bill. It's better than ours."

He became one of Wilson's most devoted supporters.

[1]Statement regarding the Geran bill given to the press on February 15, 1911.

VI. WILSON'S CHARACTERISTICS AS A POLITICIAN

When dangerous issues were put up to Wilson, he often delayed, sought conciliation, awaited understanding, but when the time came to declare himself, he did not hedge or dodge. One of the knottiest political issues then, as now, was the liquor problem. The reformers were strongly for local option; the brewers, who were staunch supporters of the Democratic machine, were against it. Wilson left no doubt as to where he stood.

May 1, 1911

MY DEAR MR. SHANNON:

The question asked in your letter of April twenty-seventh about my attitude toward the important question of local option is, of course, a perfectly legitimate one, and you are entitled to a very frank answer. I would have replied sooner had I not been prevented by imperative public engagements. I have explained my views to you in private but of course have no objection to your making them public.

I am in favour of local option. I am a thorough believer in local self-government and believe that every self-governing community which constitutes a social unit should have the right to control the matter of the regulation or of the withholding of licenses.

But the questions involved are social and moral and are not susceptible of being made parts of a party programme. Whenever they have been made the subject matter of party contests, they have cut the lines of party organization and party action athwart to the utter confusion of political action in every other field. They have thrown every other question, however important, into the background and have made constructive party action impossible for long years together. So far as I am concerned, therefore, I can never consent to have the question of local option made an issue between political parties in this State. My judgment is very clear in this matter. I do not believe that party programmes of the highest consequence to the political life of the State and of the Nation ought to be thrust on one side and hopelessly embarrassed for long periods together by making a political issue of a great question which is essentially non-political, non-partisan, moral and social in its nature.

Very sincerely yours,<br>WOODROW WILSON

REV. THOMAS B. SHANNON,
  17 Clinton Street
    Newark, New Jersey.

In the matter of appointments—always a touchy subject both for the political leader and for the political organization—Wilson was the despair of his supporters. He was interested not in men, but in principles. The business of patronage irked him.

"It's a weary business being governor. I have literally *no* time to myself, am at everybody's disposal but my own, —and, like every other man in similar case, the question of appointments drives me nearly distracted, it is so nearly impossible to get true information or disinterested advice about persons—and so many persons are trying to impose upon me. I shall get used to it, but am not yet, and it goes hard."[1]

Wilson had not the remotest idea of building up an organization of his own by the familiar method of placing his strong political supporters in the best offices. The fact that a man had laboured hard, had spent his money, in helping elect the Democratic ticket was to Wilson no reason why he should be rewarded with a fat office for which he might not be remotely fitted. Were they not all serving a common cause? And was it not imperative to find the best man, not a mere political supporter, to fill each office?

Such an attitude might be ideal; it might delight the people of the state; but it was at variance with the common political practice. It was too cold, too disinterested. To the

[1]Woodrow Wilson to Mary A. Hulbert, February 5, 1911.

ordinary leader or organizer, it was "inhuman"; Wilson was an "ingrate."

"Governor Wilson's appointment of William P. Martin to the Common Pleas Judgeship in Essex County was a painful surprise to some machine politicians and an agreeable one to about everybody else in the state."[1]

The Governor filled half a dozen of the best, most responsible, and highest paid offices in the state with men whom he knew and respected as experts. Not one of them was a politician; and unfortunately some of them had no idea of meeting political problems in a political world. Two Princeton professors, old and trusted friends, he brought into the service, Winthrop M. Daniels as a member of the Public Utilities Commission and Henry Jones Ford as a member of the State Board of Education, and when the school system was reorganized, he went outside the state for the ablest educator he knew, Calvin N. Kendall of Indianapolis, to become its head. He appointed his old friend and classmate, Colonel E. A. Stevens, to the important office of Road Commissioner and he elevated a Jewish lawyer, Samuel Kalisch, to the Supreme Court— the first of his race to be appointed to high office in New Jersey. He also appointed George L. Record, a Republican—though not without urging by Record's friends, who thought he should have a far more important office—as a member of the State Board of Railroad Assessors.

While every one of these appointments was made upon the basis of merit and fitness—all were men of a quality rarely brought into public service—yet each fat office so filled bitterly disappointed some hopeful aspirant who had supported Wilson, and discouraged the group of eager little politicians who had hitched their wagons to his star and were hoping to make him "think politically." He gave

---

[1] The *Observer* of Hoboken, April 4, 1911.

them some chance, however, with the long lists of minor appointments.

"You and Tumulty get together," he said to Judge Hudspeth, "and make out a list of the men you think ought to be appointed."[1]

Once an office was filled, Wilson dreaded any change, often enduring criticisms and attacks rather than displace an appointee.

## VII. THE MAN WITHIN THE POLITICIAN

It is not to be doubted that Wilson's first year in politics was among the most absorbing and interesting of his entire life. When a man in an audience at Lakewood cried out, "Oh, you're only an amateur politician," Wilson responded instantly:

"But I have one satisfaction: a professional plays the game, you know, because it pays him. An amateur plays the game because he loves to play it, to win it if he can by fair means in a fair field, before the eyes of all men. I'm afraid I'm only an amateur. But I'm having a most interesting time of it!"

It was interesting: it was "absorbing": was it happy?

Reading the immense correspondence of those years, one doubts whether Wilson was ever happy. Stern joy, the glory of victory, the high satisfaction of duty well done, he felt often: happiness rarely, or never. He had indeed found the place in life for which his genius, as well as his preparation, best fitted him, but there were ranges of his complex nature—the deeper inner core of the man—that went unsatisfied.

"I am a person, I am afraid, who observes no sort of moderation in anything."

He demanded too much of life. He demanded friend-

---

[1] Judge Robert S. Hudspeth to the author.

ships "without surrender," and at the same time devoted himself with unswerving loyalty to causes and principles which might disrupt those friendships. His intimate letters throughout his life show how lonely he felt himself, how dependent upon the sympathy of those who were near to him. To the outer world he turned, often enough, the "hard and brilliant shell" of the self-assured fighter.

"I am simply a Scots-Irishman who will not be conquered."

But his inner spirit starved for friendship, for free, simple, beautiful things. There was much of the poet at the core of the man. No moments of his life yielded him greater satisfaction than his long walks and his bicycle rides through the quiet lanes and byways of England in summer. He went alone, but carried a volume of Wordsworth or of the Oxford poets in his jacket.[1] As he wrote to a friend during the driven days of the governorship:

"Truly, I know what 'public life' is now! I have no private life at all. It is entertaining to see the whole world surge about you,—particularly the whole summer world,— but when a fellow is like me,—when, i.e., he *loves* his own privacy, loves the liberty to think of his friends (live with them in his *thought*, if he can have them no other way) and to dream his own dreams—to conceive a life which he cannot share with the crowd, can share, indeed, with only one or two, who seem part of him, rebellion comes into his heart and he flings about like a wild bird in a cage,—denied his sweet haunts and his freedom. Sometimes (as I must have told you more than once) my whole life seems to me rooted in dreams,—and I do not want the roots of it to dry up. I lived a dream life (almost too exclusively, perhaps) when I was a lad and even now my thought goes back for refreshment to those days when all the world seemed to me a place of heroic adventure, in which one's

[1] See *Woodrow Wilson, Life and Letters: Princeton*, p. 83.

heart must keep its own counsel while one's hands worked at big things. And *now* this is that dreaming boy's *Sunday:* he must sit at the edge of his front piazza flanked by a row of militia officers and be gazed at, while a chaplain conducts service on his lawn, with a full brass band to play the tunes for the hymns; then he must have the chaplains of the two regiments in camp, plus the Catholic priest, and anybody else that happens along, in for lunch. In the afternoon he must receive and pay military calls and attend a review. The evening brings callers galore from all along the coast. Where and when does one's own heart get a chance to breathe and to call up the sweet memories and dreams upon wh. it lives?"[1]

His letters to friends are full of his deeper feeling, his love of nature, his fondness for quiet days, and the fine comradeship of congenial friends.

"The earth is parched, the flowers wan and discouraged, the trees turning to an autumn colour, and the air pallid with dust, which covers and takes the life out of everything. There are signs of an unusually early autumn, the most noticeable of which, and the most interesting is that the swallows are gathering for their migration, quite two weeks sooner than they usually gather, sitting in innumerable companies, in quaint endless rows, on the telephone wires (where there is not current enough, I suppose, to tickle their feet), chirping away in quiet undertones of suppressed excitement. I pass under them every afternoon as I return from the golf course up on the hills by the river."

Again he said:

"How easy it is to get rid of Trenton and, even as I seem to listen to importunate office seekers, forget the great formal office in which I sit, and see out of its windows, instead of the city street on one side and the river with its

---

[1] Woodrow Wilson to Mary A. Hulbert, July 30, 1911.

uncouth banks on the other, the sights and sweet radiant spaces, the familiar houses and scenes, of dear Bermuda. It soothes and cheers and refreshes me like Wordsworth's vision of the daffodils. The mind is master of its own fate, of its own world and its own moods. It can take its pleasure as it will. And so I do not expect to grow old as fast as some men do, whose minds do not know where or whence to seek their renewal. My poor body must stay every day in Trenton, but my mind goes where it will."

Coupled with this rarely expressed sensitiveness to natural beauty he loved "people of flavour and personality." If he shrank often from meeting strangers it was because the "experience of a new human being" carried with it such possibilities of disappointment as well as of deep pleasure. But a friendship once made, what a joy was that!

"Sometimes I am a bit ashamed of myself when I think how few friends I have amidst a host of acquaintances. Plenty of people offer me their friendship; but, partly, because I am reserved and shy, and partly because I am fastidious and have a narrow, uncatholic taste in friends, I reject the offer in almost every case; and then am dismayed to look about and see how few persons in the world stand near me and know me as I am,—in such wise that they can give me sympathy and close support of heart. Perhaps it is because when I give at all I want to give my whole heart, and I feel that so few want it all, or would return measure for measure. Am I wrong, do you think, in that feeling? And can one as deeply covetous of friendship and close affection as I am afford to act upon such a feeling? In any case, you may know why such a friendship as yours is a priceless treasure to me. . . ."[1]

To another friend he wrote:

"What is more refreshing and rewarding than to turn

_____

[1] Woodrow Wilson to Edith G. Reid, February 16, 1902.

to the friend with whom you never have to consider a phrase or a thought,—with whom you can *let yourself go!* It is as if you breathed another air than that of the work-a-day world in which you toil and plan and struggle—the air of the world in which your spirit is free and native and full of the play and gaiety of an untrammelled life!"[1]

He liked especially fine women: they had "deeper sensibility," they were of "finer understanding." As the need grew for standing alone in an often unfriendly and critical world, they gave him "unarguing sympathy." He could write indeed of "helpful criticism" but what he longed for was confidence, understanding, "lightly turned laughter." Women of Southern birth understood him best.

"My dear friend," one of them wrote, "you must be content to have me, should you need me, your advocate—not your judge."[2]

His letters to his family and friends abound in his delight at meeting charming or beautiful women:

"My trip to Ky. was quite delightful, in spite of the truly terrible heat in which it was made. Lexington is certainly the place for free and gay and perfect hospitality! The men were cordial and altogether interesting, and the women were bewitching. I got, one day, into a bunch of beauties that made my head swim. They were as sweet to me as they were delightful to look upon,—partly, I hope because they liked me and not *altogether* because they thought me 'distinguished.'"

It was the Southerner here speaking, the chivalric Southerner, the romantic. He idealized, indeed, all of his real friends, both men and women, endowed them with qualities born of his own fervid imagination. He was as much the idealist in his personal relationships as in his

---

[1] Woodrow Wilson to Mary A. Hulbert, August 6, 1911.
[2] Edith G. Reid to Woodrow Wilson, June 14, 1897.

attitude toward his public duties. He made his friends
perfect before taking them wholly to him.

"We love generally without justification and there are
only two or three whom we admire with entire reverence
and perfect faith."

"Friendship is all largess. Nothing is given from a sense
of duty. It all lies in the delightful region of voluntary
service. The affection which supports it is wholly spontaneous,—and only the spontaneous is delightful."

When such a friendship failed, it tore the heart out of a
man! Friendship may be a torment for those who do not
"lack in sensibility and therefore in the power to suffer."
Of one of the greatest of his friendships he wrote:

"Why will that wound not heal over in my stubborn
heart? Why is it that I was blind and stupid enough to
love the people who proved false to me, and cannot *love*, can
only gratefully admire and cleave to, those who are my real
friends by the final, only conclusive proof of conduct and
actual loyalty, when loyalty cost and meant something?
. . . My best course, the course I instinctively follow most
of the time, is to think always of my new job, never of my
old, and to relieve my heart by devoting all its energies to
the duties which do not concern friends but that great
mass of men to whose service one can devote himself
without thought of the rewards of personal affection or
friendship. Perhaps it is better to love men in the mass
than to love them individually!"[1]

He could decide again and again in his life that it was
better to "love men in the mass than to love them individually," but always he had to have friends near at
hand to whom he could turn for understanding, whom he
could idealize, whom he could love. It was so from his
boyhood onward. In the beginning there was his father—
the rarest and deepest of his friendships—and then his

---

[1]Woodrow Wilson to Mary A. Hulbert, February 12, 1911.

devoted classmates, Bridges, Talcott, Dodge, and his Virginia friend, Dabney. Later at Princeton there were the Hibbens—Professor and Mrs. Hibben—to whom he was utterly devoted. He must see them every day: he made no plans, came to no conclusions, without talking with "Jack" Hibben. His letters to Hibben and to Mrs. Hibben were addressed, "My dear, dear Friend," "Dearest Friend," and often signed, "Yours devotedly," or "Your devoted friend." The break with Hibben over Princeton policies was one of the deep tragedies of Wilson's life: for he considered, whether rightly or wrongly, that it was a choice between adhering to his principles and keeping his friend.

His principles and his friends—how to keep them both! To solve that problem is, in some measure, to pluck the heart out of the man's mystery. What a struggle he had— all his life! He longed for friends, and love, and beauty, and quietude, but dreaded them lest they soften the iron of his purpose. He was a man of "tumultuous emotions."

"I have to . . . guard my emotions from painful over-flow. . . ."[1]

He had made up his mind with a slow but stubborn resoluteness as to his course in life. We may recall the "solemn covenant" with Charles Talcott:

". . . that we would school all our powers and passions for the work of establishing the principles we held in common. . . ."[2]

No mere boyish whim, this; he adhered to it with a tenacity of purpose absolutely unflagging. He built upon the granite of his own hard-knit, tough-fibred Scotch nature. He early perceived the "importance of single-mindedness."

". . . the singleness of his aim," he said of Bismarck in

[1]Woodrow Wilson to Ellen Axson Wilson, August 29, 1902.
[2]Woodrow Wilson to Ellen Axson Wilson, October 30, 1883.

the first article he ever wrote, "has concentrated his powers."[1]

". . . he trod steadily onward toward the ends he had marked out for himself . . ." he remarked of Pitt.

The very essence of statesmanship, he declared to be "that resolute and vigorous advance towards the realization of high, definite, and consistent aims which issues from the unreserved devotion of a strong intellect to the service of the state and to the solution of all the multiform problems of public policy."[2]

But friendship may so easily weaken a man's purpose! How was one to "school the passions" that he might not be diverted? How discipline the heart? There was danger in "thinking with our emotions and not with our minds," of being moved by "impulse and not by judgment."[3]

"Hearts," he said, "frequently give trouble. . . . They must be schooled before they will become insensible. . . ."[4]

And how are they to be schooled?

". . . in all cases the mind must be their schoolmaster and coach. They are irregular forces; but the mind may be trained to observe all points of circumstance and all motives of occasion."[5]

No wonder the common world could not understand the man: the common world neither thinks clearly nor feels deeply. How could it comprehend the tragedy of the lonely spirit pledged to a far purpose, seeking to school the heart into insensibility, only to find it clamouring the more loudly for sympathy? Hearts, after all, will not be completely disciplined even by an iron will. Wilson told a

---

[1]"Prince Bismarck," published in the *Nassau Literary Magazine*, November 1877. *The Public Papers of Woodrow Wilson*, Vol. I, p. 7.

[2]"William Earl Chatham," published in the *Nassau Literary Magazine*, October 1878. *The Public Papers of Woodrow Wilson*, Vol. I, p. 13.

[3]Address before the Phi Beta Kappa Society of Yale University, March 18, 1908.

[4]*Mere Literature*, p. 45.

[5]*Ibid.*, p. 45.

friend, just before leaving Princeton, that he had learned at last the danger of yielding to friendship.[1] And yet, almost the first thing he did upon entering public life was to enter into an extraordinary relationship with Colonel House—a friendship probably without precedent in the history of our Presidents. He could indeed say that friendship must be "absolutely without reserve," and yet he himself, by compulsion of the deepest forces within him, must reserve his principles undimmed, his faith inviolate. And he was so constituted that if his friends did not continue to adhere to the principles he considered eternal —how could they be perfect if they did not?—the "sensitive chain" which bound them together too easily snapped. He was asking a surrender which he himself could not make.

And yet, throughout his life, what friends the man had —if they remained outside the fiery path of his purpose! What devotion he knew, if the relationship could be kept personal! The hero of *The Education of Henry Adams* remarks that it is the rare man who can say that in the course of his life he has had forty true friends. Wilson was one of those rare men.

In his family relationships no man was ever more greatly blessed than Woodrow Wilson. Without the complete sympathy, the unwavering devotion, first of Ellen Axson, and later of Edith Bolling, he could never have lived to do his work. In his home he truly lived and had his being. But it seemed also necessary for him to "write out" or "talk out" his problems, his joys, his aspirations, with friends. He was the veritable, the authentic "writing man," realizing himself most deeply when he was setting down without reserve his innermost thoughts and feelings. To many natural writers the diary offers the convenient medium: Wilson found it in intimate letters.

---

[1] Professor E. G. Conklin to the author.

It is unfortunate—it is in fact, tragic—that the greater part of these letters were not preserved. All through his early life he wrote at length, almost every Sunday, to his father, setting forth his ambitions and visions. This correspondence has utterly disappeared. While we are fortunate in having the letters he wrote to Ellen Axson before his marriage, and many afterwards,[1] most of those that he wrote to her during the campaigns of 1911 and 1912, and in the presidential period, while she was at Cornish—he usually wrote daily—have been lost. He wrote a large number of letters to his brother-in-law, Stockton Axson; he wrote also to his daughters, and to other relatives, but few of these letters were preserved.

Outside of his immediate family, he had also, from his youth upward, a group of "dearest friends." Many of his intimate letters to his classmates at Princeton or at the University of Virginia—Bridges, Talcott, Dodge, Dabney —have been quoted in this biography: but even here the record is not complete. We know of several series of letters to college friends that cannot be found. At Princeton, after he became a member of the faculty, his "dearest friends" were Professor and Mrs. Hibben, to both of whom he wrote a large number of letters, only a few of which have been made available to this biographer. Other "dearest friends" were Mrs. Reid of Baltimore,[2] Mrs. Toy of Cambridge,[3] and Mrs. Mary A. Hulbert,[4] to all of whom he was writing in the same years. He also included within the circle of "dearest friends" at a later time, Colonel E. M. House.

[1] See *Woodrow Wilson, Life and Letters: Youth* and *Princeton.*

[2] Wife of Professor Harry Fielding Reid of Johns Hopkins University.

[3] Wife of Professor Crawford H. Toy of Harvard University.

[4] At the time of their first acquaintance, Mrs. Thomas D. Peck. See *Woodrow Wilson, Life and Letters: Princeton,* p. 267. Mrs. Hulbert, born Mary Allen, had come from Duluth, Minnesota. Mr. Hulbert, to whom she was married when quite young, was killed in an accident when her son was a young child. She later married Thomas D. Peck from whom she obtained a divorce in 1912. Mr. Wilson first met her in Bermuda in 1907.

To all these he turned with joy as "a release from the strain" he was under. He loved to send them books— Bagehot, first of all, sometimes copies of his own writings —sometimes flowers or "small remembrances"; he loved to write them on their birthdays; he thought they would like to know one another—since he himself found them all so wonderful! Such excursions in friendship lightened the sense of duty, the devotion to the task in hand imposed upon him by his hard-grained Scotch character, his Calvinistic religious faith.

"It is *terrible* to stand in such a blaze of publicity as I now stand in,—and as the target of all attack. . . . It needs steady nerves to stand it,—and every possible release into the dear company and *confidence* of friends."

Writing to such friends, "revealing his whole mind," seemed always to have been a rest, a recreation, to one who was hard-burdened, bitterly harassed. It was next to a "long, quiet, friendly talk."

Of all the groups of later letters which this biographer has seen, the largest in number and the most revealing, are those written to Mrs. Hulbert.[1] They began in 1907 and continued until 1915. For a time he wrote to her almost every Sunday. The letters, many of which have been quoted in this biography, deal largely with a running account of the daily tasks, problems, successes, disappointments, of a governor and President—but they also contain much of personal revelation. Following is a letter of the more personal sort:

13 Jan'y, 1911

DEAREST FRIEND,
I shall have some ink in a few minutes, meanwhile, will you forgive pencil? As usual, I have only a little interspace of a

[1]The complete collection contains two hundred and twenty-one letters. Many of Mrs. Hulbert's responses remain also in Mr. Wilson's files.

few moments in which to write. We have just left "Prospect" and I am writing from a little den, quite strange to me, in the Princeton Inn. Mrs. Wilson, Nellie, and I are to live here till early summer; Jessie, who spends Monday—Thursday in settlement work in Philadelphia, will be with us over week ends; and Margaret is established in two pleasant rooms in New York, as a full fledged independent student of music,— just a city block away from her teacher. Nellie will go and come to and from Philadelphia every day, to study at the Academy of Fine Arts, as before. Alas! it is *not* pleasant: My heart aches at the break-up of the old life, interesting and vital as the new life is. I did not realize it until it touched our home and sent us into lodgings at an inn. I feel like a nomad! The idea of a man of fifty-four (no less!) leaving a definite career and a settled way of life of a sudden and launching out into a vast sea of Ifs and Buts! It sounds like an account of a fool. At any rate, there is nothing in it of private advantage! Every private comfort and satisfaction (for example and chief of all, the freedom to go to Bermuda) is destroyed and broken up and one's life is made to turn upon public affairs altogether. What can be snatched from the public (from office seekers and re-porters and an occasional serious discussion of something really interesting and important) one *can* devote to his family or his friends or some hastily enjoyed pleasure. Even his *thinking*, which used to be done deliberately and upon the independent impulse of his own mind, he must do as bidden, at any moment, upon expected or unexpected summons,—at the call of the casual acquaintance or the exaction of the newest correspon-dence! I shall get used to it, but at present I am in revolt, and wish I were—in Bermuda, sitting by my friend, for a long, intimate chat that would get my thoughts and my spirits into perfect fettle again.

Is dear old Mrs. Jones living yet? If she is, *please* give her my love. My thoughts have recently run back at tired moments to that delicious half hour (or was it more?) I spent with her one afternoon, in real human talk—chiefly of you—and how you first flashed, a radiant vision, on Bermudan ken—and in sipping cordial and eating good cake, quite as if I were a lad again sitting "on my manners," with some gracious dame of the old regime in our own dear, forgotten South. It is a balm to irritated nerves to think of it,—a rest to my spirit,—and

"Inwood," with the very spirit of peace resting upon it,—and within the most delectable suggestions of *you* and of the first time I had a real glimpse of you as I was to know you from that time on! Ah, how delightful it all is! And how different from New Jersey politics,—which is full of the devil (as well as with promise of his defeat) and of war!

I am perfectly well. Next Tuesday (the 17th) I am to be sworn in as Governor—(which will not increase my troubles) —but we are still to be here. The fight makes good progress. All join me in most affectionate messages. Bless you for your letters—they delight me now that you are happy again and Bermuda has once more got hold on your spirits.

Your devoted friend
WOODROW WILSON

Scores of his intimate letters, like this to Mrs. Reid, express the delight he has in these friendships as a relief from the strain of his tasks:

DEAREST FRIEND,

How sweet it is of you to write such notes as that you sent me on the fourth. They cheer me and hearten me and calm me as only the voice of a beloved friend can; and I bless you for them with all my heart. The turmoil and contest and confusing struggle of the life down here drains the sources of joy and confidence in me sadly, and a dear voice like your own, so generous, so full of affectionate reassurance, so sincere and so full of comprehension, is the very tonic I need. It makes the springs run full and fresh again. . . .

All unite in the most affectionate messages to you all.

Your devoted friend,
WOODROW WILSON[1]

A letter to another dear friend, Mrs. Toy, expresses the same quality of feeling—the same out-reaching for understanding: and all of them are full of references to his tasks, his problems, and to the home life in which he delighted.

---

[1] Woodrow Wilson to Edith G. Reid, March 15, 1914.

12 December, 1914.

DEAREST FRIEND,

Your letters have the rare quality of making me feel, after reading them, as if I had really seen you and had a talk with you of many things. I wish that I could return the visit by writing a like vivid epistle, with the person in it who wrote it! I seem to have fallen singularly dull. All the elasticity has gone out of me. I have not yet learned how to throw off the incubus of my grief[1] and live as I used to live, in thought and spirit, in spite of it. Even books have grown meaningless to me. I read detective stories to forget, as a man would get drunk! I am deeply grateful to you for the glimpses you give me of your dear mother and of my own lost sweetheart from the old letters you have been reading and from your diary. You know the kind of ministrations I need! . . .

When is it going to be possible for you to pay us a visit? We shall count on one as soon as it is possible. All unite in messages of deep affection. My warmest regards to Mr. Toy.

Your devoted friend<br>WOODROW WILSON[2]

Feeling so deeply for his friends, his letters were also full of anxiety for their health, and for their welfare: and if they suffered injustice he could be hotly indignant. Even when he was toiling under the heavy burdens of the Presidency, he wrote innumerable letters, often in his own hand, seeking to help solve the infinitely trivial, infinitely irritating problems of a sister, a nephew, and of more than one friend, who had turned to him in their distress. Nor were his letters confined merely to expressions of his sympathy; they often contained more practical evidences of his friendship!

Such was the deep inner life of the man who was now being drawn more and more deeply into the absorbing struggles of politics—who was, indeed, never again to

---

[1]The death of Mrs. Wilson.

[2]Woodrow Wilson to Nancy Toy, December 12, 1914.

know the fine, free life that he loved most of all. He and his family were living at the Princeton Inn—not comfortably, but they were not financially able at the time to afford a better place. Nearly every day he went, twelve miles, to the capitol at Trenton, returning in the evening. Mrs. Wilson was indefatigable not only in watching over his health, but in reading the newspapers for him, seeing that he met the right people, bringing such leaders to her table as would most help him.

"He is working under fearfully high pressure," she wrote her friend Anna Harris, on March 20, 1911. "Nobody can rest him but me."

Many of those who came into contact with him during 1911 refer to the impression he gave of vivid life; interpreting it as it appeared outwardly:

"He positively enjoyed being governor. The effect he had upon his visitors was nearly always the same. No one could be in his presence for five minutes without being charmed with the man."[1]

He looked forward to the daily luncheons at the hotel in Trenton. He liked witty people around him.

"Judge, can't you bring in someone to-day who can tell good jokes?"[2]

When people entered the Governor's office in those days, he would sometimes sit back in his chair and "swap stories." Or late in the afternoon, he liked to take a friend for a long walk in the park and along the Delaware River. He seems never at any other period of his political life to have unbent so easily; to have had more human contacts. With the coming of the enormous burdens of the presidential campaign—soon to be heaped upon his duties as governor—he became, unfortunately, less approachable,

[1]Edward E. Davis to George Barton. See *Current History*, April, 1925. "Woodrow Wilson: His Human Side," by George Barton.

[2]Judge Robert S. Hudspeth to the author.

less free. When he neared the limit of his physical strength, he cut away what seemed less important, the human relationships, for what seemed more important. Was he mistaken? It led to many misunderstandings; it lost him friends; but it enabled him to concentrate all his powers behind the causes, the objectives, toward which he was directing all his energies. How determine which was of the greater importance? It was a deliberate choice. It was what he considered necessary: he was willing to abide by the consequences.

## VIII. THE UNDISPUTED LEADER

When the legislature adjourned on April 21st, Wilson had not only become the undisputed leader of his party, and indeed of the state, but he had carried through every reform law that he had promised. He had gone further, and brought about several important reforms not originally in his programme, including an act permitting cities to adopt commission government with a modified form of the initiative, referendum, and recall. He himself gives the best account of the achievement in a letter here published in full:

Princeton, 23 April, 1911.

DEAREST FRIEND,

The Legislature adjourned yesterday morning at three o'clock, with its work done. I got absolutely everything I strove for,— and more besides: all four of the great acts that I had set my heart on (the primaries and election law, the corrupt practices act, as stringent as the English, the workingmen's compensation act, and the act giving a public commission control over the railways, the trolley lines, the water companies, and the gas and electric light and power companies), and besides them I got certain fundamental school reforms and an act enabling any city in the State to adopt the commission form of government, which simplifies the electoral process and concentrates responsibility. Everyone, the papers included, are saying that none of it could have been done, if it had not been for my influence and tact and hold upon the people. Be that as it may, the thing was done, and the result was as complete a victory as has ever been won, I venture to say, in the history of the country. I wrote the platform, I had the measures formulated to my mind, I kept the pressure of opinion constantly on the legislature, and the programme was carried out to its last detail. This with the senatorial business seems, in the minds of the people looking on little less than a miracle, in the light of what has been the history of reform hitherto in this State. As a matter of fact, it is just a bit of natural history. I came to the office in the fulness of time, when opinion was ripe on all these matters, when both parties were committed to these reforms, and by merely standing fast, and by never losing sight of the business for an hour, but keeping up all sorts of (legitimate) pressure *all the time*, kept the mighty forces from being diverted or blocked at any point. The strain has been immense, but the reward is great. I feel a great reaction to-day, for I am, of course, exceedingly tired, but I am quietly and deeply happy that I should have been of just the kind of service I wished to be to those who elected and trusted me. I can look them in the face, like a servant who has kept faith and done all that was in him, given every power he possessed, to them and their affairs. There could be no deeper source of satisfaction and contentment! I have no doubt that a good deal of the result was due to the personal relations I established with the men in the Senate, the Republican Senate which, it was feared at the outset, might be the stumbling block. You remember the dinner in New York and the supper at the Trenton country club which I described to you. Those evenings undoubtedly played their part in the outcome. They brought us all close together on terms not unlike friendly intimacy; made them realize just what sort of *person* I was. Since then Republicans have resorted to my office for counsel and advice almost as freely as Democrats (an almost unprecedented circumstance at Trenton) and with several of them I have established relations almost of affection. Otherwise I do not believe that the extraordinary thing that happened could possibly have come about: for all four of the great "administration" measures passed the Senate *without a dissent-*

*ing voice!* The newspaper men seem dazed. They do not understand how such things *could* happen. They were impressed, too, with the orderly and dignified way in which the session ended, despite the long strain of the closing night, when the houses sat from eight until three. Generally there is wild horseplay, like that on the stock exchange, but this time everything was done decently and with an air of self-respect. I took several naps in my office during the long hours of the session, coming out into the outer office in the intervals to talk and swap stories with the men who were sitting there, my secretary, the reporters who were coming and going, and interested friends who had come down to see how things ended. Then a committee from each House called on me to ask if there was anything more I had to lay before them before adjournment,—and the session was over. Most of the members dropped in to say good bye, and by four o'clock your tired and happy friend was in bed in the noisy little Hotel Sterling, with the strong odours of late suppers in his nostrils, floating in at the open window. It's a great game, thoroughly worth playing!

I literally have not had five minutes time to drop in and see the Roeblings. I have thought of them almost every day, and have wanted to go very sincerely. I think Mrs. R. charming. But I have not felt that I could relax my attention for a moment while the session lasted,—and it had already begun when I was inaugurated, you know, and plunged into the first fight, the fight for the senatorship. Winning that, by the way, made all the rest easier; but it also made the session some two weeks longer than usual. What a vigil it has been! I am certainly in training for almost anything that may come to me by way of public tasks. There are serious times ahead. It daunts me to think of the possibility of my playing an influential part in them. There is no telling what deep waters may be ahead of me. The forces of greed and the forces of justice and humanity are about to grapple for a bout in which men will spend all the life that is in them. God grant I may have strength enough to count, to tip the balance in the unequal and tremendous struggle! This week I turn to speech-making again (much the easier task of the two) and to preparation for my western trip. All through everything, as the days come and go with their tale of tasks, runs a constant thought of you, a constant solicitude for you, and an abiding consciousness of being (and of being blessed by being),

Your devoted friend,
WOODROW WILSON

Affectionate messages from all to all.[1]

Within a period of three months, New Jersey, the "Mother of the Trusts," thus became one of the most advanced states in the Union in reform legislation—and significantly quite without the use of the new devices, the initiative and referendum, which Wilson had recommended. While other reform laws were passed under Wilson's pressure at following sessions of the legislature—to which reference will later be made—his great constructive work in New Jersey was finished. As in the Princeton reforms in 1907, and in the magnificent early record of the presidency, as in the diplomacy of the Great War, Wilson seemed to succeed best in his first irresistible attacks—when he had his following securely behind him. Later, when the idealism of the people had been somewhat dampened, and Wilson still drove onward toward his far objective, he demanded more of human nature than it would quite bear; and the forces of old habit, deep-seated selfishness, dark tradition, swept in upon him.

Wilson had achieved, in an astonishing degree, the principal purposes he had set himself. He had centralized party control in the interest of the people, under a responsible governor elected by them. It had been his vision for thirty years. He had, indeed, to work with a caucus instead of with the legislature itself, but it had sufficed to take the control wholly out of the hands of the bosses and the machine. He hoped in the following year to be able to secure a revision of the rules of order of the Senate and Assembly,[2] and perhaps changes in the constitution which

---

[1] Woodrow Wilson to Mary A. Hulbert.
[2] See New Jersey Democratic platform, October 3, 1911.

would perpetuate these new relationships of the executive and the legislature—but he was drawn away into the national campaign. All his life, as we have seen, he had been revising constitutions, always with the idea of securing unity of purpose by means of responsible leadership. He sought for a time a complete revision of the antiquated constitution of New Jersey. It is a loss to progress in constitutional method in America that he should not have been able, in one state, to establish—or seek to establish— as a legitimate experiment, a system of cabinet government, with the executive functioning as a premier. It was what he wanted to do.

One other result of Wilson's first eight months in politics is also of profound importance. This was the reaction of his experience upon the man himself. He had been completely confirmed in his faith in the people—in the "mass of the people." Had they not supported him in his vision of a new leadership, a new freedom? The old leaders could not understand; the people could. If the bosses held back, he had only to appeal to the people. He could ask for a "solemn referendum." The people wanted the high things, the right things, the true things! Something mystic in the philosophy of democracy has appealed to every great leader of the people; something higher than individual selfishness, something purer than personal interest. Wilson held that belief to the end of his days. No defeat, no failure —not even the apparent apostasy of the people themselves —disillusioned him.

Even after he was a broken man, after the heart-breaking struggles with an obdurate Senate over the ratification of the Treaty of Versailles, he could say:

"In spite of all that has happened, I have not lost one iota of my great faith in the people.

"They may act too quickly or too slowly, but you can depend upon them ultimately; you can depend upon their search for the truth and for what is right, and that is more than you can say about some of the so-called intellectuals who are actuated by prejudice and are sometimes more selfish than the masses."[1]

Wilson's dramatic fight in New Jersey, given the widest publicity, made him by the summer of 1911 one of the outstanding candidates for the presidency. It was due to his own initiative, his own activity. Not one of the "President-makers" had anything to do with it. McCombs was not there, nor Colonel House, nor Bryan, nor, during the struggle, Colonel Harvey—much less any of the party leaders or bosses, who had begun to fear him or hate him.

"Republicans as well as Democrats are frankly admitting the ability with which Governor Wilson is administering the affairs of New Jersey. Those who looked on him as a dilettante in politics have been amazed by his grasp of public questions and his businesslike method of handling them. The chief asset of this scholarly statesman seems, after all, to be his fund of hard, common sense. He is proving himself as able in practice as he was illuminative in theory. It is not surprising that the country is watching Governor Wilson with interest, and that he is being viewed as a national rather than a purely local figure."[2]

---

[1]See Norman H. Davis, in *Success*, July, 1925.
[2]Washington *Post*, April 21, 1911.

# CHAPTER IV

## NATIONAL LEADERSHIP

Every statesman who ever won anything great in any self-governing country was a man whose programme would stand criticism and had the energy behind it to move forward against opposition.

*Address before the Economic Club, New York, May 23, 1912.*

I am accused of being a radical. If to seek to go to the root is to be a radical, a radical I am. . . ."

*Speech in the New Jersey campaign.*

Whoever would effect a change in a modern constitutional government must first educate his fellow citizens to want *some* change. That done, he must persuade them to want the particular change he wants. He must first make public opinion willing to listen and then see to it that it listen to the right things. He must stir it up to search for an opinion, and then manage to put the right opinion in its way.

*Woodrow Wilson, " The Study of Administration."*

### I. A NATION IN REVOLT

A MAN," says Emerson, "is a method . . . a selecting principle, gathering his like to him wherever he goes."

Wilson's call to national leadership came at the flowering of a movement of democratic revolt in America. He did not originate it; he contributed to it no new ideas; he saw it, felt it, expressed it, with incomparable clarity and power; he became its method.

American political life from the beginning has oscillated between the ideas of Hamilton and the ideas of Jefferson; between aristocracy and democracy; between the Federalist or Republican party and the Democratic party. Hamilton believed in the rule of a privileged class, which

he sought deliberately to create in order that it might
govern the nation. "The People, your People, Sir, is a
great Beast." His profound interest, as Oliver says, was
in the hive, Jefferson's in the bee. Jefferson believed in the
people—not only in their rights, but in their capacities.
"All men are created equal." Hamilton believed in the
power of wealth; Jefferson dreaded it. Hamilton believed
in centralization of power; Jefferson in local control. The
American system owes its strength to the balance between
these two ideas or ideals of government, one centrifugal,
the other centripetal.

The Civil War was extraordinary in being a struggle to
maintain both of these apparently contradictory principles. It was at once a revolt against privilege—the privilege
of slavery—and a demand for federal unity. In his struggle
to free the slaves, Lincoln was a profound Jeffersonian;
in his demand for a strong central government, the unity of
the states, he was a thorough Hamiltonian. Four American
administrations, coming at crises in our affairs, have been
great because of this saving and essential duality: those
of Washington, Jackson, Lincoln, and Wilson. Wilson, in
his international policies, was Jeffersonian in his demand
for "self-determination," Hamiltonian in his struggle for a
union of the states of the world.

After the Civil War, there were three great waves of
political insurgency, with Wilson riding into power on the
third. Each had an emotional beginning; each represented
the more or less blind revolt of the under-dog, the West
and the South, against the East. The first was the Greenback movement of the '70's and '80's. While the Greenbackers had a panacea—fiat money—the essence of their
programme was the control of privilege. They wanted more
direct power of the people over their government, they
were against land grants to railroads and corporations,
they demanded the regulation of interstate commerce and

governmental supervision of factories, mines, and work-shops. They favoured an eight-hour day and an income tax. Every item in their bill of particulars struck straight at privilege. Save upon the money question, the progressives of 1910 and 1911 agreed practically with the programme of the old Greenback and Populist parties. Upon the question of tariff privilege the later progressives even outdid the earlier radicals; and some of the specific demands which Wilson voiced in 1911—as for popular election of United States senators, direct primaries, the referendum and recall—would probably have shocked the constitution-worshipping Insurgents of the '80's. Cleveland's election in 1884 overwhelmed the party of privilege; it did not satisfy the revolters. Cleveland proved to be a conservative of the conservatives.

For several years the insurgent movement was quiescent, waiting to see what Cleveland would do. There existed still that safety valve for discontent, free land, free opportunity in the West. Men who were restless, and felt themselves exploited or oppressed, could still escape into the free life of the prairies or the mountains. The nation had not yet reached the end of the frontier.

Then came the panic of '93, with its money stringency, its vast industrial disturbances, its Coxey's forlorn armies of the unemployed, and in 1896 the culmination of the second great wave of revolt led by William J. Bryan. The programme remained essentially the same; essentially anti-privilege; essentially Jeffersonian. It had also its familiar panacea, cheap money. It was Western and Southern; the under-dog against the top-dog. But there was this great difference: The Greenbackers and Populists had both tried a hopeless third-party movement, and had finally helped the Democratic party to win with an Easterner and a conservative; but the second wave of revolt captured the Democratic party, nominated Bryan in 1896, and came so near electing him that the Easterners shook in their shoes. In 1900 Bryan was again defeated, partly owing to the new prosperity which followed the Spanish War, partly because the war had dulled the cutting edge of domestic unrest, and the privileged interests, encouraged by their victory, entrenched themselves, under McKinley, more firmly than ever before.

This second assault was far greater than the first but it did not break over the strong ramparts. The captains on guard, Hanna and Quay and Aldrich and Platt, were too strong, too able. Nor was the jury of the people fully satisfied. There had to be more evidence still, and it came in the remarkable exposures of the Muck-rakers. The public learned of the corruption of the cities, the evil partnership of privileged interests and political bosses, of the ruthless exploitation by powerful monopolies. The "Ballinger case" dramatized the purpose of private interests, by their influence within the very official family of the President himself, to seize the natural resources of the nation for their own gain. The insurgents attacked such measures as the Payne-Aldrich tariff law as "strongholds of privilege," and overturned Cannonism in Congress. Governor Hughes's investigations of the life insurance companies made a profound impression. In the West, Bryan was no longer alone. There were rising in both parties powerful and able insurgent leaders, chief among them an "incendiary demagogue named La Follette"—if one may quote the choice appellation of an enemy—who was overturning Wisconsin.

Theodore Roosevelt, who came to the presidency through the death of McKinley, played a part in the movement wholly unexpected by the leaders of his party. He hammered home, day after day, the forgotten moralities. He played well the part of the prophet and preacher.

From his tower of observation and reflection Wilson, the

scholar, had followed all of these movements for years. He had laboriously studied their origins, worked out the history of similar upheavals in other countries, written articles and books, lectured year after year to his students. He once told the present writer that no one had followed the disclosures of the Muck-rakers with more intentness than he. Beginning his career a traditional Democrat and academic free-trader, his instincts were aristocratic. He was early a critic of Jefferson. In his thoroughgoing belief in the need of a strong federal union of the states, he was a decided Hamiltonian. But he also knew well the life of the unprivileged South after the Civil War, and when he began his fight at Princeton in 1907 to establish conditions that would make the university a "genuine seat of learning," his experience amply corroborated the criticisms and complaints of the insurgents. He found the privileged interests against him. He found that the country was "not governed by principles but by interests" and interest "does not unite men, it separates them." He became more and more a convinced progressive.

It was in the address at Pittsburgh, April 16, 1910, that he came to himself politically, as in former years he had come to himself religiously and intellectually. He began to see more and more clearly the need of greater emphasis upon Jeffersonian principles in the American system.

"I have been fighting privilege at Princeton, just as I am fighting it here now," he told a friend.[1]

He strongly approved Roosevelt's course, and, later, commended La Follette. His relationships with Bryan, which will be fully treated presently, will clearly indicate this growth and change in his views. His faith in the people increased as he tested it.

"This great American people is at bottom just, virtuous, and hopeful; the roots of its being are in the soil of what

[1] William Bayard Hale in *World's Work*, May, 1911.

is lovely, pure, and of good report; and the need of the hour is just that radicalism that will clear a way for the realization of the aspirations of a sturdy race."

Roosevelt, at the conclusion of his administration in 1908, chose his friend Taft as his successor. What was wanted, he believed, was a cool-headed lawyer, wise and steady, to guide the aroused people in the enactment of the progressive measures they were demanding. There had been emotion enough, exposures enough; the time had come for law-making. In August, 1908, after Taft's nomination, the present writer had a long talk with Roosevelt:

"Well, I'm through now. I've done my work. I want to get away so that when the new administration comes in my opinion will not be asked, nor my advice sought. . . . People are going to discuss economic questions more and more: the tariff, currency, banks. They are hard questions, and I am not deeply interested in them; my problems are moral problems, and my teaching has been plain morality."[1]

Wilson had also concluded that the emotional revolt had gone far enough.

"We are thinking just now with our emotions and not with out minds; we are moved by impulse and not by judgment."[2]

Roosevelt and Wilson had thus, in 1908, much the same conception of a new leadership. And Taft, the President-elect, agreed with them:

"The chief function of the next administration in my judgment is distinct from and a progressive development of that which has been performed by President Roosevelt. The chief function of the next administration is to complete and perfect the machinery by which these standards may be maintained, by which the lawbreakers may be

[1] Ray Stannard Baker, in the *American Magazine*, September, 1908.
[2] Address before the Phi Beta Kappa Society of Yale University, March 18, 1908.

promptly restrained and punished, but which shall operate with sufficient accuracy and dispatch to interfere with legitimate business as little as possible."[1]

Moral enthusiasm never of itself gets anywhere. It must be boiled down to its insoluble residuum of hard, clear, intellectual propositions. New definitions must be struck out; the leader, with a sort of divine carelessness, must announce his course and play his part. Lincoln laid down the law, and uttered the clarion note of leadership in words that cut like a sword through the confused but none the less passionate popular emotion on the slavery question, in his Jeffersonian declaration: "This nation cannot exist half slave and half free," and when he said with Hamiltonian emphasis to the Southern disunionists, "We won't go out of the Union, and you shan't."

But the country heard nothing clear, nothing sure, nothing strong, from Taft—and felt itself drifting, drifting, toward a crisis. It was not a lawyer that was needed, but a constructive thinker, a determined leader. An amiable, likable, honest man, Taft was no match for the powerful interests which dominated his own party. By 1910 the revolt had become tumultuous. Old party lines were crumbling, old authorities suspected. Wilson saw Taft's problem clearly. He said, on November 5, 1910:

"If I were to sum up all the criticisms that have been made againt the gentleman who is now President of the United States, I could express them all in this: The American people are disappointed because he has not led them. . . . They clearly long for someone to put the pressure of the opinion of all the people of the United States upon Congress."[2]

Wilson's judgment was unmistakably confirmed in the mid-term elections of November, 1910. A Democratic

[1] William Howard Taft, in a speech at Cincinnati, July 28, 1908.
[2] At Newark, New Jersey.

landslide swept the country, in which Wilson himself
became governor of the Republican state of New Jersey.
The national House of Representatives became Democratic. It was plain enough that the country was in dead
earnest. The South and the West were thoroughly aroused.
The safety valve of free land and free opportunity had
disappeared. The admission of Arizona and New Mexico
as states symbolized the close of the free and romantic era
of the pioneer.

## II. THE CONTEST FOR CONTROL OF THE
### PROGRESSIVE MOVEMENT

Shrewd political observers had long been well aware of
the power of the revolt. The problem by the first of the
year 1911 resolved itself into the ancient business of seeking the leadership of a popular movement that could no
longer be suppressed. It was a situation calling for the
highest strategy of politics.

Both of the old parties became at once battle grounds
for factional control. Soon after the election of 1910, the
insurgent Republicans formed the National Progressive
Republican League of which La Follette, who was the
outstanding leader, soon became a presidential possibility.
A similar split existed in the Democratic party with Bryan
leading the progressives, and Underwood of Alabama and
Harmon of Ohio the outstanding conservatives.

Colonel George Harvey, shrewd political observer, had
early seen the crisis coming. The great banking and money
interests were desperately afraid of Bryan, La Follette,
and Roosevelt. At all costs leadership must be kept out of
their hands. Harvey and the bosses, as we have seen,
picked Wilson as the man best suited to lead the Democratic party and head off insurgency.

It was a shrewd political scheme. It might easily have

worked—if the leader so chosen had not happened to be a man of deep-rooted sincerity of purpose, with an extraordinary knowledge of political history and a genius for great leadership. When one considers Wilson's career from September, 1910, to June, 1912, the astonishing struggle of a leader wholly without experience in practical politics, largely without money or organization, in opposition to the shrewdest leaders of his time; when one watches the way in which he attracted and bound men to him, established himself swiftly not only as the leader of his party but of the progressive movement of the nation; how he steered the dangerous course between the Scylla of Bourbon Democracy and the Charybdis of Bryan, even a friendly biographer will not be accused of exaggeration in setting it down as one of the surprises of American politics. Wilson often impressed the little politicians around him as an amateur in political tactics. He was exactly that. He blundered in matters of appointments, he was often inept in those personal relationships which the little politicians invariably overrate. He could not easily suffer dullness or tolerate bores. He never in his life flattered anyone; he disliked promiscuous hand-shaking; he never kissed a political baby. He abominated the familiar practice of making capital out of social relationships. He was weak on details of political organization. But in the grand strategy of statesmanship he was without a peer in American annals.

Wilson might easily have made mistakes in early 1911 that would have ruined him. He might have accepted the leadership of the bosses in New Jersey as Dix was doing in New York; he might have sat back as a "constitutional governor" and avoided the struggle for party leadership and reform legislation. Above all, he might have been tempted into alliances in the tumultuous national arena which would have made his nomination at Baltimore an impossibility.

It was the intent of a considerable body of independents and progressives in early 1911 to draw together, regardless of party, those insurgent Republicans and insurgent Democrats who held practically the same views. Why should they not join forces? They had both been beaten in the past by being divided. If they could unite, the temper of the nation was such that they felt that they could win. A third-party movement such as Roosevelt headed in 1912 was not then projected, but it was looked upon as a possibility.

In January, 1911, a great gathering was planned, to be held in New York, in which progressive leaders of both parties could be brought together on the same platform. It was well known that Wilson had already taken an advanced progressive stand. He had publicly commended the Oregon system of popular government; he had written to Daniel Kiefer, a leader in the single-tax movement, regarding his attitude toward Wall Street:

"It makes me smile to think that I should ever have been regarded as the Wall Street candidate for the Presidency. I am sure that though I have many friends in Wall Street they never supposed for a moment that I would be serviceable to any interest that would be opposed to the interest of the people and to the country at large. I am not surprising them; I am only surprising those who do not understand me.

"The duty of public men in our time is so clear that I do not see how anyone can miss his way."

The progressives therefore hoped to bring La Follette and Wilson together at their proposed meeting in Carnegie Hall. Since the writer chanced to be the only member of the committee having the matter in charge who knew Governor Wilson personally, he was asked to extend an urgent invitation to him. Wilson replied, February 8, 1911:

MY DEAR MR. BAKER:-

Your letter of the seventh is very gracious and I warmly appreciate the compliment paid me by the desire of the Insurgents' Club to have me attend one of their meetings, but it is literally true that I have reached my limit. I cannot without endangering both my health and the performance of my public duties add to the already foolishly large speaking list that I have permitted myself to make.

I am in warm sympathy with the objects of the Club and wish very much that I could show my sympathy in some definite way.

Cordially yours,<br>
WOODROW WILSON

Later the writer called Governor Wilson on the telephone, urging him to reconsider his decision, arguing that the movement was non-partisan, that we were working for publicity of ideas and principles. Wilson responded with the real reason which was holding him back.

"I am heartily in sympathy with the movement," he said, "but I am convinced that I must make my fight within the Democratic party. It must be a party movement.[1]

This was a point upon which Wilson was entirely clear in his own mind. He had written to a friend on April 9, 1910, while he was still president of Princeton:

"I find that a great many men have your feeling about the Democratic party, fearing that it is impossible to dissociate its name from errors and heresies which have recently been connected with it. Theoretically, I agree with you that the formation of a new party is very desirable indeed, but practically it seems to me that that is the line of greatest difficulty and least encouragement upon which to work. I do not in the least despair of seeing the Democratic party drawn back to the definite and conser-

---

[1]The meeting, afterwards held in Carnegie Hall, and addressed by La Follette and other progressives, was highly successful.

vative principles which it once represented. It may be a
slow process and it will be a difficult one, but there is an
inestimable advantage in working upon definite historical
foundations and within the organization of a party which
is at any rate the oldest in organization in our history
which still continues to exist. I believe, from the various
signs of the times, that it is quite within reasonable hope
that new men will take hold of the party and draw it away
from the influences which have of late years demoralized
it."[1]

Wilson knew well enough the history of independent and
third-party movements in America. His strategy was
clearly to work through the party of which he was already
an accredited leader. He would not go to the progressives;
he would make them come to him. Roosevelt, defeated in
attempting the same strategy in the Republican camp, was
later forced into a third-party movement.

Wilson's course, if it was clear, was also beset with
tremendous obstacles. It might be magnificent audacity,
but what warrant had he that he could do anything with
the Democratic party? He had already hopelessly offended
the organization in his own state. Tammany Hall, with
New York in its pocket, considered him an "ingrate" and
an "upstart." After what he had said about Wall Street
and the Oregon system, the conservatives would certainly
not support him.

He knew well enough as an historian that no candidate
since Andrew Jackson in 1832 had been elected to the
presidency without the support of conservative business
men. On the other hand, he was not yet, like Roosevelt,
the leader of the progressives of his own party. A great
and vital figure, all but worshipped in the West and
South, to wit, Bryan, filled that field. And Wilson had
been a sharp critic of Bryan for many years. He had

[1]To H. S. McClure.

indeed won a spectacular local victory in New Jersey, he was much admired by thoughtful men, but compared with any one of several progressive leaders in the nation, he was unknown to the masses of the people. Where was the call to national leadership to come from? And how? After all, there is a method, a process, by which candidates are "groomed" for the presidency—and Wilson seemed to care nothing for it. He had a curious sense that "if a man is right . . . the people will support him." If anyone had troubled to ask him at the time where he expected the call to come from—if it came at all—he would probably have answered, in a way to make the heathen rage:

"From the people."

It was exactly where the call did come from; from men unconnected with politics or political organizations—the strangest group of amateurs that ever came together to help elect a President of the United States.

### III. AMATEUR ORGANIZERS

Books have been written describing the process and taking the credit for "making Woodrow Wilson President."

"I returned to New York and laid down a plan of campaign. . . . I selected the following cities for his speechmaking. . . . I laid the plan before him. . . . I then had suggestions made . . ."[1]

". . . the man [Colonel House]. . . who picked Woodrow Wilson as the logical Democratic candidate for the presidency in 1912. . . ."[2]

But the process was not a simple one; nor was Woodrow Wilson "made" by any man or group of men. For nearly thirty years, as this biography has shown, Wilson had

[1] W. F. McCombs, *Making Woodrow Wilson President,* p. 35.
[2] Arthur D. Howden Smith, *The Real Colonel House,* p. 21.

been writing vital books and essays; he had spoken indefatigably throughout the country; his struggle at Princeton had been heralded in the press. It was the gift of his
genius to make an extraordinary impression of power upon
many of those with whom he came in contact. He had
established "centers of infection" in various parts of the
country; he had won ardent supporters among many different groups of people. He was being suggested, as we have
seen, as a man capable of great leadership, a presidential
possibility, as early as 1902, before he became president of
Princeton University. Harvey had "nominated" him in
1906; his chances for the presidency and vice-presidency
were discussed by friends in 1908; he was sought in the
same year as a candidate for the United States Senate
from New Jersey. And finally in 1910 he had been elected,
after a spectacular campaign, as Democratic governor of a
state normally Republican. He had begun his service by
defeating one of the most astute political bosses in the
country; and had declared himself for a programme of
state legislation more advanced, with one exception, than
any other in the country.

Is it surprising that the call came? As the immense
accumulation of documents and press clippings relating to
these stirring times are sorted out and arranged according
to the hard logic of chronology, the exact nature of the
call of the people may be better understood. It was a
real call. It began in volume in January, 1911, especially
following the defeat of Boss Smith on January 25th. It
came in the form of innumerable letters, many from wholly
unknown and undistinguished citizens, or in articles, editorials, interviews in newspapers—most of which, sooner
or later, reached Mrs. Wilson's eye. Among the enthusiasts
were old Princeton men who had been Wilson's classmates
or his students; Southerners who admired Wilson as a
Southerner and the possible Moses of the Democratic

party; college presidents and professors who had been his associates or devoted friends—President Eliot of Harvard among them; journalists with a keen perception of the drift of public interest; certain down-trodden politicians, like those in Texas, chafing at an old or autocratic leadership; and finally a few restless, far-sighted Jews.

Many of the letters and telegrams of congratulation indicated the general feeling:

"We congratulate you and want you to be our next President. Republicans as well as Democrats of Oklahoma are for you.

"W. A. STUART, Republican
"W. WOOD, Democrat
"M. C. FRENCH, Democrat"[1]

"Heartiest congratulations. I consider the governorship merely a stepping stone.

"J. EDWIN WEBSTER"[2]

We find the citizens of Wilson's birthplace, Staunton, Virginia, organizing a Woodrow Wilson for President Club, probably the first, as early as November 26, 1910. Its leader was Peyton Cochran, a former student at Princeton, who had taken all of Wilson's courses. Wilson responded, November 27th:

"I do not feel that I have at all proven my fitness to be the nominee of the Democratic Party for the Presidency but it is very delightful that you and your associates in the new club should entertain such confidence in me, and I want to express my very deep appreciation and gratitude. . . ."

It is interesting to note that there were practically no

---

[1] November 9, 1910.

[2] November 9, 1910. J. Edwin Webster was a Princeton classmate.

radicals, or even extreme progressives, among those who joined in the early call for Wilson; the radicals at that time were following Debs, La Follette, Bryan, and Roosevelt.

Curiously, also, quite a number of the earliest and strongest supporters were, like Wilson himself, Scotch or Scotch-Irish and Presbyterian in their origin—McCombs, McAdoo, McCorkle, McCormick. Most of them were Southerners.

A representative letter is one from R. B. Glenn, former governor of North Carolina, dated January 11th:

"Doubtless you have forgotten Bob Glenn of Davidson College days. . . . I have faith in your ability . . . and know that your courage and conscientious convictions of right will cause you to win in the end.

"This is but the beginning of your political career, and both your friends of the past and present will be greatly disappointed if you are not ultimately elevated to a still higher position."

All these letters and suggestions, however indicative of a call from the people, were inchoate and confusing. Little as Wilson seemed at the time to realize it, or desire it, there had to be some concrete organization, some practical movement. Moreover friends whose enthusiasm exceeded their judgment or their experience in such matters, were demanding an opportunity to help. Wilson turned, on February 10th, to his old friend Page for advice:

MY DEAR PAGE:——

I have a very warm friend . . . who, with Mr. Walter McCorkle and other Southern friends of mine in New York, is bent upon getting up some kind of organized movement to advocate my claims for the nomination for the Presidency. —— does not seem to me a very wise person and he certainly is not considered in this State a practical man. His schemes are generally good, but for some reason are generally smiled at. I myself think that he is underrated and that it is chiefly his manner that stands against him. At the same time I am a little uneasy about any movement that he might start (or any movement at all for that matter of this ambitious kind). I have, therefore, taken the liberty of advising him to send Mr. McCorkle and others interested to you for hard headed advice. I hope that you will not mind my taking this liberty.

With warm regard,

Cordially yours,
WOODROW WILSON

Page had been talking with Wilson only a few days before about this very matter; but his idea had been to start a "little campaign of publicity." Wilson was widely known to thoughtful people, not so well to the masses—especially in the West. Page proposed sending over to Trenton a journalist, William Bayard Hale, who had written an article describing a visit of a week with Theodore Roosevelt. Wilson had replied:

MY DEAR PAGE:——

It will be a novel experience to have a man like Mr. Hale spend a week seeing how I go through the paces, but he is most welcome and I am most happy to have a plan set afoot which may serve to keep the witches off. It is certainly generous of you to wish to have this done in the World's Work.

Most faithfully yours,
WOODROW WILSON[1]

Page began also to consider how best to meet the general situation. He finally arranged for a meeting in New York, to which he invited McCorkle and William F. McCombs.

McCombs was a remarkable and erratic character. He was a cripple; and extremely sensitive regarding his affliction. He was born in Arkansas, suffered his way through a preparatory school, and came hobbling North on crutches to enter Princeton. He gradually learned to walk, became

---

[1]February 10, 1911. This article appeared in *World's Work* of May, 1911, "Woodrow Wilson: Possible President."

an able student, and a profound admirer of Wilson, whose courses he took.

"I have known Woodrow Wilson not only as governor of New Jersey, but as a student in his classroom and as a friend. . . . Wilson is a red-blooded man; he is a fighting man; he is the young man's man."

After finishing his law course, McCombs settled in New York City. Being a Democrat, he joined one of the branches of Tammany Hall, but though a strong believer in organization, had never been active in politics. He had eagerly followed Wilson's New Jersey campaign, even contributing to the state organization.

Late in February McCombs had visited Wilson at Trenton to discuss with him the employers' liability act, which was then under consideration in the New Jersey legislature. Wilson had spoken of the reaction from the country regarding his presidential candidacy, and McCombs had declared that there ought to be some organization to take the burden of detail from Wilson's shoulders.

At the New York conference, however, it was agreed that the most important thing was to get Wilson more directly before the people of the Far West. They felt that he would appeal particularly to Western Progressives, if once he could speak to them, and he would be challenging Bryan in Bryan's territory. Page suggested that they raise a small fund among themselves and employ Frank Parker Stockbridge, a capable journalist, to make arrangements for a Western trip which Wilson could begin soon after the adjournment of the New Jersey legislature.

Wilson agreed heartily enough. He told Stockbridge:

"The people of the United States are just like the people of New Jersey. If they believe in an issue, once it is stated to them in terms they understand, they will force their leaders to adopt it."[1]

[1]Frank Parker Stockbridge, in *Current History Magazine*, July, 1924.

Wilson was doubtful at this time, however, whether to become an active candidate for the presidential nomination, still more doubtful about making any public announcement. He disclosed his inner thought on the subject in a letter to a friend:

"All these men are strangely interested in the enterprise of making me President of the United States. I cannot help them in the least. There is something in me that makes it inevitable that I should go on as I have begun, doing things as it seems to me they ought to be done, square with my own individual sense and conviction of right, whether it is expedient or not; and I may, by that token, at any moment spoil all they are generously trying to do! I think every man instinctively likes to play the rôle of king-maker. I am at present, apparently, suitable material for their favourite sport, and so the game is on the boards. I do not mean that they are not generously interested in me, personally; but I must, for the working of my own mind, have something in addition to that to explain their enthusiasm. . . . It is amazing that so little performance of one's mere duty should raise such a smoke! I do not see what else I could have done than what I have done."[1]

He was also fearful at this time that the movement in his favour would develop too rapidly; and his letters of the time show that he discouraged both organization and undue enthusiasm. "I must say that the growth of this movement gives me unaffected uneasiness," he wrote a friend on March 29th.[2]

Wilson nevertheless knew well enough that he must "test out the people." Everything would depend upon the strength of the call for his leadership. The strategy of the campaign was clear enough. He must do two things. He must make sure of his hold upon the South, the cornerstone

---

[1] Woodrow Wilson to Mary A. Hulbert, February 19, 1911.
[2] Woodrow Wilson to Arthur W. Tedcastle.

of the Democracy. While he was himself a Southerner, he
had no political following. Powerful conservative leaders
like Underwood of Alabama, Bailey of Texas, Hoke Smith
of Georgia, and others dominated the field.

He must also test his leadership as a progressive; he
could do nothing, therefore, without the West, where
Bryan was the "peerless leader."

Wilson turned his attention to the South in March—
literally tearing himself away from the legislative struggles at Trenton. He had warrant for believing that there
was a considerable number of thoughtful men who were
already interested in him. Many letters, often from complete strangers, had come to him from the Old South. Recent addresses to the Southern Society and the Kentuck-
ians in New York City had been warmly received and
widely republished. Texas especially had been stirring.

Thomas B. Love[1] of Dallas, Texas, George D. Armistead, and Thomas W. Gregory[2] of Austin were among the
early and enthusiastic Wilson supporters. Love congratu-
lated Wilson by telegraph after his election in November,
1910, and a correspondence sprang up, Love expressing
his desire to "be of service in any way possible, in pro-
moting your nomination for the presidency, and I can say
that I have already ascertained that in such a movement
many of the strongest and most influential Democrats in
Texas, scattered throughout the state, are willing to
coöperate."[3] In his letter, Love said that he had been talking with Bryan about Wilson, and that Bryan had expressed doubt as to Wilson's views, especially on the
proposal for an income tax. This conference, as will be
shown later, started Bryan to thinking about Wilson as a

---

[1]Member of the Texas legislature in the sessions of 1903, 1905, and 1907.
[2]Later Attorney General in Wilson's cabinet.
[3]December 1, 1910.

possible Democratic leader. Wilson responded to Love on February 16, 1911:

MY DEAR MR. LOVE:–

Your letter of February seventh has given me the deepest pleasure and gratification. It encourages me greatly to know that I have your approval in the things I have been trying to do.

I am taking the liberty of sending you a copy of our legislative manual which happens to be the only form in which I have at hand our campaign platform. I shall take pleasure in having sent you, under another cover also, a copy of my Inaugural address. I have as yet sent no messages to the Legislature.

I am heartily in favour of the adoption by the Legislature of New Jersey of the income tax amendment to the Constitution. I have sent no message to the Legislature on the subject, but I am planning to hold a conference with my colleagues in the Legislature at an early date and hope that I shall be able to persuade them to vote for the amendment. I find that there is a good deal of honest difference of judgment among them about it, many of them fearing to practically deprive the State of this source of income by opening it to the Federal government.

You judge me very generously with regard to my political capacity. I feel a genuine modesty about the whole thing but cannot refrain from expressing my gratitude to you that you should feel inclined to commend me to the consideration of the party. I wish very much that business or other opportunity would bring you in this direction so that I might have the advantage of a personal conversation with you.

Cordially and sincerely yours,
WOODROW WILSON

Out of these beginnings grew a vigorous movement for Wilson, and the Texas delegation at the Baltimore convention was a bulwark of strength.[1]

It was on March 9th that Wilson made his first political

---

[1] For further particulars regarding the "Texas revolt" and Colonel House's connection with it see p. 297 ff., this volume.

invasion of the South—at Atlanta, Georgia. He disclosed his own attitude toward the venture with astonishing frankness in a letter to Mrs. Hulbert:

". . . I am to speak before the Southern Commercial Congress, which the President is to attend, and where all the interests of the South and of the country are to be discussed. I am to speak at the closing evening session on 'The Citizen and the State', speaking, I believe, just before the President,—not a very eligible position on the programme. I am not going because I want to go, or because I have something in particular that I want to say, but, I am half ashamed to say, because I thought it wise (which, being translated, means politic) to go. I hate the things done for policy's sake! I do not do them with any zest; and I fear the address will lack distinction and fire on that account. But I shall do the best I can in the circumstances; and I am fortunate in the fact that none of the other men who are to speak that evening is an orator or within hailing distance of becoming one. How satisfactory one's fellows' limitations are to one once in a while! The President is popular in the South, and will, no doubt, have a very hearty welcome. Just now the whole country regards him with increased respect, because of his unexpected energy in forcing through the reciprocity treaty with Canada. You will by this time have heard that he is actually going to call the extra session. And then there will be some fun: for it will be the new, not the present, Congress. I shall hold my breath till I see just how the Democrats are going to use their majority in the new House. Champ Clark, their leader in the chair, is far from being a wise person. He is, on the contrary, a sort of elephantine 'smart Aleck.' What a comfort to be able to say these things *entre nous* and without a sense of being, as usual, indiscreet! Colonel Harvey has again become eloquent, and ingenious, on the subject of my being the Democratic nominee for the presidency. I shall try to send you by the post that carries this a copy of the March number of the North American Review, in which he has an article entitled 'The political predestination of Woodrow Wilson.' The New York Times remarked upon it that it might very well turn out to be true that I would be chosen by the party as its presidential candidate, but that it was not necessary to prove it in so nonsensical a way: that the probability could not be increased by ingenious folderol. The whole thing is very amusing, and I, as usual, look on as if at what was taking place with regard to some one else. If the presidency is a governorship greatly increased in difficulty, I do not think that I want it!"

Wilson's reception at Atlanta, compared with that of President Taft and former President Roosevelt, who were both there, surprised even his friends. Judge Hillyer, in introducing him, remarked:

"Last night we had here a man who has been President of the United States. This evening we shall hear a man who is President of the United States. But we have with us this morning a man who is going to be President of the United States."[1]

During the dinners and receptions tendered to him, Wilson met many of the real leaders of the South, and he was left in no doubt as to their attitude of enthusiasm toward his leadership:

"It has been a long time since there has been a more popular speaker in Atlanta than the Governor of New Jersey . . . At night he addressed 8,000 people in the auditorium and received a great ovation. It was a magnificent effort. He speaks with decision and thoughtfulness. But there is not an element in the audience that he fails to reach. . . . He brings the audience up to his level, for he

[1] See *Woodrow Wilson, Life and Letters: Youth*, p. 149.

talks with great clearness and simplicity. He gets everybody on a plane of high thinking at once. . . .

"He is looked upon as a very reasonable presidential possibility. If he makes good in the governorship nothing can keep him from being a leading candidate. He says himself that he 'is not a Wilson man and that he is more interested in the things that he is doing than in the things he may do.'"[1]

The Washington *Times* said:

"Woodrow Wilson is coming at a rate which is the marvel of all the politicians. . . .

"Governor Wilson made a tremendous impression in the South by his recent appearance at Atlanta, where he was given a great ovation. That performance gave the shivers to the Harmon boomers who have believed that Harmon would be pulled safely into the nomination by the certainty of a solid South. Three months ago they were listening as patiently as possible to the 'foolish talk' about Wilson; they 'knew' Harmon would win. . . .

"But to-day they are not so patronizing. They have seen a light. They are not sure about Harmon, and they are watching Wilson."

In April, Wilson spoke at Norfolk, Virginia, writing of his especial reasons for a further "explanation to the South" of his candidacy:

"I have just been down to Norfolk, Va., to dine with the Pewter Platter Club. . . . I was glad to get away from Trenton and the pressure of work; and this particular engagement was very welcome to me because I wanted to say something at this particular time in the South. At this particular time because there seems to be gathering in the South a really big body of sentiment (*and* opinion) in favour of my nomination for the presidency. The South is a very conservative region—just now probably the most

[1]The Savannah *Press*, March 11, 1911.

(possibly the only) conservative section of the country—and I am *not* conservative. I am a radical. I wanted a chance to tell my friends in the South just what I thought, just what my programme is, before they went further and committed themselves to me as a 'favourite son.' I do not want them to make a mistake and repent it too late. . . . The nearer I get to the possibility of a nomination the less I feel willing to *try* for it,—the more I see the necessity that I, being what I am, should *not* commend myself for the choice, but should go my own way of speech and effort and keep my thoughts free of entanglements."[1]

When the 62nd Congress met in April, and Southern Congressmen began to discuss the coming presidential campaign, it appeared that Wilson's prestige was growing rapidly:

"While Governor Wilson has not as many friends in Congress as either Harmon or Clark or Bryan, the reports brought in by Congressmen generally of the Wilson sentiment in their districts are surprising."[2]

These manifestations, which Wilson might interpret as a "call from the people," were as satisfactory as they were deceptive. Winning popular applause was a very different thing from winning the political organizations which controlled the delegations. Georgia might be "stirred": it did not support Wilson at Baltimore.

Having "explained to the South," Wilson was ready in early May for the invasion of the West—"Bryanland."

## IV. WILSON AND BRYAN

It is not too much to say that Wilson's greatest single problem as a leader during his political beginnings—up to, and through the Democratic Convention of 1912—was

[1]Woodrow Wilson to Mary A. Hulbert, April 30, 1911.
[2]The Baltimore *Sun*, April 4, 1911.

William J. Bryan. Bryan was not only the outstanding leader of the Democracy, but he was also one of the outstanding progressives of the country. In order to achieve leadership, Wilson must step into Bryan's place—with or without Bryan's consent. He must do this without wholly agreeing with Bryan's programme or his methods; and without alienating the necessary Democratic support in the East which was suspicious of Bryan. Above everything, he must strive for a united party.

Two men more different than Wilson and Bryan in character, in temperament, in training could not easily be found. Wilson was preëminently intellectual, Bryan emotional—types never easily sympathetic; Wilson was delicately wrought physically, easily reaching the limits of his strength—Bryan, a pattern of robustness, never knew what it was to be tired; Wilson was sensitive, shy, imaginative—Bryan, a lover of crowds and shouting conventions, numbered his political friends by the thousands; Wilson was the careful, accurate, scholarly worker, every letter like copper-plate, every document dated—Bryan, swift and careless, conducted his indiscriminate correspondence from hotel writing stands, and edited his paper "by writing on his knee" in railroad trains. A stubby pencil served him well, and often he saved time by signing his name with a rubber stamp; Wilson was a thorough, deep, studious reader—Bryan snatched his knowledge from newspapers and conversation, and read almost no books, except the Bible.

While they were thus antithetical, yet the two had vital elements in common. Both were men of faith, deeply religious; both believed profoundly in the people, Bryan instinctively by heritage, because he was one of them, Wilson by reason, by historical understanding, by virtue of his Scotch-Presbyterian conviction that "all men rank the same with God." Both men were gifted orators with the power of leading and influencing the masses; and both, underneath, deep down, were sincere in their objectives.[1] It was this sense of fundamental agreement as to the rights of the people, and the iniquity of "privilege," that gradually brought the two men together.

Bryan first swam into the ken of Wilson, as he swam into the ken of the country, in 1896. A friend remembers Wilson's "jeers" at the "cross of gold" oration in the Democratic convention.[2] And Wilson was so wholly opposed to Bryan's free-silver panacea that he voted for Palmer and Buckner in the fall election of that year. From that time onward he was for several years an unsparing critic of Bryan. He plainly considered him a demagogue, using his undeniable powers as a popular orator to mislead the people:

"We might have had Mr. Bryan for President, because

[1]Bryan's true spirit is nowhere better presented than in a letter which he wrote to the Reverend Dr. W. M. Hindman of Kenton, Ohio, just after his defeat in the Democratic convention at St. Louis in 1904, for a copy of which the author is indebted to Dr. B. J. Cigrand of Aurora, Illinois:

"I do not know what my real work in life is, and I have often been impressed with our scant knowledge of the future—even of our own lives. I feel that I have been able to do something to raise political ideals and if my life is spared I hope to do much more. My great concern has for years been, and still is, to throw whatever influence I may have, be it small or great, upon the right side of each question, to the end that human rights may be sacredly defended and public interests advanced. While I have been a candidate for office, this has been merely incidental and no part of my general plan. I do not want to hold office except as it may assist in realizing the plans that I have laid for the advancement of the interests of the common people. In fact, I shall feel relieved if I am permitted to work as a private citizen and can leave the cares and responsibilities of office to others. My life now is an ideal one. With a happy home to which I can retire when weary and from which I can go refreshed; with a sufficient income for my modest needs and with nothing upon my mind or heart but the work in which I am engaged, what more could I ask? If I have been defeated in my political aspirations the defeats weigh like dust in the balance against the blessings that I have received and that I now enjoy. No one should be happier and I think no one is more contented with his personal lot than I am.

"I appreciate the loyalty and devotion of friends like yourself, and even when I cannot secure their approval of my judgment I am sure I shall do nothing to alienate their confidence or to lessen their esteem.

"Our house is open to you whenever your footsteps turn this way and the affectionate remembrance of our family will follow you and your family and bid you Godspeed in your work."

[2]Professor Stockton Axson to the author.

of the impression which may be made upon an excited
assembly by a good voice and a few ringing sentences flung
forth just after a cold man who gave unpalatable counsel
has sat down. The country knew absolutely nothing about
Mr. Bryan before his nomination, and it would not have
known anything about him afterward had he not chosen
to make speeches."[1]

Wilson did not believe that Bryan would last—the
people would find him out; but he did last. During the
campaign of 1900, Bryan against McKinley, Bryan spoke
at Princeton Junction; and the Princeton professor of
politics went down with his friend Axson to hear him.
He was unexpectedly impressed with his power and persuasiveness as a speaker. On the way back to Princeton he
said to Axson:

"The man is plainly sincere."

In the election that fall, Wilson, though still profoundly
distrustful of Bryan, voted the entire Democratic ticket.[2]

Bryan still persisted. Some of Wilson's friends began to
be interested, even converted. Roland Morris of Philadelphia, a student and ardent friend of Wilson's, and one of
the leading Democrats of Philadelphia,[3] was a delegate at
the convention of 1904, supporting Parker, who was
nominated. But after he met Bryan and heard him speak,
he came away feeling that Bryan was the real leader,
seeking to express and serve the true wishes of the people.
Immediately upon his return, Morris went to Princeton to
see Wilson, and told him of his impressions.

"Bryan," said Morris, "represents the only live part of
the Democratic party."

"The trouble is," Wilson responded, "that Bryan has

---

[1] "The Making of the Nation," in the *Atlantic Monthly*, July, 1897. See *The Public
Papers of Woodrow Wilson*, Vol. I, pp. 331–332.

[2] Woodrow Wilson to W. J. Bryan, April 3, 1912.

[3] Wilson afterward sent Morris as ambassador to Japan.

caught the spirit and instincts of the finer aspirations of American life, but, Morris, the man has no brains. It is a great pity that a man with his power of leadership should have no mental rudder."[1]

That year Wilson voted without enthusiasm for Parker as the nominee of the party.

In 1906 came the Lotos Club dinner and Harvey's "nomination" of Wilson as a candidate for the presidency. It was clear at the time that the proposal represented the desire of Eastern Democrats for a leader to "head off Bryan."

Wilson was not at all loath to play the part. He still distrusted Bryan thoroughly. It was in April, 1907, that he wrote his famous letter to Adrian H. Joline—a letter that later was near to causing a crisis in his career:

"Would that we could do something, at once dignified and effective, to knock Mr. Bryan once for all into a cocked hat!"

That fall he made it clear[2] that there were "political propositions in his [Bryan's] platform that I consider absurd, and could never endorse." "Scathing indictments" were not enough; what was wanted was "a very calm and self-possessed examination of the actual condition of things. What we need at present is not heat, but light. . . .

"Indiscriminate abuse is clearly no remedy. . . ."[3]

In March, 1908, Wilson spoke of Bryan as "the most charming and lovable of men personally, but foolish and dangerous in his theoretical beliefs"[4] and in April he asked to be excused from making a speech at the Jefferson dinner if Bryan was to be there.[5]

---

[1] Roland S. Morris to the author.
[2] See the New York *Times*, November 24, 1907.
[3] New York *Times*, November 27, 1907.
[4] From an interview published March 10, 1908.
[5] Woodrow Wilson to John R. Dunlap, April 1, 1908.

Wilson himself had been talked about as the Democratic nominee in 1908; but there was no real campaign, and Bryan was nominated. By this time Wilson's struggle at Princeton was beginning to make clear to him the power of wealth and privilege in America; and to connect it with the greater conflict going on in the nation. He was deeply stirred as we have seen by the exposures of the Muckrakers, and by the campaign of 1908. The Socialist movement was rising in power; Debs received at the polls that fall over 400,000 votes. Although Wilson was still strongly critical of Bryan's remedies, he told a friend that he "could not quarrel with a large part of his diagnosis." That fall he voted the regular Democratic ticket, swallowing Bryan in the process.[1] We know how deeply discouraged he was from a letter written on the day after the election:

". . . the results of yesterday's voting confirm the Republican party more deeply than ever in the possession of a power they have grossly misused and render it almost impossible to organize a successful party of opposition within less than another generation,—unless men as unlike Mr. Bryan as principle is unlike expediency will devote themselves to gaining influence and control as if to a daily business, as Mr. Bryan has done. He has devoted himself to creating and maintaining an immense personal influence,—and to nothing else, for 'causes' with him have been means to an end,—for the last twelve years; and even now no one can supplant him who will not deliberately enter the lists against him and do the like,—with this immense difference, that he must devote himself to principles, to ideas, to definite programmes and not to personal preferment,—that he must be a man with a cause, not a candidacy. It's a desperate situation,—for what man of that kind will be willing to risk the appearance of per-

---

[1] Woodrow Wilson to W. J. Bryan, April 3, 1912.

sonal ambition? If someone only would, how gladly I would help him! Two years from now I can retire on a Carnegie pension of $4,000. I have $2,000 of my own. I shall not willingly wait more than two years for the Princeton trustees to do what it is their bounden duty to do with regard to the reform of university life. At the end of that time I would be glad to lend my pen and voice and all my thought and energy to anyone who purposed a genuine rationalization and rehabilitation of the Democratic party on lines of principle and statesmanship! I know what you, in your partiality, will say: 'Why not take the initiative yourself, and yourself build up a leadership which will be effective?' Because I do not judge myself as partially as you judge me. I am willing to do *this:* I am willing to *seem* to take the initiative, to seem to venture upon the field alone and of my own motion, and then yield the field, with the best will in the world, to some one of the rivals who would certainly be drawn out by my action. The man who *first* adventures will be the one misunderstood and most easily discredited by the forces of jealousy which would be gathered against him, and if that sacrifice is necessary I am not unwilling to offer myself for it. Certainly I do not want the presidency! The more closely I see it the less I covet it. The 'sacrifice' would be a release from what no prudent man, who loved even his physical life, could conceivably desire!"[1]

In the following year, 1909, however, we hear him referring to Bryan as "a great preacher." Wilson was himself awakening more and more sharply to the situation in the nation; and in his addresses in 1909 and 1910 he was scarcely less direct and forceful in his denunciations than Bryan himself.

While Bryan had long been an irritant in Wilson's mind, Bryan knew nothing of Wilson until 1910. He had read

[1]Woodrow Wilson to Mary A. Hulbert, November 2, 1908.

none of Wilson's books, knew nothing and cared nothing
for the academic struggles at Princeton; but when this
strange outsider appeared in politics, to which Bryan was
as sensitive as an aspen leaf to the wind, he was at once
keenly concerned. On the day after the New Jersey election, Bryan telegraphed Wilson—it was the first direct
communication between them:

"May your administration be crowned with signal
success."[1]

After that, Bryan's interest began steadily to mount.
Who was this Wilson, and what did he mean politically?
He was a Democrat who had carried an Eastern Republican state, and he was being talked about here and there
over the country; was he for or against his, Bryan's,
programme? Was he to be encouraged, or firmly set over
into the opposition? From that time onward until the
convention at Baltimore, in 1912, the two men never for a
moment lost sight of each other; both were warily conscious of the possibilities of their relationships as a determining element in Democratic party leadership. A remarkable story, indeed, the contest of these two personalities, with so much at stake!

Early in January, 1911, Bryan was in Texas and was
plainly impressed and disturbed to find that the Wilson
fire had started on the Texas plains. Thomas B. Love told
him that Texas was going to organize in favour of Wilson's candidacy.[2] Bryan at once wrote to Wilson, from
Mission, Texas, a hastily scrawled letter:

MY DEAR MR. WILSON:-
I am expecting to come East early in March and would like
to see you for an hour or so on political matters. The fact that
you were against us in 1896 raised a question in my mind in

---

[1] November 9, 1910.
[2] Thomas B. Love to Woodrow Wilson, February 7, 1911.

regard to your views on public questions but your attitude in the Senatorial case has tended to reassure me. I could call at Trenton or if you think better to avoid publicity I can meet you at Burlington. I have a good friend there Mr. J. [T.] H. Birch whom I expect to visit at that time. In the meantime I would like to have your opinion of the various planks of the Denver platform. Many of the planks you could endorse or condemn on the margin—others you could discuss more at length.

Yours truly<br>W. J. BRYAN

He enclosed a copy of the Democratic national platform of 1908 from the *Commoner*, a worn and yellowing document still remaining in Wilson's files. Wilson was far too canny to "endorse or condemn on the margin"; but he did write Bryan that he supported, in general, the policies laid down in the platform.[1]

Bryan was a man not easily repulsed. He was warm-hearted and direct, he liked to know men of every sort, especially if they were politicians. He had something of the evangelizing middle-western Presbyterian spirit, confident that if he could meet the audience, talk with the man, conversion must speedily follow. Many a man had been snatched, a brand from the burning! It was Bryan who pursued Wilson, not Wilson Bryan.

Bryan straightway wrote an enthusiastic article in the *Commoner*[2] headed, "New Jersey Turns Toward the Light":

"It required great courage on Governor Wilson's part to take the course he adopted in New Jersey. . . .

"In the name of every lover of popular government the *Commoner* thanks Governor Wilson for his patriotic efforts. It . . . expresses the hope that from now on the fine

---

[1] The 1908 platform contained no reference to "free silver."
[2] February 3, 1911.

effort of which New Jersey's governor is so capable may
be given on the side of those Democrats who insist that
the way to win a Democratic victory worth having is to
keep the party free from corporation influences and to
write its platforms in harmony with the heartbeats of the
people who believe in 'equal rights to all and special
privileges to none.'"

The response to Bryan's editorial was seized upon by
the Democratic press as an "olive branch."

"For the first time since the great split in 1896 there
seems to be a chance that the Democratic party may be
able to get together on national policies."[1]

Wilson, however, held back. Bryan was not content
with a general acquiescence, he wanted compliance in
every detail—and Wilson distrusted Bryan's thinking.
Bryan followed up Wilson's response, like the dominating
leader he was, by advising Wilson how to direct his legislature:

"I find your letter upon my return to the city, and am
greatly gratified at your endorsement of the platform of
1908. . . .

"I notice that you do not recommend the income tax,
although I have heard it stated that you endorsed an
income-tax amendment, as you must do in endorsing the
Denver platform. I hope that you will see your way clear
to send a message to the legislature on that subject, for
one state may be important."[2]

The correspondence and the contacts between Bryan
and Wilson during the next few months, however in earnest, are not without humour. Two dominant personalities,
each trying to lead the other! And it is no exaggeration to
say that the stake of that wary struggle was the presidency of the United States. A single mistake in these

---

[1] Indianapolis *News*, February 6, 1911.
[2] March 1, 1911.

delicate personal relationships might have made all the difference in the world at Baltimore in June, 1912.

Wilson and Bryan were soon to have their first personal meeting—in which Mrs. Wilson played no unimportant part. Bryan wanted to greet the new Governor face to face; shake his hand. Wilson, it is clear, was by no means as eager. All his life he dreaded the first plunge of personal contact—and he was still distrustful of Bryan.

Bryan, who was an ardent Presbyterian, was to speak at Princeton, under the auspices of the Theological Seminary, on March 12th. When Mrs. Wilson heard of it, she immediately invited him to dinner, telegraphing her husband who was in Atlanta, Georgia, speaking before the Southern Commercial Congress, urging him to return if possible.

A great audience gathered in Alexander Hall to hear Bryan. His subject was "Faith":

"I have devoted the mature years of my life to the problems of government and expect to continue to make that my business, but, in fact, I would rather speak on religion than on governmental problems. I began to study public questions when I was twenty years old and religion six years before that. I will be in the church when I am out of politics.

"When I am discussing the problems of government I must get a majority of the people to agree with my views if I am to carry my ideas into effect, but if, in discussing religion, I do one heart good I have not spoken in vain, no matter how large may be the majority against me."

Wilson returned just in time to hear Bryan's address, and afterwards Bryan and his friend Thomas H. Birch went with the Wilsons to dinner at the Princeton Inn.

"I hurried back to greet Mr. Bryan! He was in Princeton to-day, to address the Theological Seminary, at their

Sunday afternoon conference. They held it in Alexander
Hall, which was packed; and the address, which was on
Faith, was most impressive. He held the audience easily
for an hour and a half. It was the first time I had ever
heard him speak, and I was exceedingly pleased.[1] After the
meeting he came over to the Inn and dined with Ellen,
Jessie, Nellie, a Mr. Birch (in whose car he had come up
from Burlington), and me, and I feel that I can now say
that I know him, and have a very different impression of
him from that I had before seeing him thus close at hand.
He has extraordinary force of personality, and it seems the
force of sincerity and conviction. He has himself well in
hand at every turn of the thought and talk, too; and his
voice is wholly delightful. A truly captivating man, I
must admit. He had to be off by half past seven, so I had
only a little while with him,—only through the short
dinner."[2]

At the dinner Wilson and Bryan "capped each other's
stories," and "entirely avoided politics." Bryan had
anticipated meeting a rather solemn college professor, and
was charmed by the gaiety and nimble-mindedness of the
man he met. He was "captivated" by Mrs. Wilson.
Afterwards when a friend complimented her on "playing
good politics" in bringing the two men together, she
seemed vastly surprised. "My dear, it was only good manners." As so often happened with Wilson, after the ice of
the first contact was broken, he warmed to Bryan personally—a feeling that persisted throughout all of their later
relationships.

Three weeks later, Wilson and Bryan appeared together
for the first time on the same platform. It was at a great
Democratic rally at Burlington, New Jersey, where both

[1]This was the first real address Wilson had heard Bryan make: he had attended a
brief political rally at Princeton Junction in 1900.

[2]Woodrow Wilson to Mary A. Hulbert, March 13, 1911.

men were guests of Thomas H. Birch.[1] Just before the speaking began, a large picture of Wilson was dramatically lowered from the flies. It bore the words:

"Woodrow Wilson, Our Next President"

Bryan spoke on the subject, "Watchman, What of the Night?" and Wilson on "Questions of the Day." Bryan had never before heard Wilson speak, and came away greatly impressed with the response of the audience—and especially pleased with Wilson's tribute to him:

"Mr. Bryan has borne the heat and burden of a long day; we have come in at a very much later time to reap the reward of the things that he has done. Mr. Bryan has shown that stout heart which, in spite of the long years of repeated disappointments, has always followed the star of hope, and it is because he has cried America awake that some other men have been able to translate into action the doctrines that he has so diligently preached."[2]

The political significance of the meeting of the two leaders on the same platform caused no little comment in the press—as another evidence of a new unity of the Democratic party. They met again, momentarily, a week later, at Indianapolis, where, as the guest of Governor Thomas R. Marshall, Wilson addressed the National League of Democratic Clubs. Wilson told Bryan of his projected speaking trip through the West—Bryan's stronghold—and apparently it had Bryan's approval. Nevertheless, Wilson knew the delicacy of the problem he faced. He must win the Bryan following without alienating Bryan; he must at the same time avoid being known in the country as "Bryan's candidate." As for Bryan, that shrewd politician kept his counsel. He refused to declare whether he was for Clark or Wilson for the nomination. He refused to say that he was not himself a candidate.

[1]Afterwards appointed minister to Portugal by President Wilson.
[2]Report of Wilson's address in the Newark *Evening News*, April 6, 1911.

### V. THE INVASION OF THE WEST

Wilson was now ready to invade the West.

"The figure of Woodrow Wilson is rapidly taking on national proportions. His administration as governor of New Jersey is a revelation, in a day of colourless governors like Mr. Dix of New York, of what a strong man, with an unmistakable commission from the people, can do in the way of destroying boss-rule and compelling beneficent legislation from a reluctant legislature."[1]

He left Princeton on May 3rd. Page, McCorkle, and McCombs had succeeded in raising $3,000 to pay the expenses. Stockbridge had made advance engagements in seven states, beginning at Kansas City, Missouri. Grasty of the Baltimore *Sun* was so deeply interested in Wilson's candidacy that he sent a capable journalist, McKee Barclay, to report the meetings.

They met at Philadelphia. Wilson, although indisposed, appeared with a huge suitcase—a "young trunk"—which he insisted, throughout the journey, upon carrying in his own hand. It was, assuredly, one of the most extraordinary and audacious political adventures in American annals. A David-and-Goliath adventure! No important leaders in any part of the country which he was invading were concerned in it, or even deeply interested. The group of men who were backing him were amateurs, personal friends. It was an unknown country that they were venturing into —Wilson had never been west of Denver—and while he was an experienced public speaker, he had not yet been nine months in active politics, and had no knowledge either of the leadership or of the actual political conditions in the West. His method was exactly the reverse of that of most candidates—very different indeed from that of his principal rivals in the Democratic party, Harmon

[1] Walter H. Page in *World's Work*, May, 1911.

and Clark—in that he was working up from the people instead of down through the leaders.[1]

Stockbridge had done his best to instruct the candidate in the way he should go, with slight success. He had urged him to prepare his addresses in advance. It was the only way to assure adequate publicity.

"But it is not my way," said Wilson. "I cannot make speeches to a stenographer."

Nevertheless he made the attempt—which proved more or less a failure, since his spoken addresses varied so greatly from those he had prepared in advance.

In another respect Wilson proved difficult. No sooner had the party arrived at Kansas City than the newspaper reporters and photographers descended upon him. In spite of his experiences in New Jersey, he had not become inured to this ordeal. Why could not the press be satisfied with what he said in his speeches? At first Stockbridge feared that he would refuse entirely to see the reporters—a capital offense!—but he finally yielded, and even submitted, though with a wry face, to stepping out through the window of his hotel room to a balcony to give the photographers a chance.

"Do I have to go through with this every day?" he asked Stockbridge testily.

"Yes sir, every single day—everywhere we stop. You are a national figure, Governor."

"More's the pity," Wilson responded grimly.

Kansas City was enemy country—Missouri and Champ Clark—but Wilson was warmly received. He spoke before the Knife and Fork Club, an institution famous in the city for its dinners to public men. The only other speaker was Governor Herbert S. Hadley, a progressive Republi-

---

[1]The account of this Western trip is based partly upon documents and memoranda, supplemented by conversations, supplied by Frank Parker Stockbridge and McKee Barclay, also upon conversations with William G. McAdoo, Walter L. McCorkle, and others.

can, who paid a generous tribute to the visitor from the East. It was an audience made up largely of Republicans and not at first enthusiastic—but it was interested and curious. Wilson found it highly stimulating.

"I think I never felt a greater inspiration from any audience."

The address, which Wilson called "Issues of Freedom," was sharply attacked in certain Eastern newspapers as a "radical utterance" since the speaker advocated the use, in certain circumstances, of the initiative, referendum, and recall (though not the recall of judges). McCombs, back in New York, who was far from being a progressive, much less an insurgent, was alarmed. Here were doctrines that were anathema in the East, the veritable badge of radicalism. While Wilson had boldly advocated them in his campaign in New Jersey, McCombs was for suppressing them in the West—as he wrote excitedly to Stockbridge. Wilson, however, went his own way.

As a matter of fact, the address was not radical. Among those who heard Wilson, including the solid business and professional men of Kansas City, it was not so regarded. It was the kind of tempered exposition of the situation in the country that impressed Wilson's hearers with its contrast to the unguarded denunciations and invectives of many Western insurgents. Indeed, it was widely published throughout the West because it was marked by "cooling good sense," as one editorial writer put it. The impression that Wilson gave most strongly, as the comments reveal, was that of a man vividly alive to the confused conditions of the nation, who had thought clearly and deeply upon them, and who wished to solve them—but by no violent or revolutionary methods:

"There can be no mistaking the fact that we are now face to face with political changes which may have a very profound effect upon our political life. Those who do not

WOODROW WILSON CAMPAIGNING
WOODROW WILSON ON HIS WESTERN TRIP IN MAY, 1911.
FRANK PARKER STOCKBRIDGE, RIGHT, AND McKEE
BARCLAY, ACCOMPANYING HIM.

understand the impending change are afraid of it. Those who do understand it know that it is not a process of revolution, but a process of restoration. . . ."

He then went on to say:

"The American people are naturally a conservative people. They do not wish to touch the stable foundations of their life; they have a reverence for the rights of property and the rights of contract which is based upon a long experience in a free life. . . ."

Evils have crept in, "we have changed our economic conditions from top to bottom . . . old party formulas do not fit the present problems." There must be change, but it "must be sober change."

It was not a "wild radical" who said:

"What we must devote ourselves to now is, not to upsetting our institutions, but to restoring them.

"Undoubtedly we should avoid excitement and should silence the demagogue. The man with power, but without conscience, could, with an eloquent tongue, if he cared for nothing but his own power, put this whole country into a flame, because the whole country believes that something is wrong and is eager to follow those who profess to be able to lead it away from its difficulties. . . . The processes we are engaged in are fundamentally conservative processes."

He proposed the initiative, referendum, and recall not as panaceas, not as substitutes for representative government, but as a method by which to "restore and reinvigorate" democratic institutions.

"If we felt that we had genuine representative government in our state legislatures no one would propose the initiative or referendum in America."

His treatment of the "money power," then the black beast of the Western reformer, was similarly sober. The chief difficulty in American public life was, "to sum it all

up in one sentence . . . the control of politics and of our
life by great combinations of wealth."

But he went on to say:

"Men sometimes talk as if it were wealth we were
afraid of, as if we were jealous of the accumulation of
great fortunes. Nothing of the kind is true. America has
not the slightest jealousy of the legitimate accumulation
of wealth. . . . But everybody knows also that some of the
men who control the wealth and have built up the industry of the country seek to control politics and also to
dominate the life of common men in a way in which no
man should be permitted to dominate."

The Knife and Fork Club address was the keynote of
Wilson's message to the West. It can easily be seen why it
attracted such attention and was so widely published. It
was not denunciatory, it appealed to no class feeling, it
offered no economic or political short cuts like Bryan's
free silver, or like the veiled socialism of certain other
Western leaders. All the troubles of the country were not
alone due to "railroad control" or "tariff privilege," or
"Wall Street." It was a complicated situation which
must be met by constructive thinking, "common counsel,"
"sober change." To the West there was something refreshing, something strong and sane, in such a position
after years of exposures, investigations, and revolutionary
proposals.

Wilson himself proved vastly attractive to his audience.
It was not only the charm of the finished and cultivated
orator, in contrast with some of the "rough and ready"
Western insurgents, it was also the sense that here was a
new and hopeful leadership in American public life—the
scholar, the thinker—who came in without any of the
clap-trap, the compromises, the obligations, of the ordinary political leader.

Wilson was himself greatly reassured and encouraged by

his first contact with the West. Here as in the South he no doubt misinterpreted in some degree the warmth of his courteous hearers as political support. It made him indeed more widely acquainted, it helped him later during the crucial hours of the Democratic convention, but it did not win the politicians. Missouri remained absolutely committed to Champ Clark.

Wilson was further encouraged by the prompt commendation of his mentor in the East upon whose help he so greatly depended:

"Your telegram from Kansas City has just arrived, to our great satisfaction. I was, at the moment, reading the speech at the breakfast table. I think it was *perfect!* Am very happy to know that it was 'a great success.'"[1]

Every night during the trip, Wilson sent his wife a long telegram; and her letters in response were full of encouragement, advice, suggestion. She also relieved him of many of the economic worries which then confronted the family:

"I went to see what the Peacock Inn would charge us by the week and it was more than the 'Inn'! So that is off my mind. I was afraid that if it was much cheaper we ought to go there."[2]

Wilson's principal address at Denver on May 7th was one of the surprises of his career—one of the strangest episodes certainly in the life of any American political campaigner. Before leaving New Jersey, he had made only one stipulation, that he was not to be called upon to speak or to attend political meetings on Sunday. Sabbath observance had been the practice of a lifetime.

"I have, however, agreed to speak on Sunday in my friend Dr. J. H. Houghton's church in Denver."

While he knew that the occasion of the meeting was the

---

[1] Ellen Axson Wilson to Woodrow Wilson, May 6, 1911.
[2] *Ibid.*

tercentenary of the translation of the Bible into the English language, then being celebrated in many churches, he thought of it as only the usual service of a congregation for which he needed to make no special preparation.

To the astonishment of Wilson he was met at the train by a committee of fifty citizens composed of members of the Chamber of Commerce and the Princeton Club, led by Huston Thompson, an old student and devoted admirer.[1] He discovered to his consternation that the whole city was placarded with announcements of his "little address on the Bible." Many of the churches in Denver were to be closed and the meeting was to be held in the Auditorium, one of the greatest halls in the West.

Wilson tried to find some time for further preparation, since the subject was wholly outside of the field with which he was then chiefly concerned; but his friends would not let him alone. He must attend the services at the Presbyterian church in the morning with the Thompsons to hear Dr. Houghton, he must have supper with Bryn Mawr friends. Colorado was a woman-suffrage state and one of the leaders, Mrs. Sarah Platt Decker, was to be there. When he arrived, the "little supper" turned out to be a semi-public meeting. The suffragists were out in force and he was heckled good-naturedly regarding his supposed attitude toward votes for women, and then called upon for a speech:

"From Mrs. Wilson, not only have I learned much but have gained something of a literary reputation. Whenever I need a poetic quotation she supplies it, and in this way I acquire the fame of possessing a complete anthology of poetry. From my daughters, however, I have learned what every parent knows of himself—that I do not know how to raise children."

[1] Afterwards appointed by Wilson a member of the Federal Trade Commission.

As it happened, Wilson found only a moment for preparation before being carried away to the Auditorium. He confessed afterwards that he was utterly abashed by what he saw when he stepped out on the stage. The hall was packed; over twelve thousand people were gathered to hear him speak. Governor Shafroth was there to present him, most of the ministers of the city and many of the prominent citizens of the state had places on the great rostrum.

Wilson's enthusiastic assistants perceived at once the importance of the meeting, and by making last-minute appeals to Governor Shafroth to "make a long speech," they were able, before Wilson began, to find stenographers to report the address.

"Mr. President, ladies and gentlemen, the thought that entered my mind first as I came into this great room this evening framed itself in a question, why should this great body of people have come together upon this solemn night? There is nothing here to be seen. There is nothing delectable here to be heard. Why should you run together in a great host when all that is to be spoken of is the history of a familiar book?"

It was not alone Woodrow Wilson who spoke that night. He had, after all, small need of preparation. It was the Scotch Covenanter deep in the spirit of the man that spoke. It was his father, the Reverend Dr. Joseph Ruggles Wilson, and his grandfather, the Reverend Dr. Thomas Woodrow, it was all the long line of his God-fearing ancestors, who spoke that night. It was what he was—more than statesman, more than educator, more than scholar; it was what he was by heredity, by tradition, by all the religious atmosphere of his early training—that he gave to his vast audience that night. Is it wonderful that he held his auditors under the spell of his words? Nearly every person present was of the same stock, the same deep Protestant tradition; he revivified everything that they cherished most sacredly, believed most sincerely.

For he was talking "of the Bible as the book of the people, not the book of the minister of the gospel, not the special book of the priest from which to set forth some occult, unknown doctrine withheld from the common understanding of men, but a great book of revelation—the people's book of revelation."

Few addresses of Wilson's life, except the great addresses relating to the war, were ever so widely republished in so many different forms.[1] Read in the cold after-light it lacks the firm logical texture of most of Wilson's addresses—since it was not previously organized—it is here and there perfervid and rhetorical, its facts are not startling, its criticism not vital. Its tremendous vogue was no doubt due to the subject treated and the eminence of the speaker rather than to any intrinsic merit in the address itself. Yet it contains the essential faith of the man. To thousands of Americans, after that, he might be attacked for this or that superficial political belief, he might be attacked for partisan reasons, yet they felt that here was a leader who was voicing a faith that went to the roots of the older American life—the ancient tradition.

The day following Wilson's address was notable in Denver as the first on which connections were made between Denver and New York by telephone; and Wilson's speech was nearly the first subject of conversation over that two thousand miles of wire.

"How very interesting the story about the telephone from Denver!—the New York reporter asking 'what is the news in Denver, and the answer;—'the town is wild over

---

[1] It was published in whole or in part in many religious journals, in several forms as a pamphlet, or booklet, including an edition by the government printing office; and as a part of the *Congressional Record*, 62nd Congress, 2nd Session, Vol. 48, Appendix, 499–502. For complete address, see *The Public Papers of Woodrow Wilson*, Vol. II, pp. 291–302.

Woodrow Wilson and is booming him for President.' Even the 'Times' had to put *that* in as news!"[1]

Success proved a keen tonic to Wilson. He had started the trip West in poor condition physically. He had thriven under the heavy pressure of speech-making, dinners, receptions, interviews, and he left Denver in a joyous frame of mind. The desert country was wholly new to him, and he was intensely interested in what he saw and heard, eagerly questioning men he met on the train. He liked to get off at the stations and walk up and down with his two companions who had become by now his warm friends—as they remained during his whole life. Sometimes he would exercise, to the amazement of onlookers, by dancing a kind of hornpipe on the platform, or go through exaggerated breathing exercises. "He was the finest company imaginable—full of good stories, and with a wit that was unquenchable." He looked eagerly for letters from his wife.

"You can imagine with what absorbing interest we are following your movements as far as we are able. How fine it all is! I am longing for more news though,—more papers, —a few, a very few clippings from Denver are all I have had. The 'Times' gives but little, of course, and the other papers I see, the speeches, but few other details. I am hungry for all sorts of particulars. There was one fine article in the 'Evening Post' on Sat., I think, telling exactly what I wanted to know."[2]

She could also give good advice. Wilson had remarked that he was "not thinking about the presidency" and hostile papers in the East had pounced satirically upon the phrase.

"By the way, *please* don't say again that you 'are not thinking about the presidency.' All who know you well

[1] Ellen Axson Wilson to Woodrow Wilson, May 11, 1911.
[2] *Ibid.*

know that that is *fundamentally* true, but *superficially* it can't be true; and it gives the cynics an opening which they seize with glee. The 'Sun' of course had an outrageous little editorial about it."[1]

After Denver, the newspaper publicity was such that Wilson was overwhelmed with invitations. Committees and crowds began to meet the trains, and a visit such as that in Los Angeles became a hectic round of engagements.

California was then agitated by politics, and the control of the principal meeting planned for Wilson at San Francisco, as he was informed, though organized by the combined Princeton, Harvard, and Yale clubs, had been seized by the so-called "reactionary" or "Big Business" interests. The invitations had actually been sent out on the stationery of "Pat" Calhoun's street railway company, which controlled, to a large extent, the boss-ridden politics of the city. The Governor of the state, the progressive Hiram Johnson, had expected to introduce Wilson, but when he found that the "stand-pat" element had secured the upper hand, he refused to attend. Some of Wilson's friends advised him not to venture into the lion's den; but such an emergency only whetted his purpose.

"Lay that San Francisco speech aside," he said. "I'll prepare another one for them."

Five hundred men were at the banquet—representing the financial oligarchy of the West Coast. It was an intensely expectant audience. When Wilson arose, he was more than ordinarily courteous, with a humorous assumption of perfect innocence as to local political squabbles. But for adroit and skillful castigation, the speech left little to be desired. He said to the bankers who were present:

"If you find men who will not do what you want them to do in politics, you don't let them get accommodations at the banks. More than that, you don't invite them any-

[1]Ellen Axson Wilson to Woodrow Wilson, May 11, 1911.

where. You make social as well as political outlaws of them. That is why I feel hopeful and not pessimistic—because I can say these things in the company of men who do such things and not only not be put out of the room but be met with most generous applause. . . .

"Do you approve of it? . . . you know that these things are going on.

"I do not know that this is going on in California, but I do know that it is going on in New Jersey. And I know that it is going on in many other places. That is why I make a shrewd conjecture that it has been going on in California.

"Now, being representative Americans, taken from all parts of the country, being men alert to your own interests, isn't it possible for you to assert your own judgments and see that these things do not take place?"

William H. Crocker, the multi-millionaire president of the Crocker National Bank, was down on the programme to follow Wilson. He barely waited for the toastmaster to finish introducing him before he was on his feet.

"Mr. Governor, Honourable Judges and Gentlemen of the Jury, I plead 'not guilty'! I don't know how banking is conducted in New Jersey, but I know that we do not carry on banking that way in California."

The following day, the banquet incidents were the talk of the town. "He made more than one man about the festal board wince—but wince with a smile and a vigorous wagging of the head, 'not me'!"

Wilson was now thoroughly enjoying the campaign. From San Francisco onward, the trip can be called little less than a triumphal progress. It caused an astonishing amount of publicity.

"Thank you very much, dear, for the clippings. They were most welcome, and the telegrams still more so. The one from Los Angeles was especially satisfactory and reassuring. I am inexpressibly thankful that you are standing it so well and enjoying it indeed. And what a wonderful triumph you are having . . ."[1]

There were stops at the University of California, and an address in the Greek Theatre, there was a meeting on the way north with U'Ren of Oregon, with long talks regarding the workings of the "new devices," the initiative and referendum. Wilson had a strong admiration for the devoted reformer. He said in his address at Portland:

"I read in the paper this morning just as I was approaching this city that there were two legislatures in Oregon—one was at Salem and the other was under Mr. U'Ren's hat. . . ."

Oregon received the campaigner with open arms.

"Woodrow Wilson is the unexpected. He is a national surprise. No one foresaw the sudden coming of a national leader. Nobody gave notice of the approach of a new man of big political facts with power to do old political things in a new and unexpected way. . . .

"Wilsonism is to-day one of the largest facts in American life. It is popular leadership with a safety valve. It is popular government with a balance wheel. It is statesmanship without demagogy and of calibre and character to match and master the gathering problems in our national life."[2]

And the commendation was no mere newspaper enthusiasm. He won the Democratic delegation at the Baltimore convention, and at the election he received more votes than either Taft or Roosevelt.[3]

After addresses in Washington, Wilson faced eastward again. He felt that the trip had been a success; that the

---

[1]Ellen Axson Wilson to Woodrow Wilson, May 15, 1911.

[2]*Oregon Journal*, May 18, 1911.

[3]The vote in 1912 in Oregon was: Wilson 47,064; Taft 34,673; Roosevelt 37,600; Debs 13,343. (From the *American Year Book*, 1913.)

people of the West, if not the politicians, understood him, and that he understood them. He felt that he knew what the West wanted; and that he could lead them in securing it. He had been greatly impressed by an incident that happened at Wymore, Nebraska, on the outward journey. The train had stopped to change locomotives, and a railroad man in a jumper, wiping his hands on a piece of cotton waste, came up to the Governor as he was walking up and down the platform, and introduced himself as the mayor of Wymore. It developed that he had been elected on the Socialist ticket. Mr. Wilson expressed surprise that there should be such a strong Socialist vote there. "It wasn't Socialism that elected me," the Mayor replied. "Only about 20 percent Socialism and 80 percent protest."

"That typifies a national condition," Wilson observed to his companions. "There is a tremendous undercurrent of protest, which is bound to find expression. Taft will be renominated by the Republicans; unless the Democrats nominate someone whom the people can accept as expressing this protest there will be a radical third party formed and the result of the election may be little short of a revolution."

It was during the long railroad trip to Minneapolis that he admitted for the first time that he would be an out-and-out candidate for the presidency.

"As I took pains to tell you when we started out, I had determined that I would not make up my mind as to my candidacy until I could weigh the results of this trip. . . . While there is no certainty of my being nominated, on the other hand, if I am nominated, I shall be elected."[1]

He had moments of doubt as he looked ahead:

"I don't want to be President. It's an awful thing to be President of the United States. . . . I mean just what I say. It means giving up nearly everything that one holds dear.

[1]From McKee Barclay's notes.

When a man enters the White House, he might as well say, 'All hope abandon, ye who enter here.' The presidency becomes a barrier between a man and his wife, between a man and his children. He is no longer his own master—he is a slave to the job. He may indulge no longer in the luxury of free action or even free speech."

An hour or so after this conversation on the penalties of fame, faithfully set down by Barclay, Wilson returned to the subject:

"In spite of what I said to you, I do want to be President and I will tell you why: I want this country to have a President who will do certain things. There are men who could do these things better than I can. Of that I am sure; but the question is, *would they do them?* I cannot have any positive assurance that the man who becomes President will do, or even attempt to do, the things which I want to see done. But I am sure that I will at least try to the utmost to do them."

He was frank about another serious problem of the presidency—William J. Bryan. It was clear that he must have Bryan's support, or at least the support of his following, and in that event Bryan must be recognized. Wilson could be warm in his personal regard for the man, admire his tenacity as a reformer, but how was Bryan to be used in a constructive administration?

"Make him ambassador to Great Britain," his friend suggested.

"If he were the man for that post, I don't believe he would accept it," Wilson answered. "He will not be content to be so far away from the centre of activity; yet, if he is in Washington he will want to meddle. In any Democratic Congress he will have a large following, and unless the President has a united Congress he can accomplish little. It is not Mr. Bryan so much as Mr. Bryan's friends, who will think he has been slighted if he is not given a good post, whom the next President, if a Democrat, has to fear. And what use would he be in a cabinet?"[1]

McCombs and other Eastern supporters were also deeply concerned about the problem of Bryan. They wanted Wilson to avoid Bryan and all his ways, and they had been alarmed to the point of fervid expostulation by his plan to visit Lincoln, Nebraska, Bryan's home and the heart of the "Bryan empire." After the great meetings at Minneapolis and St. Paul, where the state military salute of seventeen guns was fired in his honour, Wilson could have returned directly East—and avoided the implications of a visit at Lincoln. He decided to go straight forward with his original plan.

Arriving in Nebraska, Wilson was met by a delegation headed by Charles W. Bryan, the brother of William J. Bryan and editor of his *Commoner*. Bryan himself was speaking in the East but sent a cordial telegram:

"I regret very much that engagements in New Jersey prevent my welcoming you to Lincoln. I hope you will enjoy your visit and carry away pleasant recollections of our city and state."

It was an interesting visit. Wilson was hospitably welcomed by Mrs. Bryan, who showed him with pride the souvenirs of Bryan's three presidential campaigns. He was enthusiastically received at the University of Nebraska and elsewhere, and his address that evening, the last of the transcontinental tour, for inspirational oratory was undoubtedly the greatest of the entire series. When he reached the climax of his peroration his appeal to the unselfish public spirit of the country's business leaders brought his audience to its feet.

Wilson's visit in Nebraska was not only warmly ap-

---

[1] From notes made by Frank Parker Stockbridge.

preciated in the state,[1] but it was recognized throughout
the nation as an effort to unite the Democratic party.
While Bryan had at that time made no statement as to
his preferences among the candidates—he was supposed
to be for Champ Clark, or to desire the nomination
for himself—Wilson was delighted with the personal
friendliness of many Bryan supporters. Bryan's brother,
hearing of the difficulties the Wilson campaign was facing
owing to lack of sufficient financial support, handed a
check to Stockbridge as the party was leaving Lincoln.

It was this Western trip that made Wilson a formidable
candidate for the presidency; it determined him in his
own mind. He had travelled eight thousand miles, and
made thirty-one speeches in seven states.

It may seem that the popular success of this trip has
been here over-emphasized, but the plain fact, based upon
an examination of an immense number of letters, newspaper articles, and editorials, is that there was almost no
unfavourable reaction. The New York *Sun* kept up a
desultory fire and there were here and there alarmed
comments—an "anarchist," a railroad magnate of Minnesota called him—but, as the *Oregon Journal* remarked,
he was so "unexpected," such a "new man" in American
public life, that he took the West by storm. Not the
politicians, for he did not get the Missouri, Colorado,
California, Nebraska, or Washington delegates at the
Baltimore convention, these being firmly in the hands of
the old political leaders—but it gave him a powerful hold
upon Western people—without which he probably could
not have been nominated, and it enabled him later, in the
election of 1912, to carry every one of these states except
California[2] and Washington. The reaction, the attacks,

---

[1]He carried Nebraska in the election of 1912 by the following vote: Wilson, 109,008;
Roosevelt, 72,614; Taft, 54,029; Debs 10,174. (From the *American Year Book*, 1913.)

[2]He missed carrying California by only 174 votes. The totals were Roosevelt 283,610;
Wilson 283,436; Debs 79,201; Taft 3,914. (From the *American Year Book*, 1913.)

were to come later when the old political leaders and the powerful interests of the East suddenly discovered what a hold upon the people Wilson had succeeded in securing.

"With the conclusion of his successful Western tour, Governor Wilson of New Jersey may be said to be a candidate in the fullest sense, although he has refrained from declaring himself an aggressive contestant for the nomination. . . .

"The Wilson candidacy is one to be seriously reckoned with from now on."[1]

## VI. THE HOME FRONT

Wilson returned from the West with his mind made up. The success of his swing-around, the remarkable reaction in the press, had raised the enthusiasm of his amateur supporters to fever heat. Even his visit at Bryan's home in Nebraska, contrary to McCombs's dire prophecies, had been well received, since it presaged a new unity of the party. Washington was also waking up. Democratic members of Congress had begun to hear from home. Who was this astonishing college professor who was getting audiences and popular attention in their own states and districts which they themselves could not get! It was calculated to impress the most hardened of politicians.

"Did you see the account of the informal poll of the Democratic representatives in which four-fifths (of those voting) voted for you for nominee? It is interesting about Senator Gore too. I am very curious to know how Bryan behaved when you were in Lincoln,—if he invited you to his house. . . ."[2]

Wilson was to arrive in Washington on June 4th. Fol-

---

[1]Springfield *Republican*, May 28, 1911.
[2]Ellen Axson Wilson to Woodrow Wilson, June 1, 1911.

lowing his return from the West, he had gone into North and South Carolina for several promised addresses—one at the University of North Carolina, where he was among old friends, and another at Raleigh, where he was the guest of Josephus Daniels. He had also visited the home of his youth, Columbia, South Carolina, where he was warmly received and introduced to a great audience as the "Democratic hope of the nation."[1] In the home of a boyhood friend where he was entertained, a notch was carved on the table to show where he sat, and in after years honoured guests were placed in "Woodrow Wilson's own chair."

Wilson found the little army of the faithful awaiting him when he arrived at the Willard Hotel in Washington. Page was there, with McCombs, McCorkle, and Vance McCormick. Tumulty had come down with a great bundle of enthusiastic letters and newspaper articles. They were for organizing immediately a Wilson-for-President movement on a nationwide basis. Get in the most notable leaders, raise money, make connections with state and local organizations!—all according to the accepted political method. They found Wilson curiously doubtful, hesitant.

First he wanted to meet some of the Congressional leaders. The magniloquent Senator Martine eagerly brought in members of the Senate and House. Champ Clark, Speaker of the House of Representatives, afterwards to be Wilson's chief rival for the nomination, came to call. Underwood of Alabama, then a member of the House, spent an hour with Wilson.

When at length the impatient little group of friends got Wilson to themselves around the dinner table, he seemed far more interested in discussing his Western trip and the political situation in general than in arrangements for his own immediate campaign.

---

[1] He was the guest of William E. Gonzales and his brother and of August Kohn.

"If I could satisfy myself that Oscar Underwood had a genuine grasp of progressive principles, I should instruct my friends to make no further efforts in my behalf, and work for Underwood."

Of Harmon, he said:

"Harmon hasn't had a new political thought since Cleveland's administration. He doesn't know that the world has moved."[1]

At length Page and McCombs put forward plans for an organization. Wilson at once objected. He seemed to think that the "call of the people" was enough.

"I don't want to be promoted as a candidate for the presidential campaign. I am willing to let you gentlemen go this far. I am getting a heavy mail from people throughout the country who are asking me to make speeches or suggesting organization. I haven't time or strength to deal with them. If you gentlemen want to take the responsibility of answering these letters, it would be a great relief to me."[2]

While this did not satisfy his friends, they agreed to go ahead on that basis. A day or two later Wilson developed his idea more fully in a letter to Page:

"Thank you sincerely for your letter of yesterday. I hated to rush away from Washington without seeing you again, but it was due to the generous way in which you treated me and left me to the rush of visitors of every kind who had to be seen, but who inevitably kept us apart.

"It increases my confidence vastly to be trusted and believed in by men like yourself and the others who are so generously advising and working with me.

"I have been thinking a good deal about the matter we discussed the other day with regard to a manager. I find in so many quarters the feeling that in some sense the

---

[1]Frank Parker Stockbridge to the author.
[2]*Ibid.*

movement in my favour ought to be allowed to 'take care of itself'; that my present judgment, at any rate provisionally, is, the further we keep away from the usual methods, the better. Of course I am far too well acquainted with practical considerations to think that the matter can be allowed to take care of itself. But if we were to secure the services of a man of large caliber who would direct attention to himself inevitably and who would stand in the same category as in the case of the one who is managing for Harmon, I think we would seem to have descended into the arena and would create some very unfavourable impressions.

"I would like soon to get hold of you and talk along this line: Would it not be well for the present at any rate to maintain merely a bureau of information and co-operation . . . My idea is that we could refer everybody who wanted such information as coöperation must depend upon to Stockbridge. He could constitute the necessary clearing house and by mere diligence in keeping track of everything, prevent matters from getting into confusion, or persons in different parts of the country working at cross purposes. He could be supplied with the necessary judgment in important matters by counsel with ourselves.

"This is all too complicated a matter. I am going to see McCombs to-morrow and I shall try to arrange, through him, for a little conference. . . ."[1]

Mrs. Wilson was undoubtedly a factor in encouraging Wilson to let his friends go ahead with their little organization. She feared that he would be tempted to make another speaking trip. She was anxious regarding his health —"trying to do everything yourself"—and she thought that his absence was making an unfavourable impression in New Jersey.

"There is a persistent rumour that is worrying some of

[1]June 7, 1911.

your friends, that another 'tour' is being arranged for you, —the inference being that you are *consenting*. Of course I know that you are *not;*—that there is no truth in it, beyond the fact that much pressure is doubtless being brought to bear on you to fall in with such plans. But it is said to be making a bad impression,—in New Jersey particularly, but also in New York—and I was wondering if it could not be publicly contradicted in some way. I enclose an editorial that alludes to it. . . . What a tremendous ovation you had in Raleigh!"[1]

On June 9th, Stockbridge began his publicity work in the bedroom of his apartment in New York.

A little later an office was set up at 235 West 39th Street, with a borrowed desk and typewriter—and moved shortly to 42 Broadway. So opposed was Wilson to propagandist publicity that there was nothing on the door of the office or on the letter paper to indicate that it was a Wilson organization. McCombs raised a little money but it was only with the greatest difficulty that the expenses could be met. They never had a bank account until Wilson's old friend and classmate, Cleveland H. Dodge, sent his check for $1,000.

Stockbridge's method was to answer inquiries for copies of Wilson's addresses, or for photographs, and presently he began to send out "clip-sheets" made up of newspaper editorials or articles about Wilson—which were becoming rapidly more numerous.

Wilson's New Jersey friends were eagerly helpful. The Trenton *True American*, edited by Henry E. Alexander, offered two pages a week for material prepared by Stockbridge, and Cleveland H. Dodge and his friends provided the money for sending this weekly issue throughout the country. By fall there were 40,000 names on the lists. While McCombs fretted at not being allowed to organize

[1] Ellen Axson Wilson to Woodrow Wilson, June 2, 1911.

on a larger scale, the very quietude, the restraint, of the
movement, was a large factor in its success. Wilson was
determined that the people must come to him: must desire
his leadership. In August he was still against a "real
campaign manager."

"I wonder if you would be generous enough to have a
talk about the matter of the general concentration of effort with Mr. McAdoo. I have found him very sagacious
and very wide-awake, and I should think that you two
could get together in your thinking very quickly.

"My instinct, of course, is against having a real political
campaign manager but my mind is always to let.

"I need not tell you how it warms my heart to have you
constantly thinking of me as you do."[1]

William G. McAdoo, who was to become a bulwark of
strength in Wilson's campaign, had become interested in
July.

McAdoo was a remarkable man. Seven years younger
than Wilson, his origins were much the same: Scotch-
Irish, Presbyterian, and Southern—born in Georgia. He
came up struggling with adverse circumstances, won his
way to an education, became a lawyer in Tennessee, and
afterwards in New York City, where he had "five years of
starvation." With a genius for action and affairs, he became the leading spirit in a daring, and at that time
doubtful, enterprise for driving tunnels under the Hudson
River. He exhibited extraordinary gifts for organization,
for dealing with men, for finance on a large scale. He had
to fight every foot of his way, since many of the large
banking interests were opposed to him. Wall Street never
liked him, never accepted him. He finished the first tunnel
in 1904, the fourth in 1909.

McAdoo first met Wilson in 1909. His son, who was a
student at Princeton, had been taken suddenly ill and, on

---

[1]Woodrow Wilson to Walter H. Page, August 21, 1911.

the way down to see him, McAdoo met Wilson on the train. They found immediately that they had much in common. McAdoo was charmed with Wilson and Wilson on his part questioned McAdoo eagerly about his activities, then much in the public press, as the builder of the great tunnels.

"What I like especially," said Wilson, "is the attitude of your company toward the public. It is so different from that of the usual so-called public service corporation."[1]

McAdoo had taken as his motto, "The public be pleased," not "The public be damned."

From this time onward, McAdoo was Wilson's firm friend and supporter. He introduced him at a banquet of the Southern Society as the "next President of the United States," he watched with keen interest the New Jersey campaign, and in the summer of 1911, falling in with McCombs, he not only contributed to the campaign funds, but offered his services. McAdoo was a great accession. A man of enormous energy and vivacity— dynamic rather than thoughtful—he was fertile in all the resources of organization. Over six feet tall, a wiry, sinewy, tireless man with a hawklike face, and the Southern blur— the Georgia blur—in his speech, he was in marked contrast to McCombs, the neurotic semi-invalid, whose towering ambitions far exceeded his capacities.

Wilson soon began to lean more heavily upon McAdoo's judgment than upon McCombs's.

"I am glad you are going to confer with McAdoo. He is a true friend of right things and a real man, loving what is just and for the good of the country—a sincere friend too."[2]

The relations between McCombs and McAdoo soon became strained, McCombs being insanely jealous, and one

[1] William G. McAdoo to the author.
[2] Woodrow Wilson to Cyrus H. McCormick, May 14, 1912.

of Wilson's major difficulties during the campaign—until his election, indeed—was in holding the reins upon his high-powered, temperamental, erratic, volunteer manager. No man, however, could have been more devoted personally to Wilson than was McCombs at this period, and it was largely due to his activity, assisted by McAdoo, that the organization in New York was kept going.

"Here we are, at Sea Girt. Ellen and the girls came down on Friday, and I got here on Saturday (yesterday), riding all the way down from New York, *via* pretty Staten Island, in my campaign manager's car. (Of course I have no campaign manager in fact; but Wm. F. McCombs, of New York, a very generous friend and a one-time pupil of mine at Princeton, has insisted upon making his office a sort of clearing house of the big correspondence that is going on from one end of the country to the other about my possible nomination for the presidency,—and a splendid fellow he is. He tells me that he dictates some fifty letters a day on the subject!)"[1]

Wilson's progress as a candidate during all the summer of 1911 and into the fall was most gratifying to his supporters—as it was presently to become alarming to his opponents. Although now extremely occupied with state affairs—"I . . . am here surrounded by a mountain of work . . . ."[2]—for campaigns were under way for the adoption of commission government by several New Jersey cities, a movement in which Wilson was deeply interested,[3] he found time for various and telling activities in the national field. In the middle of June he was called to a great meeting in Pennsylvania, where his friends Vance McCormick and A. Mitchell Palmer had been

---

[1]Woodrow Wilson to Mary A. Hulbert, July 16, 1911.

[2]Woodrow Wilson to Cleveland H. Dodge, June 6, 1911.

[3]The city of Trenton adopted commission government under the law whose passage Wilson had secured on June 20th.

busy. Here he met and made a fast friend of William B. Wilson, leader of the miners' union, who was afterwards to serve in his cabinet as Secretary of Labor. Pennsylvania was the first state to come, formally, into the Wilson fold. In July he was in Kentucky and in the fall he made his famous trip to Texas in which he literally captured the state.

It was altogether a hectic summer. Part of the time the Wilson family was at its favourite resort at Lyme, Connecticut, where the hard-driven candidate was able occasionally to spend a week-end; and part of the time they were at the Governor's Mansion at Sea Girt. This was a fine home maintained by the state near the grounds where the yearly encampments of the state troops were held. It was distressingly public, the great democracy of New Jersey often stopping to sit on the wide porches, or even walking into the front rooms without invitation, but it was none the less comfortable and attractive. Ocean bathing, tennis, golf, and other sports, ably seconded by the gallant young officers, made life agreeable enough for the younger members of the family. It was here that the Wilsons first had the use of an automobile. One of the functions of the Governor was to review the state troops. We have glimpses of Wilson, upon such occasions, in a frock coat and silk hat, riding a spirited horse.

"The first review has come off—the occasion on wh. it was obligatory that I should wear a frock coat and silk hat on horseback, and ride, with a mounted staff of seven officers, around the lines, in the presence (this time) of five or six thousand people. I tried to beg off from the costume and get leave to appear in riding togs, but my staff advisers were very firm with me, and I had to do 'the usual thing.' Evidently, though 'commander-in-chief,' I am under discipline. . . ."[1]

---

[1] Woodrow Wilson to Mary A. Hulbert, July 30, 1911.

During one of the parades a lady who had come from a neighbouring ocean resort was deeply interested in the "thin man on a horse . . . wearing a frock coat and a high hat" who was reviewing the troops. She was not to meet him personally until four years later; she was afterwards to become his wife. This was Mrs. Norman Galt.

One moment of the summer Wilson found deeply delightful and restful—a short yachting trip with his old friend Cleveland Dodge. It would have been well if he could have had more such moments of ease, could have found more time for the cultivation of friends and friendships, but from these months onward, his life became more and more a driven battle.

In the early fall Wilson had to plunge again into a state campaign. The bosses were now set against him—bitterly, irretrievably. In July there had been a demonstration of their hostility at a meeting at Avon. Nugent was still Democratic state chairman, and was giving a dinner to a company of political and personal friends. A party of officers of the National Guard then encamped at Sea Girt was seated at a near-by table. Toward the close of the dinner, Nugent asked those present, at both tables, to join him in a toast. When they all arose, he said:

"I give you the Governor of the state of New Jersey"—all glasses were raised; Nugent finished—"a liar and an ingrate!"

The diners stood for a moment stupefied. "Do I drink alone?" said the host.

He did drink alone. The glasses were set down untouched; some of the officers indignantly threw out their wine on the floor.

Not long afterwards at a meeting of the State Committee, Nugent was deposed as chairman by Wilson's friends.

When the Democratic state convention met on October

3rd, the Governor was in full control, and was greeted, according to the reports, with an "unexampled ovation." Enthusiastic supporters introduced a resolution endorsing him as the choice of New Jersey Democrats for the presidency, but thinking it unwise to complicate state issues with a national campaign, he prevented its passage. His instinct was still to hold back. He wanted to be sure that the call came from the people. He would not force it. Charles H. Grasty of the Baltimore *Sun* sought his help as a party leader in a Maryland contest. Wilson responded:

"I am afraid you will chide me for putting a scruple of taste in the way of the performance of a public duty; but I feel very strongly that it would be a great mistake for me to assume, at this time, the tone or the methods of a national party leader. If I could have come and spoken in Baltimore I would have done so with all my heart, but when your telegraphic message came asking me to send some word for publication in the paper I instinctively drew back. I think it would have done more harm than good—more harm to the cause; people would only have laughed at me for assuming that I was the man to send messages to those who were fighting for the interests of the party.

"If this is too fine drawn a scruple pray blame my judgment and not my heart."[1]

## VII. THE ATTEMPT TO RUIN WILSON

All the elements opposed to Governor Wilson awakened suddenly, in the fall of 1911, to the fact that he had become a formidable national figure. It had happened in the nation as in the state of New Jersey, that the old politicians could not at first take the college professor quite seriously. He

[1]November 2, 1911.

had no organization, no money, no experience; sooner or later he would make the inevitable mistake. But he had kept on growing!

The powerful Eastern bosses had never liked Wilson— he not only challenged their leadership, he threatened the candidates they preferred, Harmon, or Underwood, or Clark. More dangerous still, the great conservative interests, grouped under the vague term "Wall Street," were now thoroughly alarmed. Wilson's well-aimed attacks upon privilege, his support of the "new-fangled devices of radicalism," above all his "fraternization with Bryan," stirred them to drastic action.

Some even of the great Democratic newspapers which afterwards supported Wilson valiantly were more than doubtful. The Richmond *Times-Dispatch* considered him "a little too advanced on some of the questions of the day" and the New York *World* inquired anxiously, "Is Woodrow Wilson Bryanizing?"[1]

It was plain that Wilson must be stopped, and stopped at once.

Wilson was of a type unprecedented in politics: he had no political past to unearth, no enemies who knew well, from former battles, the weak spots in his armour. He had proved himself such a gifted orator with such a persuasive hold upon the people that there was no one in the party who could meet him or match him in a fair fight on issues and principles—certainly not Clark or Harmon or Underwood—no one but Bryan, and Bryan, besides being still more repugnant to the conservatives, seemed not unwilling to support Wilson. What then was to be done?

The signal for a general attack came after the New Jersey election of November 7th. Wilson had fought a hard campaign for the election of a legislature which would support his policies, and had lost the Assembly, due

[1] July 31, 1911.

to the opposition of the bosses, Smith and Nugent. It was his first set-back, and his enemies seized the opportunity for pouncing upon him.

It seems perfectly clear from an examination of the entire body of the documents that the attack was deliberate and well-organized. It involved a searching examination of his record as an educator and as a writer, and above all it sought to prove that he was a cold, ambitious ingrate, a dictatorial and selfish leader. Every scrap he ever wrote was studied.

". . . there is a conservative branch of the democracy, and it is organizing to oppose Governor Wilson. His books and the speeches he made before entering active politics are in the hands of readers charged with the duty of searching them for points relating to what is bluntly characterized as his apostasy. The deadly parallel is in preparation by experts who know the business.

"And this parallel will serve twice. First, Governor Wilson's opponents for the nomination will use it, and then his Republican opponents if he is nominated."[1]

Exactly as his enemies planned, the ammunition thus gathered was made the basis of repeated and irritating attacks.

A keen political observer, Franklin K. Lane, who at that time had not met Wilson (in whose cabinet he was afterwards to serve), wrote a friend on December 13th:

"On the Democratic side all of the forces have united to destroy Wilson, who is the strongest man in the West. The bosses are all against him. They recently produced an application which he had made for a pension, under the Carnegie Endowment Fund for Teachers, which had been allowed to lie idle, unnoticed for a year or so after its rejection, but owing to campaign emergencies was pro-

---

[1] Chattanooga *Times*, November 5, 1911, quoting the Washington *Star*.

duced, at this happy moment, to show that Wilson wanted a pension."[1]

The Carnegie pension matter referred to by Lane was one of the first handfuls of mud to be flung.

Upon his resignation from Princeton University, Wilson had applied for the usual retiring allowance given by the Carnegie Foundation for the Advancement of Teaching after "twenty-five years of distinguished service." President David Starr Jordan of Leland Stanford University applied for a retiring allowance about the same time. Upon consideration of the two applications by the board, the trustees changed the former rule and declined to grant the allowance to "a man, however distinguished, who retires from educational work to undertake other work on salary."[2] Wilson accepted the decision and nothing more was heard of the matter until December, 1911, when some one of the gentlemen of the board of trustees bared the confidential records of the Foundation to the New York *Sun*, at that time Wilson's chief editorial antagonist. A sarcastic attack was launched on December 5th—"a tale of superannuation"—"and really, you know, with his youth and his prospects it didn't seem . . ."

Wilson at once issued a statement:

[1]Franklin K. Lane to John Crawford Burns, December 13, 1911. *The Letters of Franklin K. Lane*, pp. 84–85.

[2]At the time Wilson applied there were two sorts of Carnegie pensions—one an old-age pension given to all who were sixty-five years old and otherwise eligible, and the other a distinguished-service pension, given after twenty-five years of teaching in specially selected cases. At first the twenty-five year pension was given very freely by the board, but when the number of colleges under the Foundation was so greatly increased, it became clear that the money would not suffice to make that so general a rule. Then it was decided, Wilson himself being on the committee and largely instrumental in securing the decision, to make the twenty-five-year pension exclusively and conspicuously a question of distinguished service, and in no sense one of superannuation. It was thought that to have such pensioners on the list would not only benefit scholarship in America but give to the Foundation a dignity and prestige which it had not secured. It was intended that the select ones should, while still in the fullness of their powers, be set free to devote those powers to the public service, either as scientific investigators, writers, or speakers; and it was, of course, intended to be a badge of honour, as such pensions are regarded in other countries.

The Carnegie Foundation for the Advancement of Teaching is not a plan for old-age pensions, but for the granting of retiring allowances on the ground of length and quality of service. Before I was elected governor of New Jersey, when I had just entered the uncertain field of politics, I applied to the Foundation for a retiring allowance, to which I understood myself to be entitled under the rules adopted by the trustees. I have no private means to depend upon. A man who goes into politics bound by the principles of honour puts his family and all who may be dependent upon him for support at the mercy of any incalculable turn of the wheel of fortune, and I felt entirely justified in seeking to provide against such risks, particularly when I was applying for what I supposed myself to be entitled to by right of long service as a teacher under the rules of the Foundation.

I understood that upon the receipt of my application the executive committee of the trustees of the Foundation restricted the interpretation of their rule and declined to grant the allowance. Why the matter should have come up again now I do not know. I have had nothing to do with it since the early autumn of 1910. I have not renewed the application.

WOODROW WILSON

In spite of the explanation, this utterly trivial incident was seized upon by hostile newspapers as somehow damaging to Wilson. As he wrote to a friend:

"Everywhere it is beginning to be perceived that the likelihood of my being nominated is very great and must be taken seriously,—and it *is* beginning to be taken very seriously, by certain big business interests in N.Y., who know that I could not be managed to their mind, and by everybody who, like Hearst, for personal reasons, wants to see me beaten. They are looking high and low for some means by which to discredit me personally if not politically. Just at this moment (in spite of a perfectly frank statement by me of all the facts) they are trying to make me seem ridiculous and discredited because I applied to the Carnegie Foundation for a retiring allowance,—and may, by lying misrepresentations, partially succeed—with the people who always want an honourable man brought down to their level. Next they will turn to something else upon which to put a false colour. All these things are in the long run futile. They discredit only those who do them. But for a little while they are very trying."[1]

Mrs. Wilson, in a letter to an old friend, gives intimate glimpses of the reasons why Wilson had applied for the Carnegie pension:

". . . when he applied he had *not* been elected Governor and had no means of support, for he refused to take anything from Princeton after the *day* on which he sent in his resignation. We were utterly without income for three months,—and people were declaring his election impossible!

"Of course he could easily get another 'paying job,' but that would force him to give up, in large measure, his leadership in the reform movement. What he had in mind to do was to devote his time and his voice to the cause of the people. The three years of office-holding—as Governor, —if it came to him,—was a mere episode designed to gain more completely the public ear and the public confidence as one who knew what he was talking about. The urgent appeals to him for speeches have for many years numbered from four to eight a day,—a perpetual cry to 'come over and help us.' I need not say that there is no money in such work, often not even his travelling expenses,—and his income from his books averages less than $1,000 a year,— all of which goes for life insurance. You see I am talking to you now as a *very* intimate friend, because I think it will be of service for *one* person to know *just* how it stands with him. He is the most unselfish and generous of men, and has for twenty years supported in large part his

---

[1] Woodrow Wilson to Mary A. Hulbert, December 10, 1911.

widowed sister and her family and my young sister, (now married) as well as his own.

"When he was a mere professor he could and did make some money writing and lecturing, so that we even built a home for ourselves,—but for the past ten years he has given his pen and his voice to the public service absolutely free. . . ."[1]

Hardly had this bomb been exploded, when there began to circulate, as a part of the "campaign of whispers," the story of a letter supposed to have been written by Grover Cleveland regarding Wilson's attitude during the controversies at Princeton, in which it was said that Wilson was undependable if not untruthful. It was plainly an attempt to bring the Princeton controversies into politics; it was also felt by Wilson's enemies that the unfavourable opinion of the former revered leader of the Democracy would harm him. But this letter, if it ever existed, was never published, nor was Wilson's reply, until it was used in this biography.[2] That Wilson was somewhat worried by the attack is plain from his letter to his old friend Thomas D. Jones:

"Among other things, as you doubtless have heard, there is said to be a letter of Mr. Cleveland's springing out of the graduate school controversy which they are intending, at the effective moment, to print and by which they hope to damage me. It has occurred to me that such members of the Board as yourself, McCormick, McIlvaine, Jacobus, Sheldon and Garrett ought to know of what is in contemplation in order that if you choose, in your generosity to do it, you might be ready in a joint statement which would effectively meet all the counts of the indictment they evidently intend to bring against me. I think the

---

[1] Ellen Axson Wilson to R. Heath Dabney, February 9, 1912.

[2] See *Woodrow Wilson, Life and Letters: Princeton*, Appendix, p. 358, for complete copy.

country at large already pretty well understands the situation with regard to Princeton, but such a joint statement would have overwhelming force. . . .

"I do not feel that I ought to let myself be defenseless on any side, and I know how absolutely I can count on the men of the Board who stood by me so splendidly and whom I greatly respect and admire."[1]

A barrage of attacks by prominent men was also started. Everything that had been said to the detriment of Wilson since he had been in politics was collected and sent out to the press. An address by Speaker Cannon assailing him for his attitude on the New Jersey senatorship was quoted, the remark of Croker that Wilson was an "ingrate," the assertion of Governor Pennypacker of Pennsylvania that he was a "charlatan and notoriety seeker."

But the principal line of attack, then and afterwards, was upon Wilson as "selfish," as "ambitious," as disloyal to his friends. It had already been made a feature of the New Jersey struggle; it was calculated to harm him more than anything else, as his enemies well knew, with the organization politicians who would dominate the convention in the following June.

The dramatic symbol of this form of attack was the break between Harvey and Wilson—an incident that caused an immense reverberation in the press.

Such a break had for months been inevitable. While Harvey had been of the greatest service in launching Wilson upon the troubled waters of politics, and while he had continued to write and speak in his behalf as a candidate for the presidency in 1912, the political rift between the two men had been steadily widening. Harvey had behind him certain of the great business interests of the East. He had been a close associate of Ryan and Whitney, who, though Democrats, were supposed to represent all that

[1] December 15, 1911.

was devilish in Wall Street. J. Pierpont Morgan practically controlled the publishing house of Harper & Brothers of which Harvey was the president, and, of course, *Harper's Weekly* of which he was the editor.

It will be clear to any reader of the chapters of this biography relating to Wilson's record as governor how, month by month, he must have become more disappointing to Harvey and his backers, both financial and political.

On the other hand, Harvey's continued and ingenious support of Wilson in his magazine was becoming awkward for Wilson. On November 11, 1911, Harvey placed at the head of the editorial column of *Harper's Weekly*, the slogan: "For President, Woodrow Wilson." Such support laid Wilson open in the West to the suspicion that he was the candidate of the very interests he was attacking. His backers in New York were becoming more and more uncomfortable. Roosevelt, campaigning in the West as a militant Progressive, had been assailing "the great metropolitan press edited under the shadow of Wall Street."

Harvey was thus in a pretty dilemma, caught in the net of his own cleverness. There is no evidence that his personal admiration for Wilson had changed or that he had ceased to believe in "the political predestination of Woodrow Wilson";[1] nor is there any evidence that Wilson had ceased to regard Harvey as his personal friend. But the political pressure on both sides was becoming intolerable. We have a letter written by Colonel House to William J. Bryan setting forth the situation as it was on December 5th, three weeks after Harvey had flung forth his slogan. House had met Wilson for the first time only two weeks before and had become his ardent friend.

"I took lunch with Colonel Harvey yesterday. It is the first time I have met him. I wanted to determine what his

---

[1] The title of an article by Harvey in the *North American Review*, March, 1911.

real attitude was towards Governor Wilson, but I think I left as much in the dark as ever.

"He told me that everybody south of Canal Street was in a frenzy against Governor Wilson and said they were bringing all sorts of pressure upon him to oppose him. He said he told them he had an open mind, and that if they could convince him he was a dangerous man he would do so.

"He said that Morgan was particularly virulent in his opposition to Governor Wilson. I asked him what this was based upon, and he said upon some remark Governor Wilson had made in Morgan's presence concerning the methods of bankers and which Morgan took as a personal reference.

"He told me that he believed that any amount of money that was needed to defeat Governor Wilson could be readily obtained. He said he would be surprised if they did not put $250,000 in New Jersey alone in order to defeat delegates favourable to his nomination."[1]

There is no doubt that the pressure that "everybody south of Canal Street" was bringing to bear on Harvey was effective. On December 7th—two days after Harvey's talk with House—the famous meeting between Harvey, Watterson, and Wilson took place. Wilson did not seek it. The invitation came from Watterson, whom Wilson had always regarded as his loyal friend and supporter. It was held in Watterson's rooms at the Manhattan Club. The three men met in the friendliest spirit. There was considerable discussion of the political situation in Kentucky and elsewhere. Just as Wilson arose to go, Harvey asked him point-blank:

"Is there anything left of that cheap talk during the gubernatorial campaign about my advocating you on behalf of 'the interests'?"

[1] *The Intimate Papers of Colonel House*, Vol. I, p. 51.

Wilson answered directly and frankly that there was, that members of his "literary bureau" had declared that it was having a serious effect in the West. This was no shocking statement to any of those present, for Watterson himself, as far back as the previous October, had suggested to Governor Wilson that it might be well for Colonel Harvey to moderate somewhat the rather aggressive support of *Harper's Weekly*. Harvey himself was well aware of the situation.[1] He responded to Wilson's perfectly candid answer:

"Then I will simply sing low."

Watterson said: "Yes, that's the only thing to do. The power of silence is very great. For myself, too, I shall not say a word for the present."[2]

Wilson left the conference with not the remotest idea that there had been any offense, much less any "break." He had been asked a frank question regarding a difficult problem well known to all of them, by a man he considered his friend; and he had responded with equal frankness. When informed by his friend Axson a little later that his name had disappeared from the head of the editorial column of *Harper's Weekly* he was so unconscious that any offense had been taken that he did not connect it with the interview. "Was Colonel Harvey offended?" asked Axson. "He didn't seem to be," was the Governor's answer.[3]

Tumulty, the shrewd politician, "scented the danger of the situation."

" . . . I told him very frankly that I was afraid he had deeply wounded Colonel Harvey and that it might result in a serious break in their relations. The Governor seemed

---

[1]Watterson afterwards said that he had discussed the matter with both Wilson and Harvey.

[2]These questions and replies are from a memorandum made by Harvey himself at the time.

[3]Professor Stockton Axson to the author.

grieved at this and said that he hoped such was not the case. . . ."[1]

As a result, Wilson wrote a letter to Harvey, marked "personal":

> University Club,
> Fifth Avenue and 54th Street,
> Dec. 21, 1911.
>
> Personal.
> MY DEAR COLONEL:
> Every day I am confirmed in the judgment that my mind is a one-track road and can run only one train of thought at a time! A long time after that interview with you and Marse Henry at the Manhattan Club it came over me that when (at the close of the interview) you asked me that question about the 'Weekly' I answered it simply as a matter of fact, and of business, and said never a word of my sincere gratitude to you for all your generous support, or of my hope that it might be continued. Forgive me, and forget my manners!
> > Faithfully yours,
> > WOODROW WILSON

At once, and strangely enough, comments began to appear in the press regarding this wholly private conference, charging Wilson with ingratitude toward the "man who had made him."

Harvey replied in friendly, if somewhat ironic, terms to Wilson's letter of December 21st and Wilson wrote again on January 11th:

> Hotel Astor, New York
> Jan. 11, 1910. [1912]
>
> MY DEAR COLONEL HARVEY:
> Generous and cordial as was your letter written in reply to my note from the University Club, it has left me uneasy— because, in its perfect frankness, it shows that I did hurt you by what I so tactlessly said at the Knickerbocker [Manhattan]

---

[1]Joseph P. Tumulty, *Woodrow Wilson As I Know Him*, p. 84.

Club. I am very much ashamed of myself—for there is nothing I am more ashamed of than hurting a true friend, however unintentional the hurt may have been. . . .

For I owe it to you and to my own thought and feeling to tell you how grateful I am for all your generous praise and support of me (no one has described me more nearly as I would like to believe myself to be than you have), how I have admired you for the independence and unhesitating courage and individuality of your course, and how far I was from desiring that you should cease your support of me in the 'Weekly'. You will think me very stupid—but I did not think of that as the result of my blunt answer to your question. I thought only of the means of convincing people of the real independence of the 'Weekly's' position. You will remember that that was what we discussed. And now that I have unintentionally put you in a false and embarrassing position, you heap coals of fire on my head by continuing to give out interviews favourable to my candidacy! All that I can say is that you have proved yourself very big, and that I wish I might have an early opportunity to tell you face to face how I really feel about it all.

With warm regard,

Cordially and faithfully yours,
WOODROW WILSON

Harvey replied on January 16th, thanking Wilson for his "most handsome letter" and denying that he had any "personal rancour or resentment." On the 20th, he published the following notice in *Harper's Weekly:*

"TO OUR READERS:

"We make the following reply to many inquiries from the readers of *Harper's Weekly:*

"The name of Woodrow Wilson as our candidate for President was taken down from the head of these columns in response to a statement made directly to us by Governor Wilson, to the effect that our support was affecting his candidacy injuriously.

"The only course left open to us, in simple fairness to

Mr. Wilson, no less than in consideration of our own self-respect, was to cease to advocate his nomination.

"We make this explanation with great reluctance and the deepest regret. But we cannot escape the conclusion that the very considerable number of our readers who have coöperated earnestly and loyally in advancing a movement which was inaugurated solely in the hope of rendering a high public service are clearly entitled to this information."

From this time onward not only was Wilson's name removed from the head of Harvey's column, but it was not mentioned in any article or editorial up to the time of the convention. Harvey, indeed, veered to the support of Champ Clark, Wilson's foremost rival.

Wilson's enemies were now in full cry. It was exactly the ammunition they wanted in order to convict him of ingratitude. The story spread all over the country. Watterson added fuel to the flames by issuing a written statement in which he suggested that Wilson was "rather a schoolmaster than a statesman" and went on to say, after making the assertion above quoted, that he himself had doubted whether Harvey's support was helping Wilson:

"I am not sure that I had not said as much to Colonel Harvey himself, but that Governor Wilson, without the least show of compunction, should express or yield to such an opinion, and permit Colonel Harvey to consider himself discharged from the position of trusted intimacy he had up to this moment held, left me little room to doubt that Governor Wilson is not a man who makes common cause with his political associates or is deeply sensible of his political obligations; because it is but true and fair to say that, except for Colonel Harvey, he would not be in the running at all."

It was a choice morsel for the press—"first-page stuff." McCombs rushed into the mêlée with the charge that

Wilson had been "framed": that it was a "put up job"—as it undoubtedly was. He asserted that "Wall Street," bitterly hostile to Wilson, was now seeking to injure him by trickery. Ryan's name was dragged into the controversy. It was charged and denied that the Wilson managers had approached him for a campaign contribution. Watterson appeared with a new broadside: "Says Wilson lied."

Wilson deeply regretted the entire incident. While in Detroit on January 18th he wrote out, with great care, an explanation of the controversy, but decided finally not to issue it, and it has not hitherto been published:

"I must confess to being very much distressed that this matter should have taken such a shape as to involve me in an apparent ingratitude. I did not tell Colonel Harvey that the support of *Harper's Weekly* was apparently embarrassing me in many parts of the country, without having first been asked the question point-blank by Colonel Harvey himself. Had he not asked me, I should never have conveyed any such intimation to him. The question was asked at the close of a most friendly and cordial conference, which Colonel Watterson had suggested, and was, I supposed asked as a natural part of the discussion. It was very frank and generous of Colonel Harvey to ask it, and I was very much embarrassed in having to answer. I never dreamed that the frank truth would seem an ingratitude.

"I have very sincerely admired Colonel Harvey's course. I have never doubted his editorial independence. In his support of me he has written in a manner singularly lucid and effective; and has always interpreted my opinions as I should wish to have them interpreted, often with an adequacy which I sincerely envied. But the rest of the country did not give him credit for editorial independence as I did; and when Colonel Harvey asked me whether the support of the *Weekly* was embarrassing me or not, I thought myself bound in frankness to tell him that it was.

"I did not suppose at the time that my answer to his question would result in the withdrawal of his brilliant support; because immediately after the question was asked and answered, we discussed means, if any there were, by which to remove the impression of the country that the editorial policy of Harper's Weekly was under the control of special interests. I did not need to be convinced that it was not, and I wished that means might be found to disabuse the whole country of that impression. I want to add that I retain a great admiration for Colonel Harvey and for his singular ability, and that nothing he feels obliged to do will alter my personal feeling in the least."[1]

The incident was at first alarming to Wilson's amateur managers, as the letters and telegrams plainly show. While it undoubtedly helped him with the people, for it drew again the line between the progressives and the conservatives and placed him more firmly than ever with the progressives, they worried about the effect upon the politicians who would control the convention of 1912, and probably choose the nominee. He must after all win the leaders!

The very sharpness of the attack however, gave impressive evidence of Wilson's growing prestige.

"And in the meanwhile, let it be remembered that this affair is but the latest of a series of bombs exploded at the feet of Governor Wilson, which, whatever else they may be, are an indisputable evidence of the formidable character which his prospects for the presidency have assumed in the eyes of his enemies."[2]

Walter H. Page consoled Wilson with the following letter:

---

[1] Dudley Field Malone, who was campaigning with Wilson, kept this document, which is partly typewritten, partly in Wilson's own hand.

[2] New York *Evening Post*, January 18, 1912.

I must confess to being very much distressed
that this matter should have taken such a shape as to involve me in an apparent ingratitude.  I ~~of course~~ did not
tell Colonel Harvey that the support of Harper's Weekly was
apparently embarrassing me in many parts of the country, without ~~~~ having first been asked the question point blank by
Colonel Harvey himself. ˄ It was very frank and generous of
~~him~~ to ask it, and I was very much embarrassed in having to
answer, ~~it truthfully.~~  I never dreamed that the ~~~~ ~~~~
I have very ~~much~~ admired Colonel Harvey's course.
I have never doubted ~~its entire~~ independence.  In his support
of me he has written in a manner singularly lucid and ~~admirable,~~
and has always interpreted my opinions as I should wish to have
them interpreted, often with a ~~lucidity~~ which I sincerely envied.
~~~~ But the rest of the country did not ~~~~ ~~the circumstances of his~~
~~support, as I was sure I knew them;~~ and when Colonel Harvey asked
me whether the support of the Weekly was embarrassing me or not,
I thought myself bound to tell him that it was.
    I did not suppose at the time that my ~~answer~~ would re-
sult in the withdrawal of his brilliant support; because immediately after the question was asked and answered, we discussed
~~the means~~ by which ~~it might be possible~~ to remove the ~~unjust~~
impression of the country that the editorial policy of Harper's
Weekly was under the control of special interests.  I did not
need to be convinced that it was not, and I ~~wish sincerely~~ that
means might be found to disabuse the whole country of that impression.  I want to add that I retain a great admiration for Colonel
Harvey ~~'s course in this matter,~~ and for his singular ability, and
that nothing ~~that~~ he feels obliged to do will alter my personal
feeling in the least.

FACSIMILE OF AN EXPLANATION OF THE HARVEY-
WATTERSON EPISODE PREPARED BY MR. WILSON, BUT
NEVER PUBLISHED.

MY DEAR WILSON:

As I read the public mind the Harvey incident is having a good effect and will continue to have. Harvey enabled you to speak out on Wall Street without making an attack on Wall Street. Everybody by this time is asking himself, "Well, ought Governor Wilson have lied to Harvey by evading the question or by softening his answer?" Then, too, it's pretty generally understood, except in boss and poker circles, that it is necessary to incur Marse Henry's rhetoric if you have any positive value or character. You've put him precisely where he belongs—"a fine old gentleman." That is friendly. Yet, to those who know, the area of inference is large. Leave him there. Nothing can vanquish him like silence. It's the one thing he can't understand or tilt with.

And, of course, the main matter, which Colonel Watterson has tried to obscure, hasn't been forgtoten—the popular inference about Harvey's backing. You've answered that suspicion or fear—of having the support of Wall Street—without making any attack on anybody in Wall Street.

I think the incident is working good results. And, so far as I can see, it is a positive asset. You are even saved the trouble of making any explanation!

Again, as often, the right sort of enemies turn out to be more valuable than the wrong sort of friends.

Very heartily yours,<br>WALTER H. PAGE[1]

Wilson responded to Page's letter:

"I have found it very difficult to tell just what the effect of the extraordinary performance of Colonel Harvey and Colonel Watterson has been, and I value your judgment and trust your powers of observation as I do those of few other men, and then it is always delightful to hear you put a thing. The very statement is convincing."[2]

One tremendous bomb remained to be exploded. Rumours of the impending attack were whispered about for days: "a shot that would finish Wilson," that "would

---

[1]January 22, 1912. *The Life and Letters of Walter H. Page,* Vol. III, pp. 14–15.
[2]January 25, 1912.

open Bryan's eyes," but the bomb itself was held back so that it would have the greatest possible effect upon the gathering of the Democratic clans for the annual Jackson Day dinner at Washington on January 8th. This meeting, in convention years, has long been regarded as the most important, except the national convention itself, of any held by the party. Here the plans for the convention are discussed and settled, here at the great banquet the candidates are put through their paces, and their availability thoroughly tested. It is indeed the beginning of the presidential campaign.

Two days before this great meeting, the New York *Sun* published the private letter which Wilson had written to Adrian H. Joline, a trustee of Princeton University, nearly five years before in which he said:

"Would that we could do something, at once dignified and effective, to knock Mr. Bryan once for all into a cocked hat!"[1]

Joline, a corporation lawyer of New York, a director in large enterprises, had become a bitter opponent of Wilson in the Princeton controversies,[2] and was now willing to give publicity to a private letter in order to injure him. To shake Bryan's confidence in Wilson would do more than anything else to destroy his chances.

Wilson's friends were all but panic-stricken by this incident. It was a political sensation. Wilson refused to comment upon it. Bryan was the guest of Josephus Daniels at Raleigh, North Carolina, on his way north to the Jackson Day dinner. When a reporter showed him the Joline letter, Bryan asked what paper he represented.

"The New York *Sun*."

"In that case," said Bryan promptly, "you may just

---

[1]April 29, 1907.

[2]Wilson had helped to defeat him in 1910 as a candidate for trustee of Princeton University.

say that if Mr. Wilson wants to knock me into a cocked hat, he and the *Sun* are on the same platform. That's what the *Sun* has been trying to do to me since 1896."[1]

He did not enlarge upon this statement, nor would he express any further opinion when called on the long-distance telephone by one of Wilson's excited supporters.[2] Daniels, a true friend of both men, urged him not to make any statement until Wilson could be consulted.

". . . I do not think you are the man to speak. It seems it is Mr. Wilson's turn to do the talking, if any is to be done. He may say something that will put another light on it."[3]

No other topic was more excitedly discussed by the gathering Democrats than this so-called attack on Bryan, the most powerful leader of the party, by Wilson, one of its most notable candidates. What would Bryan do? How would Wilson explain?

Wilson's own reaction was expressed in a letter written the day before the meeting:

"I am on my way down to Washington, where I am to speak to-morrow evening. The Democratic National Committee is to meet there to-morrow (which is Jackson's birth-day) and the banquet in the evening is to be a grand dress parade of candidates for the presidential nomination on the Democratic ticket. I hate the whole thing, but it is something 'expected' of me by my friends and backers, and, after all, an honest and sincere man need not be embarrassed by being put on exhibition. . . .

"There is a merry war on against me. I am evidently regarded as the strongest candidate at present, for all the attacks are directed against me, and the other fellows are not bothered. Kind one-time friends are giving to the

---

[1] Josephus Daniels, in the *Saturday Evening Post*, September 5, 1925.
[2] Thomas J. Pence.
[3] Josephus Daniels, in the *Saturday Evening Post*, September 5, 1925.

newspapers letters I wrote them before I became of public
consequence in which I expressed uncomplimentary opinions of Mr. Bryan. Rumours are sedulously set afoot that
there is a letter which various persons have seen or been
told the contents of in which Mr. Cleveland said that he
thought I 'lacked intellectual integrity,' or words to that
effect,—&c. &c. No doubt these things will have their effect and will turn various people against me, and this rain
of small missiles makes me feel like a common target for
the malicious (by the way, practically all the darts are
supplied by the Princetonians who hate me), and somewhat affect my spirits for a day at a time (the strongest
nerves wince under persistent spite); but for the most
part I go serenely on my way. I believe very profoundly in
an overruling Providence, and do not fear that any real
plans can be thrown off the track. It may not be intended
that I shall be President,—but that would not break my
heart—and I am content to await the event,—doing what
I honourably can, in the meantime, to discomfit mine
enemies!"[1]

[1]Woodrow Wilson to Mary A. Hulbert, January 7, 1912.

# CHAPTER V

# CANDIDATE FOR THE PRESIDENCY

... principles have no anniversaries.
*Jackson Day Address, January 8, 1912.*

Let those who can see lead those who cannot, but as seeing the interest of those who cannot lead as well as their own.
*Notes for an address, April 22, 1910.*

Absolute identity with one's cause is the first and great condition of successful leadership.
*"John Bright," in the University of Virginia Magazine, March 1880.*

The only thing that can ever make a free country is to keep a free and hopeful heart under every jacket in it, and then there will be an irrepressible vitality, then there will be an irrepressible ideal. . . .
*Jackson Day Address, January 8, 1912.*

## I. THE CRUCIAL JACKSON DAY DINNER

THE Jackson Day dinner has been compared with the opening day of the Kentucky Derby in which the favourite racers are paraded before the assembled spectators. Every important Democrat in the nation is supposed to be there; the party members of the Senate and House, state and city leaders, editors of notable Democratic papers—and all the candidates for the presidency.

Wilson's friends well knew the importance of this gathering. Wilson himself at first objected to being present: he thought it beneath the dignity of a presidential candidate to be thus exhibited. His friends, however, insisted. It was in a way the formal introduction of their candidate to the leaders of the party, to many if not most of whom he was still personally unknown. When the Joline letter was published they argued that he must meet the issue face to face.

Immediately upon Wilson's arrival in Washington, a conference of his close friends was called at the Willard Hotel. McCombs, of course, was there, and Henry Morgenthau and Tumulty and Dudley Field Malone. Everything was going wrong! Not only had the Joline letter caused a tremendous sensation, but the attitude of William Randolph Hearst, a problem in every Democratic campaign, required peremptory attention. One of Hearst's right-hand men, John Temple Graves, was on the ground asking embarrassing questions. Hearst's chain of newspapers might prove a formidable factor in the campaign.

Wilson's managers were also worried about one of those small miscarriages which, at such times, obscures even the profoundest issues. It was discovered that seats at the dinner accredited to New Jersey had been trickily assigned to Nugent, Wilson's most uncompromising enemy. A large delegation of Jerseymen who were the Governor's friends were angrily besieging his managers. A hostile claque at the banquet, from his own state, led by Nugent, was no matter for joking!

Wilson's advisers urged him to make an immediate statement regarding the Joline letter so that the effect might be somewhat neutralized before the dinner took place. Wilson sat down at the table, drew some of the hotel stationery toward him, and began to draft a statement.[1] He said, among other things:

"The Joline letter merely illustrates my habit,—I hope not a bad habit, however impolitic,—of speaking bluntly the opinions I entertain. I was merely expressing my judgment as a private citizen deeply concerned for the

---

[1]His fragmentary notes are still in the possession of Mr. Malone.

practical success of the party to which I have all my life belonged. . . .

"I am not singular in having been one of the many Democrats who voted for him [Bryan] at the polls while wishing that his leadership might have been that of the teacher and tribune of the people, and not that of the candidate. Office could not add to the great name and place he has made for himself in the history of the country, —and the loss of it cannot deprive him of his undisputed hold upon the affection and confidence of the people."

Before he had finished his statement, Josephus Daniels came in and was immediately pounced upon by Wilson's friends who knew that he had been Bryan's host. We have Daniels's own account of what happened:

"'What did Bryan say?' I was asked.

"'Isn't it better,' I said with a smile, to Governor Wilson, 'to let me tell you first what I said to Bryan?'

"Wilson smiled one of his inimitable smiles of inquiry and asked, 'What did you say to him?'

"My answer was:

"'I said, "Bryan, you must give these college presidents time to catch up with us."'"[1]

Wilson decided, finally, not to publish the preliminary statement he had prepared.

"After all, wouldn't it be better, without seeming to be on the defensive, for me in my address to-night to express my real sentiments as to Mr. Bryan's great service to the party and the country?"

In the meantime Malone, with Senator O'Gorman, had gone to see Bryan and found him "very generous, indeed splendid." Malone quotes Bryan:

"I believe that when Mr. Wilson wrote that letter to Joline, he believed it. It doesn't follow that he believes it now. If the big financial interests think that they are

[1] Josephus Daniels in the *Saturday Evening Post*, September 5, 1925.

going to make a rift in the progressive ranks of the Democratic party by such tactics, they are mistaken. But if
Wilson can correct any false impression in the public
mind, as I hope he will find it possible to do, it will be helpful all around."[1]

The Hearst situation came up at the luncheon which
followed, raised by Wilson's old college friend, Frank P.
Glass, then editor of a newspaper in Alabama. Glass reported that John Temple Graves was opposed to Wilson,
saying that Wilson had refused to accept Hearst's invitation to dinner, or even to meet him. Wilson told his friends
that he would make no terms with Hearst:

"I want the Democratic presidential nomination and
I am going to do everything I can, legitimately, to get it,
but if I am to grovel at Hearst's feet, I will never have it!"[2]

It was a crowded day, indeed. At five Wilson spoke before the National Press Club:

"Even if a man has written letters it ought not to embarrass him if they are published. Even if a man changes
his mind it ought not to embarrass him."

The great dinner took place in the evening at the
Raleigh Hotel. Wilson's friends had met the difficulty regarding the members of the Jersey delegation who were
unable to attend the banquet by organizing an "overflow
dinner" at another hotel. Wilson attended and made a
speech which aroused his friends to a high pitch of enthusiasm, and at the same time put him in mettle for the
crucial address later in the evening. He knew, and his
friends knew, that he might make or ruin his chances
upon this, his first appearance before the assembled party
leaders of the nation.

It was the greatest gathering of the kind ever held up to
that time. Over seven hundred guests were present.

[1]Dudley Field Malone to the author.
[2]Frank P. Glass to the author, quoting Woodrow Wilson.

Senator O'Gorman of New York was toastmaster; and there were at least five candidates for the presidency in attendance. Bryan, as the most notable leader, occupied a place of honour at the speakers' table, Wilson sat between Senator Pomerene of Ohio and Joseph W. Folk, former governor of Missouri. Champ Clark, Senator Kern of Indiana, Alton B. Parker, Democratic candidate for the presidency in 1904, and William Randolph Hearst were also at the speakers' table. Tammany Hall was represented by its chieftain, Boss Murphy, who was strongly opposed to Wilson; and the powerful leader from Illinois, Roger Sullivan, was also present. Underwood of Alabama, Marshall of Indiana, Foss of Massachusetts, though not at the speakers' table, were more or less avowed candidates. Colonel George Harvey, whose "break" with Wilson was then being hotly discussed in the press, did not come up to greet his former friend. Just in front of the speakers' table sat the little group of Wilson's New Jersey enemies headed by Boss Nugent. They refrained from joining in the applause when Wilson appeared; when they attempted, a little later, during Wilson's address, to express their disapproval, a cry of "Shame" went up from the group around them.

Every eye was on Bryan, who was received with a "flattering demonstration." What would be his greeting to Wilson? It was one of those situations, involving political drama, in which he delighted. Everyone knew that he had been hesitating—at least before the Joline letter—between Clark and Wilson. He now greeted Clark with cordiality, and then promptly stepped over to meet Wilson. He put his hand on Wilson's shoulder and "they talked for several minutes."

Harmony is always the keynote of this preliminary dinner. No matter how many feuds there may be, get the party together!

Wilson was called upon after all the speakers had appeared except Bryan. No address was awaited with such interest and curiosity as his. Would he make the same impression upon the hard-shelled politicians of the party that he had been making upon the people of the South and West? And what would he say about Bryan?

Wilson lost no time in meeting the personal issue that confronted him. Taking as his cue the appeal for harmony, he said of Bryan:

"We have differed as to measures; it has taken us sixteen years and more to come to any comprehension of our community of thought in regard to what we ought to do. What I want to say is that one of the most striking things in recent years is that with all the rise and fall of particular ideas, with all the ebb and flow of particular proposals, there has been one interesting fixed point in the history of the Democratic party, and that fixed point has been the character and the devotion and the preachings of William Jennings Bryan.

"I, for my part, never want to forget this: That while we have differed with Mr. Bryan upon this occasion and upon that in regard to the specific things to be done, he has gone serenely on pointing out to a more and more convinced people what it was that was the matter. He has had the steadfast vision all along of what it was that was the matter and he has, not any more than Andrew Jackson did, not based his career upon calculation, but has based it upon principle."

In this tribute, Wilson took exactly the position he had taken for several years regarding Bryan, that he was a great preacher, sound in his diagnosis, true in his principles. He said nothing of Bryan's remedies, nor did he refer to his presidential aspirations.

Wilson's address made a singular impression. It was a new kind of political oratory. He did not make the eagle scream. He did not invoke grandiloquently the memories of Jefferson and Jackson. His speech was short—shorter than any other made on that evening. It was direct, it was simple. It struck straight at the problems of the day.

"Now, what has been the matter? The matter has been that the government of this country was privately controlled and that the business of this country was privately controlled; that we did not have genuine representative government and that the people of this country did not have the control of their own affairs.

"What do we stand for here to-night and what shall we stand for as long as we live? We stand for setting the government of this country free and the business of this country free."

Every account of that great gathering agrees in recognizing the decisive effect of Wilson's address:

"His speech revealed to these men a new power in the party. . . . The audience progressed from rapt attention to enthusiasm."[1]

The touch at the close of the address in which Wilson turned to Bryan with "a really Chesterfieldian gesture"—"Let us apologize to each other that we ever suspected or antagonized one another; let us join hands once more all around the great circle of community of counsel and of interest which will show us at the last to have been indeed the friends of our country and the friends of mankind"—these last words brought a roar of appreciative applause.

To more than one of those present the face of the Great Commoner, during Wilson's address, was a study. He turned about in his chair, fixing his eyes on the speaker, and listened intently. For sixteen years he had been the all but unchallenged leader of his party; he had been three times its candidate for the presidency; in spite of defeat he was still its dominating figure. There is no doubt that

---

[1] Henry Morgenthau, *All In a Life-time*, pp. 142–143.

Wilson's address made a powerful, if not determinative, impression upon him. He told a friend after the dinner:

"It was the greatest speech in American political history."[1]

Some of those present looked upon Bryan's address, which followed, as his "abdication." The time had come for new men, new leaders free from the asperities of the past. For himself he was willing to march in the ranks to secure victory for the principles to which they were all devoted. He sat down amid tremendous applause. But he had given no intimation, shrewd politician that he was, as to whether he really favoured Wilson or Clark for the nomination, or whether, indeed, he considered himself wholly out of the running.

The reaction of the dinner upon Wilson's fortunes was immediate. The "rain of small missiles" aimed to destroy him had proved futile. He had actually turned the Joline letter to his advantage. George Harvey was there to observe the effect of his "break" with Wilson: what must have been his inner reaction? The newspapers on the following morning gave more space to Wilson's address than to any other; his headquarters became "the Mecca of the politicians."

"Wilson Leads in Clash of Booms," the New York *World* headed a dispatch.[2]

Some of the bosses were apparently won over. Just as Wilson was leaving to take the train for Trenton, Roger Sullivan, Illinois boss, greeted him in a friendly way and said:

"That was a great speech, Governor. I cannot say to you now just what the Illinois delegation will do, but you may rely upon it, I will be there when you need me."[3]

---

[1] Judge Robert S. Hudspeth to the author, quoting Bryan.

[2] January 9, 1912.

[3] Joseph P. Tumulty, *Woodrow Wilson As I Know Him*, p. 98.

The Jackson Day dinner was the turning point. In the meeting of the Democratic National Committee held on the following day, thirty-two of the fifty-two members present expressed a preference for Wilson as the candidate of the party.

"It begins now to 'look like business'. I like it less than I did before!"[1]

To a man of Wilson's strange, sensitive inner life, with its craving for quietude and friendship, such triumphs were always bitter-sweet. And so often they were marred by events of which the public knew nothing, so often the real and deep fruits of victory were snatched away. When Wilson returned to New Jersey he heard that his old friend Hibben, from whom he had parted, had been elected president of Princeton University. It was a blow that cut him to the heart.

"The worst has happened at the University," he wrote a friend. "Hibben has been elected president!"[2]

## II. THE ELIMINATION OF LA FOLLETTE

The strategy of Wilson's pre-convention campaign— five months, from the Jackson Day dinner to the Baltimore convention—was extremely simple. The country was now thoroughly progressive; the main stream of public opinion was setting irresistibly toward reform. It had even its revolutionary fringes. In January and February of that year (1912) great strikes, notably those in the textile centers of New England, were inspired by no mere demand for wage readjustments; they were led by Communists; they were frankly Socialist. The entire atmosphere was surcharged with emotion. "Onward

[1]Woodrow Wilson to Mary A. Hulbert, January 14, 1912.

[2]While this represented Wilson's real reaction, it was unfair to Hibben and to the University. See pp. 312–313, this volume.

Christian Soldiers" roared the delegates, a little later, at Roosevelt's convention. Bryan, La Follette, Debs had been preparing the way.

The leader who could, in all this chaos, place himself indisputably at the head of the progressive movement and yet keep his party united behind him—the second element in his strategy was as important as the first—would in all probability be nominated and elected.

Wilson and his friends were by no means alone in their perception of the grand strategy of the campaign. La Follette saw it; so did Roosevelt. Each was attempting to lead the progressive movement, and yet to keep his party behind him. From the beginning, the conservative candidates, Taft the Republican, Harmon the Democrat, had not the ghost of a chance to win.

We have, then, a political elimination race. Wilson must eliminate, one after another, his progressive rivals, those in the Democratic party that he might be nominated, those in the Republican party that he might be elected. La Follette, as we shall see, was the first to go down; Bryan and Champ Clark disappeared in the Democratic convention; Roosevelt, the greatest fighter of them all, survived until the election in November.

It was a race not the less grim for being, at that time, as impersonal as it was inevitable. Wilson frankly admired La Follette, and spoke again and again of the remarkable progressive record in Wisconsin under La Follette's leadership. He had for years approved much of Roosevelt's course. He liked Bryan. He had indeed to hold back upon some of his enthusiastic supporters who tended to become intensely partisan, and to attack his rivals rather than to advocate his principles. He wished above everything to do no injury to the progressive cause by impugning its sincere leaders. He wished to attract the liberals of the nation regardless of party. At the very beginning of his campaign he wrote to one of his old and enthusiastic Virginia friends:

"May I drop a hint to you. There are thousands of warm friends of Mr. Bryan's in Virginia and all over the country. La Follette is regarded as a very high minded champion of progressive ideas, and I think that it is bad policy not only, but essentially unjust to indulge in flings at either of those men.

"I know that you will understand, my dear fellow, my taking the liberty of dropping this hint for our hearts work together in all things.

"The progress of the 'campaign' is certainly most interesting, and, on the whole, promising, and you are doing yeoman service."[1]

For the same reason Wilson would not attack Roosevelt. Even when the battle began to be hot and Roosevelt attacked him, he would not reply; he would not make a personal issue of what he considered a "campaign of principles." This was not meekness of spirit: it was good political tactics. He preserved, indeed, an "infuriating silence."

A remarkable study in political strategy might be based upon this brief and thrilling contest. It is doubtful if any such galaxy of popular leaders and orators ever before or since strode upon the stage in an American campaign. Bryan, Roosevelt, La Follette, Wilson—masters of their art—the supreme art of leading their fellow men. They were widely different in method: Roosevelt, the rough-rider of opinion, Bryan, the silvery-tongued evangelist, La Follette, denouncing the evils of the day like some Peter-the-Hermit. Champ Clark, who was Wilson's greatest rival in the Democratic party, did not march with these oratorical gladiators. He wooed the party leaders rather than the people.

[1] Woodrow Wilson to R. Heath Dabney, January 11, 1912.

Of them all, Wilson seemed the least conscious of the contest—at any rate the personal side of it. He was not, like La Follette and Roosevelt, carried away by a fury of denunciation: he did not, like Bryan, attempt to arouse his audiences to emotional revolt. His speeches, read years afterward, appear extraordinarily calm, steady—tending to the academic and expository. They do not lack fire or fervour, they do not blink the evils of the day, but the orator seems, above everything else, to reach his effect by the cool processes of reason. And the major impression is never denunciatory, never dismal. The present writer has read many of the speeches of all these orators fifteen or twenty years after; he heard some of them delivered; he knew personally the men themselves; and it seems to him that one of the essential elements of Wilson's power, as contrasted with the others, perhaps the chief element, was the sense of confidence he inspired, confidence in the nation, confidence in himself. He seemed never to need to shout. And, like being attracted to like, what he won from the people was confidence.

Three weeks after the Jackson Day dinner these contrasts, and Wilson's position as a leader of the Progressive movement, were vividly dramatized.

The Periodical Publishers' Association of America held its annual dinner in Philadelphia on February 2nd. For years these dinners had been national events, gathering together the foremost authors, editors, and magazine publishers of the country. The dinner of 1912, which was under the general direction of Cyrus H. K. Curtis of the *Saturday Evening Post*, was designed to be the greatest in the history of the association—as it proved to be the last! Benjamin Franklin was appropriately its patron saint; and this year, for the first time, the important newspaper owners and editors of the country were invited to join with the periodical publishers. Over seven hundred men sat down to dinner at the Bellevue-Stratford Hotel.

No such inclusive gathering as this, representing the makers of public opinion in America, had ever before been held, nor has there been anything quite like it since. All shades of opinion were represented. Whatever their personal opinions might be, they recognized that the greatest political fact in the nation at that time was the progressive movement. They had therefore invited as their chief speakers the two outstanding leaders in that movement, La Follette, the Republican, Wilson, the Democrat. Many of those present had never seen or heard either of them; it was an opportunity to compare the two men, to test their appeal, to form judgments that might assist, editorially, in the advancing campaign. While it was not to be a debate, like the meetings between Lincoln and Douglas, it was nevertheless a test that might easily make or break either leader.

La Follette, at that time, was better known politically than Wilson. He had been for many years in public life. He had come up fighting every inch of his way, a bold, hard-hitting, impetuous reformer. He had fought railroad interference in public affairs, he had fought tariff privileges and the "money trust," he had fought corruption in high places. He had wrested the governorship of his state, Wisconsin, from the control of the bosses who had dominated its legislature for many years, he had himself become a veritable political dictator; he was now serving his second term as United States senator from Wisconsin. He was at that time the rising leader of the progressive wing of the Republican party, an avowed candidate for the presidency. Roosevelt, who had not yet flung his hat in the ring, had intimated that he might support La Follette. More than any other man in the country at that time, except possibly Bryan, whose star was sinking, La Follette typified Western insurgency. It did not at that time look at all improbable that he might win control of the Republican party and be nominated at the June convention. La Follette himself felt assured of success.

With such a leader as La Follette nominated by the Republicans,[1] the natural course for the Democrats would be to counter with a more conservative candidate—possibly Underwood, probably Clark, certainly not Bryan or Wilson.

The author of this biography, who was present at the dinner, recalls the hair-trigger interest with which many of those in attendance looked forward to the appearance of the two leaders. He was himself at that time a supporter of La Follette, believing that the surest way to victory for the reforms the country demanded was by way of the Republican rather than the Democratic party—if La Follette could win control.

An examination of the documents shows that Wilson gave less than his usual care to the preparation of his address. He had been in Virginia on the day before, a hard-driven programme in which he had addressed both houses of the legislature, besides making several lesser speeches. When he arrived in Philadelphia late in the afternoon, he wrote down on two sheets of the Bellevue-Stratford hotel paper a few brief notes for his address:

"Voices old and new . . .

"Old shells of every kind are being broken . . .

"All things have become new . . .

"But the fundamentals stand undisturbed, and the laws of human nature . . ."

La Follette, on the other hand, wrote out his address

---

[1] As he might possibly have been if Roosevelt, the popular Republican leader, had been as willing to subordinate his own personal interests and ambitions as was Bryan, the popular Democratic leader.

with the greatest care, working and reworking many of the paragraphs. He had been for days agitated by complications and defections in his own campaign organization; and at the last minute his daughter, to whom he was devoted, fell suddenly ill and was hurried away to the hospital for an operation. He did not arrive in the banquet hall until the dinner was over and the speaking had begun.

Don C. Seitz, manager of the New York *World*, was the toastmaster. Wilson sat between him and Cyrus H. K. Curtis. Mr. Seitz describes what happened:

"Ten o'clock came and my turn came with it. The audience settled back and Mr. Curtis shooed out the waiters. Then Woodrow Wilson, who sat on his right, said something to him. I did not hear it. A reporter from the *Inquirer* had my ear, begging on behalf of the boys that the Governor be called first, as they had La Follette's speech in manifold, but not a word of Wilson's. The break with Col. George Harvey had just occurred, and the Colonel's goggle eyes were looking straight at the speakers' table from the middle of the room. The boys scented something good. I promised to call Wilson first. Then I heard Mr. Curtis say: 'You will have to settle that with Mr. Seitz. He is to preside.' Without waiting for the Governor to express his desire, he went on: 'The Governor does not wish to speak first. He would like to be second or third.'

"'I don't know about that,' I replied. 'I have just promised a reporter from the *Inquirer* to have him speak first.'

"Mr. Wilson leaned forward. 'I have a mighty poor opinion of the Philadelphia *Inquirer*,' he said.

"'You can have whatever opinion you like,' I rejoined, 'but it doesn't pay to go back on reporters.'

"I then argued that this was a great occasion, with an audience such as he was likely never to meet again and full of expectancy. It was a great chance; and one he ought not to mislay."

When Wilson arose, "he was in a temper," remarking:

"From our introducers, as from our traducers, good Lord deliver us!"[1]

"Then followed," reports Mr. Seitz, "one of the clearest and ablest addresses it was ever my fortune to hear."[2]

Wilson had supremely the gift of putting himself at once in intimate, even confidential, contact with his audience. He was easy, he had humour, he was urbane. He had the gift of liking his audiences.

"I face this audience with mingled feelings, because I remember how much I used to respect publishers, before they published anything for me, and I knew how far they could be imposed upon. I used to be afraid that they would not publish what I offered them, but now I am afraid they will!"

Having established the contact, he proceeded to his argument, opening his subject with perfect orderliness and clarity and deepening into earnest eloquence:

"Everything is new and, therefore, every question that we touch wears a new aspect and must be approached from a new angle and, naturally, with new men. . . .

"When I hear gentlemen discuss the tariff question as if it were the tariff question that Mr. Blaine discussed, for example, I know they have been asleep ever since Mr. Blaine's day. . . .

"Progressiveness means not getting caught standing still when everything else is moving."

The men who made the Constitution were "far-seeing

---

[1]Don C. Seitz, in *McNaught's Monthly*. This differs somewhat from the official report, but it is in accordance with what many of those present remember.

[2]Owen Wister, who was present at the dinner, says: "He spoke with flawless art; his dignity and upstanding presence commanded attention, while his voice made every symmetrical sentence melodious. The whole company, easily eight hundred men, sat under the spell."—Roosevelt, *The Story of a Friendship*, p. 299.

geniuses"; but their emphasis was upon principles, not upon forms. It was the need of the hour to get back to those principles:

". . . we are not steering by forms of government, we are steering by principles of government."

The entire address, indeed, was a powerful plea to look the facts of American life in the face, to recognize the need of progress, but to guide that progress by the old principles, the deep-lying spirit of American institutions. It was a speech that held that restless dinner audience to the last man. It was progressive, but it was sane. It was, moreover, short!

Mr. Seitz goes on to say:

"Wilson received a great ovation from the audience and sat down in triumph.[1] Blankenburg[2] followed with a short talk, in the course of which La Follette came in. Wilson greeted him cordially."

It is difficult, even to one who was there, even with all the facts in hand, to explain La Follette's tragic failure. He spoke for two hours and ten minutes—to an audience that had already been for nearly four hours in their seats. "He repeated himself endlessly." He was from the first bitterly antagonistic to his audience: to the spirit of the occasion. He made a scathing attack upon the newspaper press—upon some of the very editors and publishers who sat before him, who were his hosts.

"After an hour of this the crowd became disorderly. . . . scores left the room and took refuge in the rathskeller. . . . It was twenty minutes past one when the terrible tirade came to a close."[3]

There is no possible doubt that La Follette came to the

[1]Wilson's speech was widely printed and commented upon in the press of the country. The Philadelphia *Record* on the following morning headed its report of the dinner: "Wilson Hero at Big Feast."

[2]Progressive mayor of Philadelphia.

[3]Don C. Seitz, in *McNaught's Monthly*.

dinner worn out with labour and with anxiety. But it was not this alone that led to his extraordinary failure.

He had begun his address:

"The great issue before the American people to-day is the control of their own government."

It was exactly what Wilson was saying, what Bryan was saying, what Roosevelt was saying. They were all attacking the "money-trust," the "tariff mongers," the power of privileged interests in American public life. They were demanding justice for the common man.

But La Follette was of the West, Western: he was an insurgent of the insurgents. He suspected the East: he dramatized the debtor West he had known so well, whose wrongs he had felt so deeply.

He was a powerful orator, without humour, without urbanity, but with tremendous sincerity. There was much of the old Puritan spirit in the man—fierce, incorruptible, independent. He had the kind of vivid imagination which easily transformed his enemies into veritable devils, made them targets for his ready ink bottle. No more lovable man, in his own family, in his own close circle, ever lived. But he had built his career, risen to power and place, upon remorseless exposure, relentless denunciation.

His speech at the publishers' dinner, carefully prepared, was, after all, the quintessence of La Follette and his methods, as it was the expression, raised to the $n$th degree, of Western insurgency. The result, if he had been in his usual health and strength, could not have been far different. Western insurgency, however true its diagnosis, however real its charges, was less than national in its appeal. There was an East, and it was not entirely vile. Moreover, La Follette, and the Western insurgents generally, tended to look to readjustments in mechanism for the cure of the evils they perceived with such feeling clarity: tariff changes, regulation of railroad rates, and the like. While they no longer advocated the outright panaceas of the earlier Western reformers, fiat money, free silver, there was nevertheless something panaceistic—if there is such a word—about their categorical programmes.

Wilson was far more national-minded. He went deeper. He was cautious about specific reforms: he was for restoration of the spirit upon which democratic institutions were founded. It was not, as he said, the "items of reform," but the spirit of reform, that was important. Democracy to Wilson was not a programme at all, it was not a constitution; it was a character, a habit of life. It might use old tools or new to accomplish its ends.

It was this contrast between the two men that was deeply sensed by many of those who attended the fateful dinner at Philadelphia.

La Follette's address eliminated him as a serious contender for national leadership of the progressive movement. He could retain his power in his own state: he was no longer an important factor in the great struggle of 1912.

With La Follette eliminated, Roosevelt, a far more formidable rival, a leader like Wilson with a national appeal, immediately came forward. He had undoubtedly been awaiting a favourable opportunity. After the publishers' dinner, and partly as a result of what happened there, he "flung his hat in the ring."

### III. STRUGGLE FOR DELEGATES

Roosevelt's roaring entrance upon the political scene caused Wilson no uneasiness. It actually made Republican opposition less dangerous. The virulent struggle that followed between Roosevelt and La Follette for the progressive leadership of the party, with both knifing Taft, left the Republican party in dire straits. Much as Roosevelt, at a later time, hated Wilson, he probably gave him as much real political assistance as any other human being.

"Nothing new is happening in politics, except Mr. Roosevelt, who is always new, being bound by nothing in the heavens above or in the earth below. He is now rampant and very diligently employed in splitting the party wide open—so that we may get in!"[1]

On the other hand, the threatened split in the Republican party, by vastly encouraging the Democrats, increased Wilson's difficulties. Nomination at Baltimore, it was clearly perceived, probably meant election. Everything depended, therefore, upon capturing delegates at the forthcoming primaries and conventions of the party. It was in short the kind of problem in political manipulation in which Wilson was weakest and his leading opponent, Champ Clark, an old-fashioned wheel-horse politician, most expert.

McCombs, the manager of Wilson's organization, though an amateur, was acutely conscious of the difficulties of the situation. He was eager to play the traditional and fascinating political game, dicker with the state bosses, and even build up a little machine of his own that could be depended upon in an emergency. He felt himself hampered because he dared not commit Wilson to any "recognition," or promise any favours.

He urged Wilson to modify his attitude toward the bosses—bosses were after all only local leaders—and he sought to minimize Wilson's growing understanding with Bryan—though he sought Bryan's help in certain Western states—because it was offensive to some of the powerful Eastern organizations, especially Tammany Hall.

Wilson doubted profoundly any such tactics. He had had his lesson in New Jersey. He knew what it meant to be nominated by the bosses: he knew the price a candidate was expected to pay. He was a progressive, ap-

[1]Woodrow Wilson to Mary A. Hulbert, March 10, 1912.

pealing to progressives, of whom Bryan was an outstanding leader. The party machinery was largely in the control of the "regulars," the conservatives. He must win, if at all, by going over the heads of the older leaders, by force of public opinion; by encouraging and working with the newer and younger men of the party—like the revolters in Texas, in Pennsylvania, and elsewhere. If he had followed McCombs's advice he would never, in all probability, have been nominated. An "appeal to the people," a "solemn referendum" was, throughout his political career, his sovereign method. He had unbounded faith in the people. If he could speak to enough of them, he felt that they would rise in their wrath and exert the necessary pressure upon the leaders.

Was he right in this faith? Can the people be depended upon, always, to act wisely upon great questions of state? Wilson himself in his earlier years, speaking as a political philosopher, doubted it profoundly. In a paper written in 1898, he approved the views of Sir Henry Maine:

"He is right . . . when he says that 'the fact that what is called the will of the people really consists in their adopting the opinion of one person or a few persons admits of a very convincing illustration from experience.' 'The ruling multitude will only form an opinion by following the opinion of somebody: it may be, of a great party leader; it may be, of a small local politician; it may be, of an organized association; it may be, of an impersonal newspaper.'"

When he spoke of trusting the people, was it in reality he himself, the "great party leader," he was trusting? And is it the same thing to trust the people when, after years of agitation and exhortation, their minds are made up—when there is a definite current of popular opinion, as there was in 1912—and to trust the same people when they are apathetic or in doubt? Is it the same thing to

trust the people when you are going with them and they
with you, because you believe the same things, as it would
be when the people are going one way and you quite
another? The people not only follow their prophets, they
crucify them.

Be all this as it may, Wilson's almost mystical faith
that the people would follow him if he could speak to
enough of them was not only an enormous political asset
at that time, but it reacted upon his own fiery spirit—gave
him the kind of super-power which comes in when doubt
goes out.

Wilson therefore tended to think with more or less scorn
of the scramble for delegates—even when he was helping
his own revolting organizations in states like Ohio; and he
was constantly holding back upon the chafing, high-
strung, erratic, and often undependable McCombs. He
insisted, to McCombs's chagrin, of speaking of his organization as a "literary bureau," for he thought of it
primarily as a medium for circulating his speeches, giving
wide publicity to the principles he was advocating and the
issues he was discussing. In this respect, indeed, the
service performed by a group of devoted journalists, under
the direction of McCombs and McAdoo, can scarcely be
overestimated.[1] They made Wilson the man, and Wilson
the statesman, known to the people as he could have become known in no other way, since he could not, physically, meet and speak to everybody. The radio had not
been perfected!

While McCombs was all for as many speeches as Wilson
could possibly make, he did not of course share Wilson's
mystical faith in the people. Principles were all right, reforms were all right, but a candidate to be successful at
Baltimore must, after all, have the votes. Wilson might

---

[1] Among these men were Frank Parker Stockbridge, McKee Barclay, Byron R. Newton, Thomas J. Pence.

campaign for delegates: the state organizations in most cases would dominate their choice.

Wilson, nevertheless, adhered with unshakable determination to his course. When a man really has faith, he rests upon it. In January he began a series of speaking tours, which he continued, indefatigably, through February, March, and April, the period during which most of the delegates were chosen. He was so much away from Trenton that the New York *Sun*, barking relentlessly at his heels, called the New Jersey governorship "Wilson's travelling scholarship." Some even of his friends felt that he was neglecting his official duties in his own state, regretted "his too eager chase after the nomination." He spoke in Michigan, New Hampshire, Virginia, Kentucky, Illinois, Iowa, Pennsylvania, Kansas, Tennessee, Georgia, Maryland. He literally wore himself out with these labours. His personal letters refer again and again to his "utter weariness." "Every fibre of me is tired out every day."

"Every day is, with me, a sort of mêlée,—trying to get through with more things than one day can contain. . . . Last night I spent on the road! Yesterday was observed as St. Patrick's Day and I spoke at two dinners of the Friendly Sons of St. Patrick,—one at Elizabeth, the other at Montclair (I grow more talkative every day!). I left Montclair at 12:45 A.M., to come home by motor, and reached Princeton at 4:50, just as the dawn was showing itself,—having taken the wrong road twice and wandered through the sleeping country for four hours, to make fifty miles!"[1]

He was received everywhere on these tours with convincing enthusiasm:

"Since I wrote last I've been to Virginia, my own, my native land; and they gave me a royal welcome. A special train from Staunton, my birth-place, brought some

[1]Woodrow Wilson to Mary A. Hulbert, March 17, 1912.

two or three hundred men down (with the local band) some hundred and forty miles to greet me and cheer for me at Richmond and (after speaking to each house of the Legislature) I had, in the evening, an audience of about four thousand in a huge auditorium, and won them to me, everybody said."[1]

He had what he considered flattering publicity: newspaper comments were for the most part highly encouraging:

"It cannot be denied that the Governor of New Jersey made an excellent impression here. Democrats of all kinds came to hear him, and he performed the heretofore unknown miracle of accepting them all as Democrats, instead of separating them into Sullivanites, Harrisonites, Hearstites, and so on.

"The effect was astonishingly invigorating."[2]

In April he wrote from Syracuse, New York:

"I have just finished a big job,—a swing of six hundred miles through middle and western Illinois in which I made twenty odd speeches,—from the rear of the train, from benches in railway stations, from the steps of courthouses, and from the stages of crowded halls,—ending with *four* speeches in Chicago—one in each of the four distinctly marked sections of the conglomerate town! I am here to-day to dine with the Chamber of Commerce, and am *very* dull and sleepy with the physical reaction from the fatigue and excitement. I keep wonderfully well and strong. I suppose I am like a man living on strong stimulants."[3]

Both he and his friends were convinced by the enthusiasm he excited, by the favourable newspaper comments, by the flood of approving letters, that he was

---

[1] Woodrow Wilson to Mary A. Hulbert, February 4, 1912.
[2] Chicago *Evening Post*, February 12, 1912.
[3] Woodrow Wilson to Mary A. Hulbert, April 8, 1912.

really "getting the people." Was he? La Follette and his friends were equally convinced that *they* were getting the people.

"I have said that I never witnessed a deeper and more intense public interest, with all the outward manifestations of enthusiasm and devotion, than on this tour through Ohio, Michigan, and Illinois. . . .

"It was the most remarkable series of mid-winter meetings ever held. . . .

"My tour of these states was really a triumph."[1]

La Follette then goes on to publish pages of enthusiastic newspaper comment.

Roosevelt and his friends were also certain, absolutely certain, that they had the people.

Two things are perhaps clear. The reception of all three candidates was convincing evidence of the general popular feeling of the nation. It was progressive. Probably each candidate took to himself personally some of the cheering that was meant for the cause. But it is true that Wilson made a powerful impression wherever he appeared: and compared with the other candidates who had been all their lives in politics, had wide experience and an assured following, he advanced to the front rank of leadership with astonishing swiftness.

In spite, however, of Wilson's tremendous exertion to reach the people, in spite of his undeniably favourable popular reception, when the delegates began to be chosen, he did not get them. McCombs and the practical politicians appeared to be right. One after another the states in which he campaigned most valiantly went against him. Shouting is not always voting. The old established leadership, based so largely upon personal acquaintance, favours given and received—the "vast inertia of organization"— in most cases prevailed. Politics, after all, is a close pro-

---

[1]The autobiography of Robert M. La Follette, pp. 562, 563, 571.

fession: the outsider breaks through with difficulty. Wilson's attitude toward "Jim" Smith's machine in New Jersey, however much it might please the people, did not help him with the leaders in other states. It was shrewd tactics that sought to prove him an "ingrate" in politics.

Where there were not "favourite sons" whose interests were to be advanced, Champ Clark was the kind of candidate who appealed to the organization. He knew everybody in politics: he knew every cog and wheel in the machinery of the party. McCombs wrote to Wilson, setting forth Clark's power and urging Wilson to see more of the political leaders:

"Clark's organization is built up through members and ex-members of Congress with whom he has had a long and personal relationship. This is a very strong influence and it is having its effect.

"I was in Washington for an hour on my way here and was told of the adverse result in Kansas. We had by all odds the cream of the organization there with us, and they worked very hard, I am told. This illustrates the necessity of your sending for your friends in Congress and having them come to see you. They would be very glad to do it, and I think it would have great influence . . ."

Suffice it to say that not one of the states in which Wilson campaigned that spring chose Wilson delegates— except Pennsylvania, and that was divided. Two or three of the states, with uninstructed delegations, were supposed to be favourable to him, and in two or three others he had the cold comfort of being informed that he was "second choice"; but the results, as a whole, were heavily against him. Five of the states, including Roger Sullivan's Illinois, where Wilson's hopes were high, went to Clark, Illinois by the crushing majority of 140,000 votes. Kansas had seemed hopeful when Wilson spoke there, but Clark had the delegates. Clark also won Iowa, Kentucky, New

Hampshire, Maryland. Even Wilson's own native state of Virginia, which had received him so warmly in February, refused to follow him in April, and Georgia, the state in which he had spent his youth and begun his career as a lawyer, declared for Underwood. To cap the climax, New York, with its ninety votes, controlled by Tammany, was opposed to him. At one time he began to fear that he could not win enough of the delegates from his own state of New Jersey to make a respectable, much less a triumphant, impression at Baltimore.

There were, indeed, encouraging signs in other parts of the country. Texas stood like a rock in a weary land. Forty votes! Oklahoma, where Senator Gore had been his ardent supporter, gave him part of her delegates. The bold young reformers in Pennsylvania—led by Vance C. McCormick, A. Mitchell Palmer, William B. Wilson, George W. Guthrie, and Roland Morris, were bringing in sixty votes.[1] Several other states could also be depended upon for the first ballot.

But the results of the campaign were upon the whole discouraging. Wilson's chances, which had seemed so glowing on Jackson Day, which had been advanced so definitely at the publishers' dinner on February 2nd, declined steadily through March and April. May was the "black month"—the lowest ebb of Wilson's political fortunes. There was a time when the toiling candidate, though without remitting his struggle for a moment, admitted to intimate friends—as we shall see—that he did not expect to be nominated.

He was under constant attack, irritating and petty,

---

[1] Of these five leaders in Pennsylvania, two, William B. Wilson and A. Mitchell Palmer, became members of Wilson's cabinet; two, Guthrie and Morris, were appointed ambassadors by Wilson; and McCormick was chairman of the Democratic National Committee in 1916, and during the war filled one of the most responsible positions in the administration—chairman of the War Trade Board—and served as a member of the War Cabinet.

vague or vile rumours that could not be brought up into daylight and openly met. His enemies were now using the ammunition they had accumulated as a result of the minute study of his writings. No man who expects to go into politics should ever write books! Was there anywhere a critical reference to the Italians, the Germans, the Poles; had he spoken slightingly of labour, of the Church, of woman suffrage—it was now eagerly trotted out, translated, if necessary, and circulated where it would hurt him most. He was constantly having to meet such assaults:

"I beg that you will judge the passage in Volume 5 of my 'History of the American People,' to which you allude, in connection with its full context, and not by itself. I yield to no one in my ardent admiration for the great people of Italy, and certainly no one who loves the history of liberty should fail to accord to Italians a great place in the history of political freedom.

"I should be very much pained if I thought I had been guilty of an injustice. I was, in the passage alluded to, only deploring the coming to this country of certain lawless elements which I had supposed all thoughtful Italians themselves deplored. I was thinking only of the men who have once and again threatened to give to that whole, fine body of Italians, who have enriched American life, a reputation which they did not deserve. Certainly, the Italians I have known and honoured have constituted one of the most interesting and admirable elements in our American life."[1]

At a meeting held a little later in New York, under the auspices of the Hungarian League, a letter from him was read, explaining the references in his *History* to the Hungarians:

[1]Woodrow Wilson to Agostino De Biasi, editor of the Italian review, *Il Carroccio*, February 7, 1912.

"I was not speaking of a nation, but of certain elements which had recently disclosed themselves among our immigrants. I am perfectly willing to abide by any fair reading of the passage in my history, to which you probably allude.

"I pride myself on knowing something of the great history of Hungary; that history displays a struggle for liberty which all the world must admire and applaud. I know as well as any man can know what elements of strength and of energy the Hungarian people have contributed to the variety and richness of the American people. I do not distinguish Americans in my mind, but the country from which they come.

"If I have at any time deplored certain elements that have come to us in our later immigration, I count myself very unfortunate if I have been so awkward in my way of expressing what I had to say as to bring injustice to a people whom I admire and respect."

When he was in Chicago his suitcase was stolen from his hotel room by burglars "with undoubted political affiliations." Other valuable property in the room was left untouched; but the suitcase contained letters and other documents. It was a time when scandalous stories were being whispered about and the thieves were evidently seeking some documentary proof that would ruin him. When some of his friends expressed their concern, he said:

"No letter of mine, nothing I have ever written, could injure me if published."[1]

Wilson might speak stoutly enough in one of his letters of "constant bitter attacks, winning me new friends," but as a matter of fact, they cut him to the quick. ". . . I am tired of politics . . ." he writes, ". . . there is a lot of meanness in it, and of weary futile things which disgust sooner or later. . . ".

[1]The Misses Lucy and Mary Smith to the author.

When Mayor Gaynor of New York wrote in March, deploring Hearst's attacks, Wilson replied, on March 11th:

"Misrepresentation is the penalty which men in public life must expect in the course of their efforts to render service.

"The unfortunate fact is that there are probably hundreds of men in America of first-rate intellectual force, of genuine public spirit and broad patriotism, who would be of unmeasurable value to public service, but who are deterred from entering it because they shrink from this particular penalty.

"They preferred to pursue private careers, rather than expose themselves and their families to unfounded criticism and attack, and the country is thereby impoverished. Such attacks, moreover, create personal feeling and party factions, which render the task of government infinitely difficult for anyone who undertakes it. It is the more necessary, however, as I look at it, that these things should be borne with fortitude, if not indifference, in order that our duty may be rendered without regard to our personal feeling."

Not only were the attacks upon him constant and relentless—it was largely due to Hearst's opposition that he was making a losing fight in Illinois—but there were evidences of a combination against him among the other candidates, no doubt much exaggerated by Wilson's friends. Wilson wrote to Colonel House on March 15th:

"Your kind note of the 6th brought me great cheer when I most needed it. I have been a good deal discouraged by the news from Kansas and from Michigan, where we *ought* to have won, and thought of what you are doing puts me in heart again,—as does also the knowledge that we are soon to have your counsel here.

"Signs multiply that there is a combination of Clark, Underwood, and Harmon (with a division of territory quite after the manner of the industrial combinations), and the evidence that the combination is being financed from Wall Street falls short only of legal proof. It saddens me to see things done and alliances formed which may render the dear old party utterly unserviceable (as a free unit) to the Country."

There were other serious problems. Wilson's organization, limited as it was, gave him constant anxiety. McCombs was ill and irritable and jealous, and Wilson had to settle numerous squabbles. Some of his supporters felt that everything was running at loose ends. Criticisms appeared in the press, some of which struck indirectly at Wilson's own policy of emphasizing publicity at the expense of a greater effort to secure delegates.

"Almost every day now is marked by some development which emphasizes Woodrow Wilson's need of a campaign manager with large experience in practical politics. Until recently it has seemed virtually certain that Governor Wilson would go to Baltimore with more delegates than anyone else, but, while his popularity has not declined, the other candidates are out-generalling him. The situation is becoming serious. The Washington correspondent of the *News and Courier* sizes it up well when he says that, 'While it is plainly a case of the field against Wilson, the fact remains that the field seems to be winning nearly all the instructed delegates.' . . . The campaigns of Clark and Underwood are being pressed skillfully and the favourite-son endorsements may prove a very real danger to the New Jersey Governor. In Indiana, for example, Marshall has been endorsed, but Tom Taggart really controls the delegation. In Massachusetts, the name of Governor Foss has been put forward in the primaries, but the understanding is that the Democratic organization in that state is really for Clark, with Foss for second place. So it is going all along the line, while meantime the Wilson managers apparently are doing nothing beyond continuing the publicity work upon which they have been engaged. That has been very effective, but the time has come when it will not suffice of itself. Something more is needed now, and the cry of 'conspiracy,' upon which they seem to place great reliance, may do as much harm as good."[1]

McCombs and his co-workers, smarting under such charges, declared that they could not get results without more money. They had no well-organized sources like the old party machines; and the great financial leaders were generally against them. There were times when they had not a dollar in the bank; and when they had money, McCombs spent it like a prodigal. A few devoted friends were helping substantially. Wilson's old friend and classmate, Cleveland H. Dodge, was the largest contributor; Henry Morgenthau was advancing $4,000 a month; Frederick C. Penfield had come to the rescue with a check of $10,000 when the treasury was almost empty. In March, when things were beginning to look serious, Charles R. Crane came in with $5,000. McCombs, desperately beset, used his own money freely.[2]

When they did succeed in getting more money and extending their work, they were pounced upon by eager critics. Senator James A. Reed of Missouri, a strong Clark supporter, demanded in a speech at Detroit, March 21st:

"Where is all this money coming from for the Wilson campaign? I ask this question directly and in the nature of a challenge. Where is all this money coming from to

---

[1]Charleston *News and Courier*, March 30, 1912.

[2]Other generous contributors were Abram I. Elkus, John Martin, James Sprunt, Wilson's old friend of Wilmington, North Carolina, Edward A. Filene of Boston, Hugh McRae, John Barton Payne, Edward W. Sheldon; but a large part of the fund came from small contributors. Walter H. Page, Walter McCorkle, and William G. McAdoo had contributed earlier. The total collected during the pre-convention campaign was around $200,000.

open up headquarters in almost every state? Right here in Michigan you have two Wilson campaign managers drawing $150 a week each. The country has been flooded with campaign literature."

The anxious Bryan, alarmed by Reed's attack, wrote to Wilson:

"Letters are pouring in here reiterating the charge that you have a large campaign fund. The enclosed is a sample. I only call your attention to it to emphasize the importance of publicity."[1]

Walker W. Vick, of Wilson's organization, issued a reply to Reed's charges:

"All contributions to Governor Wilson's campaign fund have been spontaneous and voluntary from his personal and political friends mainly in small amounts. A contribution of $2 from a textile worker in Massachusetts was received to-day.

"It is true that there is a Wilson organization in practically every state throughout the Union, organized and being maintained by the friends, both personal and political, of Governor Wilson throughout these states, who see in his election the embodiment of clean government and progressive Democracy, and the hope of the Democratic party in resuming popular government."

Vick responded also with the retort political by inquiring how the Clark expenditures in Iowa, Arkansas, Wisconsin, and elsewhere were being met. As a matter of fact Wilson's organization used as much money, probably, as any other in the Democratic party.[2] This was not surprising, because Wilson's managers had to build from the bottom: they had no old organization behind them, no settled channels for influencing opinion.

---

[1]April 1, 1912.

[2]Roosevelt's organization is said to have expended more money than any other in the pre-convention campaign.

To add to Wilson's difficulties at this time, his state problems had become highly irritating. Having lost the Assembly in the November election, he had now a more or less hostile legislature to deal with. Smith and Nugent were doing their best to trip him up. He was having no such triumph as he had had the year before. Instead of enthusiastic coöperation, he was more or less at loggerheads with the legislature. His opponents charged that he was not giving sufficient attention to state affairs. He vetoed many measures, sixteen in one day! He could not get favourable action on some of the bills he proposed. He had gone so far and so fast in the reforms of the previous year—Wilson's first impetuous charge, as earlier at Princeton, was always his most successful—that the reaction had set in. He was already getting ahead of his following. He wrote on April 1st:

"This has been a petty and barren legislature. It has done nothing worth mentioning except try to amend and mar the wonderful things we accomplished last year. Small men have ignorantly striven to put *me* in a hole by discrediting themselves! It is a merry world—for a cynic to live in. For a normal man it is not a little sad and disheartening. And what shall we say when we find the leader of the petty partisan band a learned and distinguished Professor in a great University . . . with plenty of independent means and plenty of brains, of a kind, but without a single moral principle to his name! I have never despised any other man quite so heartily,—tho. there are others whom I have found worthier of hate and utter reprobation—in *another* university!

"But now both the session and (it would momentarily appear) the winter are over, Heaven be praised! and we can settle to a more normal, if no less strenuous life. Now I must rush out again in search of delegates,—shy birds more difficult to find in genuine species than the snark itself! I keep singularly well, and some of my adventures I enjoy thoroughly. Last night, for example, I spoke at a chamber of commerce dinner in Plainfield and then came the twenty-seven miles back through the midnight in a motor, speeding amidst misty moonlight full of ghosts and mysteries,—everything still and asleep except the creeping chilly vapours. It does not sound very wholesome, does it? but it was good for a weary, jaded mind within the thinking box of a tired governor!"[1]

But he had not yet reached the depths: if it had not been for two things, he might well have felt entirely hopeless. One was his strong sense, his complete faith, that the people were with him; he felt it even with the state delegations going against him; the other was those deeper and more intimate resources of his life, his devoted family, and his unwavering friendships. His wife was a bulwark of strength: and his domestic life a "centre of peace." Once within his home, he felt free. The family had removed from the crowded and noisy Princeton Inn and in the preceding October, after a summer at Sea Girt, had taken a cottage in Cleveland Lane. Their old friends, the Misses Lucy and Mary Smith, were with them and bore part of the expense of the new venture. It was a rather small, half-timbered, Elizabethan house, set a little way back from the shady, winding street. Built by an artist, it had a large studio room with a skylight, beloved by Mrs. Wilson. Wilson himself wrote of it:

". . . here we are ensconced in as pretty and comfortable a little house as you would wish to see. (It is No. 25 Cleveland Lane, please note, and our telephone number is 98.) It was built and is owned by a Mr. Parker Mann, an artist, many of whose pictures (quite indifferent affairs) are on the walls, and we are using his furniture, which is both pretty and comfortable. We were lucky to find such a

---

[1]Woodrow Wilson to Mary A. Hulbert, April 1, 1912.

place, and shall find content here, I am sure, even if it *is* next door to the Hibben's."[1]

He also relieved the pressure by writing to various friends, and he rejoiced in one new one: Colonel House.

### IV. COLONEL HOUSE

Woodrow Wilson and Edward M. House first met on November 24, 1911.

It was the beginning of a friendship as interesting, as enigmatic, as potent in its influence upon public affairs, for good and for ill, as any in the annals of American public life. It ended in a "break" that was the cause of world-wide discussion. It has large biographical significance.

Colonel House was born in Texas. He was some two years younger than Wilson. His father was one of the leading business men of the state, a prosperous banker, "a great old character," who left his son a considerable fortune. Young House attended school at New Haven, college at Cornell, but did not graduate. He was an indifferent student, but intensely interested in politics.

"Every near-by political meeting I attended, and there was no one more interested in the nomination and election of the presidential candidates of 1876 than I. At every opportunity I would go to New York and hang about Democratic Headquarters which, I remember, were at the Everett House in Union Square. I used to see Mr. Tilden go in and out, and wondered then how so frail a looking man could make a campaign for President.

"Bayard, Blaine, and others I heard speak whenever the opportunity occurred, and I believe that I was as nearly engrossed in politics as I have ever been since."[2]

---

[1] Woodrow Wilson to Mary A. Hulbert, October 8, 1911.
[2] *The Intimate Papers of Colonel House*, Vol. I, pp. 13-14.

COLONEL EDWARD M. HOUSE

He became a warm friend of Oliver T. Morton, son of Senator Morton of Indiana, and visited him in Washington during the exciting Hayes-Tilden controversy of 1876.

"When the Electoral Commission was organized and began to hold its sittings in the Supreme Court Room at the Capitol, young Morton and I were permitted to slip in and out at will, although the demand for admission could only be met in a very small way. . . .

"In those days, too, I had the entrée to the White House. I remember General Grant and Mrs. Grant and several members of his cabinet. . . .

". . . I was constantly reading, constantly absorbing, constantly in touch with, public affairs. I knew the name of every United States senator, of practically every representative, the governors of all the important states, and had some knowledge of the chief measures before the people."[1]

House's and Wilson's interests were thus, from an early age, concerned with different aspects of the same set of problems. Wilson's dominating interest was in fundamentals, in measures, in the great business of political administration. House's was in men, machinery, human complications.

House's intense interest in public affairs would have led naturally to a political career; but his health was delicate, he was of small stature, and he had no gifts as a speaker.

". . . I had no ambition to hold office, nor had I any ambition to speak, because I felt in both instances that I would fall short of the first place, and nothing less than that would satisfy me.

"Yet I have been thought without ambition. That, I think, is not quite true. My ambition has been so great that it has never seemed to me worth while to strive to satisfy it."[2]

---

[1] *The Intimate Papers of Colonel House*, Vol. I, p. 15.
[2] Ibid, Vol. I, p. 16.

Having independent means, he was under no compulsion to strive for any of the conventional rewards of life. He shrank from the ordinary hurly-burly contacts. He was "inspired by the desire to improve political conditions," but he avoided, always, any personal responsibility either for the influence of his ideas or the results of his acts. If things went wrong someone else must take the punishment; public opinion could not reach him.

He had a gift of understanding and helping to adjust human relationships. He liked to get interesting and important people together, not the great audiences beloved of the orator, but friendly fireside gatherings. He liked to draw them out, learn about them, saying little himself, and helping, if he could, to advance those whom he approved, or those who, in his judgment, were going in the right direction. His friends liked him heartily. Secretary Houston, who met House when he went to Texas in 1894, says:

"I soon discovered that Colonel House was very much interested in political affairs and that he was one of the most influential figures, especially for good, in the state. He had directed the campaigns of several governors, including Hogg, Culberson, and Sayers, and was easily their most trusted and useful adviser. . . . He was human and liked the game, and, no doubt, the sense of power, and he knew how to play the game, but his first aim was to secure the best attainable thing for the people. All the public men knew that he wanted nothing and would take nothing; and they had no fear or jealousy of him."[1]

He built himself a fine house on the hill at Austin, the capital of Texas—one of the show places of the town— and it was here that he held most of his political conferences. He had been appointed a colonel on the staff of Governor Hogg, one of those "gilt-braid" offices, distinc-

[1] D. F. Houston, *Eight Years with Wilson's Cabinet*, Vol. I, p. 21.

tion without responsibility, by which political leaders of that day honoured their friends. In a hustling, bustling, pioneer life, he was that rarity, the man of leisure: the dilettante.

About the time that Wilson was entering politics in New Jersey, in 1910, House began to be more deeply interested in national affairs. He felt that the time was approaching when a Democrat might again be elected President of the United States. He moved from Austin and made his headquarters in New York. He widened his acquaintance, corresponded with many public men, and began to gather around him a group of friends like those in Texas but with a larger outlook.

Through William J. Bryan, House became interested in Mayor Gaynor of New York City as the most likely Democratic candidate for the presidency. He went to see him, became enthusiastic, urged his Texas friends to support him, and even sought an invitation from the legislature of Texas for Gaynor to visit the state.[1] For many months after Wilson had become an outstanding candidate for the presidency, House was lending his influence to another man.

Long before House and Wilson met a vigorous movement had begun in Texas to advance Wilson's candidacy. Several enthusiasts who were opposed to the old Bailey machine, and desired a new deal in Texas, were interested —among them, George D. Armistead and Thomas B. Love. They were later joined by Thomas W. Gregory, who was to become a member of Wilson's cabinet. Albert Sidney Burleson, a Texas member of Congress, had also become interested. Love had been active from the time that Wilson was elected governor and in December, 1910, as we have already seen, had begun making plans for an

[1] January 21, 1911.

organization in Texas to support Wilson. A considerable correspondence resulted.[1]

In April, Love and his friends began urging Wilson to speak at the Texas State Fair in the fall: and later, in the summer, a strong organization was formed—"Woodrow Wilson for President"—headed by Love as its president, with O. T. Holt and Thomas W. Gregory as vice-presidents and George D. Armistead as secretary. Some of the ablest younger Democrats in the state were connected with it. Several made pilgrimages to New Jersey to see Wilson, and returned thoroughly committed. Burleson, who had for several years been interested in Wilson's writings, went to see him in 1910, Gregory in 1911.

Wilson first heard of House in March, 1911, and, curiously, through the ubiquitous George Harvey. House had written to Harvey regarding certain conditions in Texas, and Harvey forwarded the letter to Wilson with the remark that "the writer is an exceptionally able man, well-to-do financially and I think sound politically."

Burleson had also spoken to Wilson about House, urging that they meet:

"You want to get acquainted with Colonel House. He is a good politician, a wise counsellor, able, unselfish, and greatly interested in politics. I think he can help you."[2]

In October, shortly before Wilson was to go to Texas to speak at the State Fair, House wrote to Wilson. His friend Senator Culberson of Texas was worried about Wilson's party regularity. Wilson responded on October 18th—the first letter he ever wrote to House:

MY DEAR MR. HOUSE:
It is very provoking how lies frame themselves and run current and I despair of keeping up with them, but I am none the

---

[1]See letter of February 16, 1911, p. 195, this volume.

[2]A. S. Burleson to the author.

less thankful to you for your referring to me the question contained in your letter of October 16.

The facts are that I voted for Palmer and Buckner in 1896, but I have never supported at any time a Republican ticket. I do not consider myself as supporting a non-Democratic ticket when I voted for Palmer and Buckner. My difference with Mr. Bryan was over the money question.

I appreciate the courtesy and fairness of Senator Culberson in making careful inquiry of you of the truth of the reports.

With warmest regards, believe me

Sincerely yours,
WOODROW WILSON

House followed with an inquiry regarding Wilson's views about the "two-thirds rule" in Democratic conventions, and Wilson's reply, in view of what happened only a few months later in Baltimore, is most significant:

MY DEAR MR. HOUSE:

Thank you sincerely for your letter of the twentieth.

I feel very strongly that the two-thirds rule is a most undemocratic regulation and puts us at a particular disadvantage as compared with the Republicans, whose arrangements respond more readily to the opinion of their party than ours can do in the circumstances.

I feel that there would be a certain impropriety in my urging a change because it would be so manifestly in my interest, but certainly any change of the sort would have my entire sympathy and approval, if it could be brought about, and I think would commend itself to the judgment of the whole country.

With warm regards,

Sincerely yours,
WOODROW WILSON

October 24th, 1911

On October 28th Wilson spoke at the State Fair at Dallas and later, accompanied by Love and Gregory, went to Fort Worth. He made a "powerful impression." He "won Texas." He never visited the state again; as Gregory says, "He never needed to." Although the old machine was against him—30 of the 31 members of the state executive committee, and 12 of the 16 members of Congress[1]—the Wilson forces at the convention in the following spring won a complete victory.

A month after Wilson's visit to Texas, Wilson and House met for the first time.

"He came alone to the Gotham quite promptly at four, [recorded House] and we talked for an hour. He had an engagement to meet Phelan, afterward Senator from California, at five o'clock, and expressed much regret that he could not continue our conversation. We arranged, however, to meet again within a few days, when at my invitation he came to dine with me."[2]

If House was delighted and impressed by the meeting— "we had a perfectly bully time. . . . Never before have I found both the man and the opportunity"[3]—so was Wilson. In the weeks that followed the friendship ripened rapidly.

"A few weeks after we met and after we had exchanged confidences which men usually do not exchange except after years of friendship, I asked him if he realized that we had only known one another for so short a time. He replied, 'My dear friend, we have known one another always.' And I think this is true."[4]

House now became tremendously interested in Wilson's campaign and used all his influence in bringing the Texas delegation to his support, he and Gregory, indeed, guaranteeing the expenses of the Wilson headquarters at Dallas. After the primaries in Texas on May 6, 1912, Wilson wrote to House:

---

[1]The four members of Congress who were for him were A. S. Burleson, R. L. Henry, Robert Smith, and Rufus Hardy.

[2]*The Intimate Papers of Colonel House*, Vol. I, p. 45.

[3]E. M. House to S. E. Mezes, November 25, 1911.

[4]*The Intimate Papers of Colonel House*, Vol. I, p. 45.

"I certainly had splendid and effective friends in Texas, and I want to express to you in particular my warm and deep appreciation of the intelligent work done. It is very delightful to have the support of the great old State."

During the early weeks of their friendship, Wilson was under fierce attack. The Harvey-Watterson break, the Carnegie pension matter, the Joline letter, if they were "small missiles," yet hurt, desperately, his sensitive spirit. He felt his isolation. He had broken with Hibben, upon whom for years he had leaned with deep affection. Though he seemed to be "cool and hard," no man was ever more dependent than he, as this biography has already shown, upon friends whom he loved and could trust.

"It is always affection that heals me, and the dear friendships I made were my real tonic and restorative."[1]

He was a lonely man: he could not live without such friendships: and yet he feared them. He feared that they would soften his purpose. His god was a jealous god: friendship, or love, or sympathy, however desperately he craved them, must not crowd in between him and his far objective. He had written of the break between Burke and Fox:

"'But there is no loss of friends,' exclaimed Fox eagerly. 'Yes,' cried Burke, 'there *is* a loss of friends. I know the penalty of my conduct. I have done my duty at the price of my friend; our friendship is at an end.' It was the price, not of his conduct, but of his nature. His passion for the principles he served was deeper than his passion for his friend. A shallower man, for whom public questions were less like the very essences of life and thought and action, might have kept his friend without giving up his opinions;

---

[1]Woodrow Wilson to Fred Yates, November 6, 1906, after a summer spent in Rydal, England.

but for Burke no such divided comradeship and allegiance was possible. . . ."[1]

Further along in the same essay, Wilson remarks:

"We should not expect a man to be easy and affable when he deems himself in a death-grapple with the enemies of his country."

And yet, however determined he was that he would not let his emotions control him ("alas, I am too intense!") he could not maintain always that "calm governance of the mind," "that discipline of the heart" that he craved. He had to have friendship.

Two months after his acquaintance with House began, he wrote:

MY DEAR MR. HOUSE:

I am so glad to hear through McCombs that you are at last about to get out and feel like yourself again physically. I have been very much distressed in thinking of your long illness, and it cheers me to think that you are now about to be released. Pray, take care of yourself. If you will permit me to say so, I [have] come to have a very warm feeling towards you, and hope that in years to come our friendship will ripen.

Cordially yours,
WOODROW WILSON[2]

There was in House something of the quality that Wilson admired in fine women: something intimate, sympathetic, unarguing. He was a listener: he drew people out. He liked to increase the assurance of those with whom he came in contact. No one who ever sat with him but felt drawn by his eager interest, his responsive "that's true, that's true," to what was said to him. He began writing to Wilson early in their friendship: "my great and good friend," "I think you never did anything better," "you

---

[1]Woodrow Wilson, "Edmund Burke and the French Revolution," published in the *Century*, September, 1901.

[2]January 27, 1912.

are so much more efficient than any public man with whom I have heretofore been in touch, that the others seem mere tyros," "no man ever deserved better of his country." As the years passed, these expressions of uncritical approval, not always confirmed by the naïve confidences of his diary, or even in his intimate conversation, increased in number and in warmth.

As a matter of fact, House never in his life openly and seriously opposed anything that Wilson desired—once he found out what it was. If he took a different tack at first, because he was unaware of the direction or depth of his chief's convictions on a given subject, he was usually quick to come about. When, as occasionally happened, he continued to believe the course was wrong—for example, Wilson's attitude on military preparedness—he either confined his expressions of contrary opinion to his diary or, by gentle arguments deftly fitted into Wilson's line of thought on other matters, sought to deflect it to the desired end. It was a relationship, indeed, that interprets Wilson quite as vividly as it does House.

Undoubtedly it was his personal feeling toward House that was at first dominant with Wilson. He liked him. His letters to House are extraordinary, both in what they contain and what they omit. Compared with his correspondence with certain other friends the early letters are disappointingly brief and noncommittal upon public matters —possibly because the two men were meeting so frequently—but they are full of the anxious solicitude for House's health, the generous appreciation, the expressions of warm friendship, that we find in his letters to such intimate friends as Mr. and Mrs. Hibben, Mrs. Reid, Mrs. Hulbert, Cleveland H. Dodge. "My dear Mr. House" became presently "My dear Friend," and "Dearest Friend."

Idealizing, as always, his deepest friendships, Wilson

was free-hearted in the tributes of his affection. The writer has never found, in all of Wilson's voluminous correspondence, however intimate, a single word of criticism of Colonel House, nor did he ever hear, not even during the inferno of the Peace Conference at Paris, a single derogatory expression from the President's lips concerning his friend.

Here is a characteristic early letter:

February 6, 1912.

MY DEAR MR. HOUSE:

It was the greatest pleasure to learn that you are really getting thoroughly well again, and I want to send my most hearty congratulations. I thought of you with real anxiety and solicitude and have been at times anxious that I did not hear of your more rapid improvement.

What you are doing is being done with the usual instinct of friendliness not only, but also for doing the right thing, and I have at present nothing to suggest, only my warm and cordial thanks.

Faithfully yours,
WOODROW WILSON

House soon proved his friendship. He had qualities that Wilson lacked. He liked to confer and adjust, and he had the time to do it. He was incurably confidential. "Just between you and me and the angels" was one of his characteristic expressions. Consultation not only pleased even the most important men since they knew he had the ear of the President, but it enabled House to bring to his chief invaluable information regarding "situations" or local leaders, facts that illuminated political alignments in various states. He was indefatigable, going about shrewd-eyed, silent, unobtrusive. These gatherings of fact he fed into Wilson's voracious mind—sometimes by word of mouth, sometimes by long letters packed with concrete information. He was swift in sensing Wilson's reactions to

the situations he reported, and his "discreet intimations"
of the President's views served not only to guide party
leaders but to enhance his own reputation for influence
upon his chief, which he strove always to build up. The
method was particularly serviceable as applied to appointments, for he was often able to inform candidates in advance, sometimes at the President's suggestion, of the
good fortune that awaited them.

While House's service to Wilson as a political reporter
and adjuster was important, as this biography will abundantly show, an examination of the immense correspondence, a minute study of many cases, shows that Wilson,
though eager for House's information, and warm in his
thanks for it, went contrary to his advice about as often
as he followed it.

Senator John Sharp Williams of Mississippi, who had
known Wilson for many years, and was his friend, set
forth the exact truth in a penetrating letter which he
wrote in answer to the charge that the Roman Catholic
hierarchy was exerting undue influence upon Wilson—a
copy of which he sent to Wilson himself:

"If you do not know it we people in Washington do
know that he is not only nominally but really the President
of the United States, and neither Mr. Tumulty, nor I, nor
anybody else controls him. The truth is, nobody influences
him very much. The further truth is, that he is not subject
to the amount of influence that he ought to be from the
arguments and knowledge of those more experienced,
perhaps, than he in public matters."[1]

House had another serviceable gift. He was the acme of
discretion.

"'What I like about Colonel House,' explained Governor Wilson one day to a group of newspapermen who
displayed curiosity about the growing friendship, 'is that

[1]March 14, 1914.

he holds things at arm's length—objectively. He seems able to penetrate a proposition and get to its very essence quickly. He wants nothing for himself. He will not hold office and is a truly disinterested friend—the most valuable possession a man could have.'"[1]

Such a letter as the following, which House wrote to Wilson on January 9, 1913—at a time when the newly elected President was harassed to the limit of his endurance by the importunities of office-seekers, must have been truly balm in Gilead:

"You can never know how deeply I appreciate your wanting me in your Cabinet. As an ex-officio member, however, I can do my share of the work and get a little of the reflected glory that I am very sure will come to your administration."

It was inevitable that House should magnify his influence with his friend. It was this relationship that was the crowning achievement of his life. Having no public place himself, he must be effective through Wilson. "He loved," says his biographer, "to play an influential if not a decisive rôle in politics." He must play it by swaying Wilson. He loved power, but he must exercise it, not directly, by his hold upon the people, or the virility of his thought, by his place in his party organization, or by office-holding, but indirectly, by his intimate contact with the dominant personality of his time.

It is not surprising, therefore, to discover in House's letters and his eagerly written diary the assumption, naïve at times, of the magic of his influence with his "great and good friend." A certain confidential expansiveness is perhaps one of the amiable sins of the diarist, especially the diarist who feels that his own record of his "silent activities," his "secret influence," furnishes the only solid confirmation of the reality of his power.

[1]David Lawrence, *The True Story of Woodrow Wilson*, p. 68.

But if the sin in House's case was amiable, it was unnecessary. As we lay out the documents, study the letters, pry into all the influences which were operative upon Wilson in making certain of his decisions, we do not doubt the pervasive if not always well-considered helpfulness of his friend House: but we find also that there were many other influential men, both experts and statesmen, with whom Wilson was also advising. We have letters and documents to show what were the real sources of his information, the real considerations which swayed him. In certain fields of the President's immense and varied activities, House was a fruitful source of information and suggestion—Tumulty was another—yet in instances cited by either as a case in which he shaped Wilson's decisions, he commonly turns out to be only one of a number of advisers who were urging the same thing. House's biographer, for example, quite needlessly makes him the "unseen guardian angel" of the Federal Reserve Act; and the implication is that the President scarcely moved without his advice. It is all too simple! The passage of the Federal Reserve Act was a complicated business in which many experts and advisers, to say nothing of hard-working congressmen and senators, played a part—as will be shown in the appropriate place.[1]

One amusing minor incident illustrating this attitude occurs in the account of the very first dinner that House gave Wilson. It is called an "important development which House suggested and carried through."[2] It was nothing short of informing Wilson, at a single session, regarding the tariff question! House had invited Houston in to do it.

"Before dinner I went over the data which Houston had

---

[1]Senator Carter Glass, one of the authors of the Federal Reserve Act, in his book, *An Adventure in Constructive Finance*, has made a searching examination of the various influences that affected Wilson.

[2]*The Intimate Papers of Colonel House*, Vol. I, p. 46.

prepared, and added to it and eliminated from it whatever seemed necessary. This data was afterwards given to Governor Wilson, who based his tariff speeches largely on it."[1]

For a man who, like Wilson, had been thinking and talking and writing on the tariff for thirty years, this seems like a large order. Probably Houston did help, for Wilson had a high respect for Houston's knowledge and advice. We have Houston's own account of this very meeting:

"After dinner, the Governor and I went aside in a corner of the room and were left alone for an hour or more. He asked me first what I thought ought to be done about the tariff and the currency. . . .

"After we had discussed both topics, the Governor asked me if I would not send him a brief on each subject. I promised that I would do so, and when I went back to St. Louis I prepared the briefs and sent them to him. When I told the Governor that I would prepare the briefs, he said: 'Please do not expect me to use the matter in my statements at great length or in the form in which you give it. I cannot deal with questions in that way. I want all the facts and interpretations of them I can get. I shall try to digest them—to get my thought permeated with them; and then I shall try to paint a word picture. I do not like to speak for over twenty or thirty minutes.' I said to myself: 'That is the artist in him.' "[2]

If we go a step further and study the speeches that Wilson made or the articles he wrote on the tariff before and after this "important development," we shall discover that Wilson continued to say practically what he had been saying for years. We shall discover another interesting thing. In the very first notable address on the tariff delivered after this meeting with House and Houston, Wilson said, courteously:

[1] *The Intimate Papers of Colonel House*, Vol. I, p. 47.
[2] D. F. Houston, *Eight Years With Wilson's Cabinet*, Vol. I, pp. 19–20.

"When Mr. Redfield came in this evening, the first thing I said to him was that I would not be here if I hadn't looked at his speeches. I primed myself on Mr. Redfield's speeches. If he recognizes these points, he must forgive me. I really thought of some of them myself."[1]

This incident is not analyzed with any empty purpose of discrediting House: but, in the interest of a real understanding of the relationship of Wilson and House, to correct the emphasis and the implication of so many similar statements in House's narrative. It was a friendship so extraordinary, so interesting, so important, that it is obscured by exaggeration, enhanced by complete comprehension. Wilson gathered information from many sources —on the tariff, not only from Houston and Redfield, but from Professor Henry Jones Ford and Professor Winthrop M. Daniels of Princeton, and many others. Senator Underwood of Alabama helped him with facts and arguments. And, as Wilson says somewhat plaintively:

"I really thought of some of them myself!"

### V. THE CRITICAL MONTH OF MAY

May, 1912, was one of the darkest months of Wilson's political career. In the latter part of April he made three speaking tours. He and Mrs. Wilson spent a week in Georgia. It was almost like going home. Mrs. Wilson was born in Savannah and they had been married there. Much of Wilson's early life had been spent at Augusta and Atlanta. They had many relatives and friends in the state. McAdoo, who was also a Georgian, with no inconsiderable acquaintance, was with them. Wilson had what everyone considered a "flattering reception." His meetings were crowded: his speeches were received with "unexampled

---

[1] Address before the National Democratic Club, New York, January 3, 1912. *The Public Papers of Woodrow Wilson*, Vol. II, p. 330. William C. Redfield, then a member of Congress, was afterward Secretary of Commerce in Wilson's cabinet.

enthusiasm." It seemed as if the state were thoroughly committed to his candidacy.

From Georgia, he went to Massachusetts, speaking at Boston and Worcester, and then to Maryland, where he had a convincing popular reception. He made a number of addresses.

"That meeting at the Lyric last night was a remarkable tribute to Woodrow Wilson. A political machine ordinarily finds no trouble in packing a political meeting. It orders out its forces, it distributes free car tickets, it brings out the marching clubs and furnishes them with bands. Moreover, it has the full party strength to draw upon. But Wilson is only one of several Democratic candidates, three of whom are on the Maryland ticket. He has no machine to help out. Yet despite these facts the Lyric last night was crowded to the doors by an audience representative of all classes of the people, and the greeting which they gave the Governor of New Jersey was one the sincerity and spontaneity of which could not be denied.

"Baltimore likes the Wilson type of man. . . ."[1]

Wilson and his friends felt absolutely certain that he was getting the people: and yet when the votes fell he lost Massachusetts, thirty-six votes, to Clark on April 30th; Georgia, twenty-eight votes, to Underwood on May 1st; and Maryland, sixteen votes, to Clark on May 6th. Body blows! Added to the results in Nebraska, Bryan's state, which went to Clark on April 19th, the situation looked dubious enough. Was Bryan also hostile? Clark was the surprise of the primaries. It is true that the Texas primaries on May 4th were favourable to Wilson, but the convention, at which final action was to be taken, was not held until May 28th.

To add to Wilson's difficulties his organization was again practically bankrupt, to say nothing of being dis-

[1] Baltimore *Sun*, April 30, 1912.

rupted by internal squabbles. One of the substantial contributors refused to advance any more money. Wilson himself fell ill; and it was even reported, publicly, that he had "broken down." McCombs was disheartened.

". . . [his] office and the headquarters at 42 Broadway were deserted. It appeared as though many of the supporters of a month or two ago were now leaning strongly toward Speaker Clark's candidacy, and from information that we recieved the Clark forces were jubilant and confident of victory. Mr. McAdoo, Senator Saulsbury, Mr. Elkus, Mr. Morgenthau, and a few other staunch friends were about all that called and conferred."[1]

McCombs himself wrote to Wilson:

"MY DEAR GOVERNOR:
"The fight seems to be going against us, but be assured I shall not abate my efforts and I still think you have a chance to be nominated."[2]

Colonel House also began to doubt Wilson's chances. He wrote to his friend, Senator Culberson, on May 1st:

DEAR SENATOR:
. . . It looks to me as if the opposing candidates might again be Bryan and Roosevelt. In that event, I think Roosevelt would beat him. He would get his share of the progressive vote and most of the conservative vote. Bryan thinks he could beat Roosevelt, but in my opinion, he could beat Taft more easily.

Wilson's best chance now, I think, is the fear of many people that Bryan will be nominated and the further fear that Hearst may succeed in landing Champ Clark and then dominate the Administration.

Faithfully yours,
E. M. HOUSE[2]

---

[1] Maurice F. Lyons, *William F. McCombs, The President Maker*, pp. 75–76.
[2] *The Intimate Papers of Colonel House*, Vol. I, p. 60.

If politics were not discouraging enough, Wilson had to meet a situation at Princeton that cut him to the heart. His old friend Hibben had been chosen president of the university, and was to be inaugurated on May 11th. While he regarded it, however mistakenly, as the last act in the tragedy of his service at Princeton, the trustees could probably have made no better choice. Hibben was "the type of man, the conciliator, the just and self-effacing administrator"[1] who was needed to hold the institution steady until it could recover from the controversies that had marked the later years of the Wilson administration. More than this, he was a devoted advocate of certain of the great essentials of Wilson's programme, and better fitted, perhaps, than any other man, to maintain an atmosphere in which they could be assimilated. He had differed with Wilson not so much in ultimate objectives as in method of approach.

To Wilson's mind, however, the choice of Hibben meant a surrender to the forces at Princeton which had opposed the reforms he regarded as vital to the future usefulness of the university. He felt that everything he had tried to do was about to be destroyed—and destroyed under the leadership of the friend who had been closest to him in all the years at Princeton. That he was mistaken did not make his own reaction less bitter.

To make matters worse, he was, as governor of the state, and *ex-officio* president of the board of trustees, supposed to be present at Hibben's inauguration, greet the distinguished guests, give his blessing upon the ceremonies. His friends urged him to go: he must not let his personal feelings influence him.

"I cannot do it," responded Wilson. "If I say what is in my heart and mind the dinner would end in a riot. If

[1] See *The Life and Letters of Woodrow Wilson: Princeton*, p. 356.

I get up and indulge in the usual platitudes, the words would stick in my throat."[1]

His letters of the time contain many examples of the intensity of his feeling. They reveal vividly certain rigorous, inflexible, unforgiving qualities of Wilson's mind.

"I am here to-day to attend a dinner of the Reform Club to-night and make a speech on the tariff (did you ever hear of anything less exciting!) but I need not have come over last night as I did, merely to be early and get a seat. I really came when I did in order not to be in Princeton any part of to-day. Jack Hibben is to be (is being) inaugurated as president of the University to-day, and I could not be present or play any part without hypocrisy. I am Governor of the State and, as such, president of the Board of Trustees of the University. I *could* not be in the town and not show myself at the ceremonies,—particularly as the President of the United States is to be there and I would be his official host. Why should I feel like a run-away, and as if I were doing an ungenerous thing? Because I love the University, I suppose, and many of the fine men who are connected with it,—and also because I am constitutionally averse from sparing myself anything hard and disagreeable,—and perhaps because it seems a less candid course to absent myself than to go there and speak out what is in my mind. *There's* the whole point of the matter! To be present and silent would be deeply hypocritical: to go and speak my real thoughts and judgments would be to break up the meeting and create a national scandal, to the great injury of the dear old place. No doubt I should stay away. But it is hard and it is mortifying. To be true to oneself and candid in the utterance of the truth is to live in a very embarrassing world. And yet what *man* would buy peace at the price of his soul.

---

[1]Roland S. Morris to the author.

"Alas! my dear friend, it is a hard world to live in! I dare say no man is so humble as not to feel the jolts and jars and clashes of it. And who shall set an estimate in such circumstances upon real, tested friendship,—friendship with insight and comprehending sympathy, that understands before the case is stated and sees as much as your own heart does? It is *that* that makes life noble and beautiful and good to live.

"The cold that knocked me out last week has almost entirely disappeared, but has left me with a little less than my wonted vigour. I am more quickly tired than is usual with me. But that is nothing. I am quite fit and in excellent spirits—except for the particular thoughts of the day.

"No letter from you yet since you sailed. I trust you are all right. All join me in affectionate messages to you all.

"Your devoted friend<br>"WOODROW WILSON"[1]

His state of mind, as well as his own attitude toward the political situation, may be best interpreted by letters that he wrote during these weeks to three of his dearest friends:

May 13, 1912.

MY DEAR HEATH:-

I am all right again and the reports about my "breakdown" were absurd. I simply had to go to bed to cure a severe cold. . . .

I think that, politically, things are in fairly satisfactory shape. As a matter of fact most of the support of Clark and Underwood is perfunctory and on the surface, and underneath, if I am correctly informed, the purpose to nominate me is as strong as it ever was. These things cannot be depended upon, of course, but this is what is reported to me by men who ought to know.

[1]Woodrow Wilson to Mary A. Hulbert, May 11, 1912.

The combination against me has certainly done wonders, and yet my chief disappointment in the primaries of various states is not that they did not result in my favour, but that they were so small in respect of the numbers who voted. The people did not take any interest in them. They were about equivalent to caucuses held through the polling places. Possibly the people will wake up later to the significance of the whole thing, but for the present there seems to be extraordinary lethargy and indifference.

I saw Dick Byrd[1] in New York on Saturday night and he is very hopeful, not to say confident, of controlling the Virginia situation in my favour.[2] At any rate, the fight there is by no means in bad shape.

With genuine affection

Faithfully yours,<br>WOODROW WILSON

Dean R. H. Dabney,
    Charlottesville,
      Virginia.

On May 14th the California primaries, twenty-six votes, went to Clark, indicating a still more pronounced drift. On the 16th he wrote to his old friend Dodge:

MY DEAR CLEVE:

Bless you for your note of yesterday! You must have known that I needed it. I do not lose heart,—somehow I cannot, *dare* not, there is so much to do,—so much that affects the very foundations of life for every man and woman in the country. But sometimes when I see vast sums of money poured out against me, with fatal success, and it begins to look as if I must merely sit on the side lines and talk, as a mere critic of the game I understand so intimately,—throw all my training away

---

[1] Richard E. Byrd, a prominent Virginia lawyer: Speaker of the Virginia House of Delegates; later, United States District Attorney for the Western District of Virginia; special assistant to the Attorney General of the United States, 1920-21. Father of Harry F. Byrd, Governor of Virginia, 1926-30; and Richard E. Byrd, aviator.

[2] Virginia, however, disappointed Wilson. Its delegation went uninstructed, controlled by the old organization leaders.

and *do* nothing,—well, I do not repine, but I grow a little sad, and need such a message, of generous love and confidence, as this you have sent me. God bless you!

Affectionately,
WOODROW WILSON

On May 26th he wrote to his friend Mrs. Reid:

MY DEAR, DEAR FRIEND,

You must have *known* that I needed a letter from you and that an expression of your generous confidence in me was just the tonic that would put me in form again! Everybody over here seems to agree that there has never been a Campaign in which there was such a systematic and malevolent attempt to destroy a man's reputation for character and intellectual integrity as has been made by my opponents all over the country, including the representatives of the other Candidates for the democratic nomination, and in such circumstances one *needs* to hear the voice of true and loyal friends to keep him in heart.

Not that I actually lose heart. I find I am of too firm a fibre, and of too firm a faith, for that; but the world grows sometimes to seem so brutal, so naked of beauty, so devoid of chivalrous sentiment and all sense of fair play, that one's own spirit hardens and is in danger of losing its fineness. I fight on, in the spirit of Kipling's "If", but that is oftentimes a very arid air; and one's heart softens and glows again and the colour comes back into the world when a dear friend speaks and call's one's heart back from its anxious quest amongst strangers. Your letter did me a world of good. You are always *there*, to think about and depend on; but when you speak the comfort and reassurance come in a flood!

The political field is hopelessly confused; no one can confidently predict *anything*,—not even the nomination of Roosevelt, though that seems daily more probable. On the Democratic side it now looks as if the choice of the convention might lie between Bryan and me. I need not tell you how I feel about it,—I am so sure you can divine. I dread the possibility and yet feel that I must offer myself and not shirk. Your judgment of Roosevelt is mine own. God save us of another four years of him *now* in his present insane distemper of egotism!

Ellen and the other girls join me in messages of deep affection. It delighted us to hear from you. I hope that you have got both health and pleasure amidst your old haunts and friends.

Your devoted friend,
WOODROW WILSON

Alas! the governor of N. J. (till 1914) cannot leave his bailiwick to travel across seas!

Wilson's friends had become suddenly alarmed regarding his own state of New Jersey. The bosses, Smith and Nugent, were working hard against him: and on the 24th he issued a strong appeal and warning to the people of the state:

## WILSON WARNS VOTERS OF PLOT TO GRAB STATE

### GOVERNOR ISSUES A REMARKABLE STATEMENT COVERING POLITICAL SITUATION IN NEW JERSEY

Declares Former Senator Is in League With Republican Machine to Defeat Him—To Upset Scheme.[1]

After reviewing his fight upon the bosses and summarizing the results of his service as governor, he says:

"What, therefore, is the present situation? What is happening now? What is happening within the Republican party is obvious to the whole country, and a very unedifying spectacle it is. But what is happening in this state within the Democratic party is not so obvious. It is, indeed, being done very quietly and very secretly, because it is being done by Mr. James Smith, Jr., who knows no other way of acting in politics and who has no suggestion to make to the voters of the state which he can quite venture to make in public. He does not, I understand, avow himself as in favour of any particular candidate for the

[1] Trenton *True American*, May 25, 1912.

Democratic nomination; he is only opposed to me: and
the men he has induced to offer themselves as candidates
to represent New Jersey in the national Democratic convention wish to be sent 'without instructions.' . . .

"Shall the Democrats of New Jersey send delegates to
Baltimore who are free men, or are the special interests
again to name men to represent them? The representatives
of special interests will be in a helpless, intriguing minority
at Baltimore. Is the progressive Democracy of New Jersey
to contribute to that minority?

"We are speaking of very practical matters now and
ought not to mince words. The question is, Do you wish
to sustain the new regime; do you wish to support government conducted by public opinion, rather than by private
understanding and management, or do you wish to slip
back into the slough of the old despair and disgrace? This
is a question to be asked on both sides of the house—by the
men who are going into the Republican primaries as well
as by those who are going into the Democratic primaries.
It involves the reputation and the freedom of the state
we love. On the Democratic side it affects my personal
fortunes, but only because I happen to have been given
the opportunity by the people of the state to represent the
great ideas and principles which every honest man ought
to represent. My heart is in them; the heart of every patriotic man in New Jersey is in them; and they are involved in this contest. . . .

"Every man who stays away from the polls on Tuesday
deliberately deserts a great cause and hands his state over
to be plundered of even her good name."

Near the close of the month the situation began to improve. On May 28th came the final Texas decision: the
expected forty votes: and the primaries in New Jersey, also
held on that day, were considered satisfactory, although
the delegation was divided, Wilson getting twenty-four

29 May, 1912

My dear Judge Wescott,

Now that there is no doubt about the willingness of New Jersey to support me, I am writing to ask if you will do me the honour of placing my name in nomination before the Baltimore Convention. I know of no one who could do it more impressively or conveniently, and it would give me great personal gratification to have you do so. Affectionately Yours,

Woodrow Wilson

Facsimile of a letter from Mr. Wilson to Judge Wescott, asking him to make the nominating speech at the Baltimore convention.

votes and Smith and Nugent, entrenched in their city strongholds, retaining four. There were also other encouragements. Daniels had made a great fight in North Carolina and Joseph E. Davies in Wisconsin.[1] South Carolina was favourable. On June 6th Minnesota, where the Wilson forces had been under the effective leadership of Frederick B. Lynch, declared for Wilson. There also began to be evidences that although Nebraska had declared for Clark, Bryan was by no means finally committed. While he had leaned toward Clark earlier in the year, he was drifting now toward Wilson. Whether this was merely to counterbalance Clark's growing strength in order to fortify his own leadership, or whether it meant a real conviction of Wilson's superiority, the reports cheered Wilson's friends.

With such a majority of the New Jersey delegation supporting him, Wilson felt assured that his friends could at least make a satisfactory showing at Baltimore in his behalf, and on May 29th he wrote to Judge Wescott:

"Now that there is no doubt about the willingness of New Jersey to support me, I am writing to ask if you will do me the honour of placing my name in nomination before the Baltimore Convention. I know of no one who could do it more impressively or convincingly, and it would give me great personal gratification to have you do so."[2]

In spite, however, of these encouragements, the drift so far as the choice of delegates was concerned was unmistakably toward Clark. It began to look as though he would have a majority on the first ballot—or, at any rate, on an early ballot. Since the convention of 1844, when Van Buren was nominated, there had been no instance in which a candidate who had received a majority of the ballots in a Democratic convention had failed ultimately

[1] Wilson got seventeen of Wisconsin's delegates, Clark nine.
[2] May 29, 1912.

to win two thirds and the nomination. Wilson himself believed that the two-thirds rule ought to be abolished, and a majority made determinative as in Republican conventions.

Although Wilson and his friends continued to keep up a determined fight the candidate himself had ceased to expect victory. He could remain "quite philosophical about the possibilities of the month," but he talked of the time "when the present battle is over, and (Beau)champ Clark or some other good Democrat of the popular stamp is nominated." And on June 9th he wrote:

"We go to the shore, to Sea Girt, on Friday, the 14th,— at least the family goes. I never know from hour to hour where sudden calls, for political conferences and the like, will take me on any given date. It is of great service to me just now to be able to look on at the political game as if I had no part in it at the same time that I am actively enlisted, and my own personal career involved. And it gives me, I think, a clearer vision and a steadier hand. Just between you and me, I have not the least idea of being nominated, because the make of the convention is such, the balance and confusion of forces, that the outcome is in the hands of the professional, case-hardened politicians who serve only their own interests and who know that I will not serve them except as I might serve the party in general. I am well and in the best of spirits. I have no deep stakes involved in this game."[1]

---

[1] Woodrow Wilson to Mary A. Hulbert.

# CHAPTER VI

# THE BALTIMORE CONVENTION

The governorship of a state is very like a smaller presidency; or, rather, the presidency is very like a big governorship. Training in the duties of the one fits for the duties of the other.

*Congressional Government, p. 253.*

What is it that a nominating convention wants in the man it is to present to the country for its suffrages? A man who will be and who will seem to the country in some sort an embodiment of the character and purpose it wishes its government to have,—a man who understands his own day and the needs of the country, and who has the personality and the initiative to enforce his views both upon the people and upon Congress.

*Constitutional Government in the United States, p. 65.*

I sometimes think it is a singular circumstance that the present Republican party should have sprung from Lincoln, but that is one of the mysteries of Providence and for my part I feel the closest kinship in principle and in political lineament to that great mind.

*Address in Chicago, February 12, 1912.*

I feel very strongly that the two-thirds rule is a most un-democratic regulation and puts us at a particular disadvantage as compared with the Republicans, whose arrangements respond more readily to the opinion of their party than ours can do in the circumstances.

*Woodrow Wilson to E. M. House, October 24, 1911.*

## I. THE GENERALS MARSHAL THEIR FORCES

THREE weeks before the Democratic convention Wilson had practically given up hope of being nominated. He and his friends kept up a bold front—McCombs could make claims with the best of them!—but the situation looked exceedingly dubious. There was even a report that Wilson was preparing to withdraw from the contest. He wrote on June 5th:

"I think that the argument that I was withdrawing from the race in what I said to the New Jersey voters will be more than offset by the action of the voters themselves."[1]

At the close of the primaries and state conventions, the situation, as regards delegates, stood as follows:

| | |
|---|---:|
| Pledged to Clark | 436 |
| Pledged to Wilson | 248 |
| Pledged to Underwood | 84 |
| Pledged to favourite sons, | |
| Harmon, Marshall, and others | 102 |
| Uncertain | 224 |
| Total delegates | 1094[2] |
| Majority | 548 |
| Two thirds, necessary | |
| for choice | 729 |

While Wilson was second in the count, his friends knew that the delegations pledged to favourite sons or "uninstructed" were largely controlled by organization politicians—Tammany Hall, the Martin-Ryan machine in Virginia, and others—and that these leaders would never of their own accord break to Wilson. If they could not get a conservative like Harmon or Underwood they would go to Clark. While Bryan insisted that the convention, on the basis of the returns, would be controlled by progressives, the wiseacres were nodding their heads. The wiseacres knew the power of organized politics, of delegations voted *en bloc*. McCombs himself was for making terms at once with Tammany Hall. Without the ninety votes from New York, what chance was there?

[1] Woodrow Wilson to N. C. Gillham.

[2] The total number of delegates in the convention, after the Credentials Committee made its report, was 1088.

Moreover, McCombs and others of Wilson's supporters were suspicious of Bryan. While he now seemed to be more favourable to Wilson, was it not merely to counterbalance the growing strength of Clark? By holding the scales even between them, they argued, he could let them kill each other off, and himself step in as the inevitable leader of the progressives in the convention. Wilson thought, at one time, that the contest was between him and Bryan.

Great pressure was brought to bear on Bryan by the friends of both Wilson and Clark. Everyone knew that he would be a power in the convention, although no one then imagined that he would be the power that he actually became. Colonel House was confident that Mrs. Bryan favoured Wilson. On the other hand, the Nebraska delegation was pledged to Clark, and Bryan was a member of it. He maintained, in his correspondence, as in his conversation, an obstinate neutrality. On the day after Wilson's victory in the New Jersey primaries, he wrote a letter that seemed to defend Clark:

"I am not able to endorse all that is done by our party or by the different leaders, but I feel sure that the progressives are going to be in control at Baltimore, and that a progressive will be nominated. While I do not take sides as between Clark and Wilson I believe that much of the criticism directed against Clark is unfair. I have known him for a great many years, and he has been on the right side of all the reform questions, and congress is making a splendid record. It is not doing everything I would like to have had it do, but progress is not usually along the line of the extreme radical. Concessions have to be made from time to time, and Clark has made but few concessions compared with the number of times he has held out for real radical legislation. I only say this in regard to Clark because you criticized him. If you had criticized Wilson

I would have presented defense of him, for I believe both of them are to be trusted."[1]

But there is evidence that at the same time he was becoming impatient with Clark. He suspected that Clark was angling for what he called the "Wall Street vote." On the day after writing to Mr. Rankin defending Clark, he wrote to Clark himself:

Ft. Wayne, Ind.,<br>May 30.

MY DEAR CLARK:

I venture to make a suggestion for your consideration. I believe the fight over wool will prove a crisis in your life as well as in the party's prospects. A leader must *lead;* it is not always pleasant to oppose friends, and one who leads takes the chances of defeat, but these are the necessary attendants upon leadership. Wilson is making friends because he *fights*. His fight against Smith was heroic. He fought for the income tax and for a primary law. The people like a fighter. You won your position by fighting and you must continue to fight to hold it. Enter into the wool fight. Don't be content to take polls and sit in the background. Take one side or the other and take it *strong*. If a tax on wool is right, lead the protectionists to victory. You can do it and it will make you strong with that wing of the party. If free wool is right, as I believe it is, lead the fight for it and get the credit for the victory if victory comes. Don't inquire about how the fight is going to go—make it go the right way if you can. If you fail you lay the foundation for a future victory. The right wins in the end—don't be afraid to wait. My opinion is that you will not have to wait long, but whether long or not, one can better afford to be defeated fighting for the right than to win on the wrong side. I hope you will pardon this intrusion upon your thoughts, but the party needs your assistance—a blast from your bugle may save the day, and it will, in my judgment, strengthen you personally.

Regards to the family.

Yours,<br>BRYAN[2]

---

[1] W. J. Bryan to E. W. Rankin, May 29, 1912.
[2] *The Memoirs of William Jennings Bryan*, p. 163.

Clark, however, was no bugle blower. His method was wholly different. He was quietly gathering in the delegates by ancient and dependable political methods. His success had surprised everyone. No one had supposed he could so easily carry so many states. While he had been a long time in public life—a member of the House of Representatives for seventeen years—his name had never been connected with notable constructive legislation, he had laid down no great principles, had illuminated no vital issues of the day. He had become Speaker by virtue of his long service and his personal popularity. Why then had he suddenly loomed so large as a presidential candidate?

Primarily, of course, Clark was the organization candidate, the dependable politician, but he also represented a condition of mind into which a considerable number of people in the country had recently fallen. They were a little weary of the more strenuous reformers who continued to urge upon them unpleasant facts, of the truth of which they were already convinced. There was an esoteric significance in the "houn' dawg" song, which came from Missouri with Clark's candidacy:

"I doan' keer if he *is* a houn',
        You gotta quit kickin' *my* dawg aroun'."

Clark thus appealed to a large group of people who, while convinced of the unhealthy and unjust conditions prevailing in the country, were not quite willing to plunge into a genuine programme of reform. Harmon and Underwood were too conservative, Wilson and Bryan too radical. What more natural than that they should turn toward the colourless Clark? In every presidential struggle there is a colourless Clark!

Clark was an old-fashioned Democrat. It was his foremost claim as a candidate that no matter what had happened in the past twenty-five years, he had always voted the Democratic ticket! He was a fine example of the old-time politician. As he stood at the Speaker's desk in his long coat—and he was a distinguished-looking figure—or appeared on the street in his broad-brimmed black slouch hat, with a touch of colour in his neck-scarf, he made one think—well, of Henry Clay.

Clark naturally appealed to the wheel-horse leaders of the party: he had also the powerful support of William Randolph Hearst and his chain of newspapers, Hearst indeed considering himself a kind of residuary legatee in case Clark could not be nominated. Clark was not unmindful of the sources of his strength, no matter how much Bryan might urge him to fight. He wrote to Hearsts's Chicago *American* after Illinois, and the Illinois organization, headed by Roger Sullivan, had given him its delegates:

"I am profoundly grateful to all who aided in carrying Illinois for me. Among them was the powerful influence of the Hearst newspapers, which have stood by me loyally, manfully, and unselfishly from the beginning, from Massachusetts to California."

With these influences behind him, and by shrewd political management, Clark was able to come to the convention with about half of the delegates, either pledged outright or sure to vote for him on an early ballot.

Aside from Bryan, who might or might not loom up suddenly as a dominating candidate in the convention, there was only one other real contender. This was Underwood of Alabama. Harmon of Ohio, the extreme right-wing candidate of the Bourbons of the party—a respectable, able, dull man—never had any chance at all. Although he controlled the entire delegation of his state under the unit rule, a group of enthusiastic Wilson supporters, led by William W. Durbin, Harvey C. Garber and John J. Lentz, had succeeded in winning nineteen out of

the total of forty-eight delegates. One of the ablest
Democratic leaders of the state, Newton D. Baker,
a thorough-going Wilson man, was to play a notable part
in the coming convention.

Underwood, however, might under certain circumstances— say if Roosevelt instead of Taft were nominated
by the Republicans at Chicago—become a real factor in
the struggle. He was an attractive figure, a conservative
indeed, but modern in his outlook. Like Clark, he was also
one of the Democratic leaders of the House of Representatives, but a man of wholly different type. He was the
youngest of all the presidential candidates in either party,
being then only fifty years old. Educated as a lawyer, and
the son of a lawyer, most of his life had been given to
politics. He was a quiet, hard-working, clear-thinking
congressman who had grown steadily in power and influence. When he first entered the House he occupied a
seat in a rear row and read his speeches in a low voice: in
1912 he was the leader of the majority in the House, and,
as chairman of the Ways and Means Committee, more
powerful even than the Speaker. The manner in which he
had led the Democratic members, formerly ineffective
because torn with dissensions, had been masterly. His
ways were quiet ways, he had the easy manners of the
South, but his hand was firm. Among his fellow members
of both parties, he was respected as a fair, straightforward,
and courageous leader. He had won a reputation, moreover, the result of studious application, for a real mastery
of the tariff question. "He was the only man in either
branch of Congress who could be shut up in a hermetically
sealed room and emerge with a complete tariff bill."

Wilson admired Underwood as much as he distrusted
Clark. He even favoured him, after his own nomination at
Baltimore, as the vice-presidential candidate. Underwood
came into the convention with the solid support of his

own state, Alabama, and of Georgia, Mississippi, and Florida—the heart of the Old South.

While Wilson, himself, felt that his chances were slim, based upon the count of the delegates, nevertheless there were certain elements of strength—very great strength—in his candidacy. He had won the support of powerful and influential newspapers. Perhaps the freest and soundest group of journals in the country at that time was the Scripps press, with twenty-seven newspapers, widely distributed. They were popular, they were non-partisan, they were progressive. They had made a careful survey of the candidates of both parties. Oliver P. Newman, one of their editors, went to see Wilson in the fall of 1911:

"We worked out a list of about fifteen or twenty questions that we wanted him to answer, not for publication but for the information of the Scripps papers, as to his attitude, from which we could determine whether we wanted to support him for President. . . . We had formerly been for Roosevelt, but had parted with him after his return from Africa."[1]

Newman says of this interview:

"When I think of the heights to which Wilson subsequently arose, I look back on that afternoon with him, there in his office at Trenton, and smile when I think of the way I cross-examined him. At that time I had no particular affection or regard for him. I was giving him an acid test to see if he met our requirements."[2]

As a result, the Scripps newspapers became Wilson's energetic supporters at the beginning of the campaign: and continued throughout his career.

Another bulwark of strength was Grasty's Baltimore *Sun*. Grasty had been greatly drawn to Wilson from the beginning: he had corresponded with him for several years,

---

[1] Oliver P. Newman to the author.
[2] *Ibid.*

and in the spring of 1912 began sending his paper to all of the delegates elected to the convention.

"The Baltimore *Sun*, chiefly through the enthusiasm of Charles H. Grasty, created an atmosphere of Wilson optimism in the city that had an undoubted effect upon the delegates."[1]

Wilson was cordial in his appreciation of Grasty's support: they remained warm friends to the end of their lives.

May 15, 1912.

MY DEAR MR. GRASTY:-

The attitude of the Sun towards my candidacy has given me so much pleasure and encouragement that I cannot refrain from the pleasure of sending you a line of warmest thanks and appreciation. Papers such as the Sun can do a vast deal towards getting our party out of the confusion into which it now seems to have stumbled.

Cordially and faithfully yours,
WOODROW WILSON

But the greatest accession of all to the Wilson cause was the New York *World*, the preëminent Democratic newspaper of the country. It had been somewhat critical of Wilson: and its unexpected declaration in his favour, made two days after the decisive New Jersey primaries, was not only encouraging to Wilson and his friends, but it established a potent counter influence in Tammany-controlled New York. The editorial, written by Frank I. Cobb, who was to become one of Wilson's valiant supporters and advisers, made a profound impression throughout the country.

"During Gov. Wilson's public career, *The World* has been compelled to take issue with him on many questions. We regarded with grave misgiving his sudden conversion to the initiative and referendum, reversing the principles

[1] Henry Morgenthau, *All in a Life-time*, p. 146.

of a lifetime. We regretted his apparent disposition to imitate Mr. Bryan's sweeping charges against the so-called Money Trust without supporting these charges with facts and specifications. We regretted his long campaign tours, his too eager chase after the nomination, and certain symptoms of instability which threatened to weaken his public usefulness. We have not hesitated to warn him when we thought he was going astray, and shall not hesitate to do so again in the future.

"But Gov. Wilson's elements of weakness are vastly overbalanced by his elements of strength. He has proved his political courage and his fearlessness. He has proved himself sound on tariff reform. He has proved himself sound on the Sherman law. He has proved himself sound on corporation control. He has proved himself sound against government by Wall Street plutocracy. He has proved himself sound on the independence of the judiciary. He has proved himself sound on the fundamental principles of constitutional government. He has proved that he is instinctively and temperamentally a Democrat. He has proved himself a free man who cannot be bulldozed by bosses or influenced against his convictions even by his personal friends. That is the sort of man who ought to be President.

"Gov. Wilson has had more public experience than Grover Cleveland had when he was elected President. He is better known to the rank and file of the party than Samuel J. Tilden was when he was nominated for President. *The World* believes that he would be a progressive constitutional President whom the American people could trust and for whom they would never have cause to apologize."[1]

If Wilson's chances sank to a low ebb before the New Jersey primaries, so that his managers were complaining

[1]May 30, 1912.

that "his offices were deserted," they began to rise again rapidly after June 1st. His friends felt that he had at least a fighting chance. Josephus Daniels and others began to consult with Wilson about the platform to be adopted at the convention and Wilson even sketched out certain planks and corresponded with his old friend Senator John Sharp Williams of Mississippi regarding them.

On June 18th Wilson headquarters were opened at Baltimore, a large suite in the Emerson Hotel, with the usual fanfare of optimistic claims. The real battle had begun.

## II. THE BATTLE ITSELF

Ten days before the Baltimore convention was scheduled to meet, Wilson and his family arrived at the Governor's Cottage at Sea Girt, New Jersey.

"Here we are at Sea Girt. We came down yesterday: the house was ready for us; it did not take long to unpack the trunks; and so we already feel very much at home again. The day is gray and drizzly; the sea makes a dismal voice across the bleak camp ground in front of us; we have had to light a fire in the huge fireplace to keep our spirits (and our temperature) up; but here we are a home group with that within us that can defy the depressing influences of the weather. What we now look forward to with not a little dread are the possibilities of the next fortnight in politics. I was saying at breakfast this morning, 'Two weeks from to-day we shall either have this sweet Sunday calm again or an army of reporters camped on the lawn and an all-day reception.' 'Which would you rather have?' Nellie asked. 'Need you ask?' I exclaimed; and that is the way I feel. Now that the *possibility* is immediately at hand (it is no more than a possibility, as things stand) I find myself dreading it and wishing most devoutly that I may escape. Not that I dread what would be really big and essential and worth while in the whole thing, but all that would go with [it]—all that is *non*-essential, *not* of the *business*, merely distracting and exhausting and hateful without counting,—the excessive *personal* tax of a campaign. May the Lord have mercy on me! My heart is not faint, but my taste and my preference for what is genuine and at the opposite pole from mere personal notoriety revolts at the thought of what I may be in for! . . .

"I am well (I do not count a teasing sick headache!) and underneath, deep down, my soul is quiet."[1]

All the preparations had been made to keep Wilson closely informed as to the proceedings at Baltimore. A private wire ran direct from the house at Sea Girt to McCombs's office in the Emerson Hotel. One telephone was in Wilson's own room, the other, where Secretary Tumulty could listen in, was kept in a little booth under the stairway. Tents had been erected on the grounds to accommodate newspaper correspondents and telegraphers. Political advisers, on their way to the great gathering at Baltimore, were constantly coming and going.

It was by no means a calm and peaceful week. The reverberations of the mighty conflict at Chicago, where the Republican convention was in session, broke the quiet of Sea Girt. McAdoo, who was at the scene of battle, was reporting directly to Wilson. Bryan, also at Chicago, never for a moment allowed the Democratic situation or the Democratic candidates to escape him. Playing the part momentarily of a newspaper correspondent, he was observing narrowly the methods pursued by the Republican "stand-patters" in dealing with their own revolting progressives. It was not unedifying to watch Roosevelt and La Follette, each bitterly hostile to the other, borne down in common ruin beneath the ruthless "steam roller" of an organization completely dominated by "the interests."

[1] Woodrow Wilson to Mary A. Hulbert, June 17, 1912.

Bryan knew well what a powerful influence the Republican convention might exert on the coming Democratic convention. If Taft won, and Roosevelt bolted, Democratic success depended upon the nomination of a real progressive.

"If the Democrats are guilty of the criminal folly of nominating a reactionary, they will supply Mr. Roosevelt with the one thing needful in case he becomes an independent candidate, namely, an issue, and with two reactionaries running for President he might win and thus entrench himself in power."[1]

No shrewder, no more experienced political manager, so far as conventions were concerned, ever lived in these states than William J. Bryan. He had become, indeed, a specialist in conventions.

"I began attending national conventions when I was sixteen years old. I have attended six Democratic national conventions and am on my way to the seventh. I have in fact attended every Democratic national convention except the convention of 1880, since 1876 (omitting, of course, the conventions of 1900 and 1908, when I was a candidate). This is my second Republican convention, the first being the convention of 1896, when a part of the Republican convention walked out as a protest against the platform."[2]

It was plain to Bryan that the same mighty forces that were ironing out Roosevelt at Chicago were preparing to control at Baltimore. They had already taken the first step, to make secure the temporary organization of the convention by choosing as chairman Alton B. Parker, the representative *par excellence* of the extreme conservative wing of the party. Parker was a distinguished figure. While he had been the nominee of the Democracy in 1904, he

---

[1]From Bryan's dispatch to the afternoon newspapers, June 21, 1912.
[2]From Bryan's dispatch to the afternoon newspapers, June 20, 1912.

represented all that Bryan and the progressives distrusted and feared. He must be headed off, and headed off at once.

Bryan, perspiring at the correspondents' desks at Chicago, wired Norman E. Mack, chairman of the Democratic National Committee:

"I have no choice among progressives for temporary chairman, but it would be suicidal to have a reactionary for chairman when four fifths of the whole country is radically progressive. I cannot believe such criminal folly is possible."

He protested in vain: the committee voted to nominate Parker. Bryan, undismayed, determined to carry the fight to the floor of the convention. As a preliminary step, he resolved to place all of the presidential aspirants on record. Would they stand with him, or with the "reactionaries"? He sent identical telegrams to Wilson, Clark, Marshall, and others setting forth the situation and asking them point-blank to help him oppose the choice of Parker.

"Kindly wire reply," added the implacable Commoner.

To a political manager, already established at Baltimore and eagerly seeking votes, such a demand for a black-and-white decision was an awkward business. McCombs was panic-stricken. He was angling for New York and wanted nothing done that would further alienate Boss Murphy. For Parker, himself a New Yorker, was Murphy's own pet candidate.

Before Bryan's message was sent out, the Baltimore *Sun* had wired Wilson, asking his views regarding the selection of Parker. Wilson responded immediately, writing his reply in pencil, on a bit of paper:

"My friends in Baltimore, who are on the ground, will know how to act in the interest of the people's cause in everything that affects the organization of the convention.

They are certain not to forget their standards as they have already shown. It is not necessary that I should remind them of those standards from Sea Girt; and I have neither the right nor the desire to direct the organization of a convention of which I am not even a member.

"WOODROW WILSON"

It was a message that made McCombs rejoice exceedingly, since it left the entire matter in his hands, as the man "on the ground."

Later, on the same day, Wilson received Bryan's message. It was indeed widely published. McCombs was newly alarmed. He called Wilson on the telephone, urging him to be cautious, and suggested a reply which beautifully straddled the issue.

Wilson talked the whole matter over with Mrs. Wilson and with his secretary, Tumulty. He inclined at first to adhere to the "hands-off" policy he had enunciated in the dispatch to the *Sun*, which was, indeed, the essence of McCombs's suggested reply. But Mrs. Wilson and Tumulty argued that Bryan's request gave the problem an entirely new aspect. Bryan was not asking Wilson to interfere in the work of the convention: he was asking him where he stood. Wilson sat down on the edge of his bed and wrote his reply to Bryan:

"You are quite right. Before hearing of your message I clearly stated my position in answer to a qu. from the Balto. Eve. *Sun*. The Baltimore convention is to be a convention of progressives—of men who are progressive on principle and by conviction. It must, if it is not to be put in a wrong light before the country, express its convictions in its organization and in its choice of the men who are to speak for it. You are to be a member of the convention and are entirely within your rights in doing everything within your power to bring that result about.

No one will doubt where my sympathies lie, and you will, I am sure, find my friends in the convention acting upon clear conviction and always in the interest of the people's cause. I am happy in the confidence that they need no suggestion from me."[1]

It proved to be a master-stroke. Wilson stood unreservedly upon Bryan's sound proposal that progressives should demand a progressive chairman. Clark straddled by making an appeal for harmony. Of the lesser candidates, Marshall of Indiana, Foss of Massachusetts, Baldwin of Connecticut, opposed Bryan. The only one, except Wilson, who supported him, was Governor Burke of North Dakota. Underwood and Harmon were, of course, favourable to the nominee of the organization.

McCombs was heart-broken. His advice had not been followed. He was "exceedingly disappointed."[2] How could he win the New York and other delegations with Wilson supporting Bryan?

As a matter of fact, Bryan's action and Wilson's unequivocal stand not only helped to unite the progressives upon a definite and simple issue, but it aroused the country to the real situation at Baltimore—and at Baltimore, to an almost unprecedented degree, public opinion was to become a dominating factor.

On Saturday the 22nd, the Republicans at Chicago adjourned, having nominated Taft. Roosevelt, raging with indignation, was branding the leaders as thieves and scoundrels, and still worse, "reactionaries"! Plans were forming for a new party. "We stand at Armageddon and battle for the Lord."

"The Republicans," wrote Wilson, "have met,—and done their worst; and now the Democrats are to meet and——?"

---

[1]From Mr. Wilson's original draft.

[2]Maurice F. Lyons, *William F. McCombs: The President Maker*, p. 80.

On Tuesday the 25th their cohorts descended upon
Baltimore. Tammany, led by Boss Murphy and accompanied by Judge Parker and August Belmont, came in a
special train with colours flying and a band playing.
Thomas Fortune Ryan, the symbol to the Progressives of
all that was terrifying in "Wall Street," was there in his
special car.[1] It was understood that he carried Virginia
safely stowed away in his pocket. Bryan had come on from
Chicago, still a busy correspondent, and, with Mrs. Bryan,
was at the Belvedere Hotel. Clark, pacing his office at the
Capitol, forty miles away at Washington, was in constant
and close communication with his managers on the floor
of the convention. Underwood, also at Washington, remained quietly at his work. Harmon was at home in Ohio.

Of all the groups at Baltimore, none was more enthusiastic and vociferous than the Wilson delegation at the
Emerson Hotel. Birch of New Jersey had brought down
an enormous portrait of Wilson to hang in the lobby, and
a delegation of Princeton men, orange hatbands and all,
paraded and sang.

The flag-decorated armoury, with the portrait of the
patron saint of the party, "WHO NEVER SOLD THE
TRUTH TO SERVE THE HOUR," was packed to the
roof.

The fine old Cardinal of Baltimore, serene-faced, robed
in scarlet, with a skullcap covering his silvery locks, stood
with raised hand:

"Let the light of Thy divine wisdom direct the deliber-
ations of this convention . . ."

Just behind Cardinal Gibbons, ready for the fray, sat
William J. Bryan. No sooner had Norman E. Mack, the
presiding officer, announced that he had been instructed to

---

[1]"For the first time one of the great money kings of America has appeared in person
at a national political convention to carry on the fight for the money interests."
(Baltimore *Sun*.)

submit the name of Alton B. Parker for temporary chairman than Bryan went into action. A wave of tumultuous cheering swept the vast gathering. To hundreds of those present he was still "the great Commoner," the "peerless leader." The New York delegation, a solid block in the centre of the floor, sat grimly silent.

The Commoner's face was pale. "His heavy black brows were contracted over his piercing eyes. His hawk nose had an extra downward twist. His lipless mouth was like a thin dagger-slit across his broad face. He held his head erect. . . . The grizzled fringe of his dark hair was ruffled and moist with perspiration. He made a fine figure, standing up there, in an old dark sack suit, with a low collar and white string tie. . . ."[1]

He motioned for silence, but the cheers kept up. Then the band began to play. Bryan sat down and fanned himself with a big palm leaf. When the cheering subsided, he began in measured tones his arraignment of Judge Parker, and nominated Senator John W. Kern of Indiana for temporary chairman to oppose him. Kern was Bryan's trusted friend. He had been the candidate for vice-president when Bryan himself ran for the presidency in 1908:

"I appeal to you: Let the commencement of this convention be such a commencement that the Democrats of this country may raise their heads among their fellows and say, 'The Democratic party is true to the people. You cannot frighten it with your Ryans nor buy it with your Belmonts.'"[2]

Bedlam broke loose when Bryan sat down. Hisses and catcalls were intermingled with vociferous cheering.

Senator Kern offered to withdraw his name if Parker would withdraw his. Parker's substantial figure, "ele-

---

[1] New York *World*, June 26, 1912.
[2] *Official Report of the Proceedings of the Democratic National Convention*, p. 6.

gantly attired," sitting with the New York delegation, did not stir. The old organization felt confident that it could dominate the convention. Let Bryan rant and Kern bargain!

Kern then electrified the convention by nominating Bryan himself for temporary chairman. The old Cardinal, who less than an hour before had prayed for peace and concord in the proceedings of the convention, gathered his scarlet cloak about his shoulders and left a hall seething with bitterness and strife.

When the vote was taken, the assurance of the old organization was confirmed. Parker received 579 votes Bryan 508. The "stand-patters" were apparently in control.

But the reaction of the convention itself was not without significance. When Judge Parker began his keynote speech, "the galleries rose . . . a brutal, noisy crowd and left a rather dazed old gentleman reading a long manuscript, nervously looking over his glasses occasionally at the vanishing crowd."[1]

If the conservatives—and indeed the Clark managers— were jubilant, Bryan only became more determined. An analysis of the vote served to drive him further toward Wilson. In his own report of the proceedings, June 26th, he said:

"Governor Wilson came out strong against Parker and so far as I know I received all the votes of the Wilson delegates. . . .

"The Clark vote was divided. . . .

"It was understood that Mr. Clark himself was not taking sides, but his managers worked manfully for Parker."

From that moment onward, the shouted assertion of an eloquent delegate from Texas, Cone Johnson, accurately described the proceedings:

[1]William Allen White, *Woodrow Wilson*, p. 254.

". . . the fight is on and Bryan is on one side and Wall Street is on the other."[1]

Great leadership consists in making issues so clear, so simple that common men who do not think may vote as they feel. Bryan's strategy was to dramatize the struggle, not only for the rank and file of the delegates, but for the people of the nation. The people would speak! In a conflict between Christian and Apollyon, who could doubt where popular sympathy would rest? When the press, and especially Bryan's own articles, clarified the issue, the "home folks" acted with astonishing vigour. They began to telegraph their delegates: a perfect inundation! No fewer than 110,000 telegrams were received by delegates during that week. The swing toward progressivism began on the second day and continued to the end. A move to continue Parker as permanent chairman was squelched, and Congressman Ollie M. James of Kentucky, a giant with a stentorian voice, upon whom the progressives had united, was chosen.[2]

The next step in the strategy of the progressives was to develop their real strength in the convention itself.

"The present issue here has been sharply defined as one between William J. Bryan and Thomas F. Ryan. . . . The bulk of the delegates here are plain people from the hills. There is no doubt where their sympathies lie. As usual, however, many of them owe allegiance to 'leaders' and are members of state delegations bound by the unit rule."[3]

Few of the old-timers thought that the unit rule, a hoary tradition of the party, confirmed by seventy-six years of

---

[1] *Official Report of the Proceedings of the Democratic National Convention*, p. 13.

[2] ". . .Ollie James's selection was a typical progressive victory, and the first one. If he had not been elected as the chairman I do not believe Wilson would have been nominated.   He was Bryan's friend and when Bryan wanted to talk he recognized him.   An unfriendly chairman could have kept him from the floor by recognizing motions to adjourn, which would have choked him off ."   (Frank R. Kent, of the Baltimore *Sun*, to the author.)

[3] New York *Evening Post*, June 25, 1912.

usage, could be modified. The progressives, however, made a strong appeal to the rules committee, arguing the manifest injustice of forcing delegates elected by districts favourable to Wilson to vote, under a unit rule imposed by a state convention, for Harmon or Clark or some other candidate in whom they did not believe. When the rules committee refused to act, they carried the fight to the floor, on a resolution introduced by Congressman Henry of Texas. The principal champion of the revolt was Newton D. Baker, "a young man with a clean-cut intellectual face," one of the nineteen delegates of Ohio who was himself a strong Wilson supporter, bound under the unit rule to vote for Harmon. Wilson had already taken a strong stand against the unit rule:

"The unit rule can have no legitimate place where delegates are elected by direct primary. It violates every principle of popular rule in such circumstances as to prevent their voting as their constituents instructed them to vote."[1]

Baker's speech was superb, arousing the convention to a high pitch of enthusiasm. In the midst of it a chance reference to Wilson touched off the fireworks. A demonstration broke loose which lasted for thirty-three minutes—an evidence of the spontaneous ardour of the Wilson support, as surprising as it was unexpected. When the vote was announced, it was a clear progressive victory, $565\frac{1}{2}$ to $492\frac{1}{3}$, and the Wilson and Bryan followers literally swept over the convention, carrying everything before them in their enthusiasm.

Wilson himself, sitting quietly with his family at Sea Girt, was called on the long-distance telephone. The news was elating. It indicated that the chances of an outright conservative candidate like Harmon or Underwood were

---

[1] From suggested platform plank drawn by Wilson some days before the convention met.

growing dimmer: but the great problem still remained—who was to be the chosen progressive? Clark, Wilson, Bryan?

With his long experience in politics, Bryan was still suspicious. While the progressives had won, it was by a rather close margin, and he knew the resourcefulness of Murphy, Taggart, Martin, and Ryan. He feared that the same forces that had ruled and ruined at Chicago would ruin if they could not rule at Baltimore. "I found that the representatives of Morgan, Belmont, and Ryan were at work."[1]

Bryan was nothing if not audacious. He did not wait for the opposition to move. He forced the fighting. He came into the convention the next day, Thursday, carrying in his hand one of the most astonishing resolutions ever introduced in a national convention. Not one of his friends who had seen it had dared to advise its submission.[2]

Bryan rose in his place and asked unanimous consent to present a resolution for immediate consideration. By this time he had become the storm centre of the convention.

"What is the resolution?" yelled a number of delegates.

"My resolution is as follows:

"'*Resolved*, That in this crisis in our party's career and in our country's history this convention sends greeting to the people of the United States, and assures them that the party of Jefferson and of Jackson is still the champion of popular government and equality before the law. As proof of our fidelity to the people, we hereby declare ourselves opposed to the nomination of any candidate for President who is the representative of or under obligation to J. Pierpont Morgan, Thomas F. Ryan, August Belmont, or any other member of the privilege-hunting and favour-seeking class.

[1] William J. Bryan, *Memoirs*, p. 173.
[2] *Ibid.*, p. 175.

"'*Be it further resolved*, That we demand the withdrawal from this convention of any delegate or delegates constituting or representing the above-named interests."[1]

For a moment the convention was stunned into silence. Here was a proposal to turn out of the convention several of the most notable delegates: one at least from the powerful New York delegation, August Belmont; one from the Virginia delegation, Thomas F. Ryan; both sitting in their places on the floor. Ryan rose to leave the hall, but the Virginians held him back.

Pandemonium broke loose. Scores of delegates leaped to their feet demanding recognition. Others stood on chairs to yell defiance at the Commoner. The sergeant-at-arms and the police were unable to quell the disturbance. Bryan himself stood immovable before the storm.

When the uproar had finally subsided, Bryan defended his resolution:

". . . this is an extraordinary resolution; but extraordinary conditions need extraordinary remedies. . . .

"There is not a delegate in this convention who does not know that an effort is being made right now to sell the Democratic party into bondage to the predatory interests of this nation. It is the most brazen, the most insolent, the most impudent attempt that has been made in the history of American politics to dominate a convention, stifle the honest sentiment of a people, and make the nominee the bond-slave of the men who exploit the people of this country."[2]

After a heated debate, in which it was argued that the convention had no right to expel delegates chosen by sovereign states, Bryan withdrew the latter part of his resolution: but he obstinately refused to withdraw the whole of it.

---

[1]*Official Report of the Proceedings of the Democratic National Convention*, p. 129.
[2]Ibid., p. 131.

"'If thy right hand offend thee, cut it off' . . . if it is worth while to cut off the right hand to save the body, it is worth while to cut off Morgan, Ryan, and Belmont to save the Democratic party."[1]

Demanding a record vote, Bryan was in a strong strategic position, for any delegate voting "nay" was in effect declaring that he favoured the nomination of a candidate favourable to "the privilege-hunting and favour-seeking class."

It was a brilliant stroke, even New York and Virginia joining in support of the resolution. As the vote was being taken, Boss Murphy leaned over to Belmont and said:

"August, listen and hear yourself vote yourself out of the convention."

The resolution carried by a vote of 883 to 201½. It accomplished the result that Bryan primarily had in mind: the vivid dramatization for the people of the nation of the lines of conflict and the forces engaged in the convention. Christian was winning over Apollyon!

It was now near midnight and hot in the teeming armoury, but a Democratic convention, once launched, regards time and weather no more than principalities and powers. Nominations were called for and the speeches presenting the various candidates continued until breakfast-time the next morning.

Oscar W. Underwood, the "favourite son" of Alabama, was the first candidate to be named—in a strong address by his friend Senator Bankhead. He was cheered for twenty-six minutes. Senator James A. Reed nominated his fellow Missourian, the "houn' dawg candidate," Champ Clark. The barometer of applause rose to an hour and five minutes. A tremendous demonstration! Connecticut then offered her much esteemed Governor, Simeon E. Baldwin; and at the ripe hour of 2:15 in the morning, Delaware

[1] *Offical Report of the Proceedings of the Democratic National Convention*, p. 136.

yielding to New Jersey, Judge Wescott stepped forward to present the name of Woodrow Wilson. Wescott, it will be remembered, had been a bitter opponent of Wilson in the state convention of 1910, but had become one of his stoutest supporters. He was an orator of the older type—a little florid, but with the real essence of eloquence, which is sincerity.

He was not allowed to proceed at once. The crowd, the galleries especially, could not wait to express their enthusiasm for Wilson. The applause was tumultuous and uncontrollable.

Judge Wescott's magnificent voice carried to the uttermost parts of the vast auditorium:

"The Democratic party is commissioned to carry on a great constructive programme, having for its end a complete restoration of the doctrine of equal rights and equal opportunity. . . . Providence has given us, in the exalted character of New Jersey's Executive, the mental and moral equipment to accomplish this reincarnation of Democracy. . . .

"He has been in political life less than two years. He has had no organization of the usual sort; only a practical ideal, the reëstablishment of equal opportunity. The logic of events points to him. . . . Every crisis evolves its master. Time and circumstance have evolved the immortal Governor of New Jersey. . . .

". . . New Jersey appreciates . . . the honour . . . of placing before this convention as a candidate for the presidency of the United States the seer and philosopher of Princeton, the Princeton schoolmaster, Woodrow Wilson."[1]

The demonstration which followed Wescott's nomination speech exceeded that of any other candidate. Wilson's friends were determined to out-yell and out-march the

---

[1] *Official Report of the Proceedings of the Democratic National Convention*, pp. 160, 161.

Clark forces, and they cheered and paraded for an hour and a quarter. A delegation appeared at the head of the parade with a huge portrait of Wilson:

"We want Wilson, we want Wilson."

Day was breaking, but Governor Marshall of Indiana and Governor Harmon of Ohio had yet to be nominated: and there was a drum fire of briefer seconding speeches, those supporting Wilson being the blind Senator Gore of Oklahoma, P. H. O'Brien of Michigan, John Walsh of Wisconsin, A. Mitchell Palmer of Pennsylvania, Ellison D. Smith of South Carolina, and Alfred Jacques of Minnesota. The name of Governor Burke, favourite son of North Dakota, was withdrawn in Wilson's favour by S. J. Doyle, a delegate from that state. It was about seven o'clock in the morning when the first ballot was taken. Clark was decidedly in the lead. The ninety votes of New York went to Governor Harmon. Underwood had the support of the Old South:

| | |
|---|---|
| Clark | $440\frac{1}{2}$ |
| Wilson | 324 |
| Harmon | 148 |
| Underwood | $117\frac{1}{2}$ |
| Marshall | 31 |
| Baldwin | 22 |
| Sulzer | 2 |
| Bryan | $1$[1] |

If the radio had then been perfected, the Wilson family at Sea Girt would probably have "listened in" on the proceedings at Baltimore. As it was, time lagged on the Jersey shore. Wilson played a round of golf and came in early to talk with the newspaper men and read the brief dispatches they had received. He was called to the telephone several times by McCombs. In the evening he and

[1] *Official Report of the Proceedings of the Democratic National Convention*, p. 196.

Mrs. Wilson sat quietly before the fireplace; for a time he read Morley's *Gladstone*—"a great book." A friend or two dropped in to call, among them ex-Governor Fort of New Jersey. When someone asked Wilson what he thought of the situation at Baltimore, he was reminded of the man, riding in a buggy, who stopped three times to ask the distance to the next town. Each time he had the same response: twenty miles. "Well, John," said the man in the buggy to his companion, "I'm glad we're holding our own."

The fourth day of the convention (Friday) was devoted wholly to balloting. It was not until the roll was called for the tenth time that the "underground work" which had been going on among the managers bore dramatic fruit. When New York was called, Boss Murphy, arising slowly, startled the convention by delivering his entire delegation to Champ Clark.

It was a tremendous moment. Everyone present knew the significance of the change. It meant that Champ Clark would carry a majority of the convention. "The fight is over," roared a Clark enthusiast. The Missouri delegation arose as one man and began a parade around the hall. Banner after banner joined in the procession. The demonstration lasted for an hour or more. A stampede was in the making. Not for sixty-eight years, since Van Buren was nominated at Baltimore in 1844, had any Democratic candidate who received a majority of the votes in the convention failed to win two thirds and the nomination. Well might Clark's friends consider that the battle was won. And Tammany Hall had won it!

Bryan had been absent during the vote. He had been worn out by the strain of two conventions. He entered at the height of the demonstration, his tall form shouldering its way through the seething marchers. When he learned what had happened he rose in his place, crying out:

"A progressive candidate must not be besmirched by New York's vote."[1]

One of Bryan's daughters, sitting in the gallery, was leading the cheering for Woodrow Wilson.

The issue hung in the balance. A stampede might easily have followed if the states on the roll next after New York had not been among Wilson's strongest supporters. When Oklahoma was called, a Clark member, hoping to break the solid Wilson vote, demanded that the delegation be polled. "Alfalfa Bill" Murray was instantly on his feet. Alfalfa Bill was lanky and collarless, wore "galluses" and a bandana handkerchief. He could roar like the bull of Bashan. Upon this occasion he not only roared but waved his arms. He had no objection to a poll, but "... we do insist we shall not join Tammany in making the nomination."[2]

He was greeted with tremendous applause: the Wilson and Bryan men went wild: Alfalfa Bill had struck the keynote of the hour.

There was no stampede, but the result of the ballot showed that Clark had eleven more than a majority. Wilson's lines, however, had held firm: he lost only two votes from the former ballot. The vote stood:

| | |
|---|---|
| Clark | 556 |
| Wilson | $350\frac{1}{2}$ |
| Underwood | $117\frac{1}{2}$ |
| Marshall | 31 |
| Harmon | 31 |
| Kern | 1 |
| Bryan | 1[3] |

---

[1] Bryan says that from this time forward he never left the hall during the sessions of the convention. "One of the assistants of the sergeant-at-arms . . . supplied me with water, keeping a large bottle under the platform, while my brother supplied me with sandwiches. My one thought was to save the Democratic party from defeat at the polls."—William J. Bryan, *Memoirs*, pp. 180–181.

[2] *Official Report of the Proceedings of the Democratic National Convention*, p. 220.

[3] *Ibid.*

It was one o'clock at night when the fateful result of the tenth ballot was announced. The Wilsons at Sea Girt had retired. Tumulty, awaiting the news, "almost collapsed."[1] As he was leaving the house for his home, Governor Wilson appeared at an upper window.

"Tumulty, is there any news from Baltimore?"

Tumulty's dejection was telltale, and a little later Wilson knew the worst. He had a long discussion with that "best of all advisers," Mrs. Wilson, as to what he should do. He had previously expressed his conviction[2] that the two-thirds rule was undemocratic and ought to be abolished. A majority should rule. And Clark had a majority! Nevertheless the rule had not been abolished: and the nominee would have to secure a two-thirds vote.

Early Saturday morning McCombs called Wilson on the telephone. McCombs was utterly discouraged, and they discussed a message from Wilson releasing his delegates. McCombs thought it would be "a good thing to have in hand." McCombs also wanted instructions as to whom, when the break came, Wilson would turn his strength. He suggested Underwood, but Wilson felt that he had no right to express a preference.

When the Governor left the telephone, tears stood in Mrs. Wilson's eyes. Their thoughts turned at once to the beloved lake country of England, and they began making plans for a visit as soon as Wilson's term as governor expired.

"Now we can see Rydal again."[3]

Wilson even considered sending a congratulatory telegram to Champ Clark.[4]

---

[1] Joseph P. Tumulty, *Woodrow Wilson As I Know Him*, p. 119.
[2] In a letter to Colonel House, October 24, 1911. See p. 299, this volume.
[3] From an interview with Mrs. Wilson, in the Baltimore *Sun*, July 3, 1912.
[4] Joseph P. Tumulty, *Woodrow Wilson As I Know Him*, p. 121.

But the battle was not ended. Wilson had powerful friends at Baltimore, men of steady nerves, like McAdoo, and long experience in politics, like Burleson of Texas, who was "quite the most active Wilson man on the floor of the convention."[1] Moreover Bryan, long wavering between Clark and Wilson, was yet to be heard from.

Later on Saturday morning—the lowest ebb of the convention so far as Wilson was concerned—McAdoo went to call on McCombs, and found him in a state of great dejection. A fatigued mind in a sickly and worn-out body! He had quite lost his head.

"The jig's up," said McCombs. "Clark will be nominated. All my work has been for nothing."

McAdoo was dumbfounded. "Do you mean that you are giving up the fight?"

McCombs said, "It is hopeless. Clark has a majority of the convention and no candidate has ever received a majority without being nominated."

McAdoo replied, "You are all wrong. Wilson is stronger now than he was last night. Under the two-thirds rule Clark can never win."

"Why, Governor Wilson himself has given up."

"What do you mean?"

"I talked to the Governor on the telephone very fully about the situation and told him I thought he ought to release his friends, and the Governor has authorized me to release them. I told the Governor that I would have to have a telegram from him authorizing me to do so as his friends in the convention might not accept my statement."[2]

McAdoo understood McCombs to say that he had such

---

[1] Newton D. Baker to the author.

[2] The writer is indebted to Mr. McAdoo for this narrative of what happened, confirmed as to the reaction at Sea Girt by Mr. Tumulty.

a telegram from the Governor,[1] and he was so "indignant and amazed" that he not only denounced McCombs— "We had some very hot words; so hot, in fact, that I can't put them on paper"—but he rushed to the telephone and urged Wilson, at Sea Girt, not to think for a moment of releasing his friends in the convention; that he was gaining strength all the time; that Clark could never get a two-thirds vote.[2] Wilson responded, according to McAdoo, that he had been acting on McCombs's advice, and authorized McAdoo to tell McCombs not to release his delegates. Upon hearing McAdoo's report, McCombs called Wilson on the telephone to confirm the decision.[3]

It seems certain that if Wilson had followed McCombs's advice at any one of several critical moments of the convention he might and probably would have lost the nomination. McCombs was obsessed with the idea that Wilson's only chance lay in winning the Tammany-controlled delegation from New York—ninety votes. When had a Democratic candidate been nominated without New York? Three times during the convention Wilson greatly ad-

---

[1] There is little doubt that some such message was sent, although there is no record among the Wilson papers of a telegram. In an interview on July 2nd a correspondent of the Baltimore *Sun* quotes Mrs. Wilson:

"There was a time when we felt dubious about this and despaired of success. Things looked so dark on Friday night, when Mr. Clark received a majority, that Mr. Wilson sent a message to Mr. McCombs releasing the Wilson delegates and asking him to tell them they were not to vote for him any longer if they felt they ought to vote for someone else. Mr. Wilson thought that it was all over, and we tried to pretend to think we were glad that it was over."

[2] Wilson was also being urged by telephone by other friends at Baltimore, among them Judge Hudspeth.

[3] This detailed statement has seemed necessary to correct various accounts indicating that Wilson, on his own initiative, sent a telegram releasing his delegates, but that McCombs "saved" him by tearing up, or, in one story, withholding, the telegram and going forward with the fight. McCombs's bitterly hostile narrative (*Making Woodrow Wilson President*, p. 143 ff.), written from memory years after the events, is wholly undependable as to its facts in this as in many other statements. He refers, for example, to Senator Stone's telegram as the cause for Wilson's action, placing it "early Friday, June 28th" when as a matter of fact the crucial tenth ballot did not take place until early Saturday morning, June 29th. Moreover the original telegram from Senator Stone remains in Wilson's files. It was not sent from Baltimore until 3:12 P. M. June 29th.

vanced his cause by acting exactly contrary to his manager's urgent advice. First, when, as we have seen, he supported Bryan's demand for a progressive chairman against the Tammany nominee, Alton B. Parker. Second, when he finally decided not to withdraw his candidacy after the tenth ballot, when Clark attained a majority. Third, as we shall see, when he refused, after McCombs's urging, to give assurance that, in the event of his election, he would not appoint Bryan Secretary of State. McCombs, although supporting a progressive candidate, seems to have had no imaginative grasp of the new forces at work in the convention. It apparently never occurred to him that Wilson might break two of the most sacred traditions of Democratic conventions: nomination without the New York delegation, and nomination after an opposing candidate had secured a majority.

Looking back, one is impressed by the hair-trigger chances of that unprecedented convention! A single misstep and Wilson would have lost.

When the convention met on the fifth day, the atmosphere was surcharged with excitement. Would there be a stampede to Clark? Would Wilson retire? What would Bryan do?

Wilson himself had been doing some hard thinking as a result of his consultations with McAdoo, McCombs, Hudspeth, and others. While the thirteenth ballot was being taken, he called McCombs—then in the convention hall— and said he had a message which he wished delivered at once to Mr. Bryan. He had written it out hastily in shorthand and had a copy made on the typewriter—the originals remain among his papers—and asked that it be taken down verbatim:[1]

"It has become evident that the present deadlock is being maintained for the purpose of enabling New York,

[1] Walker W. Vick, at the telephone, took it down in writing.

a delegation controlled by a single group of men, to control the nomination and tie the candidate to itself. In these circumstances it is the imperative duty of each candidate for the nomination to see to it that his own independence is beyond question. I can see no other way to do this than to declare that he will not accept a nomination if it cannot be secured without the aid of that delegation. For myself, I have no hesitation in making that declaration. The freedom of the party and its candidate and the security of the government against private control constitute the supreme consideration."

Such a course as Wilson here recommended would oblige every candidate to declare his position regarding Tammany support. Clark would either have to repudiate Boss Murphy or admit his obligation to him—an embarrassing decision!

Whether it was this message that influenced Bryan in making his devastating announcement after the thirteenth ballot, or whether he was already considering some such course, the strategy seemed to have been in the minds of both men.[1]

While Bryan had been maintaining his personal neutrality as between Clark and Wilson, he had all along been voting, as one of the instructed Nebraska delegation, for Clark. And Clark's managers had been doing their best— now their successful best—to enlist the support of the very interests, Tammany Hall, Belmont, Ryan, which were most repugnant to him. How could he continue to vote for Clark?

The crisis came in the fourteenth ballot. When Nebraska was called, Senator Hitchcock asked that the delegation be polled. Bryan rose in his place and demanded recognition. An expectant convention went quiet.

---

[1]Bryan does not mention, in his *Memoirs*, having received a message from Wilson. It is possible that McCombs never handed it to Bryan.

"THE PRESIDING OFFICER: For what purpose does the gentleman from Nebraska rise?

"MR. BRYAN, of Nebraska: To explain my vote."[1]

Suspecting trouble, opposition delegates clamoured for "regular order." The chairman ruled that nothing was in order but the calling of the roll. Thereupon Bryan replied:

"As long as Mr. Ryan's agent—as long as New York's ninety votes are recorded for Mr. Clark, I withhold my vote from him and cast it——"[2]

Pandemonium broke loose.

Senator Stone interceded for Bryan and asked that he be heard. The Commoner then read the statement which he had prepared. He reminded the delegates that they had passed his Morgan-Ryan-Belmont resolution by a four-to-one vote and had thereby pledged themselves against the nomination of any man connected with the "privilege-seeking, favour-hunting class."

"The vote of the state of New York in this convention, as cast under the unit rule, does not represent the intelligence, the virtue, the Democracy or the patriotism of the ninety men who are here. It represents the will of one man —Charles F. Murphy—and he represents the influences that dominated the Republican convention at Chicago and are trying to dominate this convention. . . .

". . . I shall withhold my vote from Mr. Clark as long as New York's vote is recorded for him. And the position that I take in regard to Mr. Clark, I will take in regard to any other candidate whose name is now or may be before the convention. I shall not be a party to the nomination of any man, no matter who he may be . . . who will not, when elected, be absolutely free to carry out the anti-Morgan-Ryan-Belmont resolution and make his administration reflect the wishes and the hopes of those who be-

[1]*Official Report of the Proceedings of the Democratic National Convention*, p. 232.
[2]*Ibid.*

lieve in a government of the people, by the people, and for the people. . . .

"With the understanding that I shall stand ready to withdraw my vote from the one for whom I am going to cast it whenever New York casts her vote for him, I cast my vote for Nebraska's second choice, Governor Wilson."[1]

It was a thrilling moment. The Wilson supporters broke into wild applause. Nebraska voted twelve for Wilson, four for Clark. While the change in the total vote was inconsequential—Clark lost only one and a half votes and Wilson gained only five—it was nevertheless an epoch-making incident. The Commoner had at last made his decision, placed all his power and influence behind Wilson.

Clark, hearing promptly of Bryan's shift to Wilson, came "in a rage" from Washington to Baltimore. He had been absolutely confident of the nomination. He intended to rise to a question of privilege on the floor of the convention.[2] But the convention adjourned just as he was arriving. Would he have stampeded it if he had walked down the central aisle? He was in an ugly mood, and after long talks with his managers and with Hearst, gave out a statement declaring that the "outrageous aspersion" put upon him by Bryan was "utterly and absolutely false." He demanded "proof or retraction."[3] The Clark people even made a belated appeal to Wilson himself, the telegram already referred to signed by Senator Stone and sent Saturday afternoon, June 29th:

"A majority of the national convention has voted for the candidacy of Champ Clark. No one questions his fitness and loyalty to Democracy and for seventy years the practice has been established of giving the nomination to the candidate who received a majority. We ask you in the

---

[1]*Official Report of the Proceedings of the Democratic National Convention*, pp. 234–237.
[2]Champ Clark, *My Quarter Century in American Politics*, p. 427.
[3]Baltimore *Sun*, June 30, 1912.

interests of the party and in vindication of the democratic principle of majority rule to assist in making his nomination unanimous by the withdrawal of your candidacy."

The Clark people also made frantic efforts at this time to break Wilson's solid support. They tempted Pennsylvania with an offer of the vice-presidential nomination to A. Mitchell Palmer, but Palmer himself, and Vance C. McCormick, William B. Wilson and other Wilson leaders stood firm.

Clark had reached his zenith. From that moment onward his vote began to waste away, here a vote, there a delegation. Wilson's supporters took courage. The fight became dogged, unremitting. The ballots crept up into the twenties and thirties and still no decision. Wilson at Sea Girt remarked:

"We have been figuring that at the present rate of gain I will be nominated in 175 more ballots."

June 30th was Sunday, and Wilson, with his family, escaped from the noisy camp at Sea Girt and drove to church at Spring Lake, New Jersey. After the service, the Reverend Dr. James M. Ludlow expressed surprise that the Governor should have come such a distance.

"Why, Doctor," he replied, in tones of deep emotion, "where should a man in my straits be on such a day, except in the House of God? I could not remain at the camp."[1]

But, if the convention was not in session on Sunday, the politicians were busy enough. Wilson's opponents were charging, bitterly, that his managers were "making deals," promising patronage. Some of the accusations were specific: McCombs loved political manipulation! To make it clear that he would be bound by no such "arrangements," Wilson issued a statement:

"Of course I do not know in detail what my friends and

---

[1] Dr. James M. Ludlow to the author.

supporters are doing, but I am morally certain that they are not making arrangements or attempting to come to an agreement with anybody. I am certain that they are doing nothing more than could be done in full view of the country, and that their only means of getting support is argument. There cannot be any possibility of any trading done in my name; not a single vote can or will be obtained by means of any promise."[1]

Nevertheless a political convention is a political convention. Manipulation, tit-for-tat, is the breath in the nostrils of its impresarios. Wilson might protest. McCombs was on the ground. And McCombs's problem, in luring the shy conservatives to Wilson's support, was Bryan. It had been Bryan from the beginning. Bryan stood like a rock in the way. On Sunday McCombs called Wilson on the telephone and told him that the feeling against Bryan was so intense among many delegates that his nomination depended upon the assurance, which McCombs was eager to give, that Wilson, in the event of his election, would not appoint Bryan Secretary of State."[2]

The Governor declined to make any such commitment. "I will not bargain for this office. It would be foolish for me at this time to decide upon a cabinet officer, and it would be outrageous to eliminate anybody from consideration now, particularly Mr. Bryan, who has rendered such fine service to the party in all seasons."[3]

On the other hand, Wilson's managers had moments of panic lest Bryan, deciding that neither Clark nor Wilson could break the deadlock, might at some dramatic moment, which he himself would know best how to choose, rally the progressives to his own support and seize the nomination. There were many in the convention who

---

[1]Baltimore *Sun*, June 30, 1912.
[2]Josephus Daniels, in the *Saturday Evening Post*, September 5, 1925.
[3]Joseph P. Tumulty, *Woodrow Wilson As I Know Him*, p. 118.

thought all along that this was Bryan's strategy.[1] One thing stands clear in the record: having espoused Wilson's cause in the fourteenth ballot, no one could afterwards have supported a candidate with greater loyalty than he.

In the final analysis the overturn of the so-called "re-actionaries" at Baltimore, who were at first undeniably in control, was due to the pressure of the rank and file of the Democrats of the nation—the "plain people of the hills." Political manipulation counted for next to nothing at all. It was, perhaps beyond any other in our history, a people's convention. Bryan's service—and Bryan was the dominant figure at every turn—was to make the issue clear and hold the convention steady until the people, aroused by the campaigns of Wilson, La Follette, Roosevelt, and Bryan himself, could be heard from. The newspapers played a great part in the struggle. Grasty's Baltimore *Sun*, the paper that every delegate saw every day, did loyal service not only for progressivism but for Wilson's candidacy. On July 1st the New York *World*, the most influential Democratic paper in the country, appeared with a flaming editorial by Frank I. Cobb:

"It is too late to talk compromise at Baltimore.

"Ryanism and Murphyism have created an issue that makes the nomination of Woodrow Wilson a matter of Democratic life or death. . . .

"To compromise now is to send a Democratic ticket into the campaign shackled to bossism and plutocracy.

"To compromise now is to give Theodore Roosevelt the supreme issue that he needs.

"Compromise was possible until the Ryan-Murphy

---

[1] "It was and still is my judgment, proclaimed at the time and frequently repeated since, that Mr. Bryan had not the slightest idea, when he changed the vote of Nebraska, of contributing to the nomination of Wilson. He merely desired to defeat Champ Clark, with the concealed hope and expectation of prolonging the contest and receiving the nomination himself." (Carter Glass, United States Senator from Virginia, to the author.)

This belief was shared by Newton D. Baker.

conspiracy was fully revealed and the Tammany boss
carried out the terms of his bargain with the Clark managers by throwing New York's ninety votes to Champ
Clark. Compromise was possible until Mr. Bryan was
compelled by the inexorable logic of events to repudiate
Champ Clark's candidacy and vote for Woodrow Wilson.
Compromise was possible until it became apparent to
every intelligent man that the Ryan-Murphy-Belmont-
Hearst coalition had set out to strangle progressive
Democracy, destroy Mr. Bryan politically, and prevent
the nomination of Woodrow Wilson at any cost.

"Compromise is no longer possible. There can be no
Democratic harmony, there can be no Democratic unity,
there can be no Democratic integrity, until the convention
overwhelms this shameful alliance between corrupt finance
and corrupt politics. . . .

"As Stephen A. Douglas once said, 'There can be no
neutrals in this war—only patriots or traitors.'"

The New York *Times*, which in the pre-convention
campaign, "had no favoured candidate,"[1] was now supporting Wilson vigorously.[2]

It grew clearer every hour to the perspiring delegates
at Baltimore that the mighty forces of public opinion were
behind Wilson. But it was not until the thirtieth ballot, on
the sixth day, that Wilson passed Clark, the vote standing:

| | |
|---|---|
| Wilson | 460 |
| Clark | 455 |
| Underwood | 121½ |
| Foss | 30 |
| Harmon | 19 |
| Kern | 2[3] |

[1]Elmer Davis, *History of the New York Times*, p. 250.

[2]On July 5, 1912, Wilson wrote to Louis Wiley, its business manager: "The support
of the Times has given me peculiar gratification and I feel that I must owe it in part
to your own generous friendship."

[3]*Official Report of the Proceedings of the Democratic National Convention*, p. 300.

When the newspaper correspondents, rushing up from their tents at Sea Girt to inform the Governor—"You've passed him, you've passed him"—requested a statement, Wilson remarked:

"You might say that Governor Wilson received the news that Champ Clark had dropped to second place in a riot of silence."

Wilson continued to creep up, slowly, irresistibly. What was needed was the dramatic swing-over of some powerful delegation. And this came in the Tuesday session, the seventh day of the interminable convention. Just before the forty-third ballot got under way, McCombs went over to Roger Sullivan of Illinois:

"Roger, we've got to have Illinois, or I'll withdraw."

It was the irritable plea of a sick man.

"Sit steady, boy," replied the boss.[1] A few minutes later, when his state's name was called, he rose and delivered fifty-eight votes to Governor Wilson.

Illinois was followed by Virginia and West Virginia.

It was the beginning of the end. Wilson had 602 votes, Clark had dwindled to 329. Underwood held $98\frac{1}{2}$. The convention was now in the wildest confusion. When the forty-sixth roll call began, Senator Bankhead withdrew Underwood's candidacy, and Senator Stone released the Clark delegates, but announced that Missouri would cast her last vote for "old Champ Clark." John F. Fitzgerald followed by withdrawing Governor Foss's name, giving the Massachusetts vote to Wilson. Thereupon John J. Fitzgerald of New York moved that Wilson be nominated by acclamation. A wild outburst of cheering arose from every section of the armoury. All the delegates, with the exception of those from Missouri, were on their feet. Bryan had a broad smile on his face. Senator Reed objected to the motion, assuring the convention that, while

[1] Maurice F. Lyons, *William F. McCombs, The President Maker*, p. 102.

the Missourians cherished no ill-feeling toward the Governor of New Jersey, they must insist on giving their forty-sixth vote to the Speaker. The Harmon men were then released, the roll proceeded, and Wilson polled 990 votes. Missouri paid its last tribute to Clark.

Stone then moved that the nomination be made unanimous. At 3:30 o'clock in the afternoon, Chairman James pronounced Woodrow Wilson the Democratic nominee for President of the United States.

A candidate for Vice-President had now to be nominated. Wilson wanted Underwood: but Underwood refused to allow his name to be considered. Burleson telephoned to Wilson that the convention was leaning toward Thomas R. Marshall.

"But, Burleson," said the Governor, "he is a small-calibre man."

Burleson argued that Marshall was well located geographically and was an extremely able politician.

"All right, go ahead," answered Wilson.[1]

He did not know that McCombs had pledged the Wilson vote to Marshall during the presidential balloting, and was now expecting to deliver it.

An attempt was made by a Bryan enthusiast to nominate him for the vice-presidency. It gave the Commoner an opportunity to deliver his valedictory:

"To-night I come with joy to surrender into the hands of the one chosen by this convention a standard which I have carried in three campaigns, and I challenge my enemies to declare that it has ever been lowered in the face of the enemy."[2]

---

[1]A. S. Burleson to the author.

[2]*Official Report of the Proceedings of the Democratic National Convention*, pp. 382–383 Wilson wrote to Bryan a few days later:

". . . your 'valedictory', spoken in the last hours of the Convention at Baltimore, seems to me a peculiarly noble thing and constituting a fitting close to a Convention in which you played a part which the whole country now recognizes and assesses at its true significance." (July 8, 1912.)

So the ticket became Wilson and Marshall.

When word came from Baltimore that he had won, Governor Wilson walked slowly up the stairs, and said to his wife:

"Well, dear, we won't go to Rydal after all."

# CHAPTER VII

## THE CAMPAIGN OF 1912

If you believe in me, make it possible for me to do something.
*Speech in New Jersey, October 30, 1912.*

I regard this campaign as I regarded the last one, and the one before the last, and every campaign in which people have taken part since the world began, as simply a continued struggle to see to it that the people were taken care of by their own government.
*Speech in New Jersey, August 15, 1912.*

A presidential campaign may easily degenerate into a mere personal contest and so lose its real dignity and significance. There is no indispensable man . . . men are instruments. We are as important as the cause we represent. . . .
*Acceptance Speech, August 7, 1912.*

Politics ought not to be considered as a mere occasion for oratory. Politics ought to be considered as a branch of the national business and a man who talks politics ought to tell his fellow citizens very distinctly what he thinks about their affairs and what his own attitude towards them is.
*Speech in New Jersey, August 15, 1912.*

### I. THE CANDIDATE ACCEPTS

IT IS related that on the afternoon of Wilson's nomination "a brass band of forty pieces had been held in readiness down the road." When the good news arrived from Baltimore, it "blared forth," descending upon the quiet cottage at Sea Girt. "Hail to the Chief." " The Conquering Hero Comes."

Symbol and portent! A brass band blaring forth. No more Rydal Water and Wordsworth! No more, ever again, the blissful privacy of the scholar.

It was a strangely mixed experience. The victory itself was sweet, however tinged with the inner depression of spirit so characteristic of Wilson's temperament. "Success," as he had said years before in a letter to Ellen Axson, "does not flush or elate me, except for the moment." To a man of his deeply serious nature, victory was sobering. A sense of the responsibilities confronting him overtook and dimmed the joy of the moment.

Much in the immediate experience was as stimulating as it was wholly delightful. The elation of his family and close friends no doubt came first. Nothing could have pleased him more than the heart-warming letters from the old and tried friends of Princeton and Johns Hopkins, men he knew deeply and could trust.

"You have always more than fulfilled the dreams I have had for you—and finest of all, the noblest way."[1]

"I am so happy," wrote Cleveland H. Dodge, "I can hardly think."

"I can't resist an expression of my joy," wrote Walter H. Page. "To see a sincere effort made to work out democratic ideas in government and to have the democratic philosophy of society worthily formulated once more and with authority and fitted to present conditions—these are exciting prospects and most cheering."[2]

It was a rare delight to Wilson to reply to these personal letters with all the warmth of regard that he felt. He wrote to Page:

7 July, 1912

MY DEAR PAGE,

I have wanted to write you a line of grateful appreciation ever since I received that delightful little note of hope from you written on June 19, but it has been impossible until this moment. Even now I can write only a line; but it is full of warm feeling. Your friendship and your generous faith in me are a source of cheer and of strength to me all the time.

Sincerely Your Friend,
WOODROW WILSON

[1] Robert Bridges to Woodrow Wilson.
[2] July 3, 1912.

Even at his busiest he struggled to keep up the close
friendships so necessary to his life; "...the more these new
things crowd upon me the more I seem to be dependent for
peace and joy upon those I love. The more public my life
becomes the more I seem driven in upon my own inner life
and all its intimate companionships."

He wrote to Colonel House:

"I need not tell you how warmly I appreciated your
message of congratulation or how eagerly I shall wait your
return. It is selfish to wish for you and I hope that you
will not risk anything in regard to your health by coming
too soon, but it will be delightful and reassuring to see you.

"With warmest regard,

"Gratefully yours,
"WOODROW WILSON"[1]

He wrote to his old friend Dabney on August 13th:

"Your letters, my dear fellow, have cheered me tremendously. . . .

"My own days are so full of every kind of engagement
and distraction that I hardly have time to think. I only
exist from moment to moment, but somehow nothing
shuts out thoughts of my friends wherever they are, and
your letters come like a voice in response to my thoughts.

"Always faithfully and affectionately yours,
"WOODROW WILSON"

The approval of the country at large, abundantly expressed in a downpour of telegrams and letters, certified
by innumerable newspaper articles and editorials, was not
only gratifying in itself, but kindled his confidence in the
future.

Nevertheless, the experience as a whole, to a man of

[1] July 17, 1912.

Wilson's temperament, was infinitely difficult and disquieting. Roosevelt might swim happily through such seas
of indiscriminate excitement, Bryan might ride the waves
with joy; but Wilson found it hard sailing.

"You cannot . . . *imagine* such days . . ." he wrote.
". . . an invasion by the people of the United States! I had
read of the like, and *dreaded* it, but of course had never
*realized* what it was to be the principal victim. . . . I am
wondering how all this happened to come to *me*, and
whether, when [the] test is over, I shall have been found
to be in any sense worthy. It is awesome to be so believed
in and trusted. It makes me feel a sort of loneliness, because I cannot speak of it without seeming to be thinking
of myself—and reporters haunt me the livelong day."[1]

It was indeed an invasion by the people of the United
States. They came on foot, by train, by automobile. They
swarmed across the open grounds, they sat on the porch
of the house, they even wandered about the lower rooms—
good-natured, enthusiastic, eager to shake the hand of the
candidate; Wilson could not leave the house without being
surrounded by earnest Democrats who wanted to meet
him or have their pictures taken in his company. Jackson-
ian Democracy had returned!

Much the worst ordeal of all was the descent upon the
modest, rather exclusive, home-loving family at Sea Girt
of several score of newspaper reporters, artists, photographers. They were not the skilled political writers who
had been attending the conventions, now momentarily
on leave, but "human interest" reporters, eager for the
spectacular, the bizarre, the dramatic, the personal. Some
were "sob-sisters." No member of the family could escape.
"Turn around. Take your hat off. Smile."[2]

The candidate endeavoured to meet the situation generously. He was eager to come into closer contact with the

---

[1] Woodrow Wilson to Mary A. Hulbert, July 6, 1912.

people of the country. He set an hour on the evening of the second day for receiving all of the reporters.

"We swarmed into his little office and stood in a solid semicircle facing the desk. The Governor came into the room dressed in white flannels, handsome, springy-stepped, bright-eyed, with a smile on his face.

"'I am sorry, ladies and gentlemen, that you have to stand up. Our quarters here are very limited, and I hope you will pardon me for not being able to make you more comfortable.'" [1]

"Well, Governor," remarked a New York police reporter, "You've got the first page now. Hang on to it. You've got the edge on Teddy and we want a lot of good stuff from you."

Another chimed in:

"We are all on space down here, Governor, and the more we can play you up the more we can increase our checks at the end of the week."

The Governor looked over at the first man and smiled: he thought it was a joke. He did not smile quite so broadly at the second man.

"You had some politicians come to see you from Washington, didn't you?"

"I believe there were some gentlemen from Washington."

"Who were they, Governor?"

"I recall that Senator Reed was here."

"Is Reed United States senator or a state senator?"

Governor Wilson's face grew still more serious.

"He is a United States senator."

"What's his initials, Governor?"

Wilson's face was hardening. "James A."

"As this questioning continued," says Newman, "I

---

[1] Major Oliver P. Newman, then a representative of the Scripps papers, in conversations with the author.

watched Wilson's face grow sterner. I knew that he was thinking of his nomination with the deepest seriousness. He felt the responsibility that had been placed upon him, and he looked forward to the campaign with a feeling of consecration. I could see him thinking, as he looked around the room and listened to these questions, 'Is my destiny in such hands?'"

The reports from Sea Girt on the days that followed were far from reassuring. In response to one of the reporters who had asked about the mail he was receiving he remarked lightly that he felt, in trying to reply to all the letters he was receiving, somewhat like the frog that fell into the well. "Every time he jumped up one foot he fell back two." The next morning one of the New York newspapers headed its dispatch from Sea Girt: "Wilson Feels Like a Frog."

It was not only disheartening: it was offensive. It confirmed Wilson in the strong dislike he had always felt for personal publicity. He felt that he could not be outspoken with men who could not understand, or with editors who permitted or required their writers to treat what he considered a solemn undertaking in a spirit so trivial, so personal.

"For myself, I feel very solemn about the whole thing. It is a very deep responsibility. . . ."[1]

From this time onward he was never quite free with groups of correspondents. He continued to receive them, then and afterwards, but they felt that he was on his guard, that he was "cold," that he gave them as little as he could. No man could have been franker than he with writers whom he came to know and to trust: he numbered among them many friends, several intimate friends: but he came more and more to shrink from miscellaneous interviewing.

[1]Woodrow Wilson to his nephew, George Howe, July 6, 1912.

Other visitors came in swarms to Sea Girt. For the first time in sixteen years the Democratic party felt certain that it had a winning candidate, and all the leaders wanted to tell him exactly what he should do: all the yearning office seekers sought his immediate acquaintance. The Democratic National Committee came in a body on July 4th. They were followed by practically all of the Democrats of the Senate and the House. Champ Clark, still smarting with his defeat, was prepared, like the staunch party man that he was, to support the ticket. Wilson was especially glad to welcome Underwood—"a splendid man, with singular frankness and charm."[1] The political leaders of Wilson's own state, excepting Boss Smith, arrived in a body to congratulate their candidate.

Followers who could not come personally wrote loyally:

"I have prayed to live to see a real Democrat President before I die. Next March my prayer will be answered. Congratulations to you and to our country."[2]

The progressives of the party pledged themselves anew:

"... I am more anxious for your success," wrote William J. Bryan, "than you are—if that is possible."[3]

George Harvey who had scarcely mentioned Wilson's name since the "break" in December, 1911, wrote in *Harper's Weekly*:

"Intelligent choice ... was restricted to Speaker Clark, the sturdy representative of the Old Order, and Governor Wilson, the virile champion of the New. ... The foundation of Mr. Wilson's two thirds was the feeling that he was a winner, enhanced by admiration of his exceptional intellectual capacity, consideration of his freedom from entanglements, and respect for his moral courage. ... If

---

[1] Interview in the New York *Times*, July 17, 1912.
[2] United States Senator Benjamin R. Tillman to Woodrow Wilson, July 2, 1912.
[3] July 12, 1912.

the Democrats cannot elect Woodrow Wilson, they could not elect anybody.

"No Democratic national canvass since Jackson's has been inaugurated more auspiciously."[1]

There was the perplexing business of reorganizing the National Committee which met in Chicago on July 15th. Some of Wilson's friends urged him to "sidetrack Mc-Combs." McCombs's health was wretched: it did not seem possible that he could last through a grilling political campaign: and Wilson did not have complete confidence in him. Nevertheless, as Burleson, Daniels, Hudspeth, and others advised him, it would be poor politics to leave him out. He was, accordingly, chosen chairman, but with a strong executive committee to support him, which came to be called the "veranda cabinet," and upon which Wilson really leaned. The members were: W. F. McCombs of New York; R. S. Hudspeth of New Jersey; Josephus Daniels of North Carolina; T. P. Gore of Oklahoma; Willard Saulsbury of Delaware; A. Mitchell Palmer of Pennsylvania; Joseph E. Davies of Wisconsin; J. A. O'Gorman of New York; W. G. McAdoo of New York; A. S. Burleson of Texas; Daniel J. McGillicuddy of Maine; Robert Ewing of Louisiana; James A. Reed of Missouri; and W. R. King of Washington.

With all of these activities crowding upon him, Wilson found no opportunity for working out his speech of acceptance. How could he think? Where could he work? The confusion was growing utterly intolerable. He wrote on July 14th:

"The life I am leading now *can't* keep up. It is inconceivable that it should. I wish I could describe it to you, but I fear it is as indescribable as it is inconceivable. Not a moment am I left free to do what I would. I thought last night that I should go crazy with the strain and confusion

[1] July 13, 1912.

of it,—and so I ran away! I am not at Sea Girt. I am just outside the little village of Atlantic Highlands, by Sandy Hook. A good friend here, Mr. Melvin Rice, has a big place ('Drynoch Farms') where he lives in lonely state with his wife (no children). He saw my distress, beset and helpless at the Governor's Cottage, and took pity on me. He insisted that I take asylum with him whenever the hunt harassed me beyond endurance. Last evening, therefore, after an intolerable day, in desperation, I telephoned him I was coming. At six I got in a motor, at seven thirty was here; had a delightful dinner and a quiet chat (ah, what a luxury!) on the lawn under the trees, and at half after nine turned in. I slept till noon to-day. . . ."[1]

When he could delay the writing of his speech no longer, he retired again to the "asylum of my good friend Rice's quiet place," later "escaping to sea" on the *Corona*, his friend Dodge's yacht.

". . . I not only needed rest and refreshment, I also needed five or six days in which to prepare my speech of acceptance and so (nobody knowing whither we were bound—for I am even now supposed to be 'in retreat' with a friend near Atlantic Highlands) Ellen and Margaret and I,—with Dudley Malone, a young *fidus Achates* of mine,—bundled into an automobile, went down to the dock at Atlantic Highlands, which is just by Sandy Hook, and came aboard *The Corona*; since when we have been cruising in the Sound."

He took with him the official certified copy of the platform adopted at Baltimore. It was bound in blue paper with a red border. Slipped in among its pages were several newspaper clippings dealing with various aspects of the Democratic situation, including an editorial from the *World* of July 21st entitled "Planks To Be Broken." On this some friend had written, "Important for speech of

---

[1]Woodrow Wilson to Mary A. Hulbert.

acceptance." With these documents before him, Wilson sat in the quiet cabin of the yacht as it cruised in the waters of the Sound, and wrote in shorthand his speech of acceptance.

"... [the speech] is ready, poor thing, such as it is,—and we have had a truly delightful and refreshing little cruise, away from everybody, safer in our seclusion than if we had been at sea,—for sailing yachts have no wireless."

He wrote to Dodge:

"You have given us six of the happiest days I remember and my heart is full of gratitude to you. You are an ideal friend: you do everything in the best and most generous way. The speech is written, and I am at the same time refreshed and reinvigorated."[1]

Wilson insisted upon having the ceremony of acceptance conducted with simplicity. There were no formal invitations, no special decorations. Governor Marshall, his running-mate, was the only personal guest. Wilson had come, upon closer acquaintance, to have a warm liking and respect for Marshall. He enjoyed Marshall's play of wit. He could "swap stories" with him. Upon parting after the ceremonies, Marshall presented Wilson with a book—an "Abe Martin" Indiana book:

> "From your only vice,
> "Thomas R. Marshall."

For the address itself, Wilson stood on the veranda of the cottage. He wore a business suit. There were grouped closely and informally around him many of the leaders of the Democratic party, among them, "eight Democratic governors." Tammany sent half a dozen braves.

For the vast majority of the great crowd that assembled at Sea Girt, the speech-making was merely an incident in a long day of jollification. The grounds about the "Little

---

[1] July 29, 1912.

White House" wore all the aspects of a great picnic.

Senator Ollie James of Kentucky delivered the notification speech:

"I hand you this formal letter of notification, signed by the members of the committee; I present to you a copy of the platform adopted there, and upon that platform I have the honour to request your acceptance of a tendered nomination, and, on behalf of the Democracy of the whole Republic, united, militant, I pledge you their hearty support, and may God lead you to a glorious victory in November."

Wilson spoke with impressive seriousness, confining himself at first closely to his manuscript—a method always irksome to him. At one point, after throwing in an effective aside, he stopped altogether. "I wish I did not have to read this."

The address, a little grave for a restless crowd upon a summer day, was "even better in the reading than in the hearing."

One of the hits, since it seemed aimed at Roosevelt, delighted the crowd.

"There is no indispensable man."

And again, when he said:

"The government will not collapse and go to pieces if any one of the gentlemen who are seeking to be entrusted with its guidance should be left at home."

The three months which were to follow, until the election on November 5th, were among the most strenuous of Wilson's life.

## II. VITAL ELEMENTS AND ISSUES OF THE CAMPAIGN

Wilson's conception of a political campaign disconcerted his managers.

"My private judgment is that extended stumping tours

THE HOUSE AT SEA GIRT, NEW JERSEY, WHERE WOODROW WILSON
SPENT THE SUMMER OF 1912, SHOWING THE CROWD GATHERED FOR
THE NOTIFICATION CEREMONY, AUGUST 7, 1912.

are not the most impressive method of conducting a campaign."

He considered that a few addresses, well thought out, presenting his entire programme, delivered at strategic points, would suffice. He disliked, especially, "rear-platform oratory." He thought it undignified for a presidential candidate; it gave him no time to develop well-rounded ideas. Lacking the robustness of either Roosevelt or Bryan, who throve upon such campaigning, outdoor oratory took too much out of him in voice and in physical strength.

He was soon overborne by his insistent managers. The people wanted to see Wilson: they wanted to hear, directly, what he had to say for himself. Compared with Roosevelt or Taft, familiar figures upon the great stage of American public life, he was little known. His very unfamiliarity as a popular leader—the scholar, the author, the professor—piqued the public curiosity.

"When I first began campaigning, the people seemed to regard me as some remote academic person. They came out to see me, of course, but many of them wanted to see what manner of man I was, what sort of human animal, what freak of nature I might be."[1]

He even developed a ready and witty impromptu political oratory. A crowd mounted on the tops and in the doorways of box cars liked it when he addressed them with a wave of his hand: "Fellow citizens—Gentlemen in the boxes."

"I remember distinctly when the first feeling came over me that I had 'arrived' in politics. It was when an old fellow back East a few weeks ago slapped me on the back and shouted:

"'Doc, you're all right; give it to 'em!'"[2]

---

[1]Interview in the Baltimore *Sun*, October 7, 1912.
[2]*Ibid.*

He could relate, with humour, amusing incidents of the campaign:

"I drew a picture of a group of men sitting around the stove in a country store chewing tobacco and spitting in a sawdust box, conferring about the affairs of the neighbourhood, and I got into trouble by indulging in this harmless pleasantry. I said, 'Whatever may be said against the chewing of tobacco, this at least can be said for it, that it gives a man time to think between sentences.' An enterprising newspaper published only that part of my speech and headed it, 'Advocates the Chewing of Tobacco.' And a facsimile of that article was, I understand, circulated with the advertisements of certain tobacco firms. The whole point of the thing was missed. I wasn't advocating the chewing of tobacco, but I was advocating thinking between sentences!"[1]

Toward the end of the campaign his speeches, read afterwards, seem in places to descend to positive cheapness. His natural method, in public speaking, was marked by distinction, scholarly precision both in thought and in delivery, but he was evidently carried away by the feeling that he must get to the people—by standing more nearly on their own level. He came down from his professorial platform, and gave them what they wanted—and they liked it. But he never did it gracefully; for he could not, at any time in his life, get out of character and maintain his dignity.

Such campaigning might be necessary to his election—his managers assured him that it was, since Roosevelt was charging up and down the smiling land and attacking him in every speech—but what he wanted was to "clarify certain ideas and principles," "make the people think." It was not personalities that counted, but issues.

"Why, every man concerned in this great contest is a

[1] Speech at the Monmouth County Fair, Redbank, New Jersey, August 30, 1912.

pygmy as compared with the issues. What difference does Mr. Taft's record make to me? What difference does Mr. Roosevelt's career so far make to me? What difference does my own character, what do my own attainments—whatever they may be—make in the presence of these tremendous issues of life? I tell you truly I can't afford to think about Mr. Taft or Mr. Roosevelt when I am thinking about the fortunes of the people of the United States. . . . What are men as compared with the standards of righteousness?"[1]

Wilson's conception of the issues of the campaign lay crystal clear in his mind. He had, in reality, only one speech to make. He made it in accepting the nomination at Sea Girt: he made it again and again afterwards—but with such consummate skill as an orator that he seemed always to be making new speeches.

"Newspapermen who travelled with him were impressed again and again by his versatility in handling from day to day the same topic in a different way. If his speeches were to be examined and compared, it would be found that, while he employed the same argument, he never used the same phraseology. Reporters never knew what he was going to say—they found themselves listening always for the unexpected."[2]

Great emphasis during the campaign was placed upon such issues as the tariff, the trusts, immigration. To Wilson they were the items of the programme, the practical application of it, not the programme itself. They were indeed important issues, not *the* Issue.

"In practically every speech I make, I put at the front of what I have to say the question of the tariff and the question of the trusts . . . because I believe the solution of these questions to lie at the very heart of the bigger

---

[1]Speech at Pueblo, Colorado, October 7, 1912.
[2]David Lawrence *The True Story of Woodrow Wilson*, p. 56.

question, whether the government shall be free or not."[1]

It cannot be made too clear that Wilson's primary interest was in a spirit of approach, an attitude of mind, rather than in a set programme.

"You can build a flimsy platform and stand on it successfully, provided its basis is in the right kind of spirit."[2]

Wilson's mind was deductive rather than inductive. Principles first, application afterwards. When he worked out a political "credo" in 1907, he did not at first study public utilities, or municipal graft, or the evils of tariff-grown trusts: he began to restudy Thomas Jefferson. Earlier he had absorbed Burke, Bagehot, and Gladstone. Few American scholars have known their American origins, their Constitution, better than he. And few have more clearly recognized that it was the spirit, not the dogma, of the Constitution that mattered: "Government is not a machine, but a living thing, modified to its environment... shaped to its functions by the sheer pressure of life."[2]

The process of regeneration in politics, as in religion, therefore, involved a turning back to truth. It was as deep in his own consciousness as his Calvinistic religious convictions. A man must "come to himself"; with a new spirit "all things are plain."[2]

We find exactly this process set forth in his acceptance speech—and in many that followed.

"The nation has been unnecessarily, unreasonably, at war within itself. Interest has clashed with interest when there were common principles of right and of fair dealing which might and should have bound them all together, not as rivals, but as partners."[3]

---

[1]Public letter written by Woodrow Wilson "to the voters of America," October 19, 1912.

[2]Address at Nashville, Tennessee, February 24, 1912. *The Public Papers of Woodrow Wilson*, Vol. II, p. 418.

[3]Speech of acceptance, August 7, 1912. *The Public Papers of Woodrow Wilson*, Vol. II, pp. 452–474, for this and the following quotations.

But there has been an "awakening," a "turning," a "new unity":

"We stand in the presence of an awakened nation. . . ."

It is "a turning back from what is abnormal to what is normal." The nation has "lost certain cherished liberties" which are now being recovered.

"I am happy to say that a new spirit has begun to show itself in the last year or two. . . ."

"Plainly, it is a new age. The tonic of such a time is very exhilarating. It requires self-restraint not to attempt too much, and yet it would be cowardly to attempt too little."

The address of acceptance closed with these words:

"I feel that I am surrounded by men whose principles and ambitions are those of true servants of the people. I thank God, and will take courage."

What, then, was the task of such an awakened spirit? What, but the familiar task, well known also in religious awakening, of "resuming self-control"? In a democracy this meant nothing short of restoring to the people all of the instrumentalities of their government and of their life. "Every form of special privilege and private control" must cease. That which was unrighteous and unjust must be swept away "in order to vindicate once more the essential rights of human life."

Private control of politics—the boss and the machine—must be abolished: leaders must be "servants of the whole people." Private interest, special favours, must not be encouraged by government.

These principles he went on to apply, all through his campaign, to the specific items of the programme, the tariff, the trusts, conservation, labour. In a discriminating editorial, the New York *Times* of August 8th, commenting on the acceptance speech, sets forth the crux of the matter:

"It is a system of political philosophy, not a plan of

action that Gov. Wilson presents in his speech. . . . His philosophy is no abstraction, however. It is very practical, and has a direct bearing upon our national problems and policies. It is applicable."

As contrasted with Wilson, Roosevelt's emphasis during the campaign was upon particulars, upon the items of reform. The Progressive platform was a strange mélange of new ideas. It contained everything that every reformer wanted. There were scraps of Hamilton in it: also scraps of Jefferson. It was socialistic: it was also individualistic.

Reformers and agitators had done the spadework; the people generally were convinced that "the interests" ought to be curbed, but they were confused by the clamouring variety of the methods suggested. Wilson warmed them with his faith, appealed to old and simple principles, and refused to be drawn into minute controversy over the specific treatment of the issues. If this method suited the pattern of his mind, it was also good politics. His own party, as well as the Republican Progressives to whom he was also appealing, if they were united upon the conviction that certain vital things must be done, might easily split upon the manner of doing them.

To many progressives, Wilson's method of approach was irritating: to many radicals, all but infuriating. "Glittering generalities." "Why doesn't he get down to cases?" Bryan, "en route," wrote Wilson a hasty letter, scrawled in pencil:

"While I would have preferred to have you more specific in your treatment of issues still most of the Democrats are not as exacting as I am and I think it [the acceptance speech] is quite favourably rec'd."

Oswald Garrison Villard of the New York *Evening Post*, who was intensely interested in various reforms, made the same criticism. He desired "an utterance from you which we can quote" on the Negro problem, observing:

"May I add, also, that I find as I go about that the only criticism of your addresses since nomination which seems to be widely held, is that your speeches lack definite proposals. I trust you will forgive my frankness, but I want to be helpful, and lay the situation before you precisely as I see it."[1]

Emphasis upon Wilson's concern with general principles must not, however, be overemphasis. Upon most of the important issues of the time he took a perfectly definite position. He also made it clear wherein he differed from Taft and Roosevelt. Where he was uncertain he frankly confessed that he did not know, but characteristically laid down his underlying principle of solution. With reference to the legislation which was to prove the greatest domestic achievement of his administration—that relating to banking and currency reform—he said:

"I do not know enough about this subject to be dogmatic about it; I know only enough to be sure what the partnerships in it should be and that the control exercised over any system we may set up should be, as far as possible, a control emanating not from a single special class, but from the general body and authority of the nation itself."[2]

He considered the tariff the dominant issue: and the trust question, which in his view was closely associated with tariff privileges, was of equal importance.

"The tariff has become a system of favours, which the phraseology of the schedule was often deliberately contrived to conceal. . . .

"We denounce the Payne-Aldrich tariff act. . . . Tariff duties as they [the Republican party] have employed them have not been a means of setting up an equitable system of protection. They have been, on the contrary, a method of fostering special privilege. They have made it easy to

---

[1] August 28, 1912.

[2] Acceptance speech.

establish monopoly in our domestic markets. Trusts have owed their origin and their secure power to them."

There was need of a reconsideration of the tariff schedules, "reconsideration from top to bottom in an entirely different spirit." But the nominee hastened to add that there would be no rash or hasty action in the matter:

". . . the business of a country like ours is exceedingly sensitive to changes in legislation of this kind. . . . When we act we should act with caution and prudence, like men who know what they are about, and not like those in love with a theory. . . . But we shall not . . . act with timidity. . . . There must be an immediate revision, and it should be downward, unhesitatingly and steadily downward."

He made clear the distinction between his own essential policy and that of both Taft and Roosevelt:

"Neither [of the other parties] proposes to make a fundamental change in the policy of the government with regard to tariff duties. . . . Neither does either of the other parties propose seriously to disturb the supremacy of the trusts. Their only remedy is to accept the trusts and regulate them, notwithstanding the fact that most of the trusts are so constructed as to insure high prices, because they are not based upon efficiency but upon monopoly."[1]

There was a wide divergence between the positions of the parties in their attitude toward the trust problem. Taft stood for a judicial application of the Sherman law, Roosevelt for the regulation of business, Wilson for the regulation of competition. Roosevelt contended that "monopoly is inevitable"; let us regulate it and try to make the monopolists be good to us.

The Governor countered:

"Monopoly is not inevitable, except in those industries which economists have all along recognized as 'natural monopolies.' The other sort of monopoly I will not recog-

---

[1] Public letter, written by Wilson "to the voters of America," October 19, 1912.

nize. I will not accept it, I will not legalize it. . . . I will fight it, for in fighting it I am fighting for democracy, I am fighting for freedom, I am fighting for the ideals of this American Republic."

Wilson was not against wealth, nor even against bigness.

"We propose to introduce . . . competition again, and if these gentlemen [the Steel Corporation] can stand the competition, we don't mind how big they get, but they have got to get it on the proof of their merit. If the American Steel Corporation can so improve its methods, can so get rid of the water in its stock, can so economize its processes, can so recoördinate all its scattered parts so as to beat everybody also in selling a cheap thing, made as it ought to be made, then I, for one, will be glad, not sorry."[1]

While the tariff and trust issues furnished the main points of controversy, there were many lesser issues that affected no inconsiderable groups of people. Upon all of them, at some point in the campaign, Wilson was explicit.

In the matter of immigration, for example, he had been hotly attacked upon the basis of a passage in his *History of the American People:*

". . . now there came multitudes of men of the lowest class from the south of Italy and men of the meaner sort out of Hungary and Poland, men out of the ranks where there was neither skill nor energy nor any initiative of quick intelligence . . . the Chinese were more to be desired, as workmen if not as citizens, than most of the coarse crew that came crowding in every year at the Eastern ports."[2]

Representatives of these nationalities promptly turned to Wilson for an explanation of his position on immigration. In a letter to Mr. L. E. Miller of *The Warheit,* he wrote:

---

[1] Speech in Gary, Indiana, October 4, 1912.
[2] Woodrow Wilson, *A History of the American People*, Vol. V, pp. 212–213.

"The Democratic party may almost be said to have originated in a defense of the 'open door' to immigrants, for one of the things which brought it into life was opposition to the Alien and Sedition laws. . . . I, like other Democrats, have always held liberal views with regard to immigration. I feel that it would be inconsistent with our historical character as a nation if we did not offer a very hearty welcome to every honest man and woman who comes to this country to seek a permanent home and a new opportunity.

"At times, this privilege of settlement and naturalization has been abused. The steamship companies have taken advantage of it . . . for their own profit, and men have been brought over who did not come of their own initiative. Conditions arose which made it necessary for Congress to pass laws regulating the matter somewhat strictly and I think that every American, whether born in this country or not, must feel that there may arise from time to time conditions with regard to labour in this country and with regard to the safeguarding of the various interests, both temporary and permanent, when regulation of one kind or another may become necessary. But these things are not inconsistent with the general policy of liberal welcome with which I myself heartily sympathize."[1]

Wilson's letter was not a mere attempt to explain away a statement previously written and without basis in conviction, for during his administration he twice vetoed what he considered unfair restrictive immigration measures.

The liquor question, though not then as acute as it became later, was an irritant in the campaign. Here the reformers, deeming their particular issue the most vital of all, pursued Wilson relentlessly. He had been a tem-

[1]August 23, 1912.

perate man all his life but he was not a prohibitionist. From the beginning he had believed in local option. He had said so clearly in his letter to the Reverend Thomas B. Shannon, the head of the Anti-Saloon League of New Jersey, and refused to be drawn into further controversy.[1] It made him enemies among the reformers: but it also won him friends.

Similarly he refused to change his position on woman suffrage, as a means of catching votes. In a letter to Governor Foss of Massachusetts, written at the opening of the campaign, advising against the injection of the woman suffrage question, Wilson said:

"It is not a national question but a state question.

"So far as it is a state question, I am heartily in favour of its thorough discussion and shall never be jealous of its submission to the popular vote. My own judgment in the matter is in an uncertain balance, I mean my judgment as a voting citizen."[2]

Subsequently, when he found two of his own daughters and many fine women enlisted in the cause, when he saw what women were doing in the Great War—"The women have earned it"—he urged the ratification of the woman-suffrage amendment.

To one plank in the Democratic platform, that providing for a single term for Presidents, he gave considerable thought, but took no public position upon it until after his election. It awakened, indeed, almost no interest in the campaign. Neither Taft nor Roosevelt was interested in commenting upon it and Wilson ignored it. The only indication we have of Wilson's own view of the matter at this time is a brief reply to a letter from Thomas D. Jones. Jones had written that, had the plank specified a single term of six or eight years, he would have favoured it, but

[1]See Shannon letter, published in full, pp. 151-152, of this volume.
[2]August 17, 1912.

four years was too short a period to accomplish large results. [1]

"I quite agree with you on the whole about that single term plank matter," responded the Governor, "and am steadied by your judgment regarding it."[2]

Another question, destined in later years to grow greatly in importance, was that of Roman Catholic influence in political affairs. It came up sharply upon two charges: first, that Wilson was in league with the Catholics—that he had actually joined the Knights of Columbus; and second, that he was a "black Presbyterian," opposed to the Catholic Church. Wilson met the situation squarely in a letter to William G. McAdoo:

"My attention has been called to the statement that I have become a member of the Knights of Columbus. This is, of course, not true. I have not been asked to join the order either as an active or an honorary member, and am not eligible because I am not a Catholic.

"I must warn my friends everywhere that statements of this kind are all campaign inventions, devised to serve a special purpose. This particular statement has been circulated in selected quarters to create the impression that I am trying to identify myself politically with the great Catholic body. In other quarters all sorts of statements are being set afloat to prove that I am hostile to the Catholics.

"It is a very petty and ridiculous business. . . .

"I am a normal man, following my own natural course of thought, playing no favourites, and trying to treat every creed and class with impartiality and respect."[3]

To meet the second charge, which Bryan considered the

[1] July 8, 1912.

[2] July 18, 1912. For his explicit views on the single term issue see his letter to A. Mitchell Palmer, February 5, 1913, published in *The Public Papers of Woodrow Wilson*, Vol. III, pp. 21–26.

[3] October 22, 1912.

more serious of the two, a circular letter drawn by Professor James Charles Monaghan was printed for distribution, showing the number of Catholics who had been placed in high positions in New Jersey by Governor Wilson and quoting from his addresses to prove that he had nothing but admiration for the fine services performed by individual Roman Catholics.

Many times later the same charges were to be made. Wilson was again and again attacked for having Tumulty, a Roman Catholic, as his private secretary. He never changed in his attitude of treating "every creed and class with impartiality and respect."

The reformers assailed him at still another point: his attitude on the race question. It was an extremely sensitive spot since Roosevelt was making a strong appeal to the coloured vote. The Negroes were naturally suspicious of any Southern man, and it was said Wilson had drawn the colour line at Princeton, and had failed to give recognition to coloured men while governor of New Jersey. A committee of representative Negroes received from him the assurance that, if elected, he would "seek to be President of the whole nation and would know no differences of race or creed or section, but to act in good conscience and in a Christian spirit through it all."

In a letter to Bishop Alexander Walters, he had also given evidence of his friendliness:

"I hope that it seems superfluous to those who know me, but to those who do not know me perhaps it is not unnecessary for me to assure my coloured fellow citizens of my earnest wish to see justice done them in every matter, and not mere grudging justice, but justice executed with liberality and cordial good feeling. Every guarantee of our law, every principle of our Constitution commands this, and our sympathies should also make it easy. . . .

"My sympathy with them is of long standing, and I want to assure them through you that should I become President of the United States they may count upon me for absolute fair dealing and for everything by which I could assist in advancing the interests of their race in the United States."[1]

After he became President, Wilson found the Negro problem extremely perplexing, and he did not satisfy the radicals.[2] The rift between the radical and the political leader is forever irreconcilable: the political leader, even though he is himself a reformer, can never go far enough or fast enough to satisfy the radical.

One other potent element or issue in the campaign remains to be considered. While Wilson himself decried personal appeal, it bulked large in the campaign. Wilson had a power of personal attraction for strong and thoughtful men that he never assessed at its proper value. He assumed that men were "converted to him," or followed him, because of the principles he advocated—since principles were to him far more important than men—when it was commonly his own power, sincerity, and charm of personality.

Brand Whitlock, then mayor of Toledo, analyzed this element with rare discrimination in a letter to Newton D. Baker:

"If Governor Wilson had not been nominated at Baltimore, we should have had a new liberal party in this country, and the alignment at last would have been clear. But in his personality Governor Wilson himself wholly satisfies and sums up that democratic spirit which means everything to you and me, and it is personality that counts, that tells, more than creeds or platforms. Governor Wilson's ability, his services, his mastery of himself and of affairs, his imagination, his literary ability, his sense of

[1] October 16, 1912.
[2] See *Woodrow Wilson: Life and Letters, President,* Vol. IV.

humour, all these qualities combine to endow him with a rare culture, and his character is the best platform."[1]

The campaign indeed became more or less a contest of personalities. No man in American public life ever capitalized his personality in all its phases with more consummate skill than Theodore Roosevelt. He was "Teddy" to the world! But his bag of tricks by 1912 had begun to be shopworn; and the interest of the people was piqued by a leader who was the antithesis of Roosevelt in almost every particular. Many of the letters of that time give evidence of Wilson's strong personal appeal:

"I do not believe in all the Democratic platform or possibly in all you believe, but I believe *in you* and have no doubt of the safety of the country's interests in your hand."[2]

Wilson's appeal was especially strong among college men:

"It has been a matter of great pride with me during the last few months that the men who lead in the college world should have come in such generous numbers to my support and it is delightful to me to think that possibly my success in this election will give the country a new conception of the relation of the colleges to public life."[3]

Enthusiastic personal supporters, though amateurs, furnished the backbone of Wilson's campaign. A large proportion of the funds used by his managers came from such personal admirers, often men quite unknown to him.

In spite of all the evidence of such personal loyalty and admiration, there was in Wilson a strange, deep distrust of himself. He had boundless confidence in his principles. He was bold in his faith in a God who sustained His prophets. But man was a pygmy: he himself counted

---

[1] September 28, 1912.

[2] A. W. Halsey to Woodrow Wilson, July 3, 1912.

[3] Woodrow Wilson to President Charles W. Dabney, of the University of Cincinnati, November 15, 1912.

for little when balanced against the "issues of life and death." A letter written during the campaign blazes with self-revelation; he compares himself with Roosevelt:

"I feel that Roosevelt's strength is altogether incalculable. The contest is between him and me, not between Taft and me. I think Taft will run third,—at any rate in the popular, if not in the electoral, vote. The country will have none of him. But just what will happen, as between Roosevelt and me, with party lines utterly confused and broken, is all guesswork. It depends upon what the people are thinking and purposing whose opinions do not get into the newspapers,—and I am by no means confident. He appeals to their imagination; I do not. He is a real, vivid person, whom they have seen and shouted themselves hoarse over and voted for, millions strong; I am a vague, conjectural personality, more made up of opinions and academic prepossessions than of human traits and red corpuscles. We shall see what will happen!"[1]

Perceiving this inner pattern of Wilson's spirit, one better understands much that seems inexplicable in his career. Bold, hard-hitting, resourceful, persistent to the point of obstinacy in the advocacy of his principles as in the declaration of his faith, he was as sensitive as a woman to personal relationships. If he was tough-minded, he was tender-hearted. He longed for deep friendship, and yet dreaded it when he found it, for he feared that it might soften his purpose. He longed to make men share his faith, accept his principles; he seemed sometimes to dread to attract them personally.

### III. WILSON'S APPEAL TO THE NATION

It was clear enough from the beginning that the real battle in the campaign was between Wilson and Roose-

---

[1] Woodrow Wilson to Mary A. Hulbert, August 25, 1912.

velt. The country was progressive: that leader would win who could command the progressive following. Taft, though the inevitable candidate of the conservatives, had lost the confidence of the nation. He had no battle cry, convinced no voters. He stood foursquare, unoriginal, amiable, honest, for the god of things as they were.

Wilson was a new personality in American public life. He profited by antithesis. He had the unfamiliar glamour, to the popular eye, of the scholar, the thinker, the historian. There had been enough heat in politics; what was needed now was light. Wilson was expository rather than denunciatory. He was asking the country to look at its problems: he was not offering panaceas:

"As a candidate for the presidency I do not want to promise heaven unless I can bring it to you. I can only see a little distance up the road."

Nor was he concerned with personalities in a campaign which reeked with personal attacks. The issues were too serious.

"We are not attacking men, we are attacking a system. The men are, most of them, honest."

Roosevelt might sneer:

"I love the implication that thought had anything to do with the Baltimore convention. There never was a platform in this country so wholly free from any taint of thought. . . ."

Wilson, ignoring the attack, could speak dispassionately of his opponents:

"The third party deserves your careful consideration. . . . I would be ashamed of myself if I did not realize and admit that some of the sober and finer forces of the country are now devoted to the promotion of this new movement and party."

In his attitude toward Taft, he was equally courteous. While Roosevelt was scarifying his old friend, Wilson, speaking at Minneapolis, the heart of the anti-Taft country, said:

"I do not believe that any man in the United States who knows his facts can question the patriotism or the integrity of the man who now presides at the executive office in Washington."

When Taft and Wilson were in Boston on the same day, Wilson called on the President at the Copley Plaza Hotel, to pay his respects.

"The country is indebted to Governor Wilson," wrote Harvey, "for continuing to do what one candidate can do to elevate the tone of the campaign."[1]

When Roosevelt was shot down by a fanatic at Milwaukee on October 14th, Wilson immediately wired:

"Please accept my warmest sympathy and heartiest congratulations that your wound is not serious."

He also decided to cancel his speaking programme until his opponent recovered. In two or three addresses for which arrangements had already been completed, he desisted from making any comments regarding the Progressive party.

Roosevelt's position in the campaign, if it was diverting and picturesque, was not without its pathos. Roosevelt had long been "the most interesting man in America." He had played his part, played it greatly. He had been a preacher of forgotten moralities, a stimulator of good resolutions. No President was ever, perhaps, closer to the real, if inarticulate, feeling of the people of his time. We called him "Teddy," sent him pet lions and bears, were entertained by his hunting and riding, and amused rather than offended when he added a new portrait to his gallery of prevaricators. We even reported to him with pride the champion families of children in our various neighbourhoods. When he made mistakes we forgave and excused

---

[1] *Harper's Weekly*, September 14, 1912.

him much as we would forgive and excuse our own mistakes—they were so completely understandable.

There are two kinds of greatness, that of height, the greatness that in some particular rises to the sky and in depth is beyond ordinary human fathoming: and the greatness of breadth. Roosevelt's was the greatness of breadth.

Roosevelt had occupied the centre of the stage for years: he was still full of energy. The thought of retirement to the dim quietude off-stage was intolerable to him. He could not see that the people had grown a little weary of political evangelism, they were seeking a prophet: they were tired of denunciation, they were asking for vision. Roosevelt's energized commonness could not touch the stars. He sought desperately to recapture the crowd: but the easy magic of former days was now strident; people no longer laughed at his personal vituperation. "He has promised too often the millennium," observed Wilson.

Another element in Wilson's strength was that he had no political past. Both Roosevelt and Taft had served in the White House and were vulnerable to attacks upon their record. They were busily engaged in destroying each other, a process in which the Republican insurgents, especially La Follette, joyously assisted both of them. With no record to apologize for and with no inclination to waste time in dealing in personalities, Wilson was free to exercise his passion for fighting on issues. *Harper's Weekly* on October 19th said that the Governor's speeches "are already a remarkable series of discussions of great public questions. . . . Not within the memory of the present generation has any candidate for the presidency done so much to illuminate issues and to clarify public opinion."

Wilson appealed powerfully to the people for another reason. He was free: he owed obligations to nobody but the people. He said early in the campaign:

"Nobody owns me. . . . I not only have not made a promise to any man, but no man has dared to ask me to make a promise."

At a time when the country was so thoroughly aroused over boss rule, this was a powerful element of strength to the candidate. Roosevelt indeed shrilled the charge from the stump that Wilson's nomination was the work of the bosses: but with the fight upon Smith of New Jersey and the memory of Baltimore fresh in the minds of the people, no one was deceived.

Wilson also appealed frankly to the progressive sentiment of the nation. The first important speech in the campaign, September 2nd, at Buffalo, was delivered on Labour Day to workmen. It was a demand that the "old partnerships between money and power which now block us at every turn" be forever broken up. He was extraordinarily successful in winning over the strongest of the labour leaders of the nation. In the beginning, for example, Samuel Gompers, head of the American Federation of Labor, had been a sharp critic of Wilson. He thought him an aristocrat.

"Woodrow Wilson was not my choice for the presidential candidate for the Democratic party. I had never met him, but what I had heard of him was not calculated to predispose me in his favour. Certain of his earlier academic writings indicated that he did not understand labour problems."[1]

But during the campaign of 1912, Gompers, with Secretary Morrison of the American Federation, went to see Wilson at Trenton.

"In that meeting I felt my prejudices disappearing before the sincerity and the obvious humanitarianism of the man. . . . I left Trenton feeling very much relieved."[2]

---

[1] Samuel Gompers, *Seventy Years of Life and Labor*, pp. 543–544.
[2] *Ibid.*, p. 544.

Gompers became one of Wilson's most ardent friends and supporters and so remained to the end of his life.

"My respect for him grew into a feeling of well-nigh reverential admiration. I admired his keen, alert mentality, his beautiful English, the perfect enunciation and modulation of his speaking voice. There was that in his personal dignity that made me feel when the door swung open to admit him that a real President of the United States was entering. While he was President, he was every inch a man. I always enjoyed talking to him and always left stimulated by a wider vision and a keener determination to service."[1]

Wilson appealed not only to labour: he won a large following among the Western insurgents, for he was attacking, hotly, the problems which also concerned them most nearly—the trusts, high tariff, an inflexible currency system.

Bryan became his consistent and enthusiastic supporter. No trip of the campaign was more successful than the invasion of Bryan's own state of Nebraska. In a single day Wilson made nine speeches, seven in Omaha, two in Lincoln—with an arduous automobile ride between. His face was covered with dust and his lungs filled with it—but he won anew the devotion of Bryan and of Bryan's following. He exhibited, indeed, an unexpected ability in developing easy and cordial personal relationships. At Lincoln, for example, coming out of the Auditorium he somehow lost his hat. Bryan offered his, saying: "I suppose you cannot find yours because it is in the ring." And the Governor appeared wearing Bryan's "immense sombrero instead of his own little felt."[2] On Sunday, October 6th, he and Bryan stole away together to an unfamiliar church; and that night Wilson wired to his wife:

[1]Samuel Gompers, *Seventy Years of Life and Labor*, pp. 545-546.
[2]New York *Times*, October 7, 1912.

"Fine Sunday rest after strenuous day yesterday. Am perfectly well and feeling quite equal to the task. Enjoyed my visit with Mr. Bryan very much indeed. Dearest love to all."

Bryan on his part was equally cordial. He said at the Omaha Dollar Dinner:

"I want to express my deep gratitude to him [Wilson] for the masterly manner in which he has led our forces in this campaign. . . . he has done better than we could have expected. . . .

"Let me ask you to do twice as much for Wilson as you ever did for Bryan. . . ."

While Wilson's campaign, outwardly, was a triumph, the inner machinery of organization was hopelessly confused and inefficient. One gets the impression from the documents and letters of hodge-podge management, of discord and discontent. McCombs, ill and irritable, was jealous of McAdoo. McAdoo, on his part, charged with inexhaustible energy, eager and ambitious, chafed at the necessity of playing second fiddle to a chairman who was his equal neither in physical strength nor in intellectual resourcefulness. He had written to Wilson:

"You are the only man living for whom I would accept this post. . . . If I do less well than you expect, only remember that I am not in command and that that necessarily restricts opportunity."[1]

McCombs's health, from the beginning, forced most of the work upon McAdoo. McCombs professed at first to acquiesce, but jealousy and suspicion quickly clouded his judgment and made him distrustful of all that the acting chairman did. Maurice Lyons, secretary to McCombs, says:

"From the month of July, when he was first stricken, Mr. McCombs was a changed man. He seemed suspicious

[1] June 25, 1912.

of everyone in any way connected with the campaign. In his abnormal condition he concluded that Mr. McAdoo, especially, sought to undermine him. . . ."[1]

Wilson found the constant dissension which more or less affected the entire organization both distressing and time-consuming. McAdoo, with Wilson's best interests strongly at heart, offered to retire altogether, but Wilson insisted upon his remaining. On the other hand he was infinitely patient with McCombs. While it is plain that he did not trust him, he felt a real affection and sympathy for him. "He is really very unwell, poor heroic chap."[2]

"McCombs is seriously thinking of resigning, and may do so to-morrow,"' wrote House.

"There are reasons why his resignation at this time would be a serious blow to the cause."[3]

Wilson replied on September 11th:

"Never fear. I shall not be so foolish as to accept McCombs's resignation. But do not take anything for granted."'

When the Brooklyn *Eagle* reported that efforts were being made to oust McCombs, Wilson promptly denied that there was any such intention.

"These reports," he said, "distress me very much. They are utterly without foundation. . . .

"Mr. McCombs will not only remain chairman, but his counsel is of constant service to the committee, even while he is confined to his room. We are looking forward with the greatest pleasure to his active resumption of his duties."[4]

Wilson bore with his manager contrary to the advice of several of his practical advisers, even when he knew that

[1]Maurice F. Lyons, *William F. McCombs, the President Maker*, p. 129.
[2]Woodrow Wilson to Cleveland H. Dodge, September 11, 1912.
[3]September 2, 1912.
[4]Letter to the Brooklyn *Eagle*, quoted in the New York *Times*, September 12, 1912.

McCombs was playing politics with the very leaders whom he most distrusted.

"McCombs is in conference most of the time with old-style politicians. The whole character of the callers has changed since he took charge, and for the worse. I fear Governor Wilson will have trouble on account of connections made at this time. . . ."[1]

Though the unfortunate situation growing out of McCombs's illness probably weakened the central organization, the work was vigorously carried forward by Mc-Adoo, Josephus Daniels, and many other loyal friends. It was the kind of disinterested support which the ordinary political leader never inspires. Some of the ablest and most distinguished citizens of the nation enlisted under his banner. President Eliot of Harvard University issued a statement favouring Wilson, Louis D. Brandeis became his adviser on the problem of the trusts; and in almost every state there were men of "light and leading" who were devoted followers. They gave their time, they gave unstintingly of their money.

From the outset Wilson had determined that no money should be accepted from men who expected favours in return for their gifts. He insisted upon complete publicity for campaign contributions.[2] In urging Henry Morgenthau to take the chairmanship of the Finance Committee, Wilson said:

"I shall insist that no contributions whatever be even indirectly accepted from any corporation. I want especial attention paid to the small contributors. And I want great care exercised over the way the money is spent."[3]

When Morgenthau finally agreed to serve, Wilson added:

[1]From the diary of Colonel House. *The Intimate Papers of Colonel House*, Vol. I, p. 77.
[2]See *Harper's Weekly*, August 3, 1912.
[3]Henry Morgenthau, *All in a Life-time*, p. 152.

"One thing more. There are three rich men in the Democratic party whose political affiliations are so unworthy that I shall depend on you personally to see that none of their money is used in my campaign!"[1]

The selection of Morgenthau as finance chairman and Rolla Wells as treasurer, both upright and widely experienced in large affairs, was a great boon to Wilson. Morgenthau instituted a budget system for the first time in American political history. With minor exceptions, it was adhered to throughout the contest and was so successful that by January 1, 1913, all bills were paid and there was a cash balance of $25,000 to the credit of the National Committee.[2]

The treasurer's final report is evidence of the popular appeal that Wilson made. There were 88,229 contributors of less than $100, and 1,625 in amounts of over $100, making a total of 89,854 donors. Of the total sum subscribed, $1,110,952.25, $318,909.50 came from those giving less than $100.[3]

One large contribution to Wilson's campaign fund was returned, a fact brought out by the Senate investigating committee. Wilson's old Princeton classmate and devoted friend, Cyrus H. McCormick, had given $12,500. McCormick was at the head of the Harvester Trust and Wilson's friends foresaw that his gift might be made embarrassing to his cause.

"The money was returned, but not at my request. It was done upon the initiative of Mr. Dodge and Mr. McCormick themselves. It was characteristic of them. They have illustrated again what they illustrated so often while they were trustees of the University during my presi-

---

[1]Henry Morgenthau, *All in a Life-time*, p. 153.
[2]*Ibid.*
[3]Report of the Treasurer of the Democratic National Committee.

dency there. They have always tried to act in such a way as to help me and yet leave me free."[1]

When the campaign was over the President-elect could say, as he said at the beginning:

"Nobody owns me. . . ."

He had gathered no support by deals with the bosses and their machines, and he had collected no funds by pledges to financial interests. He had spoken frankly and boldly in his addresses; so that the nation knew precisely what to expect.

On the personal side Wilson found the campaign a heavy burden. It was a great strain upon his health. He spoke frequently in his letters of being tired, "worn out," "desperately weary." Indeed the limitations of his physical strength prevented him from carrying the campaign as far as he desired:

"Alas! it seems a physical impossibility for me to get into the South during the campaign. I haven't a Bull Moose's strength, as Roosevelt seems to have, and it seems imperative, both to the committee and myself, that I should devote the few remaining weeks of the campaign to the debatable parts of the country."[2]

He maintained, nevertheless, a cheerful and even humorous attitude of mind.

"I've had a wretched sick headache for the last two days, due to an ill-behaved digestion, and this afternoon feel dull and stupid; but this is exceptional,—not the dullness and stupidity, but the headache and indigestion; for I keep singularly well. I've gained seven pounds and a half since I was nominated. I weigh $177\frac{1}{2}$ pounds. I am obviously becoming a person of some weight,—at any rate on the scales. If my days are trying and so full of—

---

[1]Statement authorized by Mr. Wilson and printed in the Baltimore *Sun*, October 26, 1912.

[2]Woodrow Wilson to Frank P. Glass, September 6, 1912.

everything that fatigues and distracts—as to make them quite overwhelming, they at least fly past with satisfactory rapidity, and it will not be long before I am either elected or bidden stay quietly at home. I would not dare say which I preferred—when I have a sick headache!"[1]

He wrote later, referring to the "whispering attacks" being made upon him:

"I am very well, but so tired that I can barely do the thinking necessary for the campaign,—and this new method of attack has made me sick at heart. . . .

"I am pegging away after my own fashion at this weary business of campaigning. There would be no bearing its tremendous burdens if there were not the element of large duty and serviceableness in it. There *are* great issues, the greatest imaginable, issues of life and death, as it seems to me, so far as the sound political life of the country is concerned; and therefore I keep heart and strength. The people believe in me and trust me. If they can only be suffered to continue to do so by my malevolent foes!"[2]

In another letter he gives a glimpse of his campaigning:

"I got back home this morning at one o'clock. After attending two dinners in New York last night, I caught an express which was stopped for me at the junction at 12.30 and drove home in a cab, too sleepy and tired for words. . . . It is wonderful how tough I have turned out to be, and how much I can stand—for the physical strain of what I went through this time is all but overwhelming; and yet I lost nothing but my voice—and not all of that. I was fool enough to try to make thirty-five thousand people hear me out-of-doors, and after that the old instrument, usually so sound and reliable, went wheezy and had no volume or resonance in it. It is slowly coming

---

[1] Woodrow Wilson to Mary A. Hulbert, September 1, 1912.
[2] Woodrow Wilson to Mary A. Hulbert, September 29, 1912.

back now, under the kindly influences of silence. 'The trouble with me is I talk too damn much.'"

One of the sorest of his difficulties was the utter destruction of his "private life," and above everything, the "confusion of family relationships." In a letter to a friend, Mrs. Wilson refers wistfully to "the old lost peace" and adds, "I dare not even let my mind dwell too much on that."[2]

"Our life now simply beggars description! But 'it is all in the day's work,' and it would be, in a sense, disloyalty to a great task that has been set us to repine because certain features of it are not to our taste."[1]

It was hard to have to forego the friendships in which he delighted. His English friend Yates, coming for a visit during the campaign, gives a glimpse of the household at Sea Girt:

"Mrs. Wilson came beaming to meet me—with her sweet smile and her indolent, sing-song, indistinct voice. Quite charming . . . just after having tea the Governor's car arrived bringing him from Trenton—at first I was a bit worried about his looks, as he not only looked pale but was quite an octave lower in his voice when he came in: however in half an hour he had completely recovered—it was a fifty mile ride, enough to wear out anyone. . . . He was overjoyed at seeing me and took both my hands—'My dear boy, I'm glad to see you'—and they surely were. The evening we passed quietly . . . W. W. again and again being called out of the room—telephones, reporters. . . ."[2]

Wilson tried to keep up by correspondence the friendly relationships which were so essential to his life, but he found more and more that his position, his great place, tended to isolate him. As he said soon after he entered the White House:

---

[1]Ellen Axson Wilson to the Rev. Dr. Edward M. Chapman, August 13, 1912.
[2]Fred Yates to his wife, August 8, 1912.

"It is a sad thing about this office. I should like greatly to see Harry Fine,[1] but a President has to send for his friends. It is a kind of mandate, a command, and you have a feeling that they have to come whether they really want to or not. I cannot take that attitude toward those I really love."[2]

In another way he felt himself handicapped. A man of fifty-five has certain settled satisfactions in life: work he loves to do; groups he loves to meet. All these things he must surrender. Dr. van Dyke urged him to speak before the American Academy, and he replied:

". . . I simply dare not undertake the task. I would not be willing to read anything which I could not carefully consider and somewhat lovingly elaborate, and I know perfectly well that it is futile for me to look forward to the possibility of that."[3]

He would have liked to keep up, in some degree, with his literary activity, but it was impossible!

"It sounds like old times to have an essay suggested to me. I barely have time for the hastiest line in reply to my correspondents,—to write anything more is absolutely impossible amidst these days of extraordinary abstractions."[4]

Worst of all to a man of Wilson's temperament was the glaring publicity in which he was forced to live. Roosevelt and Bryan might thrive in an atmosphere of constant excitement; to Wilson it was "slavery."

To the last, Wilson was himself "not too confident of the result." He kept up the struggle—"I . . . start out on the road again to get in the fray—now that Roosevelt is so much better and again in charge of his own fight"—but the event was on the lap of the gods.

[1]Henry Burchard Fine, dean of Princeton University.
[2]The Misses Lucy and Mary Smith to the author.
[3]September 7, 1912.
[4]Woodrow Wilson to Joseph B. Gilder, August 12, 1912.

## IV. ELECTED PRESIDENT

Wilson's campaign reached its climax in a stupendous meeting at Madison Square Garden in New York City on October 31st, five days before the election.

"Governor Woodrow Wilson of New Jersey, who has spent many years of his life in studious paths and has been referred to by his opponents as a cold and bookish professor, last night turned a regular old-fashioned political meeting of 16,000 persons . . . into a wild, waving, cheering, yelling, roaring, stamping mob of enthusiasts that needed no songs and no hymns and no encouragement to keep it at a high pitch."[1]

Old-time Democrats had never seen anything like it, not even in the halcyon days of the Boy Orator of the Platte. While there had been excellent introductory speeches by William Sulzer, candidate for governor of New York, Martin H. Glynn, Augustus Thomas, and Congressman Underwood—interrupted from time to time by roars of "We want Wilson!"—when Wilson himself appeared on the platform soon after nine o'clock, "pandemonium indescribable" broke loose.

"The orderly gathering that had listened as to a lecture to the Congressman from Alabama was on its feet as one man, and bellowing forth in a sixteen-thousand-throated roar its welcome to its new chief. Men and women jumped upon their chairs, waving their American flags, and cheering with all their might."

In spite of every effort to secure silence, that Wilson might begin his address, the cheering lasted for an hour and four minutes. It was an audience not only devoted to its leader, but absolutely confident of the results of the election.

---

[1] New York *Times*, November 1, 1912.

Wilson's audience no doubt felt that it must out-do the rally held on the preceding evening in the same vast auditorium to greet Theodore Roosevelt. That had also been an extraordinary demonstration: the last great rally of the Progressive party.

"Roosevelt's speech of the night before had been a last call to the faithful on the eve of battle in a forlorn hope. It was not the speech of a quitter, but a speech such as Custer might have made to his scouts when he saw the Indians coming. . . ."[1]

While the two rallies were not unlike in numbers and in noise, they differed widely in character and spirit. Roosevelt's was "almost fanatical" in its expression of personal enthusiasm. His had been an intensely personal campaign. Some of his wiser supporters had endeavoured to minimize the man, emphasize the cause. They knew the danger of a one-man party: but Roosevelt's own course balked every such effort. Great as he was, the man got in his own way.

> "Follow, follow, we will follow Roosevelt;
> Anywhere, everywhere, we will follow on.
> Follow, follow, we will follow Roosevelt;
> Anywhere he leads, we will follow him."

The fact that it was Roosevelt's first important public appearance since he had been shot down by a crazy fanatic at Milwaukee added a highly emotional element to the occasion—ably dramatized, of course, by the political managers. That their hero was waging a losing battle only added to the demonstration of their loyalty.

"The faithful had rallied around their leader in the spirit of a salutation from those about to die, and the funeral was celebrated after the manner of the Chinese, with all the fireworks possible."[2]

---

[1] New York *Evening Post*, November 1, 1912.
[2] *Ibid.*

Wilson's meeting was of a different character. While it was "as great a demonstration as ever had been accorded any candidate," yet it was "only an incident." It was a gathering to ratify "the victory of a great cause." It was not only "Democracy triumphant," but progressivism triumphant. For years the liberals, the insurgents, the reformers, had been agitating and campaigning: for the first time victory seemed fairly within their grasp. And Wilson had led them!

Wilson himself, the sensitive orator, well understood the serious significance of that vast gathering. When at length the shouting died away and he began his address, "there was absolute silence throughout the hall."

"Fellow citizens, no man could fail to be deeply moved by a demonstration such as we have witnessed to-night. And yet I am the more thrilled by it because I realize that it is the demonstration for a cause and not for a man. All over this country, from one ocean to the other, men are becoming more aware that in less than a week the common people of America will come into their own again."

Wilson's address touched the spirit of the occasion with perfect understanding. Triumph, with solemn responsibility: victory that involved new struggle: high and noble resolutions for the future!

"What the Democratic party proposes to do is to go into power and do the things that the Republican party has been talking about doing for sixteen years."

While Wilson made several addresses during the following week, the campaign really closed with the Madison Square Garden rally. A great Democratic parade had been planned for November 2nd in New York, but the death of James S. Sherman, vice-presidential candidate on the Republican ticket, put an end to it. Wilson was to have reviewed the parade, but requested that it be cancelled out of respect to the dead leader.[1]

November 5th was election day. Wilson was in high good humour. He had slept soundly and did not appear for breakfast until nine o'clock. It was a delight to be at home with his wife and daughters, to feel that the labour and the pain of the battle were over. The family had returned from Sea Girt and were living in the delightful, if diminutive, home in Cleveland Lane. It was a half-timbered, Elizabethan house, set a little way back from the shady, winding road. In an open space at one side the reporters had pitched their tents, but the home itself was far less public than the Governor's house at Sea Girt.[2]

During the forenoon, Wilson walked leisurely down the familiar Princeton streets, bowing here and there to old friends. He was going to vote. Captain Bill, his Texas ranger, was with him. Every nook and corner of the old town, every house, every street, was familiar to Wilson. Half his life he had spent among these quiet surroundings: here he had been educated—the "greatest days of my life" —here he had come, a young professor, to make his fame, here he had fought the bitter battles, as president, to re-form the university he loved. He stopped to point out to Captain Bill the house where he had boarded when he entered the university, a callow freshman, thirty-seven years before.

[1]Misfortune dogged the candidates in the 1912 campaign. Taft alone came out of it without being endangered. In addition to the shooting of Roosevelt, and the death of Sherman, Marshall, Hiram Johnson, and Wilson all narrowly escaped injury in train wrecks. Wilson actually did meet with a minor accident just as the campaign was closing. While motoring from Red Bank to Princeton early in the morning of November 3rd, the automobile conveying him and Captain Bill McDonald, a Texas friend of Colonel House's, who, after the attack on Roosevelt, became Wilson's picturesque bodyguard, struck a bump in the road and the Governor was thrown up against the roof of the car. His head was cut open and bled profusely, but the wound was not serious. A local doctor dressed it, and Wilson was able to keep his last two speaking engagements.

[2]The house is now owned by Mrs. Charles R. Williams. Cleveland Lane runs into Bayard Lane, and is only a few minutes' walk from Nassau Hall, the heart of Princeton University.

Wilson cast his vote, awaiting his turn among his smiling neighbours, in the curious little fire-engine house in a narrow side street, afterwards strolling slowly homeward again. Upon his arrival an altogether delightful and reassuring message was placed in his hand. It was from William J. Bryan:

". . . I beg to assure you that indications everywhere point to an overwhelming victory. But, whether you win or lose, I congratulate you on the splendid campaign you have made. You deserve to succeed."

In the afternoon, Wilson took several of his friends, including Dudley Field Malone, on a long walk in the beautiful country around Princeton. They crossed the famous stone bridge, went down the road where Washington's tattered army had marched, saw the place where, side by side, foe and friend, lie American revolutionaries and British regulars. They visited several of the university buildings. Wilson showed them the framed diploma of James Madison—"the only Princeton man ever elected to the presidency." They stopped to look at the death mask of Grover Cleveland. Wilson stood silent for some moments and then observed:

"What an extraordinarily stubborn face!"

Supper was a quiet family party of the kind that Wilson loved most of all, and afterwards, with friends gathered about, Mrs. Wilson read aloud from Browning's poetry.

During the day Wilson had remained calm and unperturbed, but as the evening wore on and the returns were almost unvaryingly favourable, "his face took on an expression of deep seriousness." It remained for Mrs. Wilson, who had herself played so great a part in the campaign, to break the news that her husband had been elected President of the United States. It came at ten o'clock; the special operator brought the message to Mrs. Wilson. She placed her hand lightly on her husband's shoulder.

"My dear," she said, "I want to be the first to congratulate you."

At ten-thirty the news was confirmed by McCombs:

"My warmest congratulations to you, our next President. You have won a splendid and significant victory. At this hour you appear to have received the largest electoral vote ever given to a presidential candidate. The indications are that your administration will be supported by a Congress, Democratic in both branches."

The event of the evening which touched Wilson's heart most deeply was the arrival in Cleveland Lane of the students of Princeton. The bell of old Nassau had begun ringing even before Wilson's victory was assured. The students now came marching with torches and flags.

"Tune every heart and every voice,
    Bid every care withdraw;
Let all with one accord rejoice,
    In praise of Old Nassau."

Presently the door opened, and Wilson appeared, standing there bareheaded in the flaring torchlight. It was an unforgettable moment—the eager faces, the cheering voices, the man bowing in the doorway.

Tumulty and Dudley Field Malone brought a rocking chair, placed it just inside the doorway, and held it firm while Wilson stood upon it. He spoke with great emotion, even with tears in his eyes:

"I have no feeling of triumph to-night, but a feeling of solemn responsibility. I know the very great task ahead of me and the men associated with me. I look almost with pleading to you, the young men of America, to stand behind me, to support me in the new administration."

He then went on to say:

"Wrongs have been done but they have not been done malevolently. We must have the quietest temper in what we are going to do. We must not let any man divert us. . . .

"I know what you want and we will not accomplish it through a single man nor a single session of the Houses of Congress, but by long processes running through the next generation."

Roosevelt and Taft acknowledged defeat early in the evening and sent congratulatory messages. Roosevelt's message read:

"The American people by a great plurality have conferred upon you the highest honour in their gift. I congratulate you thereon."

Taft's message read:

"I cordially congratulate you on your election and extend to you my best wishes for a successful administration."

Later in the evening, Thomas R. Marshall wired:

"I salute you my chieftain in all love and loyalty."

While Wilson had a plurality, not a majority, of the popular vote, it was a decisive victory. When the returns were all in, he was found to have polled 6,286,214 votes, while Roosevelt received 4,126,020 and Taft 3,483,922. But the popular vote only partly indicated the extent of the victory. Taft had carried only two states, Vermont and Utah. Roosevelt had carried five states, Michigan, Minnesota, Pennsylvania, South Dakota and Washington, and one, California, was divided, giving eleven electors to Roosevelt and two to Wilson. One of the striking aspects of the election, indeed, was the utter rout of the Bull Moose party. In not one state legislature did the Roosevelt Progressives come into control: in only two did a Roosevelt candidate for governor run even second. Wilson swept everything else, the final electoral vote being:

Wilson 435  
Roosevelt 88  
Taft 8

Nor was this all. The Wilson victory assured, for the first time in many years, a Democratic Congress, the House being Democratic by 147 members, the Senate by 6 members.

Most of all it was a progressive victory, for the combined vote for Wilson and Roosevelt was ten million compared with three million for Taft—a convincing evidence of the real mind of the nation.[1]

"A man of lesser character, of lower ideals, of smaller ability, could not have won the victory that Governor Wilson won yesterday. He could not have appealed to the imagination of the country as Woodrow Wilson appealed to it. No man has ever been elevated to the presidency who was more fully the people's President than this college professor who scorned alike the support of the bosses and the support of Plutocracy. It is a tremendous compliment that the voters have paid to him, but the responsibility is equally great.

"If he should fail, the consequences must be doubly disastrous. If he succeeds . . . a new era will have begun in American history, with a new vindication of republican institutions. . . . This nation will indeed have a new birth of freedom."[2]

Wilson made a short public statement on the day after election, his first as President-elect, and the last he was to issue for some time—"the time has come now to do a lot of thinking."

The statement was both an appeal and a reassurance to the business men of the country.

"The result fills me with the hope that the thoughtful progressive forces of the nation may now at last unite to give the country freedom of enterprise and a government

[1]The vote of the Socialists was another straw in the wind. The Debs vote grew from 420,820 in 1908 to 897,011 in 1912 although the Socialists suffered defections to the Progressives. (From the *American Year Book*, 1913.)

[2]New York *World*, November 6, 1912.

released from all selfish and private influences, devoted to justice and progress.

"There is absolutely nothing for the honest and enlightened business men of the country to fear. . . .

"Our hope and purpose is now to bring all the free forces of the nation into active and intelligent coöperation and give to our prosperity a freshness and spirit and a confidence such as it has not had in our time. . . .

"My own ambition will be more than satisfied if I may be permitted to be the frank spokesman of the nation's thoughtful purpose in these great matters."

# CHAPTER VIII

# THE PRESIDENT-ELECT

I am not going to hark back to old policies, but I shall try to find out whether there is not some new and suitable expression of those old principles in new policies.

*Address at the University of North Carolina,*
*January 19, 1909.*

. . . [the President] can dominate his party by being spokesman for the real sentiment and purpose of the country, by giving direction to opinion, by giving the country at once the information and the statements of policy which will enable it to form its judgments alike of parties and of men.

*Constitutional Government in the United*
*States, p. 68.*

I think that in public affairs stupidity is more dangerous than knavery, because harder to fight and dislodge.

*Article in the* Fortnightly Review, *February, 1913*

## I. WILSON FACES HIS TASK

ON THE tumultuous day after his election, Wilson set forth his policy as President-elect in a single characteristic, if impatient, declaration. He said to Mc-Combs:

"I must have a chance to think."

He was well aware of the political inundation which threatened him. The Democrats had been out of office for sixteen years: they were hungry.

McCombs himself was the symbol. He arrived in Princeton before the returns were all in, bringing with him a "slate" for cabinet appointments and a list of the faithful who were "entitled to immediate and generous consideration."

"I recognize your right," said he, "to name your private

secretary and other members of your confidential staff," but "members of the National Committee have some suggestions to submit as to members of the cabinet and heads of other departments and bureaus."[1]

To the victors, in short, belonged the spoils: and they wanted them immediately. Wilson's "iciness" astonished McCombs.

Other politicians, if not so barefaced, also rushed eagerly to Princeton. They wished to "grasp the hand" of the President-elect, to congratulate him wistfully, to make quite sure that he knew of the "yeoman service" they had performed in the "dust and heat of the campaign." An avalanche of letters and telegrams descended upon the quiet home in Cleveland Lane. It overflowed the professor's desk, gradually filled the chairs and the shelves, stowed itself away in bags and baskets. It was estimated that 15,000 letters and telegrams were delivered in the first few days after his election.[2]

Was he to be overwhelmed by "little problems of political office" when great "issues of life and death" confronted him? Even at the risk of offending friends and disappointing impatient leaders who had loyally supported him, he must, if he was to attain that clarity and "confident self-mastery" which he had once declared to be "the first and greatest of all political qualities in the conduct of our own affairs,"[3] he must have time and solitude.

Two days after the election Wilson announced his purpose. He would positively make no appointments for the present.

"I mean to keep my mind entirely open with regard to appointments of the first importance until a final an-

---

[1]W. F. McCombs, *Making Woodrow Wilson President*, p. 209.

[2]New York *Times*, November 9, 1912. A small part of the collection remains among the President's papers, in six wooden boxes—dispiriting to read!

[3]"Edmund Burke and the French Revolution," in the *Century*, September, 1901.

WOODROW WILSON ON THE VOYAGE BETWEEN NEW YORK
AND BERMUDA, AFTER THE ELECTION IN NOVEMBER, 1912.

nouncement is possible. It will be perfectly useless to resort to me for corroboration of any report. No announcement will have the least authority which is not made over my signature."[1]

The only important decision he made in the ten days following his election was contained in the announcement that he would call a special session of Congress not later than April 15th, to fulfill the promises of the party made during the campaign for immediate legislative consideration of the tariff and other problems.

Wilson had chosen the island of Bermuda as his "place of escape." He sailed on November 16th, ten days after the election, making the voyage as nearly private as possible. Only his family, a single private secretary, Mr. Swem, and the inevitable secret service attendants accompanied him. If he had been master of his desires he would have sought freedom even from newspaper correspondents and photographers:

"It does seem to me as if the newspapers of the United States must have enough pictures of me at the conclusion of this campaign to last them until I get back."

The beautiful, dreamy old island was a favourite haunt of Wilson's. The house he had chosen, Green Cove Cottage, was a place of retirement "encompassed by seaweed gatherers," "free to the wind, open to the sun."

If he had expected to slip into the old quiet routine of the place he was doomed to disappointment. A crowd met the *Bermudian* as she docked. An aide of the Governor General was there to greet him. Wilson responded:

"As soon as I knew that I had been sentenced to four years' hard labour my first thought was to get away to Bermuda and enjoy my liberty while I might."

While he was unable to avoid all social or semi-official contacts—he attended the island parliament and a state

[1]New York *Times*, November 8, 1912.

dinner, and in spite of his resolutions, made two brief addresses—his days in Bermuda were of laborious quietude.

"At last we are away from the crowd down here in this
calm clear land, where it seems possible to detach oneself
from all kinds of distracting thoughts and think freely
again. It was impossible while we were at Princeton to
answer letters written by those we really cared for, but
now a little leisure and peace have sufficed to mend our
spirits and it is a delight to turn to those we love
most. . . ."[1]

He spent a part of every day struggling with his overwhelming correspondence. The letters, written during this
one month, painfully transcribed for the purposes of this
biography from the stenographic notes of Charles Swem[2]—
no other copies were kept—would fill a large volume. It
was in itself a prodigy of labour. While they are mostly
brief acknowledgments, few are without some personal
impress, and they are marked by that exactitude of comprehension, compressed into a phrase, so characteristic of
Wilson's mind.

If the consideration of such masses of correspondence
was laborious, it yielded much valuable information. While
many of the letters were crass demands for place or privilege, some were from the ablest thinkers and leaders of
America—scholars, editors, trusted friends—who gave him
the best they had in counsel and in information. He felt
that he could "build his thinking" upon such letters as
those of President Eliot of Harvard, whose advice and
criticism throughout Wilson's entire administration, if
sometimes irritating, were deeply prized.

"You may be sure," he wrote Dr. Eliot, "that I shall
never consider any advice volunteered by yourself in any
sense an addition to my burdens. On the contrary, it will

[1]Woodrow Wilson to Edith G. Reid, November 20, 1912.
[2]The author is much indebted to Mr. Swem for the use of his notebooks.

help to relieve them, and I shall take great pleasure in seeking your advice from time to time about persons and matters in Massachusetts."[1]

Colonel House was also writing him long letters, reporting upon various men who had been mentioned for cabinet or other positions. They contained bits of news that House had picked up in his expanding function as the "official listener" of the new administration.

The Bermuda letters abound in references to Mexico, to the problems of the Panama Canal tolls, and even to European matters. It was during this trip that Wilson began to think seriously upon foreign affairs. He replied to an informative letter from the American ambassador in Russia, Curtis Guild:

"I realize very fully the critical character of the situation with regard to the relations between our own government and the government of Russia. Of course I have no acquaintance with details and I should welcome the opportunity to acquaint myself very fully with what is in your own mind and has fallen under your own observation while in St. Petersburg. . . .

"I feel that it is absolutely inconsistent with either the dignity or the principles of our own government to enter into any treaty relations with the government of Russia which would permit the treatment of one class of our citizens in one way and all other classes in another. But the difficulties to be faced and overcome in working out the right agreement, it is indispensable that I should understand very thoroughly."

To Sun Yat Sen, the Chinese leader, who had cabled his congratulations, Wilson wrote:

"Permit me to say that I have watched with the keenest interest the recent course of events in China and have felt the strongest sympathy with every movement which looks

[1]November 30, 1912.

towards giving the people of the great empire of China the liberty for which they have so long been yearning and preparing themselves."

A large part of the mail dealt with cabinet appointments: it had something of the character of a vote upon the eligibility of various leaders. Credit has been taken by this adviser or that for having "put so-and-so in Wilson's cabinet." These letters give evidence that Wilson had many and potent advisers.

"Anybody who speaks in behalf of Josephus Daniels speaks to my heart as well as to my head. I have a real affection for him as well as a very high opinion of him and you may be sure that suggestions such as yours carry great weight with me."[1]

He kept closely in touch with William J. Bryan:

"I appreciate more warmly than I can say the generous terms of your letter and am looking forward with the greatest pleasure to the opportunity of consulting with you, not now only but often."[2]

Perhaps the most beguiling of the letters are those to old and dear friends. They are full of affection and solicitude. To his nephew, Professor George Howe of the University of North Carolina, whom he had helped to educate, he wrote:

"I need not tell you, my dear boy, how happy your feeling about me makes me. Ellen received your letter to her and wants me to join her messages to mine. She, dear lady, will not as yet consent to learn to dictate letters and is quite overwhelmed at trying to write everything with her own hand.

"We think of you often and most affectionately . . .

---

[1] To Homer S. Cummings, member of the Democratic National Committee from Connecticut.

[2] November 23, 1912.

we shall count upon you when you are on your way home again to stop with us as long as you can in Washington. There will be a very warm welcome for you there."

He responded to a letter from his loyal friend of the "battle of Princeton," Dean Henry B. Fine:

"I cannot tell you what deep pleasure your letter of November 6th gave me. It reached me last night here in far-away Bermuda to which we have run away for four weeks of rest and escape from the turmoil, and I read it aloud to the family. I need not tell you, my dear fellow, how my affection leapt to meet yours as I read the generous sentences in which you expressed your delight at my election. The old days in Princeton, days of strain and pain, were days when men were bound together by something more than ordinary affection. The affection seemed to have iron put into it by the influences of strong conviction. . . . My heart goes out to you across the waters and we all join in hoping that your year abroad will bring you every kind of refreshment and strengthening."

He wrote to Dr. Hiram Woods of Baltimore, a classmate at Princeton:

"MY DEAR HIRAM:

"Delightful as it was the other night to see you and the other old fellows at the dinner it was tantalizing merely to sit at the table and look at you and have no chance to have personal and intimate chats.

"You may be sure that I shall never desire you in any circumstances to drop the old epithets of intimacy. On the contrary I should miss them very sorely if you did. I have now at last at least a little leisure in which to turn to the men I have known and loved so long and express to them my deep and continuing affection."

And no letters could be more appreciative than were many written by Wilson during these weeks to the men who had served faithfully in the struggles of the campaign:

"*Personal*
"MY DEAR MCADOO:

"Here we are settled in a little cottage ideally situated for refreshment and rest where I hope to get the kind of strength and zest I shall need for the things that lie ahead of me. At this first moment of leisure for correspondence I want to express to you once more the feeling I have had throughout the campaign of deep and growing satisfaction at the generous and efficient part, the self-sacrificing and sometimes painful part, you have played in pushing forward the common cause in which we both so earnestly believe. The records of my memory in these matters will be records to which I shall most often turn for satisfaction and encouragement. I want to send you at least this line of affectionate regard and appreciation.

"Pray never feel that there is anything that has to be explained to me. I think I understand both by knowledge and intuition both your motives and your feelings."

Wilson's letters to Joseph P. Tumulty, who was soon to be appointed his private secretary, give evidence of the frank and affectionate relationships which existed:

"*Personal*
"MY DEAR TUMULTY:

"We have been here a week now and I have thought very constantly of you who are so generously and unselfishly pulling away at the labouring oar at home in order that I might have this vacation. All unite in sending you the most affectionate messages.

"There is nothing to relate of our stay here. The newspaper men who came down with us are quite in despair at the lack of news and I think are evidently enjoying their outing. I am sure they already agree with me that this is an ideal place for a vacation and I dare say that by the time the four weeks are out they will be content to have no news to send home, because it is a sort of lotus land, where one gets content with doing nothing.

"Just at the moment of writing I am a little under the weather because of indigestion but I shall probably work that off and I feel confident the remaining three weeks will set me up in fine condition. I have caught up with the letters I brought down with me and am now free to do some of the quiet thinking and reflecting that was my main purpose in coming here."

Wilson's correspondence during this period gives clear evidence of the course of his thought. He gave his attention primarily to the clarification and application of his "general principles and policies" to the issues that were soon to arise—the tariff, trusts, currency; in short, the relationship of government to the new problems of industrialism and capitalism. During the campaign he had so far avoided the specific discussion of these problems as to awaken sharp criticism. What he was seeking, he had told the people, was a "new freedom" for America. It was the name chosen for a book which William Bayard Hale had edited, using "the more suggestive portions" of Wilson's campaign speeches. Hale had come to Bermuda bringing the manuscript with him. Wilson reviewed it carefully and then dictated a preface in which he said that the book "is an attempt to express the new spirit of our politics and to set forth, in large terms which may stick in the imagination, what it is that must be done if we are to restore our politics to their full spiritual vigour again, and our national life, whether in trade, in industry, or in what concerns us only as families and individuals, to its purity, its self-respect, and its pristine strength and freedom. The New Freedom is only the old revived and clothed in the unconquerable strength of modern America."

But the "new freedom" must be applied to difficult and immediate problems. There must be an "orderly plan of attack"; there must be "consecrated and determined leadership."

The correspondence also gives abundant evidence that he planned deliberately and carefully for the "governance" of his own personal life during the hard years that were to come. He had discovered during the campaign the limitations of his strength. He suffered often and intensely from neuritis, he was subject to attacks of indigestion, and his letters speak often of sick-headaches. The sight of one eye was defective. Dr. S. Weir Mitchell of Philadelphia, who gave him a careful examination about the time he entered the presidency, doubted whether he could survive the overwhelming labour of the great office he was soon to fill.[1] He must therefore discipline himself sternly. It was a policy which later laid him open to much criticism, even by his friends, but it enabled him to conserve his physical strength and gave him the time he considered indispensable for thought. If he had been less stern in his self-discipline, a great, good-humoured, blundering democracy, eager to grasp his hand, and whisper in his ear, might have fumbled him to death.

The problem which many of Wilson's political friends regarded as of first importance, to which they supposed he was devoting his time at Bermuda—that of appointments —he seems to have considered least of all. While many of his letters relate to cabinet and other offices, and it is certain that much of the information conveyed to him at this time was valuable, his interest even here seems to have

---

[1] Dr. Cary T. Grayson to the author.

been in a "principle of sensible action" rather than in the tangled difficulties as to whom to appoint as Secretary of State or ambassador to the Court of St. James's.

## II. THE CHALLENGE TO BATTLE

Wilson's sojourn in Bermuda had "cleared the mind," as he said, "and set the spirit free." "Four weeks of unmixed blessing."

But the thinker, especially if he happens to be a President, must pay for his retirement. Business interests, always sensitive, recalling the slashing progressivism of Wilson's campaign, had begun to worry for the safety of their golden calf. What would the new President do about the tariff? Would he tinker with the currency system? Would he attack the trusts? There had begun to be covert references in certain newspapers, even threats, as to what the "interests" might do to protect themselves. A panic might easily develop—or be developed!

A revolt was also brewing in Wilson's own state of New Jersey. His implacable enemies there, the old party bosses with their backers, the powerful financial interests, were astir. Although Wilson was still governor, it was assumed, now that he was elected to the presidency, that he would promptly resign, and they could again have their way.

When Wilson's ship arrived in New York on December 16th he was at once surrounded by alarmed advisers. McCombs was there with doleful warnings. Wilson's leadership was in danger! Some even of his more judicious friends were disturbed.

Wilson was not only aroused but angry. Everything had been so plain in Bermuda: the ideals that shone before him there in his solitude, clear stars of guidance, had seemed almost within the grasp of his leadership. He had now to meet doubt and confusion, even revolt.

As he listened to the reports that came to him, his face hardened. His friends knew the signs, a certain blazing blue coldness in his eyes, the brows drawn down in a straight line, his jaw bone sharpening, his colour rising. At such times he did not raise his voice. It was even a shade lower and softer—there was a level quietude in it that was devastating. He made his decisions swiftly and conclusively. He told the New Jersey leaders that he would not resign the governorship until the legislature had enacted the anti-trust laws that had been promised: that he intended, personally, to conduct the fight. He declared again that he would not at present make any decisions as to appointments. He decided also, contrary to the advice of some of his cautious friends, to strike back at the charges and threats that had found their way into the press or were being "whispered about."

His first speech was on the evening after his return—December 17th—while he was still white hot. The occasion was a dinner of the Southern Society at the Waldorf-Astoria Hotel.[1] It was a large and enthusiastic gathering, certain to be widely reported, since it was the first public appearance of the President-elect since his election.

Wilson made it the occasion for departing widely from his intended address. As in so many other instances in which he was deeply stirred, he revealed, as he rarely revealed even in his intimate conversation, his innermost thoughts:

"It has been my function in the past, perhaps because of a naturally combative nature, to stand often in this room and say to the audiences before me what I knew beforehand they would not like to hear, and to say to them what I believed they would not agree with me in thinking.

---

[1]Wilson's friend, Walter L. McCorkle, presided. Other speakers were Augustus Thomas and Judge Almet F. Jenks.

I have been very disagreeable in this room, not of set purpose, but because I believed at the time that I was speaking what the men before me would ultimately think. . . ."

What he wanted now to do was to impress upon the people the clear vision of his retirement—a vision of the spiritual life of a democracy as contrasted with the clamouring material demands of the moment.

"A nation is not made of anything physical. A nation is made of its thoughts and its purposes. Nothing can give it dignity except its thoughts. Nothing can give it impulse except its ideals."

He desired "a passion so great for an idea" that men would be ready to "lay down their lives for it."

While he was here speaking from the heart it was not until he came to close grapples with his opponents that the audience sat forward to listen. First, he paid respects to "some gentlemen in New Jersey":

"Mr. Thomas quoted a remark of mine that the man knew the strength of the stream who was swimming against it. I have been swimming against it all day in New Jersey, and therefore I have come here in a somewhat grim and solemn humour. Yes, we straightened things out in New Jersey, but they are not going to stay straightened out of themselves, and the happiest circumstances in the minds of some gentlemen in New Jersey to-night is that they can now count the day when they can get rid of me. That is the reason I informed them to-day that they were not going to get rid of me."

He then turned to the opposition known as "Wall Street"—which had charged him, as he had heard, with threatening prosperity. "This anonymous authorship of iniquity!" The opposition, he declared, must and would be brought out into the daylight.

"I say that not as a threat to this company, because, of course, there is nobody here who has the least nervousness about the future, but I say it in order to convey more or less playfully—*more or less playfully*—this intimation, that men have now got to stand up and be counted."

What was real prosperity anyway?

"Prosperity does not exist for a nation unless it be pervasive. Prosperity is not a thing which can be consumed privately or by a small number of persons, and the amount of wealth in a nation is very much less important than the accessibility of wealth in a nation. The more people you make it accessible to the more energy you call forth, until presently, if you carry the process far enough, you get almost the zest of a creative act."

He had his eye on classes of men in America who were not prosperous:

"God knows that the poor suffer enough in this country already, and a man would hesitate to take a single step that would increase the number of the poor, or the burdens of the poor, but we must move for the emancipation of the poor, and that emancipation will come from our own emancipation from the errors of our minds as to what constitutes prosperity."

He turned then directly to the charges that had been made:

"People make all sorts of sinister predictions as to the trouble we are going to get into down at Washington. . . .

"They say that business is going to be disturbed by the changes which are going to be undertaken by the Democratic party in the economic policy of the country."

He challenged not only those who feared a panic, but even more, those who threatened a panic to influence his course at Washington:

"Business cannot be disturbed unless the minds of those who conduct it are disturbed. A panic is . . . merely a state of mind, because obviously when a panic occurs there is just as much wealth in the country the day after the panic as the day before. Nothing in material circumstances has changed, but the whole state of mind of the financial community has changed. They dare not part with their money. They call in their loans. They are excited, and they do not always know exactly why. That is a natural panic, but you know there are unnatural panics, and sometimes panics are said to occur because certain gentlemen want to create the impression that the wrong thing is going to be done."

". . . frankly I do not believe there is any man living at the present moment who dares use that machinery for that purpose. If he does, I promise him, not for myself but for my countrymen, a gibbet as high as Haman. . . ."

It was this challenge, of course, that went home. It dramatized the issue. "Hanging as high as Haman" appeared in scores of headlines. The *Sun* in New York published a cartoon of "Lord High Executioner Wilson" with the caption "The New Gallows-Freedom" and a gibbet bearing the words, "I will hang him on a gallows as high as Haman's."

Some of Wilson's friends were dumbfounded by the reaction. He had gone too far! He had been intemperate in his challenge. But if the address gave an impression of radicalism which belied Wilson's real programme, it was an exact expression not only of his indignation but of his determination to go forward, regardless of powerful opposition, with the promised reforms. It was the ardent inner spirit of the man, grown robust in solitude, that had declared its faith and voiced its passion. And the response among the progressives of the nation, where his real strength lay, was unmistakably favourable. He dared to say the same thing after election that he had said before.

In the weeks that followed he made four other important

addresses all of which aimed at the single purpose of arousing the nation to a realization of its moral and spiritual obligations.

On December 28th, his birthday—he was fifty-six years old—he attended a celebration at his birthplace, Staunton, Virginia. It had been eagerly prepared for and the trip through his native state was a triumphal procession. Crowds turned out at every station, students of the University of Virginia, where Wilson had studied law, gathered at Charlottesville to cheer him, and when he and Mrs. Wilson with their party (including McCombs) arrived at Staunton they were met by a torchlight procession, a military escort, and the Stonewall band played "Home, Sweet Home." They were taken to the old Presbyterian manse on the hill, where they were guests of the Reverend A. M. Fraser, and they occupied the room where Wilson was born. The celebration was marked by an outpouring of generous emotion:

"He went out from us as a very little boy, laden with the prayers and benedictions of a small congregation of Christian people. He comes back to us to-day, by the favour of an overruling Providence, a proven leader of men, wearing the plaudits of the whole civilized world, and chosen to fill the highest civil office ever given to a man by the suffrages of his fellow men."[1]

Wilson delighted his audiences by his references to his early associations with Staunton—especially in his address at the Mary Baldwin Seminary for girls, which occupied the old church of which his father had once been pastor and in which he himself had been baptized.

"I have no vivid recollection of the first two years that I spent in Staunton. But I have some vivid recollections of subsequent years when I was permitted to visit this, my birthplace. For I have visited here a number of times when

---

[1]Speech of welcome delivered by Dr. Fraser.

you paid me no attention whatever. I stood in the place where I am now standing when I was a student of law in the university at Charlottesville. I had the very singular good fortune of having five cousins studying at this seminary. I was very fond of those cousins; and I paid them many attentions, and there were numbers of my confreres at the university who accompanied me—out of courtesy— on my visits. And on one occasion when I brought a somewhat numerous company of friends to the spot upon which I am now standing, I remember the great embarrassment with which I submitted to the cross-examination which preceded my entrance at these portals. I have, therefore, not always been welcomed to this spot with open arms."

It was a cool day but Wilson insisted upon speaking bareheaded. Mrs. Wilson, who sat just behind him, kept urging him in a whisper, to put his hat on. Finally someone in the audience cried out:

"Put on your hat. You'll catch cold."

"I will, being requested in front, and commanded behind."

But pleasantries and recollections soon gave way to the deeper purposes which weighed upon the President-elect. He returned powerfully to the theme of his New York address: the new ideals, the new duties of the nation—that vision he had seen so clearly in Bermuda.

"My friends, we are clearly entered into a new age."

"Moral forces" were now to prevail, "service" must be the new keynote:

"The one thing that the business man of the United States is now discovering, some of them for themselves, and some of them by suggestion, is that they are not going to be allowed to make any money except for a *quid pro quo*, that they must render a service or get nothing. . . . 'Are you giving anything to society when you want to take something out of society?' . . . I want to proclaim for my fellow citizens this gospel for the future, that the men who serve will be the men who profit."

But if the new President could set forth his prophetic ideals with convincing power, the address did not leave his audience with the impression that they had elevated a "mere dreamer" to the White House. They discovered that this Scots-Irishman—a type familiar enough to Virginians—was also a grim fighter. In fact, he left them in no doubt at all:

"This is not a rosewater affair. This is an office in which a man must put on his war-paint. . . . And there must be some good hard fighting, not only in the next four years, but in the next generation, in order that we may achieve the things that we have set out to achieve."

He went even further than this, to the point of shocking some of his friends.

"I could pick out some gentlemen, not confined to one state, gentlemen likely to be associated with the government of the United States, who have not had dawn upon their intelligence what it is that government is set up to do. There are men who will have to be mastered in order that they shall be made the instruments of justice and mercy."

At the banquet in the evening it appeared even more clearly who these "gentlemen" were. He let it be known that he understood the political situation in Virginia. He did not hesitate to say:

". . . Virginia, herself, . . . showed no great enthusiasm for my nomination. . . ."

If Wilson's address was delivered with a "banquet smile," nevertheless it cut deep. Some of the newspapers attacked him sharply, regretting that he should "unnecessarily antagonize" the Virginia leaders. When his friend Dabney wrote him of this reaction, Wilson replied:

"I hope this is not the general impression, because my friends will have to get used to my way of always having a dart for somebody, and when I speak I try to say it in as good-natured a way as I can contrive on the spur of the moment. Indeed the whole passage was on the spur of the moment."[1]

In January he carried his evangel to Chicago, where he spoke on the 11th at a great gathering of business and industrial leaders at a dinner of the Commercial Club. It was an address of great power and eloquence. There had been statements in the press that Wilson, noting the increasing anxiety of the financial interests, would "speak reassuringly." If that was what his audience went to hear, they were disappointed. If they expected the "detailed proposals" which some of his critics were demanding, they listened in vain. Wilson spoke with a frankness that made them gasp:

"The business future of this country," he declared, "does not depend upon the government of the United States. It depends upon the business men of the United States. . . . only the temper and the thought and the purpose of business men in America is going to determine what the future of business shall be."

He suggested that four things must be done, intimating that if the business men of the country would not correct themselves, the government must see that they were corrected. It was as clear and definite a programme—this Four Points speech—as the more famous Fourteen Points of a later time:

1. ". . . we must husband and administer the common resources of this country for the common benefit."

2. "The raw materials obtainable in this country for every kind of manufacture and industry must be at the disposal of everybody in the United States upon the same terms."

3. "There is a third thing which you must do which has

---

[1]To R. Heath Dabney, January 7, 1913.

not yet been done. You must put the credit of this country at the disposal of everybody upon equal terms. Now, I am not entering into an indictment against the banking methods of this country. The banking system of this country does not need to be indicted. It is convicted."

4. "And then in addition and on top of all this, we must see to it that the business of the United States is set absolutely free of every feature of monopoly. I notice you do not applaud that. I am somewhat disappointed because unless you feel that way the thing is not going to happen except by duress, the worst way to bring anything about. . . ."

Hard, blunt proposals, a tremendous indictment, striking at all the entrenched "interests" of the nation. His audience sat spellbound. He might well say, "I notice you do not applaud that." But the fact that his auditors were critical made him only the more eager to win them, to make them understand. He was convinced that the people were in a mood of revolt, they demanded reforms. Were these to come with the help and sympathy of business, or were they to meet mere blind and ugly opposition? He wound up with an eloquent note of appeal to these mighty men of the financial world:

"Don't you know that men everywhere are looking to you with confidence and with hope, on the assurance that you are not waiting for the whip of the law . . .?

"I have no intimate knowledge of the processes of business. I never was engaged in business in my life. I must take counsel with the men who do understand business, and I dare not take counsel with them unless they intend the same things that I intend. . . . The man who does not hold their interests dearer than his own, I cannot admit into my council. . . . I am a trustee for the prosperity of the United States in council, and the counsel that is not common counsel, the counsel that does not include you, is imperfect counsel, is counsel which will mislead. Won't you come in? . . . There is no bright prospect otherwise."[1]

Wilson was sharply disappointed by the reaction from his addresses. There was a wave of criticism, even by newspapers and by leaders who had been his staunch supporters.

The New York *Times* said editorially that Wilson's address "betrayed only too clearly not only a lack of intimate knowledge of the processes of business but a certain confusion of mind as to the fundamental conditions under which the affairs of the American people are conducted."[2]

Wall Street eagerly attributed a depressed condition of the stock market to Wilson's speeches.

On the other hand many of the audience at Chicago were deeply impressed. They had not only been carried along by the eloquence of Wilson's appeal but they knew, better than the East, the tone and temper of the Middle West. They knew that something had to be done: and they entertained an abiding confidence in Wilson's intelligence and good sense in proceeding by evolutionary rather than revolutionary methods. Some of them wished he had amplified certain of his statements, but they agreed with his general thesis.

Harold F. McCormick of the International Harvester Company pronounced the address "a masterpiece," and was "most impressed by his willingness to bring into his confidence the business men who listened to him. . ."[3]

Two days after speaking in Chicago, Wilson delivered a brief address at a luncheon in Trenton, tendered him by the New Jersey Electors, the Democratic State Committee, and the Democratic members of the legislature. Here

---

[1] January 11, 1913.
[2] New York *Times*, January 13, 1913.
[3] *Ibid.*

he bluntly announced that none but progressives would be put "on guard" in his administration.

". . . I feel first, last, and all the time that I am acting in a representative capacity. I am bidden to interpret as well as I can the purposes of the people of the United States and to act, so far as my choice determines the action, only through the instrumentality of persons who also represent that choice. I have no liberty in the matter. . . . Therefore, I shall not be acting as a partisan when I pick out progressives, and only progressives."

The reaction to these remarks, in powerful conservative circles, was unfavourable. The following day the New York *Times* capped its report of the speech with a headline saying Wilson would pick a "radical cabinet."

Here was fuel for the flames of discussion. Again men asked: "What does he mean?" "Progressives" was a vague term. The *Times* complained editorially that Wilson was saying a good deal and revealing nothing and that the doubt and guessing resulting from his utterances was favourable to the speculators. It suggested that he speak no more before his inauguration lest there be more "indefinite and disquieting phrases."[1]

On the other hand there is no doubt that his white-hot campaign bound the overwhelming progressive opinion of the nation more strongly than ever to Wilson. It was good politics. If he was to accomplish anything it would not be with the support of Wall Street, or powerful conservative newspapers, but with the enthusiastic faith in him of the aroused West and South. And after all, he was recommending now, after the election, only what he had recommended before the election. How could he do less?

Nor did he confine his activities merely to making addresses. He was still governor of New Jersey and he had determined to carry through his reforms at the session of

_____
[1] January 15, 1913.

the legislature which opened in January (1913). At his request a series of seven regulatory bills designed to curb the abuses of the great corporations in the state were drafted. They were aimed particularly at price-fixing and the restraint of trade and applied the doctrine that Wilson had long advocated: "Guilt is personal." Directors of corporations violating the law would be liable to fine and imprisonment.

The "Seven Sisters" acts were hotly opposed in the legislature, the attempt being made to delay action until after March 4th, when Wilson would necessarily have to resign as governor to become President. Wilson accepted the challenge, and carried the fight with tremendous vigour. His prestige in the state was now so overwhelming, his power so great, that the opposition crumbled before him, and by the middle of February the battle was won. On the 19th he signed the bills.

While the "Seven Sisters" laws put New Jersey in the vanguard of states having rigid anti-trust laws, they were, as a matter of fact, too hastily drawn, and poorly considered even by Wilson himself, since he was then overwhelmed with national problems. Some of the opposition which Wilson, in the heat of the conflict, had considered selfishly unreasonable had been based upon honest doubt as to the wisdom of the legislation proposed. The laws have since been repealed. But the determined and resourceful fight which Wilson carried on in securing their passage not only served to increase his power and prestige in his own party but further cemented the confidence of the country in his sincerity of purpose.

So determined was Wilson not to let the old forces return to power in New Jersey that he did not resign as governor until March 1st, three days before his inauguration as President of the United States.

While there was considerable complaint that Wilson

was "talking in generalities" when he discussed the great national questions of the hour, he was going forward steadily and patiently to the formulation of specific measures. He must work with the leaders of Congress: he must make no statements regarding specific legislation until he knew what he could do. While at Bermuda he had corresponded with a number of congressmen and senators, and he now began to call them in for conferences.

"Burleson, I want to talk with you briefly of some of the things I wish to accomplish during my administration."[1]

He told Burleson that he regarded the reform of the antiquated banking and currency system of first importance: the tariff and farm problems must also be considered. On December 26th, Carter Glass of Virginia, head of the subcommittee on banking of the House of Representatives, came to New Jersey to confer with Wilson. Dr. H. Parker Willis, the expert of the committee, was with him, and details of proposed financial legislation were thoroughly discussed. Wilson's grasp of the business made a profound impression upon the Virginia congressman.

"The President-elect," he said, "has more ideas about currency reform and expresses them more incisively than any man I know of."[2]

The same course was pursued in whipping into shape other features of the new administration's plans. The record shows that many leading congressmen and senators were meeting with Wilson in January to discuss legislation as well as appointments, but they were invariably men of liberal views on the matters discussed. Underwood, while generally labelled a conservative, was progressive in his tariff views. Colonel Goethals was summoned to familiarize him with various aspects of the Panama Canal and the government of the zone.

---

[1]A. S. Burleson to the author.
[2]New York *Times*, December 27, 1912.

Nor were the advisers all Democrats. What Wilson wanted was a genuinely progressive programme, and he welcomed conferences with such congressmen as William Kent of California, a Roosevelt Progressive, who came in January to talk with him on the conservation of the nation's natural resources.

If the month in Bermuda had clarified Wilson's general principles and programme, the correspondence and conferences of late December, January, and February served to prepare him for the specific consideration of the measures he was advocating.

### III. CHOOSING HIS CABINET

Wilson approached the task of choosing his cabinet with anxiety if not with dread.

"The task ahead of me, so far as it is a task of appointment to office, is wholly hateful. . . ."[1]

When it came to selecting his advisers, Wilson knew too much, had thought too much. He knew the mistakes of every President from Washington down. Read his prescient article on "Mr. Cleveland's Cabinet," written for the *Review of Reviews* in 1893. He knew all the problems, the constitutional limitations, the political complications, of a new President coming to the leadership of the democracy. He could analyze—no one has done it better—the question, "What *is* the cabinet?"

"Are we to have a purely administrative cabinet, and individual choice of policy by the President; or are we to have responsible party government, parties being made responsible not only for the choice they make of Presidents, but also for the character and motives of the men they bring forward to give him counsel. . . ? Either system would be constitutional under the existing provisions of

[1] Address before the Southern Society of New York, December 17, 1912.

our fundamental law; the former literally constitutional, the latter within the permissions of the Constitution. The practice of our Presidents, too, whenever at least they have not been mere military chiefs like Jackson and Grant, with imperative preferences of their own, has been in the direction of the latter system, until Mr. Cleveland, a man as truly taken from outside the regular lines of civil promotion as either Grant or Jackson. He has broken, more than most Presidents, with what I may call the historical method of appointment. That method has unquestionably regarded the cabinet as a party council."[1]

But when it came to deciding, outright, whether Bryan should be his own Secretary of State, Wilson found the task immensely difficult. If he could have made a cabinet out of the men whom he had known and trusted—men like President Eliot, Richard Olney, Louis D. Brandeis, David B. Jones, Walter H. Page, or Dean Fine of Princeton, it would have been clear sailing, but such men were practically or politically unavailable. His experience in public life had been so brief that he knew little of the qualifications and limitations of the leaders of his party. It would indeed have been no easy task for any Democrat in the same position. The party had been long out of power. Men who had served under Cleveland were now, for the most part, dead or too old to be of usefulness, and many of those who had succeeded to the leadership of the Democracy were men in whom Wilson had no confidence. One great advantage that the Republican party has had in the last seventy years, since it has been most of the time in power, has been the training and inheritance of experienced national leaders of cabinet size. The transition from McKinley to Roosevelt, Roosevelt to Taft, Harding to Coolidge, Coolidge to Hoover was easy and natural.

Wilson's problem was immeasurably more difficult. His

[1] *The Public Papers of Woodrow Wilson*, Vol. I, pp. 215–216.

election represented not only a change in party, but a deep-seated shift in geographical control, as well as in fundamental policies. The government for years, whether Republican or Democratic, had been steadily conservative, Eastern, urban, industrial. Wilson had determined to make it progressive, Western, Southern, agricultural. It meant bringing in not only new men but a new type of man.

"I wish to find the very best men for my cabinet, regardless of consequences," Wilson told Page. "I do not forget the party as an instrument of government, and I do not wish to do violence to it. But I must have the best men in the nation." Page adds that Woodrow Wilson spoke in "a very solemn tone as he sat bolt upright, with a stern look on his face. . . ."[1]

With such a bill of qualifications is it any wonder that Wilson hesitated? That he refused to announce his decisions until the last moment?

His delay irritated the political leaders, bringing down upon him an avalanche of advice—literally thousands of letters—and no little criticism. He quizzed the visitors who came to Princeton and to Trenton, but he gave them no satisfaction.

". . . nobody comes back from Trenton knowing anything more than when he went . . ." wrote Lane.[2]

It was exasperating to men who had fought the good fight and now expected to be admitted to the council table —and to the patronage. McCombs was terribly cut up about Wilson's reticence. So were the reporters. Their papers were pressing them for authentic information, but they could furnish nothing but gossip and inferences.

Bryan was, of course, the greatest problem. While Wilson knew from the beginning, before he was, indeed, an

[1]*The Life and Letters of Walter H. Page*, Vol. I, pp. 112–113.
[2]Franklin K. Lane to J. N. Teal, January 20, 1913.

active candidate for the presidency, that if he were elected as a progressive with Bryan's support, he could scarcely escape giving the "peerless leader" a high place in his administration; yet he dreaded doing it. He had come to have a whole-hearted admiration, even affection, for the man personally—an affection that persisted to the end of his life—but he distrusted his political thinking, doubted his wisdom.

Nevertheless Bryan had made Wilson's nomination possible; he had stumped the country for seven weeks in the campaign, and by his support had brought his great following into the Wilson camp. Furthermore, he had been the untiring leader of the party for sixteen lean years and was, more than any other man in the Democracy, entitled to recognition.

In certain ways Bryan would prove valuable. He would help establish party harmony both outside of Congress and in, and thus assist greatly in securing the reforms in which Wilson was so deeply interested. And, as Mr. Dooley sapiently remarked, Wilson might find Bryan more manageable "in his bosom than on his back." On the other hand Bryan was not only without executive experience but he knew nothing of diplomacy: he was in reality an evangelist, a reformer, rather than a statesman.

While it is clear that Wilson had practically accepted the inevitable, even before he left for Bermuda, he continued to hope that there might still be some way out, although he seemed to have had no one else in his mind save, perhaps, Richard Olney, who was too old. Possibly Bryan might be sent off to Europe as an ambassador. Colonel House's notations in his diary illustrate Wilson's hesitant state of mind:

"November 16 . . . He asked again about offering Mr. Bryan the Secretaryship of State or Ambassadorship to

England, and I advised him to do so. He said that he would."[1]

"December 18 . . . Bryan was also discussed freely. I advised him to offer Bryan the Secretaryship of State, but afterwards to suggest it would be of great service if he would go to Russia at this critical time."[2]

"December 19 . . . Governor Wilson called me over the telephone. . . . He wanted to know again about Bryan and my advice about it. I advised being cordial in making the offer, [Secretaryship of State] and to make it plain afterwards that he would appreciate his taking the foreign post [the Ambassadorship to Russia]."[3]

Another entry under the same date adds:

"I called up Governor Wilson to talk things over, and he asked if I still held to my advice about Mr. Bryan, and I answered 'yes.' This is the third or fourth time he has asked me this. It shows how distrustful he is of having Mr. Bryan in his cabinet. . . ."

Bryan himself did nothing to further his interests. He even advised Wilson through the *Commoner* to avoid appointments based upon "past service rendered":

"The men selected by Mr. Wilson for the cabinet should be selected, not because of personal service rendered to him, nor even because of past service rendered to the party. The individual counts for little; the cause counts for much."[4]

It is plain, however, that he had no intention of being sent away into the foreign service. He was far too much interested in the problems that he had been discussing for years. He told a friend in December, evidently after he had been sounded out by Wilson as to an ambassadorship:

[1] *The Intimate Papers of Colonel House*, Vol. I, p. 90.
[2] *Ibid.*, p. 97.
[3] *Ibid.*
[4] The *Commoner*, early in January, 1913.

"I do not intend to get that far away from Washington. I intend to watch this administration and see what it is going to do."[1]

If Bryan was silent his friends and enemies were not. It is to be doubted if any President ever received such a deluge of letters concerning any appointment whatsoever. The West took pen in hand and wrote to Trenton demanding recognition for the leader whom they not only admired but loved; and the East, fearing the "wild Nebraskan," if not so voluminous, was equally emphatic in its opposition.

Conservative papers like the New York *Times* hoped for deliverance from such a choice. The *Courier-Journal* doubted if the administration would be big enough to hold two men of such positive views and suggested the British ambassadorship for the Nebraskan. Watterson blithely argued that on his very substantial income Bryan "could trip it with old Tripides and cant it with old Cantharides, along with the best that the Court of St. James's turned out, six-abreast, outsiders and all. . . . Besides, we do so want to see Mr. Bryan in knee-breeches and silk stockings."[2]

The question was settled between Wilson and Bryan at a private conference on December 21st. It was a meeting that Wilson had dreaded, but it passed off beautifully. Bryan was in fine humour and "very reasonable." They spent several hours discussing a wide range of subjects, including cabinet possibilities. Later, at lunch, the offer of the Secretaryship of State was made and tentatively accepted. The Commoner felt obliged, however, to inform Wilson of the objection of Mrs. Bryan and himself to the serving of intoxicating liquors at their table. This

---

[1]Carter Glass to the author, quoting W. J. Bryan.
[2]Louisville *Courier-Journal*, November 21, 1912.

might prove embarrassing at state functions in which they would have to take part. Wilson replied that they could serve what they pleased.

While Bryan later wrote Wilson that he would have preferred no office and accepted only because he was persuaded he could render more service in the administration than as a private citizen, the truth of the matter is that he was as happy with his post as a child with a new toy. He became doubly interested in the plans for the new administration and dashed off suggestion after suggestion regarding the cabinet. And a curious collection they were —local celebrities and faithful, honest Democrats, but most of them without any distinction whatever.

Two other appointments, McAdoo and Daniels, seem to have been practically determined in Wilson's mind before he left Bermuda, although he had not decided regarding the posts they should fill. Wilson told Bryan when he conferred with him on December 21st of his intention to bring McAdoo into his cabinet, probably in the Treasury.[1] He liked and trusted McAdoo and respected his knowledge of business affairs. McAdoo had been a bulwark of strength in the campaign though he brought no great political support to Wilson, nor could he be of much assistance with Congress. He was also under fire, as the protests show, as a "promoter," though Wilson probably gave no weight to this objection.

There were several other outstanding candidates for the Treasury, notably McCombs and Henry Morgenthau. On the evening of the election, when it had become certain that Wilson had won a sweeping victory, McCombs hobbled into the room at the Waldorf-Astoria where Colonel House was sitting and remarked:

---

[1] W. J. Bryan to Woodrow Wilson, December 25, 1912, referring to their earlier conference.

"If I cannot be Secretary of the Treasury I will take nothing."[1]

He was doomed to bitter disappointment, for Wilson had already become convinced that his manager was unfit for a cabinet position. Soon after the election he remarked in the family circle:

"I fear that I am going to hurt McCombs. I know he expects a cabinet position, and I do not think him cabinet material."[2]

Wilson appreciated McCombs's services and sacrifices, but aside from any question of his capacity for handling the great problems of the Treasury, it had been painfully apparent during the campaign that he was physically and temperamentally disqualified for working in harmony with others.

Josephus Daniels was much harder to place. A man of cheerful energy and no little shrewdness, with a gift for making warm personal friends of men who at first regarded him lightly, he had risen to a position of considerable influence in the party. The editor of an important Southern newspaper, he had been a faithful lieutenant in the Bryan following since 1896—free silver and all. Wilson had come to like him heartily. Bryan was his strong supporter, as were practically all the members of the Democratic National Committee, on which Daniels had served for sixteen years as the member from North Carolina. Moreover, Daniels had thrown his support to Wilson early and rendered fine service in the campaign. He had been a godsend in the "cocked-hat" incident.[3] Wilson hesitated regarding him for the same reason that he hesitated regarding Bryan. When Walter Page learned that Daniels was slated for the Navy he was astonished.

---

[1]Maurice F. Lyons, *William F. McCombs, The President Maker*, p. 128.
[2]Miss Mary W. Hoyt to the author.
[3]See p. 256 ff., this volume.

My dear Friend,

I have been scrutinizing those over the Cabinet choices, and have decided to beg that you will do me the very great service of accepting the Secretaryship of the Navy. I know of no one I trust more entirely or affectionately; and I am sure that you will trust and believe me when I assure you that you will, in my judgment, best serve the party and its two leaders by accepting this post. I cannot

23 Feby, 1913

PRINCETON, NEW JERSEY

spare you from my Council table

Faithfully & affectionately Yours

Woodrow Wilson

Hon. Josephus Daniels

May this be confidential between us for the present

Facsimile of a letter from President Wilson to the Hon. Josephus Daniels, tendering him a place in the cabinet.

445

"Why, don't you think he is cabinet timber?" asked House.

"Timber!" exclaimed Page. "He isn't a splinter!"[1]

As a matter of fact, although Hugh Wallace and several other prominent leaders were suggested for the Navy, Wilson never seriously considered anyone but Daniels. And in the years that followed—years of stupendous conflict that tested men to their souls—Daniels, although often under attack, never lost the confidence of his chief. And Wilson had no more loyal friend and supporter in his cabinet.

Wilson wanted "one thorough-going politician" in his cabinet, but here, as in other cases, he hesitated because he could not discover his irreproachable ideal. Burleson of Texas, a stout party leader, who had served for eight terms in Congress and was thoroughly conversant with all the inner workings of the legislative machine on Capitol Hill, was early suggested. We find among Wilson's papers evidences of strong support from Burleson's colleagues, such men as Ollie James of Kentucky and Hoke Smith of Georgia. Burleson had also been an early and powerful advocate of Wilson: a supporter in Texas even before Colonel House had become active. Wilson liked Burleson, but thought him too much identified with the old organization and old organization methods. Wilson told House in November that he thought Daniels more suitable as Postmaster General than Burleson, House arguing that his fellow Texan's closer relationships with Congress, together with his aggressiveness, fitted him ideally for a department so dependent upon legislative coöperation as the post office. Nevertheless Burleson's name seems for a time to have been entirely dropped. In the "slate" which Colonel House sent on January 9th for his chief "to ponder over," Burleson's name was omitted even from the

[1] *The Life and Letters of Walter H. Page*, Vol. I, p. 119.

list of "reserves." Charles R. Crane, a warm personal supporter, and Thomas W. Gregory, another Texan, afterwards Attorney General in Wilson's cabinet, were now suggested for Postmaster General.

Burleson himself did not turn a hand in his own behalf. In fact, he discouraged his friends from working for him, for he felt that in the selection of a cabinet the President-elect should be perfectly free. It is probable that a strong letter written about this time by Congressman Underwood, whose judgment Wilson highly regarded, turned the tide in Burleson's favour: and when Wilson offered him the place he accepted promptly. He said to Wilson:

"I will be loyal to your administration and sympathetic with your policies. When I reach the point where I cannot give you my undivided loyalty, I will tender my resignation. When I talk to you, I will always tell you my candid views. I can't know what is in your mind, but I can tell you what is in mine."

"Burleson," Wilson replied, "that is just the kind of man I want."[1]

The subsequent relationships of Wilson, the philosopher and idealist, and Burleson, the practical politician, are interesting aspects of Wilson's career.

Colonel House was of great assistance to Wilson in the business of choosing his cabinet. It was not so much in making original proposals as it was in the quiet persistence with which he sought information regarding the various men suggested, fed the material in concrete form into Wilson's mind, and thus helped to clarify his thought. Many of the men investigated by House, many even who reached a position on the "tentative slate," and had House's support, disappeared from consideration. It was a method admirably suited to the pattern of Wilson's mind, since it furnished him the

[1] A. S. Burleson to the author.

abundant raw material of information upon which he could exercise his analytical and critical—possibly overcritical—intellectual machinery.

When Wilson suggested to House himself that he accept a place in the cabinet the Colonel promptly refused—convincing Wilson anew of that disinterestedness of purpose which, above almost any other quality, he respected.

"As an ex-officio member, however," wrote House, "I can do my share of the work, and get a little of the reflected glory...."[1]

How greatly Wilson appreciated House's help, on these generous and loyal terms, is clear enough from the letter he wrote to House on February 7th—House being then in Florida:

DEAR FRIEND:

I feel the need of seeing you, for a final conference about the official family.

If you do not deem the weather too severe then (for your health is the first consideration with me) will you not spend Thursday, the 13th with me at Princeton? ...

Meantime would you be kind enough to sound H.[ouston] of St. Louis on the Secretaryship of Agriculture for me? On that case I am clear and my choice made; but I think it best for you to open the matter with him, if you will be so kind.

The Treasury has been offered and accepted, as we planned.

I am in town for an evening with Cleve Dodge.

With warmest regards from us all to you both,

Affectionately,<br>WOODROW WILSON.

February 7th, 1913.

As to Houston, Page seems to have been the first to present his name to the President-elect. Page had called upon Wilson soon after the election to plead the cause of agriculture and the development of country life. To his

---

[1] E. M. House to Woodrow Wilson, January 9, 1913.

mind the problems of the soil offered opportunities second to none for the new administration and he was anxious to have Wilson meet them. At Wilson's invitation, he sent to Bermuda while the Governor was resting there a memorandum regarding men who might be fitted to head the Department of Agriculture. Houston, he thought, was the best man for the place.[1]

At this time Houston was chancellor of Washington University, in St. Louis, and enjoyed a wide reputation as an economist. While not at all intimate with Wilson, they had met on several occasions.

"The first time I saw Woodrow Wilson," writes Houston, "was in his uncle's house in Columbia. I saw him only for a few seconds, but I never forgot him."[2]

No candidate for his cabinet appealed to Wilson more strongly than Houston. Both were scholars, thoughtful men, with a background of historical and economic knowledge, both were educators of long experience, both were what Wilson called "emancipated Southerners." It was the type of mind—as was that of Newton D. Baker—that Wilson felt most at home with: but even here he doubted and hesitated. Houston had no public following, no acquaintance in Congress. Nevertheless he appointed Houston with genuine satisfaction.

The Attorney Generalship and the Secretaryship of the Interior proved the most difficult places to fill.

"I find no search quite so difficult as that for an Attorney General, because I want a man of experience and balance and yet a man thoroughly on the people's side.

"I am delighted that you should feel as you do about my recent speeches."[3]

---

[1] W. H. Page to Woodrow Wilson, November 27, 1912.
[2] *Eight Years with Wilson's Cabinet*, Vol. I, p. 17.
[3] Woodrow Wilson to W. J. Bryan, January 22, 1913.

Wilson was anxious to have a progressive and distinguished lawyer as Attorney General, for there was much important work to be done; and the West demanded that the Interior Department be directed by one who was sympathetic with its problems. For both positions a considerable number of names were presented. Louis D. Brandeis, A. Mitchell Palmer, J. C. McReynolds, H. D. Clayton, W. A. Glasgow, Joseph W. Folk, and Edgar H. Farrar were most prominently mentioned for the Attorney Generalship, and of these McReynolds, Palmer, and Brandeis most seriously considered. McReynolds's name was steadily advocated by House. Wilson himself appears to have preferred Palmer but was obliged to drop him because of the concerted opposition to him. It is perfectly certain that Wilson would have been gratified to have had Brandeis at the council table, either as Attorney General or as Secretary of Commerce, but Brandeis was bitterly attacked and opposed. The strongest objections came from the "upper social crust" and wealthy business men of Boston. James Ford Rhodes, the historian, wrote on December 19th:

"The best men here, men of affairs as well as lawyers, all of whom voted for you or President Taft will regard the appointment of Mr. Brandeis as a member of your cabinet, should it be made, with profound regret."[1]

Some of the objections were based upon professional charges, others were no doubt due to hidden racial prejudice, for Brandeis was a Jew.

On the other hand, there were distinguished men who rushed to Brandeis's defense and urged that he be included in the official family.

Wilson himself sought information from friends whose fairness he could rely upon. To his friend Arthur Tedcastle he wrote on January 3rd:

[1]James Ford Rhodes to Woodrow Wilson, December 19, 1912.

"I want to get all the disinterested opinion I can collect about Mr. Louis D. Brandeis. He is a man of such originality and force and might be made so serviceable to the public that I want to know just what his neighbours whom he has not prejudiced by his action with regard to them personally think about him."

Liberals like Edward A. Filene, Felix Frankfurter, Henry Moscowitz, and Norman Hapgood interested themselves in Brandeis's behalf, Hapgood investigating and disproving the charges made against Brandeis's practices.

Up until the moment when the full cabinet became known, it was generally believed that Brandeis would be chosen, probably as Secretary of Commerce. Wilson finally passed him over, not because he had any belief in the charges, for three years later when pressing for Brandeis's confirmation as a Supreme Court justice, Wilson wrote Senator Culberson:

"I myself looked into them [the charges] three years ago when I desired to make Mr. Brandeis a member of my Cabinet and found that they proceeded for the most part from those who hated Mr. Brandeis because he had refused to be serviceable to them in the promotion of their own selfish interests, and from those whom they had prejudiced and misled."[1]

McReynolds's reputation as an able and progressive lawyer rested chiefly on his prosecution of the Tobacco and Anthracite Coal trusts while acting as special counsel for the government during Roosevelt's time. He was a Southerner and a traditional Democrat and was thought to be a strong progressive. Wilson met McReynolds for the first time on February 15, 1913, at House's apartment. He liked him and about a week later invited him into the cabinet.

[1]May 5, 1916.

No post gave Wilson greater concern than the Secretary-ship of the Interior. The conservation of the natural resources of the nation had been a burning issue since Roosevelt's time. It was a problem that especially aroused the Middle Western progressives. During Taft's administration charges of corruption and favouritism had been widely made: the Ballinger-Pinchot case filled the newspapers. The East and the West were widely at variance as to policies. Many of Wilson's politically independent supporters felt that his appointment to the Interior Department would be the acid test of his progressivism. Could he or would he resist the great lumber, oil, and water-power interests which were seeking to seize control of government lands in the West to exploit for their own profit? Progressives generally approved the course of Walter L. Fisher, then Mr. Taft's Secretary of the Interior, and some of them urged Wilson to retain him in the new administration so that he might carry through the excellent policies he had inaugurated. Wilson listened, respectfully enough, to the proposals,[1] but it would have been a departure wholly foreign to his policy as a party leader.

Many names were put forward, most notably, those of Walter H. Page, Newton D. Baker, and Franklin K. Lane.

Lane was thought of by his friends for a cabinet position even before the election, but he himself seems not to have taken their suggestion seriously. He was content with his chairmanship of the Interstate Commerce Commission, and believed his means would not permit him to enter the cabinet. Also, he questioned his fitness:

"They ought to be the very largest men that our country can produce, and I am not fool enough to think that I am entitled to be in such a group."[2]

---

[1] ". . . I attach no small importance to what you say about the present Secretary of the Interior," he wrote on January 9th to Ray Stannard Baker.

[2] Franklin K. Lane to E. S. Simpson, November 26, 1912.

Lane was fairly well acquainted with Colonel House and was with him on several occasions during the winter of 1912–13, but seems to have made no effort to advance himself. Writing to Wilson on November 22nd, House said:

"Lane is fine material, but he is contented with his present position and would not change it."

Again, in January, Lane said in a letter to House:

"As I have told you, I am to be eliminated from consideration."[1]

The more House thought of Lane, however, the more satisfied he became that it would be a mistake to omit him from the cabinet. February 16th, the day after Wilson met McReynolds, at House's request Lane paid him a visit. The Colonel informed Lane that he was being considered for Secretary of the Interior, and received from him the assurance that he would serve wherever asked, but was quite content to remain at the head of the Commission. The meeting confirmed House's judgment.

"My opinion of him increased materially. . . . There will certainly not be a stronger or more dominant force in the cabinet."[2]

Wilson himself, though he did not then know Lane personally, had been greatly interested and impressed by a letter which Lane had written to him suggesting his friend James D. Phelan[3] for Secretary of the Interior. In setting forth Phelan's qualifications, Lane's understanding of the functions and requirements of the Interior Department was so clearly revealed that Wilson is said to have exclaimed:

"Why not Lane himself?"

But the President-elect's own first choice was Newton

---

[1] January 22, 1913.

[2] *The Intimate Papers of Colonel House*, Vol. I, p. 107.

[3] Ex-mayor of San Francisco; afterward United States senator from California.

D. Baker of Ohio. Baker was a West Virginian by birth and had been a student under Wilson at Johns Hopkins. He was, like Wilson, a scholarly reformer in politics, an able lawyer, a brilliant orator. He had been the virile lieutenant of Tom Johnson in the progressive movement in Ohio. At the Baltimore convention Baker had proved an effective supporter of Wilson and he had taken no small part in the campaign that followed. Wilson asked him to come East for a conference. When the offer was made Baker felt that he could not conscientiously leave his office as mayor of Cleveland, since he had been elected on pledges to accomplish certain definite reforms. He therefore declined the appointment.

Page was also seriously considered, but the party leaders protested that a Southerner must not be put in charge of the department that controlled the pensions, and Wilson then turned to Lane, who was finally appointed only four days before the inauguration. Lane did not meet the new President until he was summoned to the White House to be sworn in. "Mr. President," he introduced himself, "I am your Secretary of the Interior."

One of the leaders that Wilson wished especially to bring into his cabinet was A. Mitchell Palmer of Pennsylvania. The Pennsylvania Democracy, while it was weak numerically, had rallied early to Wilson's support and had served well his cause in the Baltimore convention. Palmer was an outstanding leader, a lawyer of ability, and a man of prominence in his state. He was considered for several places in the cabinet, and finally, after Hugh Wallace had declined the position, he was offered the War portfolio. Wilson confidently expected an acceptance, but Palmer, who was a Quaker, immediately declined, writing on February 24th:

"Many generations of my people have borne strong testimony against 'war and the preparations for war' . . .

"As a Quaker War Secretary, I should consider myself a living illustration of horrible incongruity."[1]

Palmer's answer brought Wilson to the "end of his rope." Time was now short and none of the men suggested seemed to him suitable for the War office. He referred to his dilemma in a conversation with his secretary, Mr. Tumulty, who remarked:

"There ought to be a New Jersey man in your cabinet."

Tumulty suggested Lindley M. Garrison, then vice-chancellor of the state, a man of cultivation, a lawyer, a judge who had endeared himself especially to the younger members of the bar, of whom Tumulty was one. Wilson knew of him chiefly by reputation, but he summoned him at once, and was so greatly impressed by the incisive quality of his mind that he offered him the War office on the spot. Garrison was vastly astonished. He protested that he knew nothing either of the army or of politics and that he felt himself "temperamentally unfitted" for such a position. "I have been a lawyer all my life and nothing but a lawyer."[2] But Wilson only urged the harder and the next day, February 25th, Garrison accepted. House, with whom the President-elect had not consulted, was astounded by the speed with which he acted. He confided to his diary:

"The thing that impresses me most is the casual way in which the President-elect is making up his cabinet. I can see no end of trouble for him in the future unless he proceeds with more care."[3]

The appointment, indeed, proved to be unfortunate.

The two newest departments, Commerce, and Labor remained to be filled. Wilson, still seeking a place for Brandeis, would have liked him in the Department of

---

[1] James Kerney, *The Political Education of Woodrow Wilson*, p. 301.
[2] L. M. Garrison to the author.
[3] *The Intimate Papers of Colonel House*, Vol. I, p. 111.

Commerce. When his selection seemed impracticable Wilson turned to William C. Redfield. Many names had been suggested but Wilson thought that Redfield came nearest to what was demanded in a department dealing so largely with the industrial and commercial affairs of the nation. Redfield had been a manufacturer who had maintained while a member of Congress a strong belief in low tariffs. Wilson had been impressed by several of Redfield's tariff speeches, and attracted, as he often was, by his facility in expression. Redfield had recently been around the world and visited the Philippine Islands, which seemed to Wilson an added qualification. Redfield promptly accepted.

The Labor portfolio was not formally filled until the last moment, for it was not until March 4th that Mr. Taft signed the bill creating the new department. Wilson had, however, his chosen candidate in mind—William B. Wilson of Pennsylvania. Wilson was a rough-hewn character of a type unfamiliar in the highest councils at Washington. He had been a coal miner, had risen to power in the miners' union, and had become an important element in the Democratic organization in Pennsylvania. He had served three terms in Congress where he had, in his quiet way, made staunch friends. A North-of-Ireland Scot with a stout Presbyterian background—a heritage similar to the President's own—he was a man of the soundest common sense, the soul of simple loyalty.

So the cabinet was completed. Toward the end Wilson was compelled to resolve his doubts and fill the places, even though he had not fully satisfied his critical requirements. And when once an office was filled, Wilson disliked to change—he was of those who would "rather bear those ills we have than fly to others that we know not of."

With no member of the new cabinet can it be said that Wilson was truly intimate. He knew McAdoo, perhaps, the best personally; Houston was a familiar spirit intellectually. He liked and dreaded Bryan. Daniels was comfortable and devoted. He knew Garrison and McReynolds and Wilson scarcely at all and had never met Lane until Inauguration Day. It was a cabinet largely made up of unknown and untried men. Bryan was the only member with a national reputation: and he was looked upon with doubt by a large part of the country. But Wilson's own prestige was so great, he was so widely trusted, that the comment upon his appointments was not unfavourable. It was felt that in any event he would himself dominate; and the temper of the nation was tolerant. "Wait and see."

As a matter of fact the cabinet, considered as a whole, really had a pattern and character. As Frank Cobb pointed out in the *World:*

"This cabinet . . . has to be taken largely on trust. . . .

"No cabinet ever wrecked the administration of a truly great President. No cabinet ever saved the administration of a mediocre President. The genius of a Daniel Webster could not make a Tyler anything but a Tyler. The corruption of a Cameron and the intrigues of a Chase could not shake public confidence in the leadership of Abraham Lincoln.

"But of vastly greater moment than any individual in the cabinet, or all of them combined, is the method by which the cabinet was obviously organized. Here is the first concrete example of Mr. Wilson's attitude toward the presidency—his first official interpretation of his office and duties.

"Whether strong or weak in its various elements, this is no cabinet of political trade and barter. It was fashioned by no political boss. It was fashioned for no political boss. It was fashioned to placate neither sordid political interests nor sordid financial interests. Every member stands on his own merits, as Woodrow Wilson sees these merits."

And finally, as Cobb says, "It is no cabinet of corporation lawyers. It is no cabinet of hack politicians or machine henchmen. It is a cabinet of public servants, and appointed because the President who selects them believes that they are qualified for their work.

"A President capable of performing his task in this spirit may sometimes go astray in his judgment of men, but he has given to the country a convincing proof of his political sincerity."[1]

One other extremely important appointment was made before Wilson was inaugurated. This was his private secretary—in some respects a place of more consequence in the smooth functioning of his administration than any cabinet appointment. Wilson would have liked Newton D. Baker; and the name of Dudley Field Malone was suggested. Baker, however, was cabinet material, and could not in any event leave his task at Cleveland. Wilson turned therefore to Joseph P. Tumulty with whom he had already worked, whom he knew thoroughly, whose loyalty and devotion he trusted.

Tumulty had served as Wilson's secretary throughout the governorship. Mrs. Wilson liked him and advocated his appointment. He had been especially useful as an adviser in local New Jersey political affairs. Some of Wilson's counselors were opposed to him—he was "not big enough" —and there were many letters arguing that the appointment of a Roman Catholic would be a sad mistake. To Wilson the idea that Tumulty would "let the Vatican into the secrets of the White House" was puerility of the lowest order. Tumulty's limited experience, his want of national contacts—he was then, indeed, only thirty-three years old—and his "interest in the mechanism of small politics" were more serious objections. But Wilson had a genuine

---

[1]March 4, 1913.

liking for Tumulty. He trusted his devotion and depended upon his information. No other candidate, save Baker, was even seriously considered; and Wilson made his decision early in February.

With such a captain and such officers the Ship of State was ready to sail.

# INDEX

# INDEX